Liberation against Entitlement

Liberation against Entitlement

Conflicting Theologies of Grace
and Clashing Populisms

Tim Noble

☙PICKWICK *Publications* • Eugene, Oregon

LIBERATION AGAINST ENTITLEMENT
Conflicting Theologies of Grace and Clashing Populisms

Copyright © 2022 Tim Noble. All rights reserved. Except for brief quotations in critical publications or reviews, no part of this book may be reproduced in any manner without prior written permission from the publisher. Write: Permissions, Wipf and Stock Publishers, 199 W. 8th Ave., Suite 3, Eugene, OR 97401.

Pickwick Publications
An Imprint of Wipf and Stock Publishers
199 W. 8th Ave., Suite 3
Eugene, OR 97401

www.wipfandstock.com

PAPERBACK ISBN: 978-1-6667-1306-0
HARDCOVER ISBN: 978-1-6667-1307-7
EBOOK ISBN: 978-1-6667-1308-4

Cataloguing-in-Publication data:

Names: Noble, Tim, author.

Title: Liberation against entitlement : conflicting theologies of grace and clashing populisms / Tim Noble.

Description: Eugene, OR : Pickwick Publications, 2022 | Includes bibliographical references and index.

Identifiers: ISBN 978-1-6667-1306-0 (paperback) | ISBN 978-1-6667-1307-7 (hardcover) | ISBN 978-1-6667-1308-4 (ebook)

Subjects: LCSH: Liberation theology.

Classification: BT83.57 .N625 2022 (print) | BT83.57 .N625 (ebook)

07/27/22

Scripture quotations are from New Revised Standard Version Bible, copyright © 1989 National Council of the Churches of Christ in the United States of America. Used by permission. All rights reserved worldwide.

This book is a result of a grant project entitled "Latin American Liberation Theology: Prospects and Challenges," (GAČR 18–1543S) and is also the result of work carried out under the following project, Charles University Research Centre No. 204052, "Theological Anthropology in Ecumenical Perspective."

Contents

Preface | vii
Introduction | 1

1.   The Disheartening of Societies | 15
2.   Populisms in Conflict | 52
3.   Grace as Entitlement | 82
4.   Liberation from Dis-grace | 116
5.   A Liberating Theology of Service | 146
6.   *Fratelli tutti*: The Grace-Filled Path to Liberation | 175
7.   Transformation through the Spirit | 214

Bibliography | 233
Index | 255

Preface

THE JOURNEY OF THE writing of this book has been a long one and the times have been, to say the least, interesting. It is part of a research project entitled "Latin American Liberation Theology: Prospects and Challenges," (GAČR 18–1543S), funded by the Czech Science Foundation (GAČR), that ran from 2018–2020. Initially I had planned to write something else, but the results of the Brazilian presidential elections in 2018, combined with other political developments in the Czech Republic where I live, in my native country of the United Kingdom, and elsewhere, caused me to re-focus. The question of how to respond to the experience of social division was a key challenge for liberation theology, and one that I was convinced it could respond to in a way that would be inspiring also for very different contexts, such as ours in the Czech Republic. That is what this book is about.

But to write a book is always more than just typing words on a computer screen. It involves engaging with the ideas and challenges of other people in conversation and through their writings. There are moments of inspiration and enlightenment, moments of darkness and despair. Towards the end of this book I turn to Pope Francis and especially his encyclical *Fratelli Tutti*, which appeared as I was about halfway through writing the book and which I recognized I would have to include as it treated of much the same content. Pope Francis describes his encyclical as a "modest contribution." I offer this book in the same vein, aiming not at definitive answers, but at least to show the important questions to be asked and the criteria necessary for responding to them.

The main global companion to the writing of this book has been the coronavirus pandemic. I started writing in February 2020, when news of a new virus in China was coming out. Very soon we entered our first lockdown, and most of the past year and a half have been spent in varying degrees of lockdown. This has slowed many processes. Libraries have done amazing work to make sure that we have had access to material, but we have not been able to visit them in person for much of the time. Teaching and accompanying students has required a lot of very worthwhile effort, and travel has been severely restricted, so the renewed energy from meeting friends and colleagues at conferences and elsewhere has disappeared. These are very minor inconveniences compared to those who have suffered illness and long-lasting side effects or have lost those close to them. In writing this book, such people (too many of whom I can name) have been at the forefront of my thought, especially friends in Brazil who have suffered so hard during the past year or so.

Focusing on the Czech Republic and Brazil, the two countries that have been at the center of my life for the past thirty years (I am writing this preface thirty years to the day since I first arrived in Brazil), has meant that this book is also personal. I have refrained from using my friends and experiences too much as proofs for my points, but underlying what I write are stories, friendships, time spent together with people. Much of the book will focus more on the problems and the negative side of the two contexts, but that is neither the whole story nor even the majority story. There are simply always far more good people around, who strive to help the other, to make the world a better place. I know many such people, in the Czech Republic and in Brazil, and that is why I believe that we can transform society towards the fullness of the Kingdom, even if it is a slow journey and we will never fully arrive there. God's salvific activity is present, not only future.

There are many examples of this, but I want to recall one group with whom I worked when I was in Brazil. This group, known as *Grulae*, which stood for *Grupo de Libertação Alternativa Estudantil*, or Student Alternative Liberation Group, was for students from the town of Justinópolis, on the periphery of Belo Horizonte in Brazil. To get into university in Brazil, students had to pass an examination, the *vestibular*. Especially to gain a place in a public university the competition was immense. Public education was underfunded and classes overcrowded and thus poorer students were at a huge disadvantage compared to those who had been to private schools. One of the aims of *Grulae* was to prepare students for these examinations to complement their school education so that they could go to university and return to help build up their neighborhoods. For a number of years I taught (I use the word loosely) English and then French, as they had to do an exam in a modern foreign language. Every night Monday to Friday the students would come along in the evening, usually after a day's work that would also involve travelling two or three hours by bus into the city. They would study the different subjects they needed.

Although not everyone succeeded in getting to university, many eventually did and as a result there are doctors, actors, teachers, journalists, pharmacists, and many others who are still actively engaged in their communities and in doing good for other people. Over the last year I have also been accompanied by messages on a *Grulae* WhatsApp group, bringing me news of triumphs and tragedies. But what impressed me thirty years ago and impresses me today is the goodness and the desire to change things for the better. It is a slow path, but like the journey to university, constantly trying eventually brings results. So I want to dedicate this book especially to my friends from *Grulae* and to other members of the group who came after I had left but whose example is no less impressive.

I also want to thank a number of people and places. My stay in Brazil was made possible thanks to the generosity of the Jesuit community of FAJE (the Jesuit Faculty of Philosophy and Theology) in Belo Horizonte and the kindness of the Rector of the institution. I am also grateful to the Protestant Theological Faculty of Charles University in Prague, where I work. I am fortunate to be part of such a supportive faculty that presents the very best of Czech society in its engagement and openness. I am also grateful to the International Baptist Theological Study Centre in Amsterdam, where I am a research fellow and where I am part of an international community of engaged and committed Christians who inspire me in much of what I do. In both these institutions I have wonderful students, whose questions and comments have enriched my thinking for this book. Last but definitely not least, I want to thank all at Wipf and Stock. It is a pleasure and an honor to work with such a publisher and I am deeply grateful for all that they do to make theological texts available at accessible prices. It is a great service to the discipline of theology and the life of the churches.

Apart from the grant project mentioned above, the publication of this book and additional research for it has been supported by the Charles University Research Centre No. 204052, "Theological Anthropology in Ecumenical Perspective," under the leadership of Professor Ivana Noble of the Ecumenical Institute of the Protestant Theological Faculty of Charles University in Prague. Ivana is not only the leader of the project, but more importantly for me, my wife. Because I have been slow in writing this book, she has not had the chance to read the manuscript, but she has supported me, talked to me about it, made helpful suggestions and raised interesting (sometimes difficult) questions. It would not have been possible to write this book without her and for that and for so much more I remain more grateful than words can say.

Introduction

IN 1844 A TWENTY-FIVE year old German exile in Paris published a short piece in a journal he had co-edited with a fellow exile, Arnold Ruge. His name was Karl Marx and the short piece became the Introduction to *A Contribution to the Critique of Hegel's Philosophy of Right*. The rest of the work would only be published after his death, but it can be considered as marking the beginning of his attempts to understand why people were suffering from or had imposed on them a sense of alienation. The introduction itself contains Marx's most famous description of religion. He writes: *"Religious* suffering is, at one and the same time, the *expression* of real suffering and a *protest* against real suffering. Religion is the sigh of the oppressed creature, the heart of a heartless world, and the soul of soulless conditions. It is the *opium* of the people."[1]

This, at least, is the standard English translation. The German text, however, while it does speak of a "heartless" (*herzlos*) world, speaks not of religion as its "heart" (*Herz*), but as its "*Gemüth*." This word, more normally written today as *Gemüt*, is defined by a leading German dictionary

---

1. Marx, "Zur Kritik der Hegel'schen Rechts-philosophie," 71–72. The passage reads in the original German: "Das *religiöse* Elend ist in einem der *Ausdruck* des wirklichen Elendes und in einem die *Protestation* gegen das wirkliche Elend. Die Religion ist der Seufzer der bedrängten Kreatur, das Gemüth einer herzlosen Welt, wie sie der Geist geistloser Zustände ist. Sie ist das *Opium* des Volks." The translation is from Karl Marx, *A Contribution*. For a brief commentary on the text, see Jerilyn Sambrooke Losch, "Introduction to a Critique of Hegel's *Philosophy of Right* (1843–1844)," in Diamanti et al., *The Bloomsbury Companion to Marx*, 3–8.

as "the totality of the psychical and spiritual forces of a person."[2] And the word that is translated as "soul" is "*Geist*," more commonly translated as "spirit." The same dictionary defines "*Geist*" as the "thinking consciousness of a human being."[3]

But that is enough of the German lesson.[4] The translation is not entirely inaccurate and it certainly gives an alliterative force to the phrase that even transcends the original. My aim in this book, however, is to return to the idea of a search for an all-encompassing unity, both on the personal level (the *Gemüt* that Marx speaks of) and on the communal level (here I shall speak more of *shalom*). As Marx saw it, religion had up till that point served as the force for the restoration of this sense of integration both on a personal and a communal level. This force, Marx recognized, was already falling apart. Marx himself broadly welcomed this,[5] but he also recognized the need for something that would serve the same end.

In this book I want to engage not so much with Marx himself as with the question of what role faith can play for Christians in giving the courage (*Mut*) to work for the restoration of wholeness against a backdrop of division and exclusion. This will involve taking seriously Marx's critique, but also recognizing that both Christianity and Marxism work with what Johann Baptist Metz called "an eschatological reserve."[6] As we

---

2. Gemüt: "Gesamtheit der psychischen und geistigen Kräfte eines Menschen" (Duden, "Gemüt"). The word is not used much today, though it persists in the classic German term "gemütlich." I will use the form *Gemüt*, rather than Marx's older form. In other languages, words like "spirit" or "soul" are used: so, for example, in Portuguese: "o ânimo de um mundo sem coração"; in Spanish: "el alma de un mundo desalmado"; in French, similarly: "l'âme d'un monde sans cœur." Italian shares with English the translation into "heart": "il cuore di un mondo senza cuore." Russian also uses the translation "heart" (*serdce*). Czech uses the word for "feeling," "cit." See on the passage Jandourek, "Jak to Marx myslel."

3. "Geist: denkendes Bewusstsein des Menschen, Verstandeskraft, Verstand" (Duden, "Geist").

4. Almost! *Gemüt* is also related to the word *Mut*, normally translated as "courage." Another dictionary page says the word "represents a collective concept for the psychological (*seelisch*) sensibilities and thoughts that are described through the substantive Mut." The word *seelisch* is related to the English word "soul" and could also be translated as "spiritual," or "mental."

5. For a recent assessment of Marx on religion, see Jan Rehmann, "Religion," in Diamanti et al., *Bloomsbury Companion to Marx*, 387–94, especially 388 on this passage.

6. Metz, *Theology of the World*, 118.

will see in chapter 5, this idea resonates with one of Pope Francis's four principles, that time is superior to space. Here it means that political engagement is both necessary and in some ways obligatory, but that all political choices are penultimate and need to be judged against the claims of a faith that works for the restoration of *shalom*, for the instauration, though not complete construction, of the Kingdom of God. But Marx's insistence that this is not an excuse for inaction must remain clear.

Contexts

Three divided societies in particular shape my discussion. I was born and raised in the United Kingdom (more specifically, in England). Although I have not lived in the country for twenty years now, the toxic aftermath of the Brexit referendum has been a constant presence for me over the past five years. Whether British society is irrevocably destroyed is a moot point, but it has at least suffered severely, with the pro-Brexit minority of the overall British electorate imposing its destructive and exclusionary view of the world on the majority. This manifestation of small-minded entitlement is one that Pope Francis will condemn in *Fratelli tutti*, as we will see in chapter 6. However, my predominant focus will be on two other countries, Brazil and the Czech Republic.

I lived and studied in Brazil for four years in the early 1990s, worked with Brazilians in London for six years, and have returned a number of times in the past twenty-five years. I have many friends in Brazil, and it is a country that remains deeply important for me on many levels. Chapter 1 will offer a closer reading of contemporary Brazilian society, but here it is enough to say that the election of Jair Bolsonaro as President in 2018[7] poured oil on the fire of discontent in the country, and divisions remain as strong as ever. The Brazilian context will offer the sharpest relief for my central argument, that underlying two forms of political populism, of the right and of the left, there are competing theologies of grace. What I will call the theology of entitlement is countered in Brazil equally strongly by the theology of liberation and their conflicting views of how the grace of God operates provide a strong backing for two different political programs.

My third focus is the Czech Republic, my home for some twenty years, and a country of which I am now also a citizen. It is a beautiful and

---

7. He assumed office on January 1, 2019, but the elections occurred in October 2018.

impressive country, situated in the heart of Europe, seeking to negotiate between competing worlds. As a Slavic-speaking nation that is nevertheless turned more towards the west, there is a continual pull between east and west. Finding a place, under attack or dominance by more powerful neighbors (from the Franks in the ninth century, through the Habsburgs to the Soviet Union), has been a constant struggle. But like many other postcolonial countries, the Czech Republic (a country that, as such, has only existed since 1993) has more recently faced severe internal divisions, torn between a culture of openness and welcome, and one of fear and small-mindedness. This is part of my daily life too and the background, as I explain later, against which I write.

The other event within which I have written this book is the coronavirus pandemic, which has transformed our world in ways that we hoped would never happen. The effects of this pandemic will take years, decades even, to play out. For my purposes, the most important feature has been how reactions to lockdown, to apparently straightforward and simple matters like wearing masks or getting vaccinated, have created another level of division in society. Division is not a competition, and I do not wish to claim that our societies are any more divided today than they were in the past. My reading of history would suggest that this is not a contemporary problem but a common experience of humanity through the ages. Nevertheless, that still makes it a problem today, and one that we have to face up to.

There is a temptation for Christians, even for theologians, to seek to find ways of reconciliation that will enable a meeting and a coming together of disparate positions. However, for reasons that I will explain in much more detail over the course of the following pages, I no longer believe that this is the right approach. Supping with the devil comes at too high a price, and some positions are irreconcilable. It is possible, necessary even, to approach the other "speaking the truth in love" (Eph 4:15). But love, as Pope Francis will make clear, is not a synonym for letting everything go. The passage from Ephesians concludes with the exhortation "Be angry but do not sin; do not let the sun go down on your anger" (Eph 4:26). Anger is sometimes the right response, because some things are wrong. Anger is not enough, though, and we need to find ways, not to reconcile, but to continue to stand up for what is right, what is of God, whilst recognizing that the other also is a child of God.

Two Conflicting Theologies

The question of how to deal with division and disagreement has not passed theologians by, and there have been a number of attempts to look at political theologies that take into account opposition. What I want to do, however, is related but different. In his doctoral dissertation, published as *Teologia e Prática*,[8] the leading writer on methodology in liberation theology Clodovis Boff[9] speaks in the subtitle (and frequently thereafter in the book itself,) of *"teologia do político,"* a theology of the political. So I offer in these pages an investigation of theologies that underlie two different political positions. My reason for focusing on this dimension is also connected to the fact that in the situations of conflict referred to above, in the United Kingdom, Brazil, and the Czech Republic, Christians are found on both sides of the debate and both lay claim to what they consider biblical or theological backing for their positions.

In seeking to present two very diverse and irreconcilable theologies, it needs to be made clear from the outset that I neither think it possible, nor do I claim, that I operate from some neutral position. I will look at two positions, one that I will refer to as a theology of entitlement, and the other a theology of liberation. My aim is to show why a liberating theology of grace is best able to give a sound basis to a political engagement for the other, and most especially for the other who is excluded, on grounds of social status, race, gender, nationality, sexual orientation, or whatever other ingenious ways human beings discover to marginalize other human beings.

I write from a particular political stance that might be broadly described as social democratic,[10] and out of the experiences of life in

---

8. The English translation is *Theology and Praxis*.

9. Whether Clodovis Boff is still a theologian of liberation is a moot point. On this point see Noble, "Teologie osvobození"; Noble, *Poor in Liberation Theology*.

10. The problems of political parties associated with this name are many. In Britain, support for Brexit and fear of losing voters has made the Labour party unsure of what it stands for. In the Czech Republic the party that bears the name Social Democrat (the Czech Social Democratic Party) has spent the last ten years or so shooting itself so often in the feet that it has nothing left to stand on. And although as will become clear in the first chapter I am broadly supportive of the *Partido dos Trabalhadores* (PT–Workers' Party) in Brazil, there are features of the behavior of some of its members that render it far from perfect. So I am under no allusion that all attempts to realize a political vision are tainted with injustices, on both sides. But the vision remains and, as we will see Pope Francis argue in *Fratelli tutti*, a vision that seeks to work with and for the excluded is more appealing than one that seeks to make the rich richer and at best hopes that some benefits will accrue to the poor as a side effect.

Britain, Brazil, and the Czech Republic. This political choice is no doubt the result of many influences, but at least consciously it is for me closely related to my understanding of what it is to be a Christian, and therefore what it is to be a theologian. Although I will listen to the voices of others, especially when I look at theologies of entitlement, I do so from this critical perspective. Where reconciliation is possible and desired, it can be sought, but if not, the dust must be shaken from our feet as a testimony against them (slightly paraphrasing Mark 6:11).

Whether reconciliation is possible or desirable in political differences is debatable. In the language of Chantal Mouffe and Ernesto Laclau, two political philosophers with whom I engage most directly in chapter 2, there is always at best an agonistic, or at worst an antagonistic relationship between conflicting political positions. The first means that both sides recognize what we might term a level democratic political playing field, within which opposing and irreconcilable positions can be put forward. The second means that there is not even an acceptance of shared rules of engagement. But both positions insist that ultimately difference is inevitable. There are (at least in principle) positions on the right and the left that have the desire to end inequality and exclusion, even if the means for doing this are a matter of irreconcilable difference. However, there are also political positions that, from a Christian perspective, are wrong, because they are fundamentally opposed to the gospel. In the image used in the story of the final judgement in Matt 25:31–32, there are sheep and goats and they must be separated.

The wrong positions have to be condemned, but in order to be condemned they have to be understood. Even political leaders who act in evil ways[11] cannot be simply written off as purely evil, and much less so those who vote for them or support them. Political choices have to be made, and when the choice is between two unsatisfactory options, people have to decide what they consider the least unsatisfactory. I turn to criteria for this in the conclusion, but it has to be recognized that much of contemporary culture is unappealing to many people. The proliferation of private languages, where people choose what words should mean and

11. Examples of such leaders, from the countries I referred to above, include, but are by no means limited to, Boris Johnson in the United Kingdom, Andrej Babiš, and Tomio Okamura in the Czech Republic, or Jair Bolsonaro (among many others) in Brazil. All these (and of course others) have been directly responsible for lies, corruption, and the stoking of xenophobic attitudes. Final judgement is God's, and we can hope that they may have redeeming personal qualities, even if they hide them resolutely from public view.

seek to impose their meanings on others, the increasing individualism and denial of the possibility of human empathy, wild and short-sighted pendulum swings in attitudes to just about everything, all these cause problems. Protests about discriminatory attitudes to gender, to sexuality, to race, are important, but exclusion is rarely solved by counter-exclusion, and certainly not without engagement, argument, and explanation.

For that reason, though I aim to show how theologies of entitlement are fundamentally and necessarily idolatrous, we need to understand why people are tempted by them. In his Spiritual Exercises, St. Ignatius of Loyola has two sets of Rules for Discernment, more appropriate for respectively the First and Second Weeks.[12] The fourth rule for the Second Week says:

> It is characteristic of the bad angel to assume the form of "an angel of light," in order to enter the devoted soul in her own way and to leave with his own profit; i.e. he proposes good and holy thoughts well adapted to such a just soul, and then little by little succeeds in getting what he wants, drawing the soul into his hidden snares and his perverted purposes.[13]

The positions espoused by political leaders, which are enthusiastically received by significant minorities among electorates, are, it seems to me, helpfully read in this light, as the activity of the bad angel. This is not to diminish the responsibility of those who propagate the lies and promises of plenty, but it may help to depersonalize and ultimately relativize their actions. It is neither enough to blame one individual for what transpires, nor will such positions ultimately persist.

The *Gemüt* that I seek to recover, then, is not a compromise between contrasting positions that will allow all to claim victory and all to be dissatisfied. The dictionary definition of this word that I gave above spoke, in German, of *Gemüt* as the "Gesamtheit der psychischen und geistigen Kräfte eines Menschen." To translate *Gesamtheit*, in this definition, as

---

12. The Ignatian Spiritual Exercises are divided into four stages, known as weeks. The First Week focuses mainly on a recognition of the exercitant's sinfulness and an experience of God's mercy. The Second Week has as its main focus the incarnation and ministry of Jesus, combined with exercises for determining one's way of life. An accessible translation, along with other writings of Ignatius, such as his Autobiography, can be found in Munitiz and Endean, *Saint Ignatius*.

13. *Spiritual Exercises* 332, in Munitiz and Endean, *Saint Ignatius*, 352. "Angel of light" is a reference to 2 Cor 11:14: "Even Satan disguises himself as an angel of light." Paul here is speaking of "false apostles."

"totality" is accurate, but potentially misleading. For it is not a totalizing force, but more precisely, in theological terms, it is *pleroma*, the fullness of life in God (cf. Eph 3:19; Col 2:10). This is what grace, I shall argue, is about, the active intervention of God in the life of his people to bring them to the fullness to which and for which they are created and called, to *theosis*, to life in Christ. At its most fundamental level, politics must serve this end and no other and it is arguably theology's most urgent task to call politics to this end.

Taking Sides

One of the aims of this book is to argue that, as one author puts it, the "church does not have a political party, but it does have 'a side.'"[14] The problems caused when the church has taken sides are evident in the history of many countries. At one level it is correct that the church in most cases cannot simply equate taking sides with support for one particular party, because there may be legitimate, if irreconcilable, paths to achieving the same ends. However, liberation theology has reminded us constantly that God does takes sides, God has made an irrevocable option for the poor. In any given political situation there are a limited number of ways to engage. One either votes for a candidate or party, or one abstains or records one's dissatisfaction with what is on offer in some other way. It may be the case that in these circumstances at the very least the church can point negatively to those for whom people should not vote. Unfortunately when it does this, it is often on very narrow grounds, frequently to do with candidates' alleged attitudes towards abortion or some forms of sexuality or partnerships. These are of course important issues, and not to be ignored, but as we will see later they cannot be the only grounds on which the church chooses which party to support. To seek to protect the unborn whilst supporting the destruction of the lives of the born on so many other levels (education, family life, employment, health, justice, etc.) is not only incongruous but also immoral.

So, although my intention is not to offer a theological justification for supporting a particular political party, I do contend that particular choices have to be made and that there are, or should be, theological underpinnings for these, as far as Christians are concerned. It will not always be possible to accuse one's political opponents of acting in bad faith. The fundamental opposition I have spoken of above and to which I

---

14. Bakker, "O 'mensalão/petrolão,'" 841.

return in greater detail in the second chapter means that there are indeed competing discourses, both of which genuinely believe that they provide the best solution, and yet are fundamentally incompatible. Epithets like "left" and "right," "liberal" and "conservative," "socialist" and "capitalist," are frequently bandied about. Sometimes they help, mostly they are excuses not to engage, but they do point to some of the dividing lines.

Despite the inevitability of antagonism, sincerely held differences are possible. For that very reason, argument and disagreement will occur among Christians, with mutual examinations and questionings of the underlying theology. It is important to avoid biblical proof-texting, partly because the diversity of the biblical record in terms of concrete political engagement is similar to the diversity of political beliefs among Christians today. So I will not engage in detailed biblical exegesis in what follows, though I do insist that a "canonical" reading of the Bible, that is, one that at least seeks to interpret the many individual books using an overarching hermeneutical key, rules out self-centered theologies of entitlement and encourages theologies of liberation (properly understood).

One principle of such a canonical reading is that God is a God of justice and that therefore injustice is antithetical to God. So God is always on the side of those who in Spanish and Portuguese are called respectively *injusticiados* or *injustiçados*. There is no simple English translation of this word. Frequently in texts from liberation theology it is translated as "victims of injustice," which is partly correct. However, there is a danger of reduction to victimhood, to add injustice to injustice. I will therefore move between translating the phrase literally as "the injusticed," or, at least a touch more elegantly, as "those to whom injustice is done." But, as José Maria Vigil, in whose writings I first came across this word, argues:

> God is against injustice and places himself on the side of the "injusticed" (the victims of injustice). God does not make nor can he make a "preferential option for justice.... The option of God for justice is based on his very being: God cannot be other, nor could he not make this option without self-contradiction or without denying his own being. God is, "by nature," option for justice and this option is neither gratuitous (but rather axiologically inevitable), nor contingent (but rather necessary), nor arbitrary (but rather based per se in the very being of God), nor "preferential" (but rather alternative, exclusive, and excluding).[15]

15. Vigil, "Opção pelos pobres," 243–44. The paraphrase of *injustiçados* as "victims of injustice" is Vigil's own, but for reasons given in the text above I will not follow him in this.

The political choice is therefore not strictly speaking a choice. For Christians there is no decision needed to stand on the side of justice. It is a necessity of faith. The unjust are excluded, as the gospels make clear. "Weeping and wailing and gnashing of teeth" may be metaphorical language, but it expresses the results of injustice, namely, a self-exclusion from the Kingdom (see Matt 8:12; 13:42, 50; 22:13; 24:51; 25:30).

The Argument of the Book

It is now time to introduce the argument of this book. Competing political positions cannot simply be reduced to categories of "right" and "left," or "conservative" and "liberal." Attitudes are shared across this spectrum, and so I will look at two clusters of positions that I will call those of entitlement and liberation. The first concentrates on the potential gains for the individual, be that the individual human being or individual group, such as a nation. The major focus is on what is of advantage for us and depends on a sense of deserving whatever is perceived as good as a right. The second cluster of positions has as its focus the needs of the other and of a restoration or creation of a world in which all live together and seek harmony and peace (*shalom*).

My fundamental claim is that these conflicting political positions carry with them, mostly implicitly, sometimes explicitly, underlying theologies. Particularly I want to look at the theologies of grace that are present in these positions. That is to say, how do they perceive God at work in the world, and what do they see as the relationship between God and humanity? This second question is strictly one of theological anthropology, but grace is the action of God in the world, and that action necessarily and inevitably impacts on human existence before, with, and on the way to God.

These theologies are always embodied. So, I begin with a focused socio-analytical reading of the situations in Brazil and the Czech Republic. For Brazil, I will concentrate mainly on the last thirty years or so, since the first post-dictatorship elections in 1989. A necessarily curtailed survey will look at the problems of political failures and successes, and see how they have led to the shaping of current Brazilian society, bringing about a deeply divided and fractured country, with support on both sides from groups who are (or claim to be) Christian. Drawing on the work of sociologists, political scientists, and theologians, I will present an overview of the situation in the country that will help to explain the political choices that have been made. Although a tendency to "entitlement" has been evident across the political spectrum, I will also argue that the election of Jair Bolsonaro has seen a politicization of religion in favor of the narrow interests of theologies of entitlement and prosperity and in favor of exclusion against an option for the poor.

My treatment of the Czech Republic, though having a similar end in mind, will be slightly different. The conscious history runs much deeper.[16] I begin, then, with what from a historian's point of view, will be a grossly inadequate overview of the country's[17] history. My aim is to show the "mythic" understanding of that history, what people regard as important and why. I argue that it is precisely these events that combine to form a modern narrative of what it means to be "Czech." After this rapid recounting of some major turning points in the history of the country, I will focus, as with Brazil, on the past thirty years, since the effective end of the Communist regime, a period that began in November 1989. As I examine the country, I will also look at religion, given that the Czech Republic is often labelled (misleadingly, I will argue) as one of the most atheist in the world.

Governments in both Brazil and the Czech Republic have been labelled populist. In chapter 2, I examine in more detail what this means. Populism studies has been a leading academic growth area since around 2004 with the publication of an article by the Dutch scholar Cas Mudde.[18] Here though I focus on the reading of the phenomenon offered by the Belgian-born Chantal Mouffe (b. 1943) and her intellectual and life partner, Ernesto Laclau (1935–2014), born in Argentina and a

---

16. First traces of the existence of *homo sapiens* in the Czech Republic date from around 45000 BCE. The archaeological and written of the country are often better preserved than in Brazil. The dating of the first humans there is contested, from around 45000 to around 13000 BCE. The latter date is of the first human remains, but the earlier date points to alleged human-generated artefacts. See Martin, *Pré-história*, 61–66. There is obviously a very long history prior to the arrival of Europeans that is both largely unknown, because of the scarcity of archaeological records, but also largely ignored. The way history is told can lead to entitlement or to liberation, and it is also important to take sides here.

17. The Czech Republic came into being as an independent state on January 1, 1993. I will use the name Czech Republic, since this is what most Czechs use. The government tried to introduce the barbarism Czechia, to translate the Czech "Česko," but the term has not caught on in Czech, except sometimes in sports commentaries.

18. Mudde, "Populist Zeitgeist."

near-contemporary of Pope Francis.[19] For me the advantage of Mouffe and Laclau's work is that it allows for, indeed insists on, populisms of both the "right" and the "left," thus avoiding making populism one of those things, like ideology, that is always someone else's problem.

Instead, populism can be seen as a fundamental part of the political reality. In one sense, there are no "non-populist" positions; the question is how one uses and deals with the "people" who are constructed through or around the populist discourse. Although this chapter will not appear to be directly theological, it does have an important underlying theological concern. This concerns the nature of the "people," and can be summed up in a simple question. To what extent does a given populist political discourse lead to the building up of the people of God, and to what extent does it lead to the construction of a people that "hardens it heart," that puts God to the test (cf. Ps 95:8–9)?

These two questions will serve as the basis for chapters three and four. In the third chapter I look at theologies of entitlement. Because of their prevalence in the Latin American (and particularly in the Brazilian) context, I will focus first on theologies of prosperity. Because the crude behavior of money-grasping pastors and a rather rough and ready theological approach can be often easily dismissed, I will try to understand and present the appeal of these theologies, since they are also theologies of liberation, offering escape from poverty and hardship. Not only do they offer such escape, but they frequently appear to provide it too, so they have to be taken seriously. Nevertheless, I will show how theologies of prosperity, linked to populist political movements primarily of the right, end up producing an idolatry, or what we might term an "idology" (the discourse about an idol) in place of a "theology." The chapter then goes on to show how this broader sense of entitlement produces a similar situation in the Czech Republic, not, for the most part, in terms of official church discourse, but in terms of how a significant part of the Czech population regards the other, especially the other who is from elsewhere. The disregard, fear, or hatred of the other may not be expressed in formally theological language, but draws often on a kind of atavistic semi-theological memory and requires theological judgement.

The fourth chapter will then turn to liberation theology. This chapter will concentrate especially on the way in which liberation theology points to the problem at the heart of theologies of entitlement and of all

---

19. On Laclau's reading of Latin American populism, and its similarity to Pope Francis, see Simeoni and Vespasiano, "Primacy of Reality," 278.

political iterations that seek to build on positions of entitlement. Political engagement from a faith perspective arises from a broadly personalist or relational perspective that demands a commitment to the other, most especially to the other who is excluded. This broadly personalist position is necessarily social, and theologies of entitlement are examples of the presence of social sin, one way of characterizing what Leonardo Boff calls "dis-grace."[20] Social sin is condemned by liberation theologians, but I also point to the way in which sexual ethics has come to define many Christians' understanding of "the social." This in itself becomes a form of masking, since it hides or ignores other social evils that destroy life. Against this is a liberating grace that seeks to return a true understanding of freedom for the other. Freedom is also the basis for love, the living out of grace against dis-grace, which seeks to build a new world, knowing that the journey must be undertaken, even if the fullness is never achieved.

The fifth and sixth chapters will then focus in on the expression of a very particular form of liberation theology, by examining Pope Francis and his liberating theology of service, of seeking to be the means through which God's grace can be experienced. After a brief comment on Francis's relationship to liberation theology, I will give special attention to his use of the Argentinean theology of the people, with its strong emphasis on the culture and construction of a people. Then I will look at the four principles that underlie his theological vision, all of which go against theologies of entitlement and support theologies of responsibility and service. His non-synthesising dialectics[21] both allows for difference and points to the weakness of populisms of entitlement and exclusion, because of their deficient theological basis.

Having established this theological base, the sixth chapter then goes on to offer a detailed reading of the encyclical *Fratelli tutti*, issued on the eve of the feast of St. Francis of Assisi (October 3) 2020. The encyclical addresses the issues that are at the heart of this book, so I use it to look at them from the perspective of Pope Francis as he seeks to portray a grace-filled path to liberation. His analysis of the world both shows the problems and the possibilities and then he argues for the need to engage in a politics that welcomes and embraces the other. Without excluding the other who believes in entitlement, he refuses to accept such positions and argues for

---

20. The word in Portuguese is "des-graça." As in English, without the hyphen it means simply "disgrace." I will look more at Boff's negative definition (the absence of grace or opposition to God's grace) in chapter 4.

21. On this, see Noble and Noble, "Non–synthetic Dialectics."

the power of social love to transform societies towards the reconstruction of *shalom*, having the courage to seek for the renewal of *Gemüt*.

The book concludes through a consideration of the role of the Holy Spirit, the giver of life and justice and the one who gives the strength to speak out against the false prophets of entitlement. The gifts of the Holy Spirit enable an engagement with the situation in Brazil and the Czech Republic, always seeking to do good for those who are excluded and oppressed. Political choices require both a commitment to and a rejection of imperfection, since they must be made and they will always fail. The task of the Christian (the task of the saint) is to search out and enable good to be done, so that, as the opening lines of Ephesians put it, through the grace of God, the power of the Spirit at work in the world, and the love of the Father, all may return under the headship of Christ:

> In him [Christ] we have redemption through his blood, the forgiveness of our trespasses, according to the riches of his grace that he lavished on us. With all wisdom and insight he has made known to us the mystery of his will, according to his good pleasure that he set forth in Christ, as a plan for the fullness of time, to gather up all things in him, things in heaven and things on earth. (Eph 1:7–10)

1

The Disheartening of Societies

IN SEPTEMBER 2019 I visited the city of Belo Horizonte, capital of the state of Minas Gerais in south-east central Brazil. It is a city I know well, having lived and studied there for four years in the early 1990s. My previous visit had been in March 2014, a few months before the World Cup in Brazil. A few months after the World Cup ended, Uber entered the Brazilian market and Brazil is now Uber's second biggest market.[1] My friends around the city insisted on ordering Uber rides for me, which gave me the chance to talk to various drivers, all of whom were doing it as a second or third job.[2] All of them complained about the problems of life in Brazil, in a way that I had never heard before. Previously, despite the many hardships, there was a sense that things could and would get better. Now there was only despair, and, with the coronavirus pandemic, hope has only faded even more.

Because I want to examine in this book how liberation theology can contribute to a grace-filled response to political division, it is important first of all to try to understand the causes and nature of this division. This is to evoke and employ the first phase of liberation theology's traditional

---

1. According to data from 2018 cited in Team Machine, "O mercado de aplicativos de transporte no Brasil," Brazil is behind only the USA, and the city of São Paulo has the most Uber rides of any city in the world.

2. Accurate information on how many Uber (and the like) drivers use it as a second source of income is not available, but it could be between 70 and 80 percent. Presumably this also varies from place to place.

See—Judge—Act methodology.³ So in this chapter, I look at the reasons behind this deep sense of despair, as cause and effect of the current sociopolitical situation in two different contexts. The first is that of Brazil. But as I also aim to investigate in what ways a liberation theology of grace can speak to the post-Communist Central European reality of the Czech Republic, in the second half of this chapter I will turn to the Czech sociopolitical situation. In both contexts, I will present an overview of the main political and social questions, to try to understand some of the reasons behind the divides present in both societies. Because I want to look at conflicting underlying theologies, I will also offer a brief oversight of the role of religion in each society.

Reading Brazil

In the first years of the new millennium much of Latin America was marked by "a pink tide," the election of leaders from parties of the political left.⁴ Liberation theology had emerged in the 1960s and 1970s in a period when the majority of Latin American countries were ruled by dictators, led or backed by the military. As countries returned to democratic rule from the mid-1980s on, centrist⁵ or centrist-right governments initially predominated. But the election of Hugo Chavez in Venezuela in 1998 led to various forms of left or left-centrist governments in a majority of South American countries.⁶ Many of these governments were able to achieve significant social change, using money generated by the boom in the price of commodities at the beginning of the twenty-first century. However, the financial crisis that began in 2008 led, as one important contributory factor, to a radical reduction in income and was, along with widespread suspicions of corruption, a major reason in the disappearance

---

3. I have investigated this method in much greater detail in Noble, *Poor in Liberation Theology*, especially in the fourth chapter where I consider the contribution of Clodovis Boff.

4. On this, see Chodor, *Neoliberal Hegemony*. An important analysis of the way in which this tide turned is found in the work of the Brazilian political scientist, Silva, "Fim da Onda Rosa." I return to this below.

5. Despite the inadequacy of the terminology, which often says more about the speaker than the reality, it is both frequently used and retains some residual interpretive power, so reluctantly I will use it.

6. Such governments were found in Argentina, Bolivia, Brazil, Chile, Ecuador, Paraguay, Peru, and Uruguay. In Latin America, there were also socialist governments in El Salvador, Nicaragua, Honduras, Guatemala, and the Dominican Republic.

of many of these governments from power.[7] In Brazil the Workers' Party (*Partido dos Trabalhadores*, known by its initials PT) held power from 2003 till 2016, when the serving president Dilma Rousseff was removed from office after a process of impeachment. What led to this fall?

Before answering this question, we need to consider the long prehistory, especially since the arrival of the first Europeans in Brazil. Pedro Álvares Cabral (c. 1467–1520) led an expedition that arrived on the coast of Brazil on April 22, 1500, making contact with the indigenous people on the following day.[8] For the past five hundred years, then, there has been a complex history of encounter, sometimes peaceful, often violent, that has created both good and bad. The stories can and have been read in many ways. Earlier accounts that sought to downplay conflict and stress harmony[9] have given way to those that look at the deep roots of violence and disregard for the life of the other. Finding a place from which to read the history of Brazil has turned out to be more complex than finding Brazil itself was for Cabral.

I begin my reading of the contemporary situation by turning to a Brazilian political scientist, Fabricio Pereira da Silva. In an article published in 2018, Silva reflects on his own trajectory as an observer of Latin American politics. He writes:

> What in the near past was improbable may appear obvious from an analysis carried out *a posteriori*, and new predictions will be made that will probably prove to a large extent to be wrong in the future. Why then offer one more analysis of the situation? In order to discuss the reality in this moment and find ways to intervene in it: this is what Latin American social scientists have tried to do throughout almost all their history as intellectuals in marginalized and profoundly unequal societies, but something that they have almost not done at all in the past decades. It needs to be done, whilst recognizing that our capacity to influence reality and to predict it is almost zero, in large part because the

---

7. After a brief interlude, Argentina now has a left wing government, as do the Dominican Republic, Ecuador, Mexico, Panama, and Uruguay. Whether the Nicaraguan and Venezuelan governments can be termed leftist, or simply dictatorships, is an open question, though rather an important one, since their actions were once used as positive examples by theologians of liberation. Cuba has a special place in the history of liberation theology in Latin America.

8. For more on this, see the excellent history of Brazil, on which I draw in this chapter and subsequently, Schwarcz and Starling, *Brazil*, 5–12.

9. The classic account is by Freyre, *Casa-grande & senzala*.

eyes of our disciplines, and in particular of Political Science, have not always been constructed for our specific realities, frequently distorting them. And yet we cannot abstain from going on trying—preferably seeking to construct more appropriate eyes, thus hoping to contribute to the effort of a conceptual reconstruction that goes beyond the text.[10]

This lengthy quotation points to the difficulties of trying to give an overview of the current situation in Brazil. What will happen remains unknown at more than a simply banal and obvious level. I am writing during the coronavirus pandemic, with its attendant economic shocks. More tragically, the pandemic, even as I write, continues to have a devastating effect on Brazilians. And, as Silva laments, how do you read the situation in Latin America using tools developed for Europe and North America? The attempt to "think from Latin America"[11] is gaining ground, but to some extent always suffers from having to construct itself, implicitly or explicitly, over against other forms of thought. And still, it is necessary to try to understand.

The desire to search out meaning in the events of any society is not purely a matter of intellectual curiosity, or a kind of voyeurism, watching the falling apart of the kind of commitment to democracy that once united both left and right. From my perspective as a theologian, it also has a theological impulse, to do with the importance of discernment, something that is key for Pope Francis. Where is God at work, and what criteria do we use to determine where God is at work? But to answer those questions requires a more detailed look at what Silva calls the "reality," and an acceptance that there is a reality to be looked at. To find a way to acknowledge there is a reality, however seen, implies a desire to find a way. This involves the willingness to accept that what appears entirely clear may not be. The freedom to acknowledge that we might just be wrong is perhaps the most necessary grace that we need.

Nevertheless, recognizing that societies are even more complex (polyhedrons[12] rather than two-dimensional), I am going to start with the hope that there is a reality about which we can talk, even if we judge it differently. So let us start with some comments on the social and political reality of Brazil in the past years.

---

10. Silva, "Fim da Onda Rosa," 166.
11. Bautista, ¿*Que significa?* The book was published in Madrid.
12. To use a favorite image of Pope Francis, to which I return below.

Transitions

In the late evening of March 31 to the early morning of April 1, 1964, a military coup occurred in Brazil, overthrowing the government of President João Goulart. Goulart had been planning a reform program, including agrarian reform and the nationalization of oil refineries.[13] The military, acting in collaboration with and support of the country's traditional elites, decided that the country needed safeguarding against possible moves towards a more "socialist" political system and seized power. The military dictatorship lasted until 1985, when a new president was indirectly elected, with the first full democratic elections taking place in November and December 1989.[14] In a sign of things to come, the president elected in these elections, Fernando Collor de Mello, was impeached after two years as a result of involvement in corruption scandals. From 1994–2002 the country was led by Fernando Henrique Cardoso, who in a previous life as an academic was one of the founders of the theory of dependency that had a considerable impact on early versions of liberation theology.[15]

Cardoso's government had already made moves towards reducing the inequality gap in the country,[16] but by the end of his government there was considerable unrest at the size of public debt and what were perceived by his critics as neoliberal economic policies. In October 2002, Luiz Inácio Lula da Silva, or Lula as he is almost universally known, the leader of the PT, finally succeeded in winning the presidential elections, after three previous unsuccessful attempts. He assumed office on January 1, 2003, for his first four-year term.

13. See Schneider, *Brazil*, 87; Schwarcz and Starling, *Brazil*, 505–12.

14. The first round of the Brazilian presidential elections took place on November 15, 1989, just two days before the demonstrations that led to the downfall of the Communist regime in Czechoslovakia, which began on November 17. The second round of elections occurred on December 17, 1989. A week before, December 10, 1989, a government of national understanding had been installed in Czechoslovakia to prepare national elections for the new post-Communist state.

15. On Fernando Henrique Cardoso as sociologist and president, see Whitehead, "Fernando Henrique Cardoso." See also Anderson, *Brazil Apart*, 2–51. These pages represent two chapters in Anderson's book, one written in 1994 at the beginning of Cardoso's presidency, the second in 2002 at the end. The first is more optimistic, the second damning.

16. For one indicator of this, see Sobreiro Filho et al., "Beyond Agrarian Reform Policies," 1110–12.

The Workers' Party (PT)

The PT had its roots in attempts to unionize metalworkers in São Paulo in the 1970s. Already in the late 1960s Lula, born in 1945 in the north-east of Brazil, had begun to engage in union activity and by the mid-1970s he had been elected as leader of the Metalworkers' Union in São Paulo. The party itself was founded on February 10, 1980, at a meeting held at a Catholic school, the Colégio Nossa Senhora de Sion, where one of the founding members, Marta Suplicy,[17] had studied. One writer has suggested that six different segments were involved in its formation. These were the growing popular movement against the military dictatorship; the part of the academic elite who had aligned themselves to popular movements and were influenced by the theory of dependency; the wing of the church influenced by Vatican II, Medellín, and Puebla, as well as by the theology of liberation and CEBs (*comunidades eclesiais de base*, Base Ecclesial Communities);[18] the workers' movements of the industrial zones of São Paulo;[19] the many "popular movements" that were politicizing the population; and finally various radical underground political movements.[20]

Over the next twenty years, the PT grew its base, winning elections for the governorship of many federal states in Brazil and mayoral elections in a number of large cities. First entering parliament in 1982 with eight seats,[21] they would eventually become the single largest party represented

17. Marta Suplicy (b. 1945) was a federal deputy and senator for the PT, as well as mayor of São Paulo and minister of tourism and culture under respectively the presidencies of Lula and his successor Dilma Rousseff. Upset by corruption in the party, she later left the PT and voted for the impeachment of Dilma. Her former husband, Eduardo Suplicy (b. 1941), was the first senator for the party, being elected in 1990.

18. CEBs is the Portuguese abbreviation for *comunidades eclesiais de base*, Base Ecclesial Communities. Medellín and Puebla were the second and third general assemblies of CELAM, the Latin American Episcopal Conference, held respectively in 1968 and 1979.

19. The district in the southern part of Greater São Paulo is often known as ABC, and more recently ABCD, after the names of four cities Santo André, São Bernardo do Campo, São Caetano do Sul, Diadema. It houses a huge part of the industrial power of the city, including many automobile works, and it was in this region that the PT came into existence and where Lula worked as a union organizer. These are large cities in their own right, with populations ranging from over 150,000 in São Caetano do Sul to over 800,000 in São Bernardo.

20. I take this suggestion of the different groups from Bakker, "O 'mensalão/petróleo,'" 825. For a detailed investigation into the role of Christians in the foundation of the PT, see Barbosa, "A Esquerda Católica," especially 117–46.

21. The PT were the party with the largest number of seats in the Chamber of

in what is, however, always a very fractured Brazilian parliament.²² It was this feature that led to the first major scandal to touch the party in Lula's first term as president. Known in Portuguese as the *mensalão*²³ scandal, it came to light in 2005. At the time, despite the fact that with ninety-one seats in the 513-seat Chamber of Deputies they were the largest party, the PT needed to find support from members of the other eighteen parties in the parliament, most of whom were not its natural allies.²⁴ The allegations were that the PT was arranging the payment of large sums of money to deputies from other parties to vote for measures that they wanted to get through.²⁵ The source of this money was often the budgets of different state organizations.²⁶

Whatever the actual ins and outs of the case, there was certainly enough evidence of wrongdoing to show that in practice the PT had behaved little better than other politicians. A number of people were charged and convicted of offences in relation to it, and several leading members of the PT had their political careers ended, perhaps most notably José Dirceu, one of its founders.²⁷ Because the PT had always claimed to be substantially different to other political parties in Brazil, it was hit hard by the scandal. In order to gain power, Lula had already had to make concessions that were hard to take for the more radical tendencies in the party, including initially agreeing to maintain the neoliberal financial policies of his predecessor, Fernando Henrique Cardoso.²⁸

Deputies in the Federal Elections in 2002, 2010, 2014, and 2018. In 2006 they received the most votes, but were just behind the PMDB (the Brazilian Democratic Movement Party) in terms of seats.

22. On the problems of the Brazilian electoral system, see Figueiredo, "Os mais relevantes problemas."

23. The word "mensal" means simply monthly, and refers in this case to a monthly salary. Brazilian Portuguese has a particular fondness for both diminutives and augmentatives (in the case of masculine nouns, as here, the augmentative ending is -ão). So it means literally something like "Big Monthly Salary" and is perhaps best visualized with a mouth open in shock horror emoji.

24. On this, see Katz, "Making Brazil Work," 92.

25. See Bakker, "O 'mensalão/petróleo,'" 822–24. See also Figueiredo, "Os mais relevantes problemas," 418–27.

26. Figueiredo, "Os mais relevantes problemas," 419–20.

27. The degree to which Dirceu was guilty is hard to determine, given that not everyone is convinced of the impartiality of the Brazilian legal system.

28. On this, see Vieira, "O *transformismo* petista," especially at 40–54, in a section tellingly headed "O PT ao serviço da burguesia" (The PT at the Service of the Bourgeoisie). See also Anderson, *Brazil Apart*, 47, 54.

Bolsa Família: Attempts at Inclusion

There were, on the other hand, many positive aspects of Lula's first period in power, most importantly the *Bolsa Família* project, which guaranteed a minimum standard of living to everyone. Someone who found it insufficiently radical describes it as follows: "The program was nothing more than a compensatory policy destined to those who could not enjoy their true rights. The government gave these people crumbs, instead of carrying out a real redistribution of income and quality public policies."[29] However, more positive readings see in it an attempt to focus resources on the very poorest people in Brazil. The *Bolsa Família* program involved

> a conditional transfer of income: transfers are made in money (not in kind) for families (not for individuals), in a focused way (they seek to reach the very poorest) and it is conditional (the families are bound to fulfil certain commitments, in general in health and education, in order to receive the benefits).[30]

It served to augment the salaries (cash transfer) of families earning less than one basic salary per month.[31] In return families had to agree to send any school age children to school and to have their children vaccinated against certain diseases (hence conditional).[32]

Although definitions of poverty are notoriously complex,[33] in most measurable terms the *Bolsa Família* program has had a significant effect on reducing inequality in Brazil.[34] Along with some other related pro-

---

29. Vieira, "O *transformismo* petista," 42.

30. Souza et al., *Efeitos*, 7. This work was published by IPEA, the Institute of Applied Economic Research, an agency of the Brazilian government's Ministry of Economy.

31. The basic salary, *salário mínimo* in Portuguese, is a fixed wage that frequently serves as the basis for Brazilian salaries (expressed in terms of how many of these "salaries" are earned—one, two, three, four, and so on). In 2021, the minimum salary was R$1,100 (1,100 Brazilian Reais), equivalent to around two hundred American dollars or 166 Euros. Estimates are that approximately twenty-seven million workers in Brazil earn the minimum salary or less; see Motada, "Cresce número." Among the major successes of the PT governments was the raising of the basic salary by 70 percent between 2004 and 2014, as noted in Bastos, "Ascensão e crise," 13.

32. See, for example, Pinto, "Meanings of Poverty," especially 134–35.

33. I have already touched on this in Noble, *Poor in Liberation Theology*, 19. For more detail, see Pinto, "Meanings of Poverty," 136–37, for the "scientific" definitions, and 137–45 on the experiential understandings of poverty among residents of a favela in Rio de Janeiro.

34. See Souza et al., *Efeitos*, 29–30.

grams, by 2016 it was helping 13.8 million families in Brazil,[35] at a total cost of just 0.44 percent of the country's GDP.[36] Despite the fact that poverty remains strongly present in Brazil, and is indeed growing again, there is ample evidence that the *Bolsa Família* program did succeed in reducing both the rate and most dramatic effects of poverty, especially amongst those living in extreme poverty. The same is broadly true in terms of inequality too. Brazil has historically had a high Gini coefficient,[37] and this still remains the case. Nevertheless, the *Bolsa Família* program is likely to have made a contribution to its fall from almost 0.6 to almost 0.5.[38]

There were, however, other factors, such as a rise in oil prices, which came as Brazil discovered large offshore oilfields, and the rise in prices of other raw materials. The Brazilian economy grew during the years 2002–14,[39] despite the problems encountered with the global financial crisis that began in 2008 and that had repercussions in many Latin American countries, including Brazil. But of course the growing wealth also brought increasing temptations for politicians and others to make

---

35. Souza et al., *Os Efeitos*, 11. The authors point out that this equates to roughly one fifth of the Brazilian population, so somewhere between thirty-five and forty million people altogether.

36. Souza et al., *Efeitos*, 9. The figures refer to 2016, when the GDP of Brazil was some R$ 6.3 trillion. The figure is higher than the Latin American average of 0.33 percent of GDP, though still clearly very low in percentage terms. For a more general overview of attempts to make Brazilian society more equitable, see Fishlow, *Starting Over*, 87–139.

37. The Gini coefficient (named after its developer, the Italian statistician and sociologist Corrado Gini) is used to measure income inequality. The lower the number, the greater the equality. Though not without problems, it is still commonly used as an indicator of levels of inequality.

38. Souza et al., *Efeitos*, 23–28. In 2001 the Gini coefficient for Brazil was 0.595. In 2015 it was 0.514, according to the figures of Souza et al., *Efeitos*, 23. World Bank figures are somewhat different, showing a figure of 0.584 in 2001 and 0.519 in 2015. They also show that the figure has risen in the past three years to reach 0.539 in 2019; see World Bank, "Gini Index." Brazil remains among the nations with the highest Gini coefficients, with anything over 0.5 regarded as highly unequal.

39. See, for example, Segala, "O grande desenvolvimento." The full title translates as "Brazil's Great Development between 2003 and 2015: Was It Really So Great?," and the answer is "no", certainly not in comparison to the particular Latin American or BRICS countries the author chooses. But even he admits that "It is undeniable that there was some growth and economic development in Brazil in the first decades of the 2000s. It is similarly undeniable that this growth was substantial." This growth was positively experienced by a large sector of the population.

sure that they benefitted from it, and it was allegations concerning this that led to the downfall of the PT government.

Lava Jato: Further Scandals and Reactions

In March 2014, a police investigation was launched under the code name of Operation Car Wash, in Portuguese, *Lavo Jato*. This operation, led by the Federal Police, brought together a number of other ongoing investigations into political corruption that had emerged with the *mensalão* scandal.[40] The investigation was far-reaching and led in many directions.[41] At its origins were accusations of bribes paid to or by the state-owned petrol company, Petrobras, many of which had occurred when the President, Dilma Rousseff (elected first in 2010 and then re-elected in 2014) had been its head. Later accusations came to include Dilma herself but most notably the former president Lula, accused of receiving money from a number of companies, both for his own personal gain and for political purposes.[42] As a result of charges laid under the operation, Lula was sentenced to a lengthy term in prison. Having served almost two years in prison, he was released in late 2019, as the appeal system had not yet run its course. In March 2021 various charges against Lula were found to have been illegally laid,[43] which means that at the time of writing in July 2021 he can once again stand for office in the presidential elections to be held in 2022.

Apart from the various allegations and trials, the scandals uncovered by the *Lava Jato* operation also led indirectly to the impeachment of the president, Dilma Rousseff. In 2016, facing increasing unpopularity, in no small part due to economic difficulties, she was impeached, mainly on the grounds of having broken budget laws. Some Brazilian

---

40. See, for example, Gonçalves and Andrade, "A corrupção," 275–76. See also Bakker, "O 'mensalão/petróleo,'" 823–24.

41. A good summary of what is a very complex case can be found in Prior, "Escândalo Político e Narratologia," 16–18. One of the difficulties is finding unbiased accounts of what happened; this article does so, without in the first instance applying judgement. See also Anderson, *Brazil Apart*, 114–18, 145–48.

42. In November 2020, Dilma was cleared of charges relating to Petrobras. The accusations that led directly to her impeachment were also dismissed.

43. See, for example, BBC, "STF anula condenações contra Lula." Technically the Supreme Court found that the accusations were made and tried in the wrong court, so it is possible that they will be brought again.

commentators have referred to this as a parliamentary coup.[44] Although in strict legal terms this may be an exaggeration,[45] the whole affair was deeply problematic, as was much of the judicial process around the *Lava Jato* operation, especially the charges laid against Lula. His supporters consider these charges to be purely political, whilst his detractors and supporters of the far-right regime currently in power in Brazil hold them as proof of the unsuitability of the left for government.

Although there are many imponderables, it is almost certainly true that there was fairly widespread corruption in Brazilian politics in the first decade and a half of the twenty-first century. Whether there was more or less than in the previous decade and a half, since the return of a civilian president in 1985, is very unlikely. The previous impeachment process in 1992 against Fernando Collor (who resigned before the process finished) also involved allegations of corruption, and even Fernando Henrique Cardoso, who at a personal level was probably one of the more honest Brazilian politicians, faced allegations that his administration had bribed members of Congress to pass the legislation that allowed a President to stand for two consecutive periods of office.[46]

Going back to the Collor presidency, it is also the case that a number of politicians have been jailed for corruption. In general terms, of course, this is to be viewed positively, though frequently it would seem that individuals have been sacrificed, without any readily observable change in the system. The effects of corruption or allegations of corruption on the country have been the subject of much study.[47] But more importantly

44. The title of Bastos, "Ascensão e crise," and the sub-heading on p. 45 of his article are very clear on this. The title is "The Rise and Crisis of the Dilma Rousseff Government and the Coup of 2016." The subheading is "O 'austericídio' e o golpe de 2016": "The 'Austericide' and the Coup of 2016."

45. See Nunes and Melo, "Impeachment." At p. 288, they specifically state that "there was no coup." However, there immediately follows a "but", which at least makes clear why others have used the word. On the other hand, Domingues, "Crise da república," 1748, writes "The event that sealed the fate of the Rousseff government, bringing the PT cycle to an end, was a *parliamentary coup*." See also Silva, "Fim da Onda Rosa," especially 170–72.

46. See Anderson, *Brazil Apart*, 43.

47. See, for example, Padula and Albuquerque, "Corrupção governamental," looking at the negative effect of corruption on the market value of government enterprises; Gonçalves and Andrade, "A corrupção," which offers a Durkheimian reading, seeing corruption as manifestation and cause of anomie; Medeiros and da Silveira, "A Petrobrás nas teias da corrupção," on the media construction of scandal; Figueiredo, "Os mais relevantes problemas"; Maragnoa et al., "Corrupção, lavagem de dinheiro."

they had serious repercussions on a Brazilian electorate that was already becoming disillusioned with the PT. In itself, this was not necessarily a bad thing, as the party had been in power, until Dilma's removal, for over 14 years. The problem lay in what was on hand to replace them.

From Frying Pan to Jair: The Election of Bolsonaro

Dilma was replaced by her Vice-President from the Brazilian Democratic Movement Party (PMDB), Michel Temer. It did not take very long for Temer himself to be accused of involvement in various corruption cases. Although he managed to avoid impeachment, he was so unpopular[48] that he withdrew his candidature for the presidential elections in 2018. It was against this background that the election campaign of 2018 was played out. Initially the PT had chosen Lula as its candidate,[49] and as the year went on, he was leading in most of the polls against any of the other candidates, including Jair Bolsonaro, a former army officer and candidate of the far right.[50] However at the beginning of September 2018, less than four weeks of campaigning before the first round of elections, Lula was forbidden to stand by the Superior Electoral Court (TSE), as he had been found guilty of money-laundering. Although the legal validity of much of the process against Lula has been considered highly questionable,[51] there was at the time no recourse against the judgement and Lula was replaced by the man originally chosen as his vice-presidential running mate,

---

The list could go on. There are, it will come as no surprise, a vast number of blogs, Facebook groups, WhatsApp groups, etc., linked to these questions, where the level of debate is not always of the highest intellectual quality.

48. According to polls he had a disapproval rating of over 80 percent; see Redação, "Temer bate próprio recorde." Another international poll revealed that Temer had the lowest approval rating of any Head of State in the world, with only 7 percent; see Schmitt, "Levantamento."

49. The Brazilian constitution allows a president to serve two successive terms of office, but then they have to step down for at least one electoral period before they are allowed to stand for office again. On the Brazilian presidency, see Inácio, "Presidential Leadership," focusing on the presidential terms of Cardoso and Lula.

50. See Lamounier and Guerra, "Eleições no Brasil 2018," 255. On Bolsonaro, see Marina Basso Lacerda, "Jair Bolsonaro: a agenda defendida em sua trajetória política," in Guadalupe and Carranza, *Novo ativismo político no Brasil*, 289–308.

51. As mentioned above, this has even been agreed by the courts. On the initial judgement, see, for example, Oliveira and Veronese, "Brasil y el 'fenómeno Bolsonaro,'" 260. For a report on the judgement from the website of the TSE, see "TSE indefere pedido de registro." See also Anderson, *Brazil Apart*, 169.

Fernando Haddad, a former minister of education and subsequently mayor of São Paulo.

After the first round of voting on October 7, 2018, Bolsonaro held a commanding lead, securing just over 46 percent of the votes, with Haddad second on 29 percent. These two went through to the second round of voting, which took place on October 28, 2018. This saw Bolsonaro win with over 55 percent of the votes cast.[52] Jair Messias Bolsonaro was born in 1955 in the state of São Paulo, and served in the army during the military dictatorship. Having left the army under somewhat of a cloud— he had criticized the authorities for not paying soldiers more and was suspected of planning bombing campaigns against military headquarters—he first became a city councilor in Rio de Janeiro in 1988, before entering the Federal Parliament in 1991. He remained a member of the Chamber of Deputies until his election as president. Not untypically in Brazilian politics, he was a member of many different parties,[53] before ending up running for president as the candidate of the Social Liberal Party (PSL—Partido Social Liberal). In the meantime, he has left that party and set about forming his own political party, Alliance for Brazil.

Bolsonaro is normally categorized as belonging to the far right of the political spectrum. Although the word "fascist" is often used more as an expression of strong disagreement with the political viewpoint of the other than as a specific political description, there are good grounds for seeing Bolsonaro as promoting a form of fascism.[54] Two Brazilian social scientists, in an initial reflection on the success of Bolsonaro in the 2018 presidential elections, borrow this definition of fascism from a Brazilian specialist in public law, João Ricardo Dornelles, who writes:

52. Brazil has a system of compulsory voting for all literate citizens between the ages of eighteen and seventy. However, in practice this law is not strictly enforced, since those who do not vote are normally cleared by an amnesty voted by the congress. In the second round of the 2018 presidential elections over thirty million voters did not vote at all (just over 21 percent of the electorate) and a further ten million (equivalent to 9.5 percent) either returned blank or spoilt voting papers. The figures in percentage terms for abstentions is in keeping with the results of elections since 2002, though the number of spoilt or blank votes was almost twice as high in percentage terms.

53. He had previously been a member of eight other political parties. On the place of political parties in political careers in Brazil, see Sandes-Freitas and Costa, "Partidos políticos." Their article focuses more on decisions to stand for mayoral office and the role of parties in this, but includes material on elections for the national parliament.

54. On fascism as a political philosophy, see Ryan, *On Politics*, 927–45. Ryan stresses the importance of irrationalism for fascism, something I return to in the next chapter.

> Fascism necessitates the continuous construction of an "enemy" who is identified in all those who are "different," failing to recognize human and cultural diversity. Denialism (*o negacionismo*) and intolerance are, therefore, characteristic of fascism. [It consists in t]he negation of human alterity, of rights, of divergent opinions, of diversity, of historical achievements, of knowledge, of dialogue.[55]

Bolsonaro and his followers seem to rejoice in being called fascists, though their definition may be different to that of Dornelles.[56]

In so far as Bolsonaro has a political program, it involves a systematic dismantling of most of the social advances of the past thirty years. He often speaks approvingly of the dictatorship. He has turned back or sought to turn back rights for indigenous people, environmental protection measures, funding for public education, and a range of other socially beneficial policies. Despite this and his apparently criminal mishandling of the coronavirus pandemic, he still retains some support in the country. Rising rates of crime in many of the largest Brazilian cities, the wave of corruption scandals (genuine or not) that afflicted the PT, and several periods of economic downturn all combined to encourage people to seek security in someone who sought to present himself as a strong and charismatic leader and for some the hope persists.[57]

Bolsonaro and the Politics of Religion

One further point needs to be made about Bolsonaro's election, concerning the role of denominational affiliation in decisions to vote for him. Although Bolsonaro is nominally a Roman Catholic, his current wife[58] is a Baptist. Bolsonaro's discourses proved highly popular with a significant number of Brazilian evangelicals and neo-Pentecostals, not least his

---

55. Dornelles, "Direitos humanos," 162, quoted in Oliveira and Veronese, "Brasil y el 'fenómeno Bolsonaro,'" 246. They attribute the quotation from Dornelles to p. 161 of his article, but it is to be found on p. 162.

56. Other politicians, such as Viktor Orbán in Hungary, Matteo Salvini in Italy, Nigel Farage in the United Kingdom or Tomio Okamura in the Czech Republic, to name just some examples, are usually less keen to be identified as fascists, though all of them meet the criteria expressed in the definition given by Dornelles.

57. On this, see Junge, "'Our Brazil.'"

58. Like a number of other politicians who claim to want to defend the family, Bolsonaro is not a prime example of marital fidelity. He is at the time of writing married for the third time.

pronouncements against abortion and homosexuality. This provided another twist to the voting patterns of "evangelicals"[59] in Brazil. Initially tending to vote for more conservative candidates, under Lula there was a surge in support for the PT, before turning back to more conservative candidates, and ultimately to the extreme Bolsonaro.

In an analysis of the elections of 2002 and 2006, an American-based Brazilian sociologist, Simone Bohn, argues that the evangelical vote is to be seen as the vote of an identity group rather than an interest group. Therefore, for example, in 2002, when one of the candidates in the first round of voting was an evangelical, there was a large vote for him among evangelicals, but in the second round, when he was no longer present as an option, many voted for Lula. In 2006 there was no evangelical candidate, and voting was thus more in line with general political interests.[60] In examining the elections, Bohn also investigated attitudes towards democracy, and already in 2007, she could note that

> evangelicals present the highest rates of dissatisfaction with the functioning of the democratic regime in Brazil and the highest likelihood of developing ambivalent attitudes towards democracy. These results are worrying, given that, as indicated by the literature, there is a tendency towards growth of this sector in the country.[61]

This tendency to vote as an identity group and to hold democracy in less esteem can be seen in the voting in the 2018 election.[62] Bolsonaro presented himself as the candidate of the evangelicals, peppering his discourses with reference to God. In itself this would not have been enough—research carried out before the election indicated that 79 percent of the population wanted a president who believed in God and for 30 percent it was important that the president was of the same religion as

---

59. The term "evangelical" is probably best used loosely. There are many genuinely evangelical Christians in Brazil, but it is becoming increasingly unclear as to how to define certain religious groupings in the country, such as the Universal Church of the Kingdom of God (*Igreja Universal do Reino de Deus*—IURD). Without doubting the faith of many of its ordinary members, its leadership can only with great difficulty be described as Christian.

60. Bohn, "Contexto político-eleitoral," on identity and interest groups at 368.

61. Bohn, "Contexto político-eleitoral," 381.

62. On evangelicals in the events of 2013 to 2018, see Ronaldo de Almeida, "*Players* evangélicos na crise brasileira (2013–2018)," in Guadalupe and Carranza, *Novo ativismo político no Brasil*, 217–36.

them.⁶³ But the combination of someone who was skeptical of democracy and who identified very strongly with evangelical interests clearly helped Bolsonaro gain the support of evangelicals.

Two researchers of the evangelical vote for candidates for election to state and national legislatures in the four largest Brazilian states in 2018 note that the three main issues were

> the moral agenda (with an emphasis on the "gender ideology" and the defense of the nuclear family, referred to as the "traditional family"), public security (in relation to the "fight against violence" and "maintaining public order"), and the fight against corruption (which had strong moral overtones and promoted a cleansing/renovation of politics, often without, however, questioning the fundamental participation of companies owned by national and foreign capital or the financial system).⁶⁴

The moralizing discourse, often centered around a rhetoric of loss,⁶⁵ appealed strongly to evangelical voters, but also to certain segments of the Roman Catholic vote in the country.⁶⁶

The latter point is important to bear in mind. In the second round of voting, some 70 percent of evangelicals voted for Bolsonaro, whilst the Catholic vote was split in half. But in absolute numbers, this meant that Bolsonaro's Catholic numbers outweighed his non-Catholic voters by almost two to one (almost thirty million Catholic voters against 21.5 million evangelicals).⁶⁷ Bolsonaro was much less successful with adher-

---

63. Noted in Cunha and Evangelista, "Electoral Strategies," 84, with reference to a survey cited in 93n1, *Retratos da Sociedade Brasileira—Perspectivas para as Eleições 2018*, which was conducted by the Instituto Brasileiro de Opinião e Estatística (IBOPE) in March 2018. As is often the case with sociological surveys, the word "religion" presumably means "the same denomination."

64. Cunha and Evangelista, "Electoral Strategies," 90.

65. Cunha and Evangelista, "Electoral Strategies," 87. See also Christina Vital da Cunha, "Retórica da perda e os Aliados dos Evangélicos na política brasileira," in Guadalupe and Carranza, *Novo ativismo político no Brasil*, 237–56.

66. See Cunha and Evangelista, "Electoral Strategies," 92. There is very little literature on Catholic voting patterns in the elections. This may be because until recently the Roman Catholic church formed a significant majority of the voting population, and thus its patterns would necessarily follow the general trends. But there is also little direct research on CEBs and voting, partly because of the difficulties in determining what counts as a base community and the somewhat loose nature of many of the groups.

67. See Gonçalves, "O mais fiel dos eleitores." As the figures and the report make clear, of course not all evangelicals voted for Bolsonaro, and some of his strongest opponents are to be found amongst more socially engaged evangelicals: the article

ents of Afro-Brazilian religions, those who declared themselves to be of no religion, and those who identified as atheist or agnostic, but he also triumphed amongst Spiritists and those lumped together under the label "Other Religions." Most notably, his majority of over 11 million among the evangelical voters was greater than his overall winning majority of some 10.8 million votes.

The victory of the far-right candidate through the support of a significant number of conservative evangelical and Catholic Christians is clearly a challenge to the Catholic left, which is closely associated with the theology of liberation, both in theory and in practice.[68] Although continuing a long history of division in Brazilian society, there are now two discourses about the aims of society that have very little point of encounter.[69] They are, as will be seen in the next chapter, both populist discourses, and both in their own ways offer the possibility of overcoming experiences of oppression or slavery.

For the right, especially the religious right, there is the feeling of being overwhelmed by demonic powers that manifest themselves in the form of public violence, and in what are regarded as forms of immorality. This immorality is sometimes found in gender and sexual behavior and sometimes in the shape of corruption, something that has been at the heart of Brazilian life more or less since the beginning of colonial times. For the left, including the religious left, there is the ongoing reality of poverty, of injustice, of hunger, of unemployment or underemployment. Both positions condemn the forms of corruption that have kept an elite in power for so long, even during the PT years of presidency. Both also combine a rhetoric of loss with the offer of utopian solutions. Despite some similarities, there are, however, real differences between

---

quotes the rather nice word "PTcostais," which in English would be "PTcostals", pronounced almost identically to "Pentecostal", only without the letter "n". See also on a more detailed breakdown of voting figures or intentions, Alves, "O voto evangélico." See further Lellis, "O Presidente pode misturar," on Bolsonaro's ("Jair Messias") appeal to voters through a series of social media messages allegedly based on John 8:32, "the truth will make you free," also a favorite phrase of liberation theologians; see, for example, Gutiérrez, *Truth*.

68. For an insightful reflection on the history of the Catholic left and politics in Brazil, see Moreira, "Esquerda Católica." I will return to the idea of antagonism in the next chapter.

69. For an analysis of the evangelical view of politics, see Ricardo Mariano and Dirceu André Gerardi, "Apoio evangélico a Bolsonaro: antipetismo e sacralização da direita," in Guadalupe and Carranza, *Novo ativismo político no Brasil*, 329–50. Mariano is one of the leading Brazilian sociologists in this field.

these clashing populisms. Before looking at them in more detail, and focusing on their theological roots, the next step is to look at whether there are similar clashes in the Czech Republic, as a comparison from a very different context.

Reading the Czech Republic

Unlike Brazil, one of the world's largest countries in terms of landmass and population, the Czech Republic is a middle-ranking country.[70] It is also, in its present guise, a new country, having come into existence on January 1, 1993, following the so-called Velvet Divorce, the decision taken by the respective leaders of the Czech and Slovak federal parliaments to go their separate ways and make two states out of the former Czechoslovakia. The country joined NATO in 1999 and became a member of the European Union on May 1, 2004. Behind this summary there lies, however, a much more complicated history.

A Very Short Version of a Long History

I cannot offer an exhaustive history of the country in its various guises.[71] But the events that I have chosen to highlight are not random.[72] The origins of the word "Czech" are debated, though probably, as with many other names, it originally meant something like "people."[73] This people

---

70. Data taken from Worldometer, "Countries in the World by Population." According to this list, out of 235 countries, territories and dependencies around the world, the Czech Republic ranks eighty-six in terms of population and almost exactly halfway (117) in terms of size. Brazil is, according to these figures, the sixth most populous country in the world, and remains the fifth largest in terms of area. However, in terms of population density, Brazil is far less densely populated, with the Czech Republic at eighty-six again, and Brazil at 187.

71. The territory of what Czechs consider their country today includes three regions: Bohemia (Čechy), Moravia, and part of Silesia. Sometimes it is referred to as the lands of the Czech or Bohemian crown. For more on this, see Heimann, *Czechoslovakia*, 1–2. Heimann's dislike of the term "Czech lands" is reasonable, but to use "Bohemian" does not entirely solve the problem (and is unworkable in Czech, anyway, as she points out). I will use both.

72. My analysis is broadly in agreement with that of the noted Czech Catholic historian, Tomáš Petráček, in his analysis of the roots of contemporary Czech religion. See Petráček, *In the Maelstrom*.

73. A classic article on this is Spal and Machek, "Původ jména Čech." See also Blažek, "Čech", which offers a lengthy overview of theories and bibliography.

would seem to have arrived some time in the sixth century, coming from the south-east. The famous legendary account tells of a Forefather Čech (Czech), leading his people on a westwards migration, until coming to Říp, a solitary volcanic hill in the middle of a plain. Climbing to the top of the hill, he is alleged to have claimed the territory visible from there for his people. The mythic power of the legend lies in its strong sense of belonging to the land and its story of the construction of a people.

Although there are archaeological remains going back far further, a key date in the history of the country is 863. In response to a request from the ruler of Greater Morava to the Byzantine Emperor, two brothers, originally from Thessaloniki, Constantine (Cyril) and Methodius, came to the region to instruct people in Christianity, translate texts into Slavonic, and form a local clergy. At this time, though, the proto-Czechs, living further west, had already come under the influence of the Frankish Empire.[74] The major outcome of this was that the Czech lands came under the jurisdiction of the Western Church, though with strong influences from Byzantium even after the Great Schism in 1054 that led to the parting of the ways between the Eastern and Western branches of Christianity. The attachment to the Western Church meant that, despite the Slavic links, there was a stronger link to Western Europe, and this was strengthened in the Middle Ages, when Charles IV of Bohemia became the Holy Roman Emperor.

Less than fifty years after the death of Charles IV, the country was rocked by what amounted to a civil war, following the execution of the Church reformer Jan Hus by the Council of Constance in 1415. Although in part this was due to ecclesial and theological conflicts, at least some of it seems to have been linked to forms of national self-understanding. As a leading contemporary Czech Catholic historian writes of the Hussite movement:

> In the history of ideas in Europe, Hussitism is one of the first instances when a messianic complex is applied to a whole nation. The ideologues of the Hussite revolution created the concept of a nation that best understood the Gospel and was therefore called upon by God to lead other nations and the universal Church.

---

74. See Petráček, *In the Maelstrom*, 9–11. Petráček entitles this section "Cyril and Methodius: Their Mission and Its Failure," which is telling. The mission was in some ways both success and failure, but as Petráček says, it did not lead to a lasting indigenization of Christianity in the region.

The salvation of the whole universal Church depended on the faith of that nation and its pushing for reform (God's truth).[75]

The conflict led to the establishment of two competing churches in the country. Peace was restored by the efforts of the king, Jiří of Poděbrad, who also attempted to gain support for one of the first multilateral European peace treaties.[76] From the sixteenth century until 1918, the country was effectively under the Habsburgs, except for a brief period in 1619–20, when it was ruled by the Elector Palatine Frederick V, known as the Winter King, who was defeated at the Battle of the White Mountain in November 1620. The seventeenth and eighteenth century saw a process of what is often called re-Catholicization, which led to a remarkable religious revival in the country.[77] In the nineteenth century, a period of national revival began, championing the use of the Czech language, the recording and transcribing (or invention) of national myths and legends, and the promotion of a new Czech national spirit. The country was also an economic powerhouse for the monarchy, with the effects of the industrial revolution being felt sooner than in other parts, including increasing urbanization.[78]

On the morning of October 28, 1918, at the statue of King Wenceslas in Wenceslas Square in the center of Prague, Isidor Zahradnik, at that time a Roman Catholic priest,[79] announced to a small crowd the liberation of the Czech nation, and soon after a telegram was sent proclaiming the founding of the Czechoslovak Republic. The first President was Tomáš

---

75. Petráček, *In the Maelstrom*, 13.

76. This document, the full title of which is *Tractatus pacis toti Christianitati fiendae* (known variously also as *Tractatus pacis* or *Cultus pacis*) can be read alongside Hus's final undelivered address to the Council of Constance, the *Sermo pacis*. Both were impassioned calls for peace among different factions, and both have a lot to say still today (as well as parts that would no longer entirely pass muster). On Jiří of Poděbrad and the *Tractatus*, see Jurok, "Mírová a propagační poselstva." The text is in Vaněček and Kejř, *Všeobecná mírová organizace*. Hus's text in Latin and with a Czech translation can be found in Hus, *Řeč o míru*. No English translation appears to exist of this work.

77. On this see Petráček, *In the Maelstrom*, 14–16, and Hošek, "Discerning the Signs," especially here 14–17.

78. See Petráček, *In the Maelstrom*, 24.

79. Born Theodor Zahradník in 1864, he took the name Isidor when he entered the Premonstratensian Order. He was a member of the Imperial Parliament in Vienna. In 1919, he left the Roman Catholic Church and after a brief period as an Orthodox Christian joined the Czechoslovak Church (later the Czechoslovak Hussite Church). He died in 1926. For more on the declaration of the new Republic, see Heimann, *Czechoslovakia*, 37–39.

Garrigue Masaryk, who was head of state until 1935, just under two years before his death in 1937. There is much to admire about Masaryk. He was born in 1850 in the town of Hodonín on the border between the current Czech Republic and Slovakia. His mother worked as a cook, and his father, who was Slovak in origin, worked as a coachman. He was nevertheless able to study and proved very capable, studying philosophy in Vienna with, among others, Franz Brentano. He later spent a year in Leipzig, where he came to know Edmund Husserl, and also an American woman, Charlotte Garrigue, whom he married in 1878.

Evaluations of what Czechs normally call the First Republic vary.[80] Following territorial conflicts especially with Hungary and to a lesser degree with Poland, by the end of 1919 the territory of the new Czechoslovakia was fixed, extending some 1800 kilometers from the western border with Germany to Carpathian Ruthenia, which bordered with Ukraine. The first census of the new country in 1921 counted over 13.3 million inhabitants, a number which by the next census in 1930 had risen to almost 14.5 million. At least until the Great Depression, the Czechoslovak economy was very strong. In the 1920s the country appeared to have established itself in short time as a successful functioning democracy.

There were however problems from the beginning. Although speaking mutually intelligible languages, Czechs and Slovaks had no real history of being one country,[81] and there was a sense of a Prague monopoly on power and decision-making that was only ever partially overcome. But the biggest problem was with the large German-speaking part of the population, generally known as the Sudeten Germans. Heavily congregated around the borders of the Czech lands, it constituted over a fifth of the population of the country according to the 1930 census. When independence from the Austro-Hungarian monarchy was declared, many Germans wanted to become part of Germany, but this would have reduced both the territory and economic power of the new state greatly (many of the factories were in these areas), and the new government took steps to ensure that it retained its land. Moreover, Sudeten Germans were disproportionately affected by the economic crisis at the beginning of the 1930s, which merely stoked resentment towards the government in

---

80. For a critical but reasonable reading, see Heimann, *Czechoslovakia*.

81. At its peak, the territory of Great Morava, with its heartlands in the border areas of today's Czech Republic and Slovakia, controlled much of the territory of the two countries. But this was for a period of perhaps a couple of decades at the end of the ninth century.

Prague. The tendency to patronize the other (as with the Slovaks) or demonize them (as with the Germans) was not the recipe for a unified state. The claims to democracy, as a historian of Czechoslovakia has argued, were suspect, because at the time and arguably still today, "What is not made explicit to the innocent outsider is that in contemporary Central European thought, democracy was popularly considered to be as much about equal standing for the 'nation,' i.e. for the ethnolinguistic group, as about voting or other rights for the individual."[82]

The First Republic came to an end with the signing of the Munich Agreement by the British Prime Minister Neville Chamberlain, which gave away the Sudeten part of Czechoslovak territory to Hitler. The deep-rooted sense of betrayal by outsiders that this has given rise to should not be underestimated. In March 1939, the Nazis marched into Czechoslovakia and the country was again divided, between the *Reichsprotektorat* of Bohemia and Moravia and a puppet state in Slovakia led by the fascist Roman Catholic priest Jozef Tiso.[83] The most devastating impact of the Nazi occupation was the deportation and murder of the vast part of a thriving Jewish community going back almost a thousand years.[84] Attacks on Jews had begun earlier, however, led by members of the major Sudeten German party.[85]

By the end of the war, Soviet troops had advanced as far as Prague, whilst American troops liberated the western part of the country. Agreements between Winston Churchill and Stalin, with the backing of President Roosevelt, meant that the country had been placed under the Soviet sphere of influence. Nevertheless, initially the republic was re-formed under Edvard Beneš, who had been Masaryk's successor in 1935 and who had led the Czech government-in-exile in London during the war. One of the most important actions was the implementation of the so-called Beneš decrees, which expelled nearly all those who had selected "German" or "Hungarian" as their nationality in the 1930 census (or for those born after that date whose parents had done so). The implementation of

82. Heimann, *Czechoslovakia*, 50.

83. See Ward, *Priest, Politician, Collaborator*.

84. On the complexity of relationships between Jews and the First Republic and of Jewish self-understanding in the period, see Čapková, *Czechs, Germans, Jews?*.

85. The first political murder of a Jew after Hitler's coming to power in Germany took place in the spa town of Marienbad on August 30, 1933, when Professor Theodor Lessing, who already in 1923 had warned of the fatal dangers of National Socialism, was shot dead in his home. See Švandrlík, *Historie Židů v Mariánských Lázních*, 26–29.

The Disheartening of Societies

the decrees led to the mass expulsion, often accompanied by violence and theft, of some three million people whose ancestors had lived since the Middle Ages in the country. Nationalist Czech leaders still defend the decrees, whilst others recognize that they amounted to ethnic cleansing. They certainly led to what had once been a multi-cultural and multi-ethnic country becoming very mono-cultural.

The first post-war elections were held in May 1946. They were won by the Czechoslovak Communist Party, led by Klement Gottwald, which obtained over 31 percent of the votes cast.[86] Gottwald led a coalition government until, in February 1948, he orchestrated a coup that led to the resignation of Beneš as president, with Gottwald himself effectively replacing him. Thus began just over forty years of Communist rule in Czechoslovakia. This period saw the execution of at least 248 people, the imprisonment or internment of many others,[87] and periods of greater or lesser repression. A brief moment of respite occurred in 1968, which ended with the invasion of Warsaw Pact troops in August of that year. This was followed by what became known as the period of normalization.

What this period entailed is perhaps best illustrated through Václav Havel's famous example of the greengrocer in his essay "The Power of the Powerless."[88] Havel speaks of the little lie of the greengrocer, who places a sign saying "Workers of the World, Unite" amidst the carrots and onions. He probably does not believe in the system, but by placing the sign there he is essentially acquiescing with and supporting it, as the price for having a trouble-free life. As Havel puts it:

> The slogan has the function of a *sign* and as such it contains—in a hidden way, yes, but still—a quite definite statement. Verbally it could be expressed as follows: "I, Greengrocer XY, am here, and I know what I have to do: I have to behave in the way that is expected of me; they rely on me and they can't hold

---

86. The Slovak Communist Party gained a further six percent, so that the Communists gained some 38 percent of the total votes cast, and ended up with 124 seats in the three-hundred-seat parliament.

87. Precise figures are difficult to determine. I take these from a report entitled "Oběti komunistického režimu", compiled by the Office for the Documentation and Investigation of the Crimes of Communism, of the Czech police. See Wikipedia, s.v. "Komunistický režim v Československu," https://cs.wikipedia.org/wiki/Komunistick%C3%BD_re%C5%BEim_v_%C4%8Ceskoslovensku#Ob.C4.9Bti.

88. Havel, "Moc bezmocných." The essay was written in October 1978.

anything against me; I am obedient and therefore I have the right to a quiet life."[89]

The only alternative is to stop living in the lie and, in spite of the threat of oppression, decide to live in the truth. Such a decision, writes Havel, has not "only an existential dimension (giving the person back to themselves), a noetic one (revealing reality as it is), and a moral one (as exemplary). It also has a clear political dimension."[90]

Havel himself was one of the signatories of Charter 77, which called on the government to uphold the rights accorded to citizens in the 1975 Helsinki Accords. These accords agreed to hold inviolable all post-war European boundaries and to non-intervention in domestic affairs. However, they also contained a clause in which signatories committed to the upholding of human rights, and thus Charter 77 could call on the government to fulfil its obligations. But even with the onset of *perestroika* in the Soviet Union, there were no immediate signs of the fall of communism in Czechoslovakia. However, on November 17, 1989, students and others gathered to march to remember and celebrate the opposition to the closing of Czech universities by the Nazis fifty years previously.[91] Reports, later found to be untrue, that a student had died during this march, and the brutal attacks on many others, led to a series of demonstrations. When it became clear that the army would not fire on demonstrators, and that the movement was too powerful to be halted, the Communist government very quickly bowed to the inevitable and by the end of November they had agreed to the transfer of power, which took place with the election of Havel as president at the end of December 1989.

After November: Events Since 1989

What Czechs call the "after November" (*polistopadový*) period has seen a number of significant changes, most significantly the appearance of two new countries on January 1, 1993, the Czech Republic and Slovakia. The

89. Havel, "Moc bezmocných." The story and comment are at the beginning of the third section of the work. See also on this, and with references to English translations, Sire, *Václav Havel*, 70–72.

90. Havel, "Moc bezmocných."

91. Protests against the Nazis had led to the death of a medical student, Jan Opletal, and his funeral on November 15, 1939, had seen significant student demonstrations against the Nazi occupiers. Nine lecturers and students were then executed on November 17, 1939.

division was agreed by the two federal prime minsters at the time, the Czech conservative nationalist, Václav Klaus, and the extreme nationalist leader of the Slovak Federal Government, Vladimír Mečiar. There was no popular consultation, nor vote, and neither of their parties had committed to the division of the country in their manifestos. On May 1, 2004, both countries joined the European Union, and since the end of 2007 the Czech Republic has formed part of the Schengen area within the EU.

Although it is a stable democratic country, Czech politicians have not for the most part shown great capabilities or honesty. Havel as president was a figure of moral authority, though not always supported in his own country. The other dominant figures for much of the past thirty years have been Klaus, as prime minister and then president for two terms, and the current president, Miloš Zeman, also a former prime minister and now in his second and final term as president. Klaus is a Eurosceptic climate-change denier, who started off badly as prime minister and has not improved. Zeman, originally nominally a Social Democrat, has morphed into a populist role based on personal prejudice. A number of his interventions have been found to be unconstitutional, though the role of the president is unfortunately unclear. Presidents have some powers, which are meant to be more theoretical than real, but Zeman, as Klaus before him,[92] has eschewed the chance to represent the whole country in order to pursue his own agenda.[93]

The Czech Republic Today

This rapid survey of Czech history has been included to show some of the problems that lie behind the current situation. One is that, for most of the past five hundred years, the Czech lands have been either directly ruled by or under the sway of others, starting with the Habsburgs for some four hundred years,[94] followed by the Nazis, and finally the Soviet Union. Although the history of European countries is not always read in postcolonial terms, the history of the Czech Republic can be partly thus

---

92. And to some extent Havel.

93. On how this has played out in the task of appointing governments, see Kopeček and Brunclík, "How Strong"; Mansfeldová and Lacina, "Czech Republic," especially here 140–43.

94. Technically the Austrian emperor was also king of Bohemia, but this meant that to all intents and purposes the country was ruled from Vienna.

understood, with many of the associated challenges.[95] An introductory text on postcolonialism suggests, among other things, that postcolonial thought looks at

> how the First/Western world represented the non-European native/world, how colonial histories, anthropology, area studies, cartography were rooted in a racial discourse, how the native was feminized, dehumanized and marginalized in both, representations and real life in the period of colonialism, the psychological effects of colonialism on colonizer and colonized, the 'instruments' of colonial domination: English literature, historiography, art and architecture, [and] the rise of nationalist discourse that resisted colonialism.[96]

Many of these features are, in direct form, absent in the Czech context. The Soviet Union did not have the anti-Slav racism of the Nazis, and neither in general did the Habsburgs. Nevertheless, the influx of migrants to Vienna in the nineteenth-century to perform frequently lower-status jobs led to at best a patronizing and in practice more racially dismissive judgement on Czechs.[97] For a long time, the dominant and official language was German, and Czechs were to some extent a sub-class in their own country. This led in the nineteenth century to an oppositional discourse, which offered resistance to forms of imperial oppression. The artistic and literary forms are more complex, but also in the nineteenth century Czech began to be used more and more as a literary language, and Czech musicians and painters were part of the national revival.[98] A somewhat related feature, which academics perhaps tend to undervalue,

---

95. On this, see Moore, "Global Postcolonial Critique," especially 19–21, where he looks both at why post-Soviet countries are postcolonial and why the epithet is often resisted. Many of the essays in this volume are relevant for the Czech context, even if the Baltic experience was more obviously and directly one of colonial occupation in Soviet times. However, this was also in practice the Czech experience during the Habsburg period.

96. Nayar, *Postcolonialism*, 4.

97. See Kopczyk, "Those Problematic Slavs." On p. 54, Kopczyk refers to postcolonial readings of central European history, here with reference to Silesia, ruled in part by the Habsburgs and in part by Prussia. This article applies rather to Prussian judgements on Polish-speaking Slavs, but is almost certainly applicable to the southern situation too.

98. A famous example is the *Slovanská epopej* (The Slav Epic), a series of twenty extremely large format paintings by the Czech artist Alfons Mucha, covering Czech and more generally Slav history.

is sport,[99] where national sporting success against the colonizer is hugely important. The Hungarian water-polo team against the Soviet Union in the Melbourne Olympics in 1956 is one example, and for Czechs, the victories over the Soviet Union in the 1969 Ice Hockey world championships served as a symbolically powerful riposte to the invasion of Warsaw Pact troops in August 1968.[100]

However, for my purposes the most important feature is the development of a national discourse that served or serves as a resistance to colonialism. One of the features of Czech history over the past two centuries has been a form of what came to be called in nineteenth-century Russia the battle between the Slavophiles and the Westernizers.[101] Was the country a Slavic country that should look to the East, and see itself as part of a larger Slavic entity (or even at times ethnicity) that was a counter-balance to the West European hegemony? Or was it a part of the West, even if not a part entirely of the hegemonic western European powers? The Czech Republic, Czechs will make clear, is most definitely not Eastern Europe, but Central Europe, and the most impressive response to the struggle between the turn to East or West has been the desire to serve as a bridge between the two.

This goes back at least as far as the arrival of Cyril and Methodius who came as missionary delegates of the Byzantine Emperor Michael III. Although under Photios, the Patriarch at the time of their sending, the first steps towards the division of Eastern and Western churches would take place,[102] the church was still one at this time, and the area of Great Morava was claimed also by the Franks. Cyril and Methodius sought to gain support from both the Pope and Patriarch for their attempts to

---

99. See, however, the brief entry, King and Moraga, "Postcolonialism and Sport." On readings of sport history from a post- or decolonial perspective, see Clevenger, "Sport History"; on forms of neo-colonialism through sport, see Melo and Rocha Junior, "Esporte, pós-colonialismo, neocolonialismo."

100. On this, see Švepešová, "Československá hokejová reprezentace," especially 101–6.

101. See Parush Parushev, "The Slavophiles and Integral Knowledge," in Noble et al., *Wrestling*, 121–55.

102. From an Orthodox point of view, one should add that the first steps had been taken earlier, around the turn of the century, by Charlemagne and his insistence on inserting the *Filioque* into the Nicene-Constantinopolitan Creed. This was one of the major novelties against which Photios complained. The actual schism created by Photios was to do with the right of the Emperor to propose or dispose of patriarchs without papal approval. On this, see Dvorník, *The Photian Schism*.

inculturate the liturgy, using a Slavonic translation.[103] Today the struggle is between three groups, one of which is more or less pro-Russian, one of which looks to the EU, and the third of which seeks to develop a language of exclusive Czech nationalist identity.

Following 1989, there was initially a turn to the West, and a desire to integrate with western Europe. However, even then, Václav Klaus was, at least for economic reasons, opposed to membership of the European Union. In 2004, when the Czech Republic joined the European Union, the majority of the population supported the move. The referendum held the previous year had seen 77.3 percent of those who voted support the accession.[104] Although the percentage of the electorate as a whole that supports EU membership has probably remained fairly constant, an increasing number of negative voices have been raised, and, as in many other European countries, the European Union has proved a useful scapegoat for the incompetence and dishonesty of local politicians.

Andrej Babiš and Politics for Profit

Since 2014 the leading political figure in the Czech Republic has been Andrej Babiš. From 2014 to 2017 he served as finance minister in a coalition government with the Social Democrats and from 2017 to 2021 he was prime minister. Babiš, who holds joint Slovak and Czech citizenship and whose attempts at Czech produce a rather garbled mixture of the two languages, is the owner of a major business concern, Agrofert, which started as an agrochemicals firm, but that now has its fingers in many pies, including owning two of the leading Czech newspapers. Babiš is among the richest people in the country, and is, according to the Slovak Constitutional Court, a former member of the Czechoslovak communist secret police (the StB, *Státní Bezpečnost*, or State Security).[105] As for his business operations, allegations that he came about his wealth by entirely legitimate means remain so far unproven.

    103. On this, see two books by František Dvorník: *Byzantské misie* and *Zrod střední a východní Evropy*.
    104. Turnout was only just over 55 percent, which means that just under 42 percent of the total electorate voted in favor.
    105. The relevant document can be seen at "Kompletní spis spolupracovníka." Babiš continues to deny any involvement, and precisely how active and useful he was as an agent is also another matter. Allegations that he was also connected with the KGB seem to be based on little direct evidence.

There is little doubt that Babiš has used his personal wealth to gain political power and his political power to increase his personal wealth.[106] It is not clear that he has any particular ideological leanings, unless increasing personal wealth is an ideology. He is generally seen as pro-Russian because of his background and his business dealings, but these may also be partly pragmatic. He is only against the European Union inasmuch as it has accused him of corruption and misuse of EU funds for his own personal gain. His initial handling of the first wave of the coronavirus pandemic in the country was highly successful, but his subsequent actions have led to the country having proportionately one of the worst records in the world. This seems to be having an impact on opinion polls, where his party is no longer the leading party in terms of voting preferences.[107]

So what kind of national discourse can Babiš provide? The first aspect is more to do with those who vote for his party, ANO 2011. "Ano" is the Czech for "yes", but the title is also an acronym, standing for "Akce nespokojených občanů", Action of Dissatisfied Citizens.[108] That most citizens in a democracy are dissatisfied is to be both expected and arguably desired. Roughly 30 percent of those who voted in the 2017 parliamentary elections clearly felt that Babiš and his party were the people to deal with their dissatisfaction. Babiš may succeed in appealing precisely by not trying to offer a clear vision of what it means to be Czech today. In practical terms his government is centrist in terms of the policies it adopts, presumably on the grounds that most voters are also centrist. He has shown an ability to know when to pick fights with Russia and when not, and likewise with the European Union. Babiš is normally portrayed as a populist, though his discourse is not overly populist, in the way of

---

106. On the problems of politics in Central and Eastern European countries, including the propensity to corruption, see Innes, "Political Economy." A recent Council of Europe report ranked the Czech Republic last of 42 countries in terms of applying anti-corruption measures: see "Czech Republic Ranks Last."

107. I am writing in July 2021. [Elections in October 2021 saw ANO winning the most seats, but being replaced by a coalition of opposition parties with a commanding majority.]

108. ANO (Akce národní obrody—Action for National Revival) was also the name of one of the pro-Nazi parties in Czechoslovakia, formed in October 1938. For more on this movement see Heimann, *Czechoslovakia*, 96, and the Czech historian, Ivo Cerman, "Název ANO." Whether Babiš's choice of the acronym was deliberate or accidental is an open question.

someone like Orbán in Hungary, though as elections approach it is becoming more directly populist again.[109]

This means that the country's identity is formed rather negatively as a general sense of dissatisfaction. Cleverly this utilizes the strong anti-institutional strain in recent Czech history, which is also a feature of its postcolonial existence. Institutions, for much of the past five hundred years, have always been the instruments of the colonizer, and are therefore not to be trusted. This is at least one of the major problems that the churches have faced in the country, as will be seen shortly. It is also a reason for the anti-EU sentiment in the country, used by nationalist politicians especially in relation to migrants. It is, therefore, rather ironic that Babiš is a migrant from Slovakia, and that Tomio Okamura, the leader of the neo-Fascist Freedom and Direct Democracy party (SPD), whose main campaigning point is racist anti-migrant policies, is the son of a Japanese father and Czech mother.

The development of the highly xenophobic and racist anti-migrant stance began, not surprisingly, around the time when significant numbers of migrants were fleeing the civil war in Syria in 2015 and 2016. There was a huge outcry in the Czech Republic against any attempts to settle migrants in the country, even though under the EU proposals the country would have had to take only twenty thousand people. The figure of just over one million refugees in 2015 that is often quoted[110] amounted to approximately 0.25 percent of the then total EU population (and approximately 0.15 percent of the total European population). To put this again into a more manageable perspective, in a small town of five thousand people, that would mean about twelve new people moving in, or in a city like Prague with just over a million inhabitants, it would have entailed maybe an extra three thousand people, considerably less than the number of students who come each year to study at the university.[111]

Against this background, it is worth asking why this nationalist populist discourse has developed and what effect it has on the role of religion

---

109. I am writing in mid 2021, with elections due in October. Babiš has been adopting an increasingly xenophobic and anti-EU (right-wing populist) discourse, in order to gain voters from the right. Like all successful politicians and business people, he can at least read the market well.

110. Eurostat, the EU Statistics Office, reports that there were 1.26 million asylum claims in EU countries in 2015, more than double the number in 2014. See Eurostat, "Asylum."

111. I appreciate that the spread would not be even, but twenty thousand people in Prague would not be a huge number.

The Disheartening of Societies 45

in the country. Overall the Czech Republic is not a poor country[112] and, in direct contrast to Brazil, it still has a high level of income equality.[113] At least until the onset of the COVID-19 crisis, unemployment was extremely low and incomes had been rising for many people. However, despite this there is a substantial minority who do not benefit, or who do not benefit to such a large extent, or who continue to perceive themselves as disadvantaged.[114] There is also a widespread perception, going back to the First Republic at least, that the decisions are made by people in Prague, who tend to look down on those from elsewhere,[115] and indeed frequently the way that people in the capital vote is at odds with the rest of the country. Although it is more expensive, it is also true that wages are higher and unemployment even lower in Prague than elsewhere. But this does not explain everything, since there are many people in Prague who are opposed to migration too. Age differences and education levels also play their roles, though again they do not explain everything.

One of the aftermaths of communism in particular, but arguably of the whole colonial experience, is that civil society has been relatively weak.[116] This is perhaps changing in the Czech Republic,[117] not least with the efforts of the Million Moment movement, which formed in protest against the government of Andrej Babiš, and with other activities at local levels,

---

112. Though see Pakosta and Rabušic, "Postoje k příčinám," who look at attitudes to poverty in the country, and report that official figures in this period were that around 9 percent of the population was living in poverty. The 2019 figure concerning those at risk of poverty was 10.1 percent, measured as those with an income of 60 percent of median income: see "Statistics on Income and Living Conditions." It is still unclear how much that percentage will rise because of the effects of COVID-19. As a comparison, the figure for the UK is about twice as high.

113. Its Gini number, around 0.24, is one of the lowest in the world, and according to Eurostat, the second lowest in the EU. See Eurostat, "Gini Coefficient."

114. For a comparative central European study of expressions of nationalism, albeit with data from the late 1990s, see Weiss, "Cross-national Comparison."

115. As someone who has lived in Prague since I came to the Czech Republic and who was born and lived a good part of my life in the United Kingdom in London, I should probably confess that this feeling is not without grounding. Both self-reflection and observation suggest that those who dwell in large capital cities do tend to have a superiority complex in regards to the rest of the country.

116. On this, see Noble, "Kirche und Zivilgesellschaft."

117. See Szent-Iványi and Lightfoot, "Determinants," concentrating particularly on the area of international development. The authors show that in this area at least Czech NGOs have had more impact than their Hungarian counterparts, though civil society in general still remains itself underdeveloped.

where change can be more effectively realized.[118] But it is precisely this part of Czech society that is open to migration and more pro-European and anti-Russian. So it is not clear whether a strengthened civil society would make Czechs more or less tolerant, or rather what the critical turning point would need to be for that to happen. In some issues (the rejection of migrants from the Middle East or Africa), the majority is clearly very nationalist, but on many other issues there is probably room for change. By and large Czech society is fairly liberal in regard to sexual issues, though there is often an overlap between extreme nationalism and the kind of rhetoric that claims to support "family life" in its traditional forms.

Religion and Society in the Czech Republic

The question that arises is if Christian believers or Christian churches have anything to offer in this situation. This requires a brief survey of the current religious situation in the country. Two claims are frequently made about the religiosity of the Czechs. The first is that the country has one of the lowest percentages of people claiming to belong to a Christian denomination in Europe, the second is that those figures do not really tell the whole story.[119] The history of this move towards what can variously be termed non-belief or non-institutional belief or perhaps even institutional non-belief is complex, and goes back at least to 1918.[120]

Although of those who claim religious belief, by far the largest number in the country belong to the Roman Catholic tradition, when the independent nation began, the Roman Catholic Church was seen by many as representative of the Austro-Hungarian Empire. Approximately one million people left the Roman Catholic Church in the first decade of the First Republic, most of them joining the Czechoslovak Church (from 1971 the Czechoslovak Hussite Church), which was formed by a group of

---

118. See, for example, Pixová, "Empowering Potential."

119. A helpful introduction to this can be found in Havlíček, "'Měřítko vytváří jev,'" 118–19. Havlíček, a sociologist of religion, points out that whether one finds religiosity in Czech society depends on what one assumes religious belief and practice are. See also, in English, Vido et al., "Czech Republic."

120. See Vido et al., "Czech Republic," 204. See also Hamplová and Nešpor, "Invisible Religion," 591–92. For a fascinating account of the religious dimensions at play in the early years of the First Republic, looking at Tomáš Masaryk, his daughter, Alice, and the Slovenian architect (and staunch Roman Catholic) Jože Plečnik, see the book by Berglund, *Castle and Cathedral*.

Roman Catholic Modernists in 1920.[121] Severe Communist repression of the churches (especially, though not only, the Roman Catholic Church) further exacerbated the situation.[122] Up to 30 percent of the clergy belonged after 1971 to the group *Pacem in terris*, to all intents and purposes a pro-regime association of Catholic priests.[123] The numbers of those who proclaim adhesion to a religious group in the census has fallen dramatically from 1991, and will presumably fall when results emerge from the most recent census in 2021.

All this would seem to support the claim that the Czech Republic is an atheist country. However, "atheism" is a notoriously polyvalent term.[124] One major problem in the Czech Republic is the absence of any socialization in religious belief.[125] With many families already three or four generations from any form of institutional religious belief, there is no passing on of traditions, except that of being a "non-believer."[126] But until recently there has not been the anti-religiosity present especially in Anglophone countries such as the United Kingdom or the United States. The word "apatheistic" has been coined[127] to describe the general lack of interest in religion, and this would be an accurate description of the situation in the Czech Republic. There is little virulent atheism or attacks

---

121. See, for example, Noble, "Various Christian Traditions," looking at how very soon other Christian traditions (especially Orthodoxy and Protestantism) came to be present in the church.

122. On the Catholic church under Communism, see Tížik, "Struggles"; Balík and Hanuš, *Katolická církev*, 132–52.

123. Balík and Hanuš, *Katolická církev*, 142, suggest a membership of 37 percent of priests in *Pacem in Terris* 1973, falling to 32.8 percent in 1983 and 29.2 percent in 1986.

124. See Vido et al., "Czech Republic", 207–13. Vido et al. considers that Czech atheism is a form of what they term "incredulous atheism." CREDs are "credibility enhancing displays," and when these are absent, religious adherence declines. See also Petráček, *In the Maelstrom*, 106.

125. See Hamplová and Nešpor, "Invisible Religion," 595. On the intergenerational dimension, see Laudátová and Vido, "Současná česká religiozita."

126. It is perhaps worth pointing out that Czech does not really have a word for religious in the sense of "having some kind of religious feelings, beliefs, tendencies". The adjective *náboženský* means "religious" as in a religious building, or religious articles, but is not applied to a person, certainly not in normal spoken Czech. There the difference is between "believer" (*věřící*) and "non-believer" (*nevěřící*). The believer would generally be understood as one who belongs to a church and attends services in it, which is obviously a fairly restricted group. This means that in most surveys little room is left for those who are "believers in something", or, as the well-known Czech theologian and Catholic priest Tomáš Halík puts it, followers of "somethingism."

127. Apparently first by Nash, *Religious Pluralism in the Academy*.

on religious belief (except on Islam, which of course most of those who attack it know nothing about, given how few Muslims there are in the Czech Republic). But in principle, the churches are not excluded from the public debate,[128] and individual church leaders or others associated with churches have spoken out on a number of issues.

However, these voices are often mixed. The Roman Catholic Cardinal Archbishop of Prague, Dominik Duka, who was a political prisoner under the communist regime, has, since his appointment as Archbishop, become an increasingly vociferous supporter of politically nationalist and conservative viewpoints, mostly agreeing with his close neighbor, the President (the Archbishop's Palace is right next to Prague Castle, the official seat of the President of the Republic). He is in general opposed to the political, social, and theological stances of Pope Francis and even went so far as to congratulate the leader of the neo-Fascist Freedom and Direct Democracy party on his party's success in the elections.[129] But other bishops and priests, such as probably the best-known Czech priest, Tomáš Halík, have been equally vociferous in their condemnation of his positions.[130] This means, though, that divisions within society are simply mirrored by divisions within the church, and it is almost certainly the case that the positions taken by leaders in the two camps are shared by opposing groups of believers within the church.

Summary

This chapter has sought to give an overview of the causes of division in Brazil and the Czech Republic. On the surface there is very little in common between the two countries. Nevertheless, I hope that it is also evident that there are points of connection between these two culturally

---

128. Even if they may not enter into it greatly. See Kratochvíl, "Analýza role římskokatolické."

129. One of Duka's protégés is leader of the electoral list of the Freedom and Direct Democracy party in Prague. Duka has not at the time of writing disowned him.

130. As I was putting the finishing touches to this chapter, the president of the Czech Bishops' Conference, Archbishop Jan Graubner, archbishop of Olomouc, issued a strong condemnation of candidates for extremist parties such as the SPD who claim to be Roman Catholic. Citing Pope Francis's principles that I examine later in this book, he insists that "it is not possible to argue in favor of a single value that does indeed correspond to a Christian view of society and the world whilst being silent or denying other Christian values." Klimentová, "Prohlášení předsedy."

The Disheartening of Societies

and geographically distant countries.[131] Both suffer from a weak and fragmented political set-up, and corruption is widely believed to be present in both societies. As a result of this, or perhaps as a cause of it, both societies are deeply divided. Brazilians, inhabitants of by far the largest country in Latin America, do not tend to worry about national identity, whereas it has become an increasing preoccupation for Czechs, who in comparison to their western and northern neighbors (Germany and Poland respectively) are a small nation.

When I first came to the Czech Republic, perhaps the most famous way of phrasing national identity was a negative one, used by sports fans, who would chant "Whoever doesn't jump isn't Czech" (*Kdo neskáče, není Čech*). But in the intervening years jumping has ceased to be a sufficient designator for national identity. Both Brazil and the Czech Republic have national myths about the kind of societies they are, and part of the problem has been the difficulty of living up to those myths. Myths, of course, are not untrue. They tell important stories for us about who we are, how we relate to each other, where we come from, where we are going. The Brazilian myth has been one of welcome, of the ability to get things done one way or another, of racial equality, of what one might call *joie de vivre*. The Czech myth stresses the independence and resilience of the people, even under occupation; it places an emphasis on humor and ridicule as weapons of choice, and it has strong links to the land.

These national myths remain strong and important for both cultures. But they do not offer enough. Encountering changing reality, they start to fall apart. The stories that people tell about themselves are, however, never quite as rigid as they may appear.[132] They can evolve in different directions. As I move on in this book, I want to look at the theological underpinnings of two countervailing moves in national myth-telling.

---

131. The President of Brazil from 1956–61, Juscelino Kubitschek (1902–76), was of Czech descent, through his mother. His maternal great-grandfather had emigrated to Brazil already before 1830. Some sources, based on unclear evidence, suggest that his great-grandfather was also of Roma descent, which would be highly positive, but evidence for this seems scant. On this, see Cairus, "De Alemão a Cigano." And Brazil beat Czechoslovakia for their second World Cup success in 1962, coming from behind to win 3–1. Also, as I mentioned earlier, both their contemporary democratic stories began at almost the same time in late 1989.

132. A good example may be the British "stiff upper lip," the attitude of not showing emotions and getting on with life. This was something that only came to be regarded as positive in the second half of the nineteenth century, and is now fading. On this, see Dixon, *Weeping Britannia*.

One is to emphasize the rights of the particular group (either the "nation," or a sub-section of it) to the exclusion of others. Such an emphasis leads to or is based on a theology of entitlement, which sees the grace of God as the tool for God to bestow his favors on the particular group. It seeks for certainty and for the rights to which the group feels are its due. The other is to seek to include and expand the story, to find fulfilment for all, especially the poor (however defined and understood). Here the theological roots are of liberation, of seeking to go beyond the shackles that prevent the fullness of life in Christ, where God's grace opens up new possibilities of growing to that fullness.

Put like that, of course, it makes the first group the problem. But the boundary line between the two almost certainly runs through most of us,[133] and it is mainly the content of the entitlement and the nature of liberation that is in question. It is always important to recognize that those one disagrees with also have an opinion, and that there is something that they perhaps rightly fear will be lost, and that whatever it is may indeed be worth holding on to. The concrete expressions may often be unacceptable, but the intuition needs to be listened to. And whichever story is told is an attempt to shape the story of the nation as a single story that excludes other versions.

In the next chapter, then, I want to look more closely at the problem of division, of the clash of two conflicting populisms. That they clash, we will see, may be inevitable and even healthy, but the real question will be how to allow the clash to happen on something approaching a level playing field and how to welcome clashes without being overwhelmed by them. An answer, at a politico-social level, to the question of whether there is or should be a way of overcoming divisions is clearly beyond the scope of this book. My interest is more narrowly theological. More clearly in Brazil, but arguably in a more "secular" form in the Czech Republic, underlying this

---

133. I draw this metaphor from Decree 4, paragraph 20, of the Thirty-Fourth General Congregation of the Society of Jesus, on "Our Mission and Culture," which noted that "the boundary line between the Gospel and the modern and postmodern culture passes through the heart of each of us. Each Jesuit encounters the impulse to unbelief first of all in himself; it is only when we deal with that dimension in ourselves that we can speak to others of the reality of God. In addition, we cannot speak to others if the religious language we use is completely foreign to them: the theology we use in our ministry cannot ignore the vista of modern critical questions within which we too live. Only when we make sense of our own experience and understanding of God can we say things which make sense to contemporary agnosticism." The text can be found at "Decree 4."

debate are different ways of understanding what it is to be human, which is linked to different understandings of how God interacts with God's creation. Is God at our service, or are we at God's service? Although I will only begin more directly to address this question in chapter 3, it is one that must be kept in mind as we move on to the question of populism.

2

Populisms in Conflict

IN THE PREVIOUS CHAPTER, I presented an overview of the current sociopolitical situation in Brazil and the Czech Republic. This synchronic reading examined the divisions present in both societies. Deep social division is not, though, specific only to these places or this moment in time. It is instead a feature of human social life in many different places and periods. In this chapter, I want to look in more detail at some of the reasons behind this apparent impulse to division. To do this, I draw on one particular interpretation of the notion of populism that enables me to read the conflicts in society as manifestations of two competing and irreconcilable worldviews. This will enable me in the following chapters to bring out the underlying theologies that are used, implicitly or explicitly, to support these conflicting positions.

Briefly to anticipate my theological reading, I will be looking at how different views of society understand what it is to be human, and how they consider the nature of human interrelations (society), and thus what it means to find liberation. Using the insights of Ernesto Laclau and Chantal Mouffe, I will present the different approaches underlying the conflict as a clash of populisms. Referring back to the first chapter, I will look at how in Brazil and the Czech Republic the struggle is between a form of right populism, heavily nationalist and exclusivist, and forms of left or center-left populism, which are more socially (though not necessarily ethnically) inclusive.

The debate around populism is already extensive and shows no sign of abating. My aim here is narrower, and focuses on the fact that any definition of "populism" includes some idea of a "people." My main interest, which will later tie in with my examination of Pope Francis's theology,[1] is to see how this "people" is constructed and for what end. I do this because in focusing later on theologies of entitlement and, in contrast, of liberation, I will also be looking at how these theologies understand the "people of God." Because much populist discourse works on the basis of appeal to the emotions, I also look at the importance of the affective, since it too has its role in theology. But first I turn to a brief account of populism itself.

Understanding Populism

To begin, then, what is populism? Frequently an accusation of populism serves as a shorthand condemnation of an opponent.[2] On the other hand, it would be wrong to assume that no such thing as populism exists. It is therefore necessary first to outline what we are talking about. Over the past fifteen to twenty years, the literature on populism has expanded enormously and definitions have become increasingly sophisticated and nuanced.[3] Broadly, I will be following what has been termed the "ideational approach to populism." In introducing this approach, two of its leading representatives, Cristóbal Rovira Kaltwasser and Kirk Hawkins, say:

> The common discourse of populist parties and movements reveals a shared way of seeing the political world: as a Manichean struggle between the will of the common people and an evil, conspiring elite. They [the scholars] argue that these ideas, expressed in the rhetoric of leaders and supporters, have a real impact on politicians' behavior in office and the resultant policies. Moreover, these ideas are one of the main factors motivating

---

1. See McCormick, "The Populist Pope?," 160.

2. Though often presented as someone else's problem, as I will understand the term, most of us are populists and all of us have ideologies. The debate is over what the populism aims at, what kind of people we are trying to construct.

3. For some recent accounts of what populism is and how it is manifested in different settings, see, for example, Torre, *Global Populism*; Fitzi et al., *Populism*; Morelock, *Critical Theory*; Mudde and Rovira Kaltwasser, *Populism in Europe*; Conniff, *Populism in Latin America*; Basset and Launay, "Latin American Populism."

people to mobilize and support populist forces. We call this the *ideational approach* to populism.⁴

Rovira Kaltwasser argues elsewhere for adopting only "a minimal definition of populism."⁵ He takes as his preferred starting point Cas Mudde's definition of populism as: "a thin-centred ideology that considers society to be ultimately separated into two homogenous and antagonistic groups, 'the pure people' versus 'the corrupt elite,' and which argues that politics should be an expression of the *volonté générale* (general will) of the people."⁶ Rovira Kaltwasser expresses this distinction between "people" and "elite" in populism by appealing, as in the description above, to the theological term "Manichean."⁷ I take him to be using it descriptively from the point of view of the "people," who view the "elite" as evil, whilst they, the people, represent all that is good. Clashes of populisms are, then, even if unwittingly, already theological clashes, opposing different moral visions of the world and the forces that shape it. The particular ways in which the populisms are expressed depend on local circumstances; since they are "thin ideologies," they can latch on to "thicker" ideologies, such as nationalism or racism, for example.⁸

But they can also latch on to other more life-giving ideologies, such as liberation. Here I follow the Uruguayan Jesuit Juan Luis Segundo (1925–96), among the most sophisticated of liberation theologians. Segundo perceived that theology is itself in its expression always necessarily ideological.⁹ To use "ideology" as a solely pejorative term—a weakness

---

4. Hawkins et al., *Ideational Approach*, 2. The ideational approach develops and expands the approach of Ernesto Laclau that I focus on below. See also on this Hawkins and Rovira Kaltwasser, "Ideational Approach to Populism," 514. In this article the authors, noting that populism studies began as a part of Latin American Studies, both introduce the ideational approach and argue for its relevance to Latin America.

5. Cristóbal Rovira Kaltwasser, "How to Define Populism? Reflections on a Contested Concept and Its (Mis)use in the Social Sciences," in Fitzi et al., *Populism*, 64.

6. Rovira Kaltwasser, "How to Define Populism?," 64, citing the famous paper of Cas Mudde, "The Populist Zeitgeist," 543.

7. See, for example, Rovira Kaltwasser, "How to Define Populism?," 65: "populism is first and foremost a specific set of ideas that is characterised by the moral and Manichean distinction between 'the people' and 'the elite.'" See also Andrew Arato and Jean Cohen, "Civil Society, Populism, and Religion," in Torre, *Global Populism*, 105: "populism invariably construes the people and the non-people, and social antagonism generally, in moralistic Manichean terms."

8. See Arato and Cohen, "Civil Society, Populism, and Religion," 102.

9. This is most clearly expressed in Segundo, *The Liberation of Theology*, especially

exclusively of other people from which I am thankfully spared—is unhelpful, since it seeks to disguise the fact that all ways of thinking take place from a particular and necessarily limited perspective. Thus, liberation theology also appeals to an ideological position, in that, from a particular interpretation of faith, it seeks both to draw on and construct a coherent set of practices that will lead to the transformation of the whole person. This has inevitable and necessary social, political, and cultural implications, since human life occurs within these contexts.

Chantal Mouffe and Ernesto Laclau

Bearing this in mind, I now turn to two of the leading writers on the subject of populism over the past thirty years. Chantal Mouffe was born in Belgium in 1943 and is a Professor in the Department of Politics and International Relations of the University of Westminster in the United Kingdom, where she also directs the Centre for the Study of Democracy. Ernesto Laclau, who was her husband, was born in Argentina in 1935, and after initial studies there, moved to the United Kingdom, becoming Professor of Political Theory at the University of Essex and a founding member of its Centre for Ideology and Discourse Analysis. He died in 2014. Mouffe and Laclau pursued related but independent careers, writing both separately and together. Mouffe continues to write on issues around populism and what she terms agonistics, to which I return shortly.

Neither of them is greatly interested in religion, though in a brief paper on religion and liberal democracy Mouffe acknowledges that "the fight for social justice has often been enhanced by the participation of religious groups."[10] When Laclau engages with religion, it is frequently as a representative of reaction. However, in 2002, he published a short work in Spanish, drawing on three papers he had given, which carries the title (in English translation) *Mysticism, Rhetoric, and Politics*. He draws

---

125–53. For a good overview of Segundo's position and references to relevant works, see Ahlert, "Fé e ideologia." See also Scott, *Theology, Ideology, and Liberation*, especially 9–74, in which he looks at ideology and then discusses whether theology is hegemonic and ideological. Scott aims to present a non-ideological theology that takes the Marxist critique of ideology seriously. I think the difference will be that for Segundo (and I follow him here), ideology is inevitable, but it requires, and here I agree with Scott, constant self-reflection and self-critique, so that theology can still make claims that are capable of going beyond the limitations of the particular theologian.

10. Mouffe, "Religion," 325.

mainly on Jewish mysticism, but argues that the "thesis that I am trying to defend is that this double movement that finds its extreme form in mysticism—that is to say, the incarnation and deformation of particular contents through the expansion of logics of equivalence—is at the root of every ideological process, including political ideologies."[11] What this means will be explained in more detail later on, but for now it is simply enough to note that a language that draws on the transcendent is not entirely alien to him. Indeed, Andrew Arato has claimed that in describing populism, Laclau "theologizes it and strongly affirms the theological structure he secretly introduces."[12]

In the preface to a dissertation written in 2010, Daniel Miller noted that his chapters on Laclau would be particularly expository, because he presumes "an overall lack of familiarity with Laclau's thought on the part of readers within the areas of religious studies and theology".[13] However, in the past decade or so, a growing number of writers in the area of theology and politics have begun to draw on the writings of both Laclau and Mouffe.[14] However, for those readers who are not so familiar with them, I turn now to their work, to see how they can help give a language to talk about division, which I will then develop in subsequent chapters by looking at the underlying theological ideas and practices. This focused reading means that I will necessarily have to leave out a lot of the complexity present in their writings.[15]

---

11. Laclau, *Misticismo*, 44. See also Laclau, "On the Names of God." Also on this see Panotto, "La dimensión política."

12. Arato, "Political Theology and Populism," 156; on Laclau, see 156–66.

13. See Miller, "Political Theory," ix.

14. For earlier attempts to bring their thought into dialogue with religion, see especially Stavvrakis, "Religion and Populism"; Stavvrakis, "Antinomies of Formalism." See also Mejía Carrillo, "Populism and Religion." For ways in which an agonistic approach can help create unity between religions, see Indralak and Giordano, "Chantal Mouffe and Religious Pluralism." On links between spirituality and radical democracy, see Stoddart, "Spirituality and Citizenship." See also Springs, "On Giving." Among more recent articles, see, for example: Peruzzotti, "El populismo"; Herrero, "Laclau's Revolutionary Political Theology"; Gabatz and von Sinner, "Populismo e 'povo.'"

15. One author, writing on populism, has noted that "Mouffe and Laclau's writings on Marxism and populism—some of which they produced together, and some separately—are famously dense and sometimes resistant to summary." Baker, "'We the People.'"

Hegemony and Socialist Strategy

In the introduction to their first major work on populism, *Hegemony and Socialist Strategy*,[16] Laclau and Mouffe note that "Political conclusions similar to those set forth in this book could have been approximated from very different discursive formations—for example, from certain forms of Christianity."[17] With their interest in the Italian Marxist Antonio Gramsci (1891–1937), shared with liberation theologians,[18] it seems to me that among the forms of Christianity would be liberation theology, but I shall return to that later. For now, it is time to turn to how they understand the crucial concept of hegemony.

Hegemony, for them, "will allude to an absent totality and to the diverse attempts at recomposition and rearticulation which, in overcoming this original absence, made it possible for struggles to be given a meaning and for historical forces to be endowed with full positivity."[19] Rather than being a fully developed set of ideological stances, then, hegemony is in this sense something akin to an eschatological reality, a journey towards fullness of meaning and sense. Given the insistence on hegemony having to do with the development of discourses, it can be understood as an enabling discourse that makes it possible to find meaning amidst the contingency of life. This means, for example, that at one level there is indeed no such thing as society.[20] That is to say, society is not "a thing," an objective existent that can be appreciated and understood and accepted by all.[21] As they put it, "We must, therefore, consider the openness of the

16. Laclau and Mouffe, *Hegemony*. The first edition was in 1985, the second in 2001.

17. Laclau and Mouffe, *Hegemony*, 3.

18. For an overview, see Pagnelli, "Gramsci." For a short overview of Gramsci's life and thought, see Buttigieg, "Antonio Gramsci."

19. Laclau and Mouffe, *Hegemony*, 7.

20. The former British prime minister, Margaret Thatcher, once famously claimed in an interview that there is no such thing as society. She did go on to say that there is "a living tapestry of men and women and people and the beauty of that tapestry and the quality of our lives will depend upon how much each of us is prepared to take responsibility for ourselves and each of us prepared to turn round and help by our own efforts those who are unfortunate." In a sense, then, Mrs. Thatcher was echoing Laclau and Mouffe, though no doubt this would have horrified her. A transcript of the interview is available at Thatcher, "Interview."

21. One of Laclau's first articles, published in 1983, was entitled "The Impossibility of Society." The article is also cited in Herrero, "Laclau's Revolutionary Political Theology," 15.

social as the constitutive ground or 'negative essence' of the existing, and the diverse 'social orders' as precarious and ultimately failed attempts to domesticate the field of differences."[22]

All attempts to define the social order, to articulate a normative understanding of society (which is frequently of course presented as a descriptive account), will, for Laclau and Mouffe, ultimately fail, because society or the social is not a fixed reality, but a fluid one,[23] with competing discourses (or hegemonic orders) seeking to describe it. As they put it, in relation to Louis Althusser:[24]

> The symbolic—i.e., overdetermined—character of social relations therefore implies that they lack an ultimate literality which would reduce them to necessary moments of an immanent law. There are not two planes, one of essences and the other of appearances, since there is no possibility of fixing an ultimate literal sense for which the symbolic would be a second and derived plane of signification. Society and social agents lack any essence, and their regularities merely consist of the relative and precarious forms of fixation which accompany the establishment of a certain order. This analysis seemed to open up the possibility of elaborating a new concept of articulation, which would start from the overdetermined character of social relations.[25]

It is worth unpicking this quotation, before applying it to a reading of the situation in Brazil and the Czech Republic.

For Althusser, as Laclau and Mouffe explain, overdetermination,[26] a concept drawn from Freudian psychology, means that, for any given political situation, there are multiple contradictions in play that cannot be simply reduced to one general contradiction but combine to produce an effect. So, for example, Althusser asks, why did the Russian Revolution succeed, whilst others failed? Even if the general contradiction

22. Laclau and Mouffe, *Hegemony*, 95–96.
23. See Blühdorn and Butzlaff, "Rethinking Populism."
24. Louis Althusser (1918–90), a French Marxist philosopher, was an influential figure for Clodovis Boff in his classic work on method in liberation theology, *Teologia e Prática*. On this see also Noble, *Poor in Liberation Theology*, 107–9. Boff, however, works with Althusser's theory of generalities, not the concept of overdetermination.
25. Laclau and Mouffe, *Hegemony*, 98. The rejection of the two planes is at least reminiscent of the rejection of the two planes (the supernatural and the natural) in Roman Catholic theology in the 1950s and 1960s.
26. His classic statement on the theme is "Contradiction and Overdetermination" in Althusser, *For Marx*.

between capital and labor was present everywhere, there were many other contradictions in Russia, and it is the interplay between these that led to conditions in which the revolution could take place. It was thus overdetermined. To call the "symbolic" overdetermined is to draw even more, though, on Freud's use of the term, especially in his *Interpretation of Dreams*, where many events in one's life, both more or less banal occurrences of daily life and deeply repressed thoughts, can combine to give content and shape to the dream.[27] For Laclau and Mouffe this leads ultimately to the importance of discourse.

For even if there is no such "thing" as society, this does not mean that society does not exist. It simply means that it is contingent and a result of a whole gamut of actions and interactions, expressed in different competing discourses. Hegemony, fundamentally, is the explanation of the particular contingent relationality that dominates at any given time. In this sense, then, all forms of social organization are hegemonic. For hegemony is about the construction of a social order, and that happens through articulation, which Laclau and Mouffe understand as "any practice establishing a relation among elements such that their identity is modified as a result of the articulatory practice."[28] Although this is not precisely the language that Laclau and Mouffe would use, we can understand this as being about the construction of the stories that a people tells about themselves.

Hegemonic Constructions in Brazil and the Czech Republic

This already points to one of the problems that underlies the situation analyzed in the previous chapter. In both Brazil and the Czech Republic (and of course elsewhere) there are conflicting narratives (discourses), which is also to say there are attempts to construct very diverse social orders. A key element in both settings is to do with who counts as an actor in the narrative. In the 2018 Brazilian election campaign Bolsonaro even tried to use the anti-foreigner trope in Brazil, though probably with little success.[29] The word "marginalized" already implies people on the

27. Motta and Serra, "Ideologia," 143, argue that Laclau and Mouffe's turn to the symbolic ignores the fact that Althusser applies the concept of overdetermination to the real.

28. Laclau and Mouffe, *Hegemony*, 105.

29. Safarik, "Melting Pot," 231. I have only once been able to go to Brazil with my wife. While there we were travelling with some friends, and spent a night in a town

edge: Bolsonaro and his supporters have tried to push such people over the boundary to become outsiders. This is a clear attempt to construct a hegemonic discourse about the nature of Brazilian social order. This discourse is the articulation of a praxis of exclusion, of concentration of power and wealth, of the abuse of the rights of those who are considered as not belonging. The fact that this discourse may be unacceptable to many (and should be unacceptable to all) does not mean that it is not a construction of a social order.

Against this, there are other narratives. At the end of May 2020 in a live television interview, a Brazilian economist Eduardo Moreira, noted, in response to a poll on attitudes to Bolsonaro, that some 70 percent of the Brazilian population were against him, and that they needed to affirm their rights and their voice.[30] This, in the way of things, led to a hashtag with the words "Somos 70 por cento," "We are 70 percent," a statement of rejection of Bolsonaro, which also includes a very different vision of how the country could be, or, to put it another way, offers a competing hegemonic discourse. Stronger discourses of this nature, since they also seek to have something positive to say, come from supporters of the PT and former president Lula. This oppositional discourse will emphasize the importance of education, of democracy, of the reduction of inequality, and the promotion of greater opportunity for all.

Similar differences can be noted in the Czech Republic too. Here the extremes are for the most part less marked, since the extreme right, though represented in parliament, is not as numerically strong as it is in Brazil, and the anti-migration stance is actually a racist anti-Islamic stance, rather than a campaign against migration as such. The country needs labor, and no one, as far as I know, complains about Slovak migration,[31] though Slovaks are the second largest group of migrants in

---

of some ninety thousand inhabitants in the state of São Paulo. We stayed with some friends of our friends (a nicely Brazilian thing to do) and not only their children but even they were intrigued to meet my wife, from the Czech Republic, and all of them found the sound of Czech very bizarre. The children and some of the other adults we encountered had never met a foreigner before.

30. For more information see Moreira, "Porta-voz do #somos70porcento"; BBC, "O que é o movimento." This latter article reports that the poll found that 33 percent of the population thought at the time that Bolsonaro was doing a good or excellent job, with 65 percent thinking he was doing a bad or below average job, and 2 percent who did not know. Presumably "We are somewhere between 65 and 67 percent" was not judged such a memorable slogan.

31. At some point during one of the coronavirus lockdowns, when the Czech

the country.³² Nor indeed is there much complaint about Ukrainians, who are the largest group of migrants.³³ So the problem is not migration, but the fear of terrorism and a fear of the unknown and differently pigmented other (racism).

But if the division in the Czech Republic is not quite as extreme as in countries like Brazil, the United States or the United Kingdom, the struggle to provide the dominant hegemonic discourse is still strongly present. This is connected with how the past is integrated into the present, a problem that the Czech Republic has never really dealt with.³⁴ After 1989, the then President, Václav Havel, took the apparently magnanimous decision not to seek to punish unduly those who had actively served the Communist state. Havel's decision was a mixture of pragmatism and principle. The principle was that a democracy should not seek revenge, but set about constructing a new just society, which is of course a hegemonic discourse itself. More pragmatically, as Havel notes, some seven million people had been "members"³⁵ of the Communist Party, and there was a practical need to have people around to do some of the work that a state needs (police, army, civil service, university teachers, and so on).³⁶

Thus many people who were to some extent or other complicit in the former regime are still in positions of responsibility and authority, or are simply still doing their jobs or having to come to terms with what happened in the past. Even the Communist Party was not banned and

---

Republic was already showing a high number of cases, Slovakia closed its borders for a while with the country. The internet joke was that this was to make sure that they kept the Czech Prime Minister Andrej Babiš (originally Slovak) out of the country.

32. The latest figures for 2019 show that there are just over 120,000 Slovaks living in the country, which is approximately 20 percent of the total (the exact figures are 121,278 Slovaks out of 595,881 foreigners, which is 20.35 percent). See "Cizinci."

33. Officially there are 145,518 Ukrainians in the country. Slovak and Czech are still mutually intelligible languages, and Ukrainians who speak either Ukrainian or Russian or both, can usually pick up another Slavic language relatively well, so linguistically life is simpler. The third largest group of migrants is from Vietnam (61,952), and that story is a more complex one. Migrants from the UK, like me, do not in general experience any xenophobia.

34. See Noble, "Living."

35. Of course membership of the Communist Party was a bit like membership of majority Christian churches. Not everyone who was a member of the party was a convinced and active Communist.

36. Havel, *Prosím stručně*, 54. There are laws to prevent former secret police agents or others with a close connection to the regime from holding various offices, but implementation is not always easy.

continues to be represented in parliament, where it has offered tacit support to shore up the minority government of Andrej Babiš. The consequence of the inability or unwillingness to come to terms with the past is that the discourse of the past may have changed its colors, but still holds considerable sway. Words like "democracy," "justice," "honesty," "truth," have an almost Orwellian ring to them. The very name of the neo-Fascist Freedom and Direct Democracy party is indicative of this.

The opposing hegemonic discourse seeks to rescue these terms and to draw on the more multi-cultural and multi-ethnic memories of Czech history. Following the election of the Babiš government, a protest movement, under the banner *Milion chvilek pro demokracii* (A Million Moments for Democracy) formed, to call for Babiš's resignation. Led mainly by young students (its first chair, Mikuláš Minář, a former student of the Protestant Theological Faculty of Charles University, was born in 1993), it has succeeded in gaining considerable support, gathering at one demonstration almost a quarter of a million people. Like all protest movements, its discourse is phrased more negatively, but again like most protest movements the negative contains an implicit positive, calling for honesty and truth in public life, for government to be for the people, not for a private company, and for people to come clean about the past, to name just a few of the demands.[37] These demands offer a vision of society, and it is too a hegemonic discourse. So, for now, I take from this brief look at hegemony the importance of recognizing that all political movements utilize discourses to justify their position. And so, of course, do theologies, mine and others. The implications of this will become clearer as we progress.

Hegemonic Discourses of Populism

It should be clear now that the attempts to develop a hegemonic discourse are both common and conflictual. In an interview given in 2008 Chantal Mouffe summed up what she and Laclau had understood by hegemony:

> To speak of hegemony means that every social order is a contingent articulation of power relations that lacks an ultimate

---

37. In late 2020, Minář left the leadership of the movement to try to establish his own political party. However, the problem of having no positive program has meant that this has gained little traction and the party will no longer seek to contest elections. A channel for protest is important but insufficient.

rational ground. Society is always the product of a series of practices that attempt to create a certain order in a contingent context. These are the practices that we call "hegemonic practices." Things could always be otherwise. Every order is predicated on the exclusion of other possibilities. A particular order is always the expression of a particular configuration of power relations.[38]

These hegemonic practices are closely tied up with the question of populism, and it is to populism that I now turn.

An American journalist, Peter Baker, began an essay on populism published in the British newspaper, *The Guardian*, by noting:

> When populism appears in the media, which it does more and more often now, it is typically presented without explanation, as if everyone can already define it. And everyone can, sort of—at least as long as they're allowed to simply cite the very developments that populism is supposed to explain: Brexit, Trump, Viktor Orbán's takeover of Hungary, the rise of Jair Bolsonaro in Brazil. The word evokes the long-simmering resentments of the everyman, brought to a boil by charismatic politicians hawking impossible promises. Often as not, populism sounds like something from a horror film: an alien bacteria that has somehow slipped through democracy's defences—aided, perhaps, by Steve Bannon or some other wily agent of mass manipulation—and is now poisoning political life, creating new ranks of populist voters among "us." (Tellingly, most writing about populism presumes an audience unsympathetic to populism.)[39]

In other words, populism, as noted at the beginning of the chapter, is a negative descriptor that only ever applies to other people, like terrorism or proselytism.[40] As the examples given by Baker indicate, outside of Latin America, but now also within it, populism is also seen as a problem principally of the right, where those who are seen as less intelligent than

---

38. Elke Wagner, "Interview with Chantal Mouffe," in Mouffe, *Agonistics*, 131. The interview was originally published as Wagner, "'Und jetzt, Frau Mouffe?'"

39. Baker, "'We the People.'"

40. "Des einen Populismus ist des anderen Demokratie, und umgekehrt" ("The Populism of the One Is the Democracy of the Other, and Vice Versa"). Dahrendorf, "Acht Anmerkungen," 156, quoted in Mudde, "The Populist Zeitgeist," 543. I have altered Mudde's translation of the original German. The German article and an English translation can be found in the bibliography under Dahrendorf, "Eights Remarks on Populism." The implication of the article that freedom can be obtained in a shop opens up all sorts of trains of thought that I cannot follow here.

"us" are easily manipulated by characters who are often portrayed like a Bond villain.

But already in 2004 the Dutch scholar Cas Mudde had examined the growing use of populism as a descriptive marker. As we saw, he understands populism as a "thin" ideology, that can be widely applied, on the left and the right. The problem that remains, however, is to what extent such descriptions of populism actually allow for any input from the "people," the *populus*. For most expressions of "anti-elitism" are led by the elite (the main supporters of the Brexit movement in the UK, the former US president, Bolsonaro and his supporters, Babiš or Okamura in the Czech Republic, and so on).

It is, therefore, to his credit that Laclau in his book, *On Populist Reason*,[41] argues for populism to be taken seriously as the expression of the voice of the "people." His interest is in how a "people" is constructed. This is one of the ways in which Laclau positions himself as a post-Marxist, since he desires to move beyond class struggle as the defining antagonism that drives social change.[42] Already we can note that this will be important for liberation theologians. In its early stages, there was a segment of liberation theology discourse that drew heavily on the notion of class struggle.[43] But the significance of class struggle as a helpful theological tool rapidly diminished, not least because, as Marxists have found, it does not seem to work, or at least alienation is so strong that it has proved hard to overcome. For all that there would be differences,

---

41. Laclau, *On Populist Reason*.

42. In a debate with Slavoj Žižek, Laclau notes that "my notion of the people and the classical Marxist conception of class struggle are two different ways of conceiving the construction of social identities, so that if one is correct the other has to be dismissed—or, rather, reabsorbed and redefined in terms of the alternative view." See Laclau, "Why Constructing," 647.

43. In an article defending liberation theology against the 1984 Instruction on Certain Aspects of Liberation Theology, Anselm Min argues that liberation theology "boldly accepts the reality of class struggle and the necessity of revolutionary change." Min, "The Vatican, Marxism," 446. For an earlier reflection, see Foroohar, "Liberation Theology," 44–50. Cuda, "Latinoamérica en el siglo XXI," uses Juan Carlos Scannone's fourfold typology of liberation theology as a base, and points out that the second type, associated by Scannone with Hugo Assmann, is a revolutionary theology that works with the notion of class struggle, though not necessarily with a violent version of it (see p. 63). Cuda's article makes use of Laclau to look at a post-Marxist reading of Latin American theology, especially the theology of the people that emerged from a similar broadly Peronist background to that of Laclau himself.

Laclau's notion of the construction of the people will be far closer to the perspective of most contemporary liberation theology.

Empty Signifiers

On several occasions Laclau uses the concept of the empty (or Master) signifier, originating with the French psychoanalyst, Jacques Lacan (1901–81), who describes it thus:

> When have we passed over into the order of the signifier? The signifier may extend over many of the elements within the domain of the sign. But the signifier is a sign that doesn't refer to any object, not even to one in the form of a trace, even though the trace nevertheless heralds the signifier's essential feature. It, too, is the sign of an absence. But insofar as it forms part of language, the signifier is a sign which refers to another sign, which is as such structured to signify the absence of another sign, in other words, to be opposed to it in a couple.[44]

Moreover, and this is perhaps the key point to take from Lacan, "every real signifier is, as such, a signifier that signifies nothing."[45] Essentially, the point of the empty signifier is that it is a concept that everyone can understand, but only insofar as it is not defined, because ultimately it is not definable (and it is not definable because it does not as such exist).[46]

For Laclau the empty signifier is indicative of the way in which the political enterprise functions.[47] Essentially, the partial becomes the universal and this occurs through a form of relationality that is based on difference. Things are what they are (and his claim is indeed an ontological one) in relation to other things that are different. This starts from a Saussurean linguistic perspective.[48] Because language is a series of relations,

---

44. Lacan, *The Psychoses*, 167.

45. Lacan, *The Psychoses*, 185.

46. Compare what I was saying above about society. It should be noted that, perhaps somewhat ironically, there is a very real danger of the Master-Signifier or Empty Signifier itself becoming what it describes—that is, to paraphrase Macbeth, a concept full of sound and fury, signifying nothing. On this, see Hook and Vanheule "Revisiting the Master-Signifier."

47. For more on this, see also Laclau, "Why Empty Signifiers Matter." The original is from 1994, and it also appears in Laclau, *Emancipations*.

48. Laclau, *On Populist Reason*, 68.

"the *totality* of language is involved in each single act of signification."[49] And in order for a system of signification to be established this totality is necessary. But how can we move from this relation of difference to find something that holds together the different parts? Laclau explains it thus:

> (i) Given that we are dealing with purely differential identities, we have, in some way, to determine the whole within which those identities, as different, are constituted (the problem would not, obviously, arise if we were dealing with positive, only externally related, identities). (ii) Since we are not postulating any necessary structural center, endowed with an a priori "determination in the last instance" capacity, "centering" effects that manage to constitute a precarious totalizing horizon have to proceed from the interaction of the differences themselves.[50]

In other words, what is available to us to help us move beyond the given of difference to some kind of shared vision or understanding? Laclau points out that, if difference is constitutive, then we are always faced by a kind of Platonic Third Man conundrum, because whatever is posited as unitive is so in distinction to something else (the proletariat is not the bourgeoisie, for example). The only way out of this, according to Laclau, is to come up with some form of what he calls hegemonic identity, which "becomes something of the order of an *empty* signifier, its own particularity embodying an unachievable fullness."[51] Or, as he puts it elsewhere, "a certain particularity, without ceasing to be particular, will assume a certain role of universal signification."[52]

Each signifying system is also necessarily exclusionary. This is because, in Laclau's words:

> On the one hand, each element of the system has an identity only as far as it is different from the others. Difference = identity. On the other hand, however, all these differences are equivalent to each other as far as all of them belong to this side of the frontier of exclusion. But, in that case, the identity of each element is constitutively split: on the one hand, each difference expresses itself as difference; on the other hand, each of them cancels itself as such by entering into a relation of equivalence with all the other differences of the system. And, given that there

49. Laclau, "Why Empty Signifiers Matter," 67.
50. Laclau, *On Populist Reason*, 69. See also Laclau, "Why Empty Signifiers Matter."
51. Laclau, *On Populist Reason*, 71.
52. Laclau, "Why Constructing," 652.

> is only system as far as there is radical exclusion, this split or ambivalence is constitutive of all systemic identity. It is only insofar as there is a radical impossibility of a system as pure presence, beyond all exclusions, that actual systems (in the plural) can exist. Now, if the systematicity of the system is a direct result of the exclusionary limit, it is only that exclusion that grounds the system as such.[53]

To put it simply, then, each word within a language has an identity as part of that language because it is different to other words, but it is equivalent to the other words because it belongs within this language. So for example an elephant is not a mouse is not a duck, and so their identity is in difference. But they all belong to signifiers of types of animal within the English language and they exclude as signifiers within the system, for example, "*slon*," "*myš*," or "*kachna*," (the Czech signifiers for these animals).

At the same time, this very example shows that there is some kind of broader relationship and that somehow we never quite get there. Translation is possible, one can move from one system to another, but they remain exclusionary, and this is true with political systems too. What things like poverty or justice or democracy mean within each system are clear, but they are also exclusionary of what these terms mean in other systems. Each system is a totality. And, says Laclau, "This relation by which a particular content becomes the signifier of the absent communitarian fullness is exactly what we call a hegemonic relationship."[54] The attempt to make the particular system universal is hegemony.

In politics this is driven by a lack, and the same is also true in liberation theology, where it is precisely the lack of freedom that provides the driving force for theological enquiry. Laclau notes, then, that "Any term which in a certain political context becomes the signifier of the lack plays the same role. Politics is possible because the constitutive impossibility of society can only represent itself through the production of empty signifiers."[55] All forms of political discourse are partial, but each form also seeks to become constitutive of the whole, to develop a hegemonic discourse that successfully articulates social relations.

---

53. Laclau, "Why Empty Signifiers Matter," 67.
54. Laclau, "Why Empty Signifiers Matter," 72.
55. Laclau, "Why Empty Signifiers Matter," 72.

Constructing a People

The articulation of social relations is another way of explaining what Laclau and Mouffe mean when they talk about the construction of a people. This construction may begin with a single request, but this soon moves on to demands and claims. So, for example, a local community in an area on the periphery of a major conurbation in Brazil might want better bus services, and may start by asking the local transport service to increase the number of buses. But as it investigates more, it also realizes other areas where it is badly served—education, healthcare, housing, for example—and it starts to demand that it receives equal treatment in these areas too. Thus we move from request to demand to claim. And though not everyone may have an equal investment in each claim (for example, those who are not parents may not have the same investment in education as those with school-age children), an equivalential relationship is recognized.[56] It is precisely the group that gathers around this demand(s) that comes to be a people, but for Laclau it is important that the demands come first. It is not a group of people who start looking for something to campaign for, but a need that has to be met and that brings people together.

This raises the question of who Laclau understands "the people" to be. A people, as we have just seen, forms around demands and claims that are expressed hegemonically: "The aims of any group in a power struggle can only be achieved if this group operates hegemonically over forces broader than itself that, in turn, will change its own subjectivity."[57] This means, though, that the people are in fact always a particular group, and those Laclau has principally in mind are essentially the excluded or marginalized. He uses the terms *populus* and *plebs*: "*Populus* is the totality of the community; *plebs* are those at the bottom of the social pyramid."[58]

What happens, though, is that the *plebs* identifies itself as the whole, as the *populus*,[59] so the interests of a particular group are regarded as the interests of all. Again, then, we see the claim that the partial is made into the universal. Antagonisms occur because there are different partial groups claiming universality. One of these divisions is the classic Marxist distinction between the proletariat (as a kind of conscientized[60] class)

---

56. On this, see Laclau, "Why Constructing," 655.
57. Laclau, "Why Constructing," 672.
58. Laclau, "Defender of Contingency."
59. See also Laclau, *On Populism*, 81, 93–94.
60. Conscientization (*conscientização* in Portuguese) is a term, sometimes

and the *Lumpenproletariat*, the unorganized rabble.⁶¹ Laclau reworks this distinction to show how the "otherness" (or heterogeneity) of the *Lumpenproletariat* breaks down barriers between different groups and is a crucial basis for understanding social relations. It is not, for Laclau, that the *Lumpenproletariat* is in some sense simply what the proletariat is not, but that it forms a part of history. In a phrase that would meet with agreement among liberation theologians, he says that the "'peoples without history' have occupied center stage to the point of shattering the very notion of a teleological historicity."⁶² This is why Laclau has been called and indeed has understood himself as "post-Marxist," seeking to confront the limits and aporias of Marx's own thought. The other is not a problem to be overcome through dialectics, but "heterogeneity is constitutive."⁶³

Perhaps the simplest way to understand Laclau here is to consider the notion of "democracy," the rule of the *demos*, or in Latin *populus*. In practice, democracies are always in fact oligarchies, or at least oligocracies: that is to say, a minority of a population decides on the course of the country's politics and politicians claim to represent the "people" (the *populus*), when in fact they represent a relatively small proportion of it. In Brazil, more than 60 percent of the electorate did not vote for Bolsonaro,⁶⁴ whilst in the Czech Republic Babiš was voted for by only around 18 percent of the total

---

expressed in English as "critical consciousness," that comes from, or at least is closely associated with, the Brazilian educationalist Paulo Freire. On Freire, and his relation to liberation theology, see Kyrilo and Boyd, *Paulo Freire*; they consider conscientization on pp. 77–86.

61. Marx's description can be found first in *The German Ideology* and is developed in the fifth chapter of *The Eighteenth Brumaire*. On this, see also Stallybrass, "Marx and Heterogeneity," an article to which Laclau also refers in *On Populist Reason*, 143–46.

62. Laclau, *On Populist Reason*, 148. Those Laclau calls "peoples without history" are similar to those Gustavo Gutiérrez calls "non-persons"; see Gutiérrez, *Power of the Poor*, 57: "In Latin America the challenge does not come first and foremost from the non-believer. . . . It comes from the non-person. It comes from the person whom the prevailing social order refuses to recognize as a person." Laclau's expression is perhaps slightly more felicitous, but both need to be understood correctly, not as descriptive claims (because obviously all peoples have history, all persons are persons), but as indicative of how the dominant hegemonic discourse treats them.

63. Laclau, *On Populist Reason*, 148. On how Laclau and Mouffe manage to move beyond a more general Levinasian position on heterogeneity (which to some extent they obviously share), see Grebe, "Contingency, Contestation, and Hegemony."

64. He received the votes of just under 40 percent of the total electorate, though 55 percent of the votes that were actually cast.

electorate.⁶⁵ Of course these groups may not be the *plebs*, but nevertheless a segment of the population determines the fate of the whole, imposing its hegemonic discourse on an admittedly fractured majority, for whom other hegemonic discourses were more appealing.⁶⁶

Nonlinear Understandings of History

Following on from his insistence on the constitutive nature of heterogeneity, Laclau insists on the nonlinear nature of history, arguing that "history is a discontinuous succession of hegemonic formations."⁶⁷ This is one of the ways in which Laclau seeks to escape the Hegelian determinism present in much of Marx's writings, or at least in interpretations of them.⁶⁸ History is not an inevitable journey to some pre-defined *telos*. On reflection, this must be so, since the types of *teloi* that are proposed, the end to which history is leading, are plural. For Hegel it is the World Spirit, for Marx the dictatorship of the proletariat, and the examples could proliferate. The question of whether there is progress in any sense in human history is only answerable if there is an agreed set of criteria for determining what progress is. For Laclau, though, such a debate would be to miss the point.

His argument is, after all, not for or against the idea of progress, but aims at showing how societies change. The claim that he makes is that this is through a clash of hegemonies. It is debatable whether or not this clash in fact produces a discontinuity. At one level it obviously does. Especially in two-party political systems, such as the United Kingdom or the United States, there is a tendency to propose political programs in terms of "not-X," where X is the other party. We are defined by not being the other hegemonic program that we have managed to defeat. Recent

---

65. Again, he received almost 30 percent of votes actually cast, but ignoring people who do not vote is precisely to try to do away with heterogeneity.

66. For example, in the United Kingdom, only 38 percent of the total electorate voted for Brexit and just under 30 percent voted for the Conservative party in the 2019 general election. And though they received the highest percentage of votes cast since 1979, the Conservative party only received some 43.6 percent of those votes, meaning that over 56 percent of voters cast their votes against them. Nevertheless, the government claims to speak for "the British people." Of course, they are not alone in this and it is an obvious reason for the fragmentation of society, since governments do not and do not even want to speak for a majority of the population.

67. Laclau, *On Populist Reason*, 226.

68. On determinism in Marx, see Sherman, "Marx and Determinism," 63–64.

governments in both the UK and USA, and certainly Bolsonaro in Brazil, may give further support to this view, with more radical differentiation in discourse than before. But even here, the alleged discontinuity can be seen in terms of continuity too, as we saw when looking at the nature of difference. By defining oneself over against a disputed other, the other becomes an ongoing part of the discourse. From this perspective, it might also be argued that history is a continuous succession of heterogeneous hegemonic formations.

In the end, this may not matter so much, however. The point that is being made is that history is not a straight line, but a series of points. Bolsonaro cannot be understood without the various PT governments of Lula and Dilma, but Bolsonaro presents a very different kind of hegemonic formation to that of the preceding governments. Babiš cannot be understood without the corruption scandals that have rocked the Czech Republic more or less since its beginning as an independent nation in 1993. In his case, it is not clear that he presents an alternative hegemonic formation—the major difference seems to be that sufficient people are prepared to accept corruption if it goes hand in hand with some kind of administrative competence. The name of Babiš's party,[69] it will be recalled, is an acronym that refers to "dissatisfied" citizens, and dissatisfaction is another way of seeing the clash of competing hegemonies.

(Ant-)agonisms

Chantal Mouffe has termed this clash of hegemonies "agonistics," the struggle between competing populisms. Disagreement is not an unfortunate outcome of the political, but is at its very heart. The conflict of hegemonic formations means that there is not and indeed cannot be any ultimate single social structure. Mouffe's choice of agonistics as opposed to antagonisms comes from her desire to find a way of talking about liberal democracies that allows for a struggle between adversaries rather than between enemies.[70]

69. ANO—*Akce nespokojených občanů*, Action of Dissatisfied Citizens.

70. Mouffe, *Agonistics*, 7. However, Mouffe often uses the term "antagonism" and it is frequently more or less a synonym for agonistics: for example, "It is only when division and antagonism are recognised as ineradicable that it is possible to think in a properly political way" (Mouffe, *Agonistics*, 15). Nevertheless, the intended distinction is important, since it depends on whether the other is perceived as rival or enemy. The rival is to be beaten, the enemy is to be overcome and excluded. For those who

Mouffe's approach, which I find attractive, does, however, rely very heavily on the presence of "a kind of 'conflictual consensus' based on divergent interpretations of shared ethico-political principles."[71] Although she is keen to emphasize that liberal democracies, with their already conflicting pulls between "liberty" and "equality," cannot necessarily be seen as a universal solution to the political,[72] she does have to assume that there are shared ethico-political principles: there is "a real confrontation, but one that is played out under conditions regulated by a set of democratic procedures accepted by the adversaries."[73] In such a case, an agonistic approach is possible. The hegemonic formations are certainly conflictual, but, and here I return to my point about continuity and discontinuity made earlier, they are in relation. But what happens if these principles are not shared? Given a rejection of a common ground, only antagonism, the struggle against enemies, is possible.[74] How, then, can we be certain that both sides are playing the same game on the same playing field with the same rules?

Mouffe's response would concentrate, it seems to me, on her understanding of democracy. In the introduction to her book *The Democratic Paradox*, she argues that democracy as currently practiced is

> a new political form of society whose specificity comes from the articulation between two different traditions. On one side we have the liberal tradition constituted by the rule of law, the defence of human rights and the respect of individual liberty; on the other the democratic tradition whose main ideas are those of equality, identity between governing and governed and popular sovereignty. There is no necessary relation between those two distinct traditions but only a contingent historical articulation.[75]

---

prefer cultural references, agonistics is the Olympics, antagonism is Hunger Games. An agonistic approach is probably preferable, but in reality antagonism may be the most common experience.

71. Mouffe, *Agonistics*, 23.

72. See Mouffe, *Agonistics*, 35–40.

73. Mouffe, *Agonistics*, 9.

74. It seems to me that Mouffe herself realizes this problem. In conversation with Iñigo Errejón, one of the founders of the *Podemos* movement in Spain, she says that "we first need to restore democracy so that we can radicalise it." See Errejón and Mouffe, *Podemos*, 24.

75. Mouffe, *Democratic Paradox*, 2–3, quoted in Laclau, *On Populism*, 167.

Many recent profound disagreements in politics can be understood as manifestations of the clash between the liberal tradition and the democratic egalitarian tradition. A clear example is in responses to the COVID-19 pandemic. The liberal tradition has strong reservations about any government edicts about wearing masks, for example, not because there is any problem with the mask itself, but because it involves being told what to do. An egalitarian tradition has no problem with everyone being treated the same, but ultimately finds it hard to deal with intolerance. The hegemonic clash is precisely then about where the fault line is drawn that divides these two traditions, and which pole is dominant. Mouffe and Laclau will also both insist that there is no neutral ground in this debate. It is not that there is a "right" answer to which both sides are approximating. The positions are radically different and consensus is neither possible nor desirable. As Mouffe puts it, "it is vital for democratic politics to understand that liberal democracy results from the articulation of two logics which are incompatible in the last instance and that there is no way in which they could be perfectly reconciled."[76]

My argument is that this irreconcilable difference is not a matter only of the political in its widest sense, but also a part of theology. In the next chapters, I will look at two competing theological visions that accompany the different political approaches. These theological visions are essentially competing hegemonies in the sense that Laclau and Mouffe use the term. Admittedly as theologians we might want to claim that, unlike with the social order, there is a "right" answer. However, to attempt to articulate faith in God (that is, to engage in theology) is to make assumptions about God, and about the possibility of truth. But one of those assumptions is that the fullness of God is unknowable, at least on earth (the dull reflection of the ancient world's mirrors, as Paul puts it). So in this case we can certainly approximate towards the right answer, but we can never claim to have it, and therefore, any theological position is trying to establish its own hegemonic position.[77]

---

76. Mouffe, *Democratic Paradox*, 5. On this, see Smith, *Laclau and Mouffe*, 10–12, 119–21.

77. Obviously, writing a book is nothing other than an attempt at establishing a hegemonic formation. This is as true for this book as it is for Laclau and Mouffe. Critics, then, either seek to build up the hegemony or provide a conflicting hegemony. This is most definitely not relativism. Hegemonies are not relativist, though they are evidence of plurality. However much we may desire it, there is no drone that can give us a view of things as they are *sub specie aeternitatis*. That does not mean, however, that such a position does not exist, it simply means that we have no definitive access to it.

Left Populism

I turn now to how Mouffe understands left populism, since political positions associated with many Latin American liberation theologians are best categorized in this way. The first, and broader, step is what she terms the construction of a people. As we have seen already with Laclau, without a people (*plebs*), there is no populism. Remembering Laclau's claim that a people emerges around a social demand, Mouffe writes that what is needed is

> the construction of 'a people' around a project which addresses the diverse forms of subordination around issues concerning exploitation, domination or discrimination. A special emphasis must also be given to a question that has gained particular relevance in the last thirty years and which is of a special urgency today: the future of the planet.⁷⁸

The introduction of the ecological question, mirrored in liberation theology, points to the ever more heterogeneous nature of the people, given the ever more diverse nature of subordinations.⁷⁹

The presence of experiences of subordination is a crucial starting point for Mouffe and Laclau. The obvious danger with talk of a people is that it opens up space for the forms of collectivization created under Communist regimes.⁸⁰ In practice that led to the identification of the people with the state and of the state with the leader: as Stalin may not have said, both "L'état, c'est moi" and "Le peuple, c'est moi." But this militates against a genuine political engagement of a people, who are simply informed of their will by those in power. From what we have seen so far it is evident that Laclau and Mouffe both want to avoid such a position. So the question remains of how response to subordination, always at one level personal, can lead to the formation of a people that allows for a plurality of experience in search of a common goal.

In their preface to the second edition of *Hegemony and Social Strategy*, Laclau and Mouffe write that a chief principle of the book concerned

---

78. Mouffe, *For a Left Populism*, 61.

79. In *The Democratic Paradox*, 124, Mouffe mentions, for example, "gender, race, environment and sexuality." All of these can be used to subordinate (exclude) the other.

80. On the collectivization of agriculture in Czechoslovakia, see Rychlík, "Collectivization." The chapter examines the whole process, from before the Communist takeover in 1948 up to the end of communism in 1989. On the first phases of collectivization see Pernes, "Kolektivizace."

"the need to create a chain of equivalence among the various democratic struggles against different forms of subordination. We argued that struggles against sexism, racism, sexual discrimination, and in the defense of the environment needed to be articulated with those of the workers in a new left-wing hegemonic project."[81] The people comes together, then, as persons.[82] It is constituted through a series of what Mouffe and Laclau term equivalential relationships. An equivalential chain is formed, in which "each individual demand is constitutively split: on the one hand it is its own particularized self; on the other it points, through equivalential links, to the totality of the other demands."[83]

Equivalential relations allow, then, for both particularity and difference and for unity. To use an example from Brazil, the needs of a landless rural worker, part of the *Movimento Sem Terra*, are not precisely the same as a union member in a factory. One wants, among other things, access to land to farm, the other wants, again among other things, employment rights (and the point being made by Laclau and Mouffe is that each of them and others around them will have a whole range of demands). Nevertheless, at the same time their demands are related because there is an equivalence or a logic of equivalence between them (both want justice, both want access to their rights, and so on).[84] A people is constructed, we could say, when there are sufficient links in the equivalential chain to produce an articulable demand of a collective will.

This collective will can be expressed when there is a demand (or demands) around which people can unite and a way of acting out their

---

81. Laclau and Mouffe, *Hegemony and Socialist Strategy*, xviii.

82. I use "person" rather than "individual", not least because person encourages the view of relationality. It would be fascinating to compare Laclau and Mouffe's post-Marxism with Emmanuel Mounier, whose position could be termed something like a Catholic Marxism and whom I consider in chapter 4. On the influence of Mounier's personalism on Paulo Freire, another thinker who is often categorized as post-Marxist, see Kyrilo and Boyd, *Paulo Freire*, 27–39. On Mounier and Marx, see Hill, "Emmanuel Mounier"; Čulo and Šestak, "Recepcija Emmanuela Mouniera," examining the generally favorable reception of Mounier in communist-era and later Yugoslavia, because his personalism was seen as compatible with Marxism.

83. Laclau, "Populism," 37; Mouffe, *Agonistics*, 63.

84. See Mouffe, *Agonistics*, 62–63. There is a certain overlap here with Clodovis Boff's distinction between a correspondence of terms and a correspondence of relations model of linking the present situation with the Scriptures. Boff argues that a correspondence of relations model allows us to both relate to and draw from the Bible and to retain the specificity of our own situation, which is not that of the Bible. See Boff, *Teologia e Prática*, 262–67; Boff, *Theology and Praxis*, 146–50.

demands. Mouffe sees this in terms of a radical citizenship.[85] This claims that participation in "a 'we' of radical democratic citizens does not preclude participation in a variety of other 'we's.'"[86] This is expressed concretely in different movements, such as Black Lives Matter, Extinction Rebellion, Occupy,[87] or *Podemos* in Spain.[88] Other groups also show signs of radical citizenship—the Brexit coalition, ranging from the far right to the far left, including a range of different opinions, desires, and hopes, was and is a distinctly odd set of bedfellows, but it is also an excellent example of an equivalential chain.

The Affective Dimension of a People

Another crucial emphasis for Mouffe is the importance of what she terms the affects, or an affective turn. This is important, because, for most of us, political opinions do not operate solely or even mainly on the plane of rational argument. She suggests that "artistic practices can play a decisive role in the construction of new forms of subjectivity . . . because, in using resources that induce emotional responses, they are able to reach human beings at the affective level."[89] Given the power of the affects in political discourse, it is worth delving more deeply into this dimension of populism. We are all aware of the kind of short and meaningless phrases—"Law and Order," "Family and Stability," and so on—that get plastered around our cities as elections approach. These are an example of the power of the "Empty Signifier." This "Empty Signifier" is, as we saw, something around which a people can form, but that in itself ultimately has no existence or even meaning, at least not in an independent verifiable form. But that is precisely why it is so good at giving people a rallying point, since each can attribute their own meaning to the idea.

What "the nation" is, for example, can be understood in all sorts of ways, exclusively or inclusively, nationalistically or in terms of relationships with other countries, as target of pride, criticism, fear, love, and so on. What populisms do is gather people around such ideas, which can

85. Mouffe, *For a Left Populism*, 67–68.
86. Mouffe, *For a Left Populism*, 68.
87. Mouffe, *For a Left Populism*, 19.
88. See Errejón and Mouffe, *Podemos*.
89. Mouffe, *For a Left Populism*, 77, with reference to Mouffe, *Agonistics*, 85–105, a chapter entitled "Agonistic Politics and Artistic Practices."

and must never be cashed in. This is why, for Mouffe, "a left populist strategy cannot ignore the strong libidinal investment at work in national—or regional—forms of identification and it would be very risky to abandon this terrain to right-wing populism."[90] This is very important because otherwise there is a tendency for those on the left to turn up their noses at certain manifestations of popular discourse. The nation may not exist, but it can serve as a nodal point for people, and this can be used in many different ways to achieve different ends.[91] Czech national identity can be built, for example, on narratives of exclusion and homogeneity, or on narratives of multiculturalism and inclusivity. It is there that the hegemonic discourses collide.

Ignoring the role of affects is, as Mouffe notes, often disastrous.[92] The left especially is a product of modernity, and of a particularly Gnostic form of modernity. Those who share the views of the particular left-wing group or political party are the enlightened and the problem with the rest of the population is that they have not yet come to enlightenment. So all that is needed is time and education and all will understand the power of the rational arguments being made. To say that rationalism is not the be-all and end-all of politics is a descriptive rather than prescriptive statement. Most Brazilians who voted for Bolsonaro did not do so because they had drawn up a spreadsheet in which they listed the reasons for and against and came to a rational decision based on all available information. They voted for him because he was not the PT candidate, because they were fed up with the perceived corruption around that party, and disappointed with the way their lives were going and the fact that no matter what they did and how hard they worked and how many sacrifices they made, at the very best they were managing to stay in the same place. They wanted a country that felt safe, that did not seem to pay more attention to minorities than to the majority, and so on. Rational arguments will not change those basic instincts and feelings, though affective ones may.

What needs to be done, rather, is to "recognise the role of this libidinal energy and the fact that it is malleable and can be oriented in multiple

---

90. Mouffe, *For a Left Populism*, 71.

91. I am revising this text just after the end of the European Football Championship, in which the English national team did unexpectedly well. Although it helped that the manager and players are a very impressive group of committed human beings, it was nevertheless interesting to observe and reflect on reactions to the team that do seem to say something about experiencing national identity as not simply negative.

92. Mouffe, *For a Left Populism*, 72.

directions, producing different affects."[93] One way that this can be done is through the use of art "to foster the development of those new social relations that are made possible by the transformation of the work process."[94] It is not, of course, that art and politics are two distinct spheres that can come together, but that they are implicit at least in one another. In the various protests under the banner of the Black Lives Matter movement, this was very clear. Removing statues and replacing them with others is both a political and an artistic decision, and as Mouffe argues,[95] museums and art galleries become spaces in which education and political statements can be made.

In terms of liberation theology, this emphasis on the affects is helpful. It mirrors the debate in early liberation theology about the role of "popular religion," the beliefs and practices of ordinary people.[96] By coming to see these as expressive of the desire for liberation and often as subversive of official narratives, the affective dimension of belief was incorporated into liberation theology, even if this theology frequently suffered (and suffers) from its links to modernity and an insistence on over-rationalization. In this respect the Base Ecclesial Communities have been especially important, as they offer a space for celebration and artistic expression of political and religious beliefs.[97]

Both in politics and in theology it is, of course, necessary to avoid the paternalistic assumption that art is what is useful for those who are unable to think. This is not Mouffe's point, though. What is been sought is something else, at two levels. One is the overcoming of a very limited version of rationality that reduces it to something like a topic of analytic philosophy and acknowledging that reason can be expressed in a number of ways. The second is the acknowledgement that the affective plays a much larger role in most political identification than anything else, existing on the level of what the Baptist theologian James McClendon has called convictions.[98] These are those beliefs and practices that make us who we are and they are ultimately affective. I can of course give reasons for what I believe, but the reasons are post hoc and incomplete.

93. Mouffe, *For a Left Populism*, 73.

94. Mouffe, *Agonistics*, 87.

95. Mouffe, *Agonistics*, 99–103.

96. A key figure here is usually considered to be the Chilean theologian Segundo Galilea, who sought to reinterpret popular religiosity in a liberation perspective.

97. On this, see, for example, Domezi, "Devoção."

98. See McClendon and Smith, *Convictions*.

Summary

Populism, then, is to do with the construction of a people around a specific social demand, that seeks to construct a new hegemonic order that is in agonistic (or in practice more frequently antagonistic) relation with the current order. Hegemonies are always contingent, seeking to establish a set of practices that order society in a particular way. They do not have an ultimate (transcendent) rational foundation, and they need to engage with the affective as well as with the rational. Mouffe and Laclau are deeply committed to the construction of a left populism, which can further be described in the above terms as the attempt to install a left hegemony, where the equivalentially related demands of excluded groups for greater justice and participation against the dominating paradigms of the current neoliberal hegemony are met.

It should be readily apparent that this approach is not without problems. As a Brazilian political scientist, who would, I suspect, be broadly in favor of left populisms, has noted, in seeking to make a positive case for populism, Laclau can end up making everything a form of populism, in which case the term ceases to have any useful interpretive role.[99] Moreover, in times of fractious conflict, is there really no place for looking for some form of reconciliation? And if not, at least is there any way in which competing hegemonies can lead to something positive, rather than to violence? I will look at this later, when I discuss Pope Francis' encyclical *Fratelli tutti*.

Neither Laclau nor Mouffe are exactly easy reading and both of them have the tendency to move rather seamlessly between the descriptive and the normative. And of course their position itself must be subject to the criticisms and comments they make about other positions. It can only be contingent. I am not sure that they would object to that point, since they are not making a claim to finality, but are seeking ways to reignite the left in and against a neoliberal hegemony. What is needed to develop a politics that can take on this hegemony within a broadly democratic setting? As they note, many of the attempts to do this have ultimately had to accept the rules of neoliberalism: examples are Tony Blair and New Labour in the United Kingdom, or the first PT government in Brazil. What they want is to enable a resistance that can articulate a new social order that denies the basic tenets of neoliberalism.

---

99. Silva, "O Fim da Onda Rosa," 167.

In this, at least, they are joined by many liberation theologians. So far, at least that I can discover, liberation theologians have not worked a lot with Laclau and Mouffe,[100] but there is considerable overlap in interests.[101] Both are searching for how to engage in transformative social activity. Liberation theologians see faith as having an integral political dimension, and thus as bringing a kind of transcendent, though self-questioning, basis for a particular hegemonic discourse. And Laclau and Mouffe see politics as having a much wider impact than purely party politics or even government in the narrow sense. Even if Laclau and Mouffe do not refer to religion much, they would certainly recognize that it has a political dimension and would welcome forms of religious faith that side with the poor and excluded. Both liberation theologians and especially Mouffe also stress the need for the affective, for the recognition that the political and the religious echo in the whole of human existence and in the whole of the person.

It seems to me that left populism is an excellent way to describe the political engagement of liberation theologians. This is both a strength and a weakness. It is a strength because political engagement necessitates making choices and those choices, in the terms of Laclau and Mouffe, have to form part of an equivalential chain. Theologians on their own and as such have no real political impact, only in conjunction with others who share some of their demands for a more just society. Not all of those will have the same motivations. In some ways that does not matter, except, of course, when it does, and that leads us on to the weakness of the choice of left populism. If we accept that the PT in Brazil has provided a form of left populism—and that is a debatable question—then allying themselves with the PT has proved problematic for liberation theologians. For all the good the PT has undoubtedly done, there were problems, of corruption and of abuse of power, that cannot be ignored. My enemy's enemy may be my friend, but if they are defined in terms of their enmity, they may also turn out to be my enemy too. This at the very least makes it clear that, as Mouffe and Laclau argue, there are a large number of "we's," and sometimes we need to break the chain.

---

100. An obvious exception is Emilce Cuda, cited above. Cuda, a lay Argentinean theologian, is among the leading representatives of Latin American theology of her generation. I will turn to her work on Pope Francis later in this book.

101. See the early works on ideology in liberation theology: Libanio and Taborda, "Ideología," 580–83; Taborda, *Cristianismo e Ideologia*, especially 91–98,

The question that remains is how to deal with conflict. Mouffe argues for the importance of agonistics, of encountering the other as adversary and not as enemy. To do this, it is necessary to go beyond the moralizing discourse of much of contemporary politics.[102] This is an obvious temptation for theology, to reduce the differences to a rather Manichean battle between good (my side) and evil (the other side).[103] But that ends up ignoring the conflict, since, for Christians, in the battle between good and evil there is only one winner, even if there may appear to be temporary setbacks in the campaign. It prevents listening to the other and it prevents any attempt to work to transform the other, to put across our position in a way that the other can hear and respond to. What then can a theological reading of the conflict bring? It is to that question that I turn in the following chapters.

---

102. Elke Wagner, "Interview," in Mouffe, *Agonistics*, 141–44.

103. Recall the description of populism offered at the beginning of this chapter, drawing precisely on this Manichean reading of society.

3

Grace as Entitlement

So far, I have looked at Brazil and the Czech Republic, as examples of divided societies and the competing hegemonic discourses behind the politics of exclusion and inclusion that are manifestations of this division. In doing so, I intimated that these conflicting discourses, present also within different Christian churches, have a theological underpinning, based on very diverse understandings of theologies of grace. It is to this difference that I now turn, looking first in this chapter at what I will call theologies of entitlement.

Entitlement

In a text published in 2020 to mark the Feast of St. Ignatius of Loyola (July 31), the Provincial of the British Province of the Society of Jesus (the Jesuits), Fr. Damian Howard, SJ, addressed the question of entitlement. He defined it as "an over-powering, unspoken, usually unconscious conviction that resides in the dark, inarticulate recesses of our minds that we have a right to something, a possession, a person or experience."[1] The manifestations of this conviction are, needless to say, manifold. A greater awareness of human rights is welcome, but hijacking or abusing the language of rights to describe desires and aspirations seeks to make such language meaningless. As Emmanuel Levinas says, despite arguing

---

1. Howard, "St. Ignatius."

so strongly for the importance of the other as constitutive for who I am: "My resistance begins when the evil that [the Other] does to me is done to a third who is also my neighbor."[2] Theologically, there are human rights, but they are rights granted by God, not an entitlement to be sought at the expense of the other.

In his text, Howard looks at how Ignatian discernment offers one way of confronting this sense of entitlement, "disentitling" as he puts it. Towards the end of his text, he says that what

> we *are* called to renounce is our sense of entitlement, because we can never experience the gifts which God showers upon us every day if our fundamental sense is that they are due us. When we renounce entitlement, we liberate a space, the space of gratuity and gift, a space in which the Spirit can act. And in that space it becomes possible to discover the love of the Father in all its surprising richness.[3]

The phrases he uses here, "the gifts which God showers upon us every day," "the space of gratuity and gift, a space in which the Spirit can act," are essentially what is summed up by the word "grace." What is not in question is that God does indeed present us with gifts, that life is an experience of what the French philosopher Jean-Luc Marion has called "givenness."[4] However, what is in question is the degree to which that experience of givenness is simply that, a living out of life as gifted, or whether it is the other side of a bargain, an economic process of exchange, either in crude material terms or in terms of what we are due because of our experiences.

In this chapter, I begin with this broadly economic understanding of grace. In different forms it enjoys a very powerful presence in contemporary Christian discourse, including in Brazil and, differently, in the Czech Republic. Christianity is presented as a redemptive discourse that rewards the righteous and punishes the unrighteous, frequently, though not inevitably, in the economic terms suggested by the word "redemptive" itself. I will then turn in the following chapter to liberation theology and its understanding of grace, as the in-breaking of the transformative power of God's love in and against a world of injustice and oppression.

Because my starting point is one of profound disagreement with the manifestations (and presuppositions) of theologies of entitlement and

2. Levinas, *De Dieu*, 134.
3. Howard, "St. Ignatius."
4. For more on this, see Noble, *Mission*, 81–83.

prosperity, I begin with an introduction to such theologies that seeks to take them seriously and to understand why they are so appealing. This is necessary because in one way or another the risk of focusing on some sense of entitlement is present in most Christian theologies. Most of what are called heresies, especially those that occupied the minds and hearts of the early Church Fathers, eventually come down to questions about salvation—how can we be assured of salvation, who must Jesus and, by extension, the Holy Trinity be, in order to guarantee the promise of salvation? The search for this assurance is a dominant theme through the history of Christianity. It is present already in the famous words of St. Paul to the Corinthians, "If Christ has not been raised, your faith is futile and you are still in your sins. Then those also who have died in Christ have perished. If for this life only we have hoped in Christ, we are of all people most to be pitied" (1 Cor 15:17–19).

Paul, of course, goes on to affirm the reality of the resurrection, but he does so without recourse to a theology of entitlement. It is because Christ was raised from the dead that we too can hope in turn to be raised, but this is because of the action of God, not because of what we have done. Nevertheless, very soon the tendency developed to see salvation as an entitlement. If we keep our side of the bargain, then God must save us. So the crucial question became if we could be sure that God could indeed save us, and then what "keeping our side of the bargain" entailed. Because one of my focuses in this book is on Latin America, and more specifically Brazil, I will focus on the theology of prosperity, especially in its Latin American form, as one manifestation of a theology of entitlement. Only then will I turn to another more specifically Czech "theology" or practice of entitlement. To see how a much more overt theology of prosperity developed, it will, however, be useful to examine the pre-history.

Antecedents of Prosperity Theology

In the Cape Town Commitment, issued on behalf of the Third Lausanne Congress that took place in Cape Town in 2010, prosperity theology or prosperity gospel is defined as "the teaching that believers have a right to the blessings of health and wealth and that they can obtain these blessings through positive confession of faith and the 'sowing of seeds' through financial or material gifts."[5] By pointing to the language of "rights" this

---

5. Third Lausanne Conference, *Cape Town Commitment*, 99: "Walk with simplicity, rejecting the gospel of greed."

definition, issued by a major Evangelical gathering, picks up and heavily criticizes the sense of entitlement that some believers have regarding God's duty towards them. But even if this particular manifestation of the gospel is a modern phenomenon, theologies of entitlement have a longer and far more complex history.

In the early church, calls to generosity towards the poor were many,[6] and the duty of Christians to give alms was a common topic of sermons and writings.[7] This was more than just an expression of compassion. As one writer on the topic puts it, "almsgiving emerged as central to the sanctification process. . . . The wealthy were urged to give, not simply to be compassionate and to address a need, but to save their souls."[8] At this stage, there is not a direct relationship between giving and salvation, and there is no suggestion that the one who gives will benefit materially from so doing. Indeed, those with resources are urged to liberate themselves from them to the greatest extent possible. Nevertheless, it is easy to see how almsgiving could lead to the view that God is duty-bound to recompense the giver for their generosity by bestowing salvation on them, so there is already the beginning of the possibility of a theology of exchange.[9]

During the Middle Ages, especially in the twelfth to fourteenth centuries, before the Black Death recalibrated social existence, and then again in the second half of the fifteenth century, many of these themes returned. At this period, though, it was impossible, at least in most of Europe, to think economically outside of thinking theologically.[10] As early capitalism began to spread around Europe, it is not surprising that this

---

6. For a detailed compendium of texts from a wide range of Church Fathers, on different topics, see Sierra Bravo, *Doctrina Social*; see, for example, the words of St. Cyprian of Carthage on almsgiving, 595–610, 613–14 (paragraphs 1240 to 1280, and 1287).

7. See Devin Singh, "The Economic Theology of Late Antiquity," in Schwarzkopf, *Economic Theology*, 279–86, especially 280–82.

8. Singh, "Economic Theology of Late Antiquity," 281.

9. As Devin Singh points out, there is an ambiguous relationship towards debt and exchange in Late Antiquity that would resurface over the course of Christian history: see Singh, "Economic Theology of Late Antiquity," 284–85.

10. See Raymond Benton Jr., "The Economic Theology of the High Middle Ages," in Schwarzkopf, *Economic Theology*, 287–94, here especially 287. To use the phrase "High Middle Ages" is obviously to focus on Europe, which, even if it was where most Christians resided at the time, was not by any means the sole place where Christians lived and thought.

era saw strong condemnations of usury, as both unnatural and unscriptural.[11] But if this meant that the time was in principle strongly averse to the ideas of theologies of entitlement, two factors tend to suggest that this is not the whole story.

First, we cannot ignore the ambivalent influence of Anselm and his theory of atonement. Anselm wants to demonstrate how we can know that we are saved. Positively, Anselm acknowledges that we cannot do anything to recompense God for our sin. So at that level no matter how many alms we give or how much good we do, we will not be able to make ourselves worthy of salvation and a just God would have to punish us. Thus it is only through the voluntary self-giving of Christ, the Son of God, on the cross that salvation can be made possible. But the other side of that argument is the historical one. Christ has died on the cross and thus we are saved, for the ransom has been paid by the only one who can do so. Thus God is in some sense bound to respond to the self-offering of Christ. Again, this is not about material reward, but it does open up the way to a sense of entitlement. Because Christ died for our sins, we deserve to be forgiven (even if at this stage it is demanded of us that we also be repentant).

The second element is one that fills the landscape of many European countries, namely, the presence of vast churches, built with the proceeds of different forms of mercantile activity. The more magnificent the church, the more one had been blessed by God and the more God was expected to have mercy on the donor's soul.[12] This was backed up by having massing priests to say masses for one's soul and all the other trappings of medieval religion. These can be dismissed as somehow an impure form of Christianity, but at their heart lay a deep faith and an acknowledgement of the precariousness of any individual. This was both because of the many threats, from disease, famine, war, and so on, that even the richest could not entirely avoid, and because of a kind of disposition of anti-entitlement, the realization that nothing was guaranteed. The transformation of purgatory[13] into a debt-clearing house is only one manifestation of this.

Such a rapid summary necessarily leaves many exceptions unnoted, not least the role of different religious orders, and the ongoing attempts

---

11. Benton, "Economic Theology of the High Middle Ages," 290–91.

12. On medieval churches in England, see Varnam, *Church as Sacred Space*, especially 179–240.

13. The classic work remains Le Goff, *Birth of Purgatory*.

to reform the church from within, and their economic implications. Nevertheless, up to the time of the Reformation, although there were possibilities of theologies of entitlement, they do not seem to have equated that entitlement with a material prosperity here and now. Rather, they implied a bargain between a donor and God, in which by giving money to alleviate the sufferings of the poor or to honor God through beauty and the construction of churches, the donor would at least greatly increase their chances of being rewarded with eternal life.

It was against this background that Martin Luther began to preach. In many ways Luther continued and further developed medieval teachings on the church and the economy.[14] As a Nigerian Lutheran scholar Ibrahim Bitrus argues, Luther saw nothing wrong in prosperity in itself, as long as it was not assumed to be necessary for salvation.[15] To this end Bitrus quotes Luther's Commentary on the Sermon on the Mount: "For, outwardly to have money, property, and people, is not of itself wrong, but it is God's gift and arrangement."[16] Luther's highly spiritualizing account of the Sermon of the Mount is one that liberation theologians (and others) would strongly disagree with, but for now the point is that Luther did not see the accumulation of wealth as in and of itself problematic, but rather a sign of God's generosity. God provides to those who ask, as Luther makes clear in his comments on the Our Father in the Small Catechism.[17]

In pointing this out and in arguing that the poor do not need to be told that they are suffering,[18] Bitrus is not seeking to defend most current forms of prosperity theology. For him, ultimately Luther does not preach a theology of entitlement.[19] Bitrus suggests that much Neo-Pentecostal prosperity theology seems to claim that

> salvation is not simply a deliverance from sin, but is also a victory over poverty, disease, and evil powers which thwart human prosperity. In other words, justification by grace through faith begets prosperous and successful life here and now on earth. As a result, whoever believes in Christ will enjoy abundant

---

14. Philipp Robinson Rössner, "Martin Luther as Economist," in Schwarzkopf, *Economic Theology*, 296.

15. Bitrus, "'Give Us Today,'" 23.

16. Bitrus, "'Give Us Today,'" citing Luther, *Commentary*.

17. Bitrus, "'Give Us Today,'" 26–27.

18. Bitrus, "'Give Us Today,'" 24–26.

19. For another critical reading of Neo-Pentecostal prosperity theologies from a Lutheran perspective, see Deifelt, "Teologia luterana."

prosperity of wealth, health, and success in every aspect of life. This is believed to be achievable through positive confession of faith, and "sowing seeds of faith" in the form of faithful giving of tithes and offerings. But for Luther, there is only one gospel—salvation from devil, sin, and death by grace through faith. Anything in addition to this is idolatry.[20]

There is then no entitlement to prosperity or even to salvation. There is the possibility of faith and through faith all else becomes conceivable. Assurance of salvation is not identical with entitlement to salvation.

This very brief survey, which has left out more than it has included,[21] allows us to make some summary points before moving on to look at current theologies of entitlement. The long tradition of the church points always to the grace of God as something unearned. Wealth is rarely condemned as such, but it is to be used for the good of the other and of the community, because to care for one's sister or brother in need is a God-given task. There is very little attention to the material benefits of belief, though there are many occasions when the danger of a theology of entitlement comes into play. Generally this is to do with a sense of entitlement to salvation because of one's economic contribution, even if not phrased in quite such brutal terms. Although mostly avoided, this element is present throughout the history of the church, and when stressed it leads to theologies of prosperity.

Prosperity Theology

For the time being, I will leave aside the alleged scriptural basis for prosperity theologies,[22] though for proponents of such theologies this

20. Bitrus, "'Give Us Today,'" 29.

21. To name one obvious example, I have not looked at Weberian theories of the power of the Protestant work ethic, arguably deriving from Calvin.

22. I will move between the singular and plural in what follows. That is because, as with liberation theology or any other kind of theology, there are differences of emphasis, divergent starting points, and so on, that both allow for and demand a more pluralistic reading. But on the other hand, also like liberation theology, there are some shared positions that permit a more universal reading. Because my interest is not in the history of prosperity theology as such, I will not go into the divisions and differences. For more on different strands of prosperity theology, see Vincent, "Formation," looking at what he terms "Word-Faith prosperity teachers" and "non-Word-Faith prosperity teachers." See also Freston, "Prosperity Theology," 69, who, drawing on Amos Yong, offers five different strands of prosperity theology (each in turn with its own variations).

is the most important part. I want, instead, first to look very briefly at the historical development of the doctrine or practice of prosperity. Its roots are usually traced back to nineteenth-century America and in particular to the "New Thought" movement, whose adherents "shared the idea that God is Mind, humans are spiritual beings, and thoughts can manifest change in the physical world."[23] The New Thought movement, whose initial proponents included Phineas Quimby (1802–66) and the founder of Christian Science, Mary Baker Eddy (1821–1910), emphasized the idea of God as Mind. Among its adherents there were different attitudes to matter, from regarding it as illusory to seeing it as secondary to the mental sphere. Not all such positions led to an opening to a form of prosperity gospel,[24] but many did. Thought could lead to reality,[25] so to concentrate one's thought on prosperity would lead to achieving it. All this can explain why, in the words of a Brazilian writer on prosperity theology, much of the research on the topic has related it to "so-called self-help literature, aspects related to the psychology of religion, to so-called spiritual warfare or battle, [or] to theodicy, as a kind of negation of the latter."[26]

But these more psychological or mental antecedents led, directly or indirectly, to a more focused emphasis on material success and prosperity. The founding father of contemporary prosperity theology is frequently held to be Kenneth Hagin (1917–2003),[27] who began as a preacher in the Assemblies of God, performing healing ministries. In 1962 he founded his own ministry, based on conversations he claimed to have held with Jesus.[28] The "Word-Faith" approach of Hagin and his disciples was based on the power of Positive Confession, namely that "once believers strengthen

---

23. Hutchinson, "New Thought's Prosperity Theology," 29.

24. As Hutchinson, "New Thought's Prosperity Theology," 31, points out, Mary Eddy Baker's rejection of the material meant that she did not adopt a success theology. Acquiring something that is not really there is obviously a futile exercise.

25. See Hutchinson, "New Thought's Prosperity Theology," 32, in reference to Nona Brooks (1861–1945), one of the founders of the Divine Science movement.

26. Dusilek, "Traços pagãos," 200.

27. See, for some examples, Neto, "Teologia de Prosperidade," especially 6–7; Oliveira, *Retribuição e Prosperidade*, 79–81; Vincent, "Formation," 27; Shayne Lee, "Prosperity Theology," 227–28.

28. Neto, "Teologia de Prosperidade," 6.

their faith by memorizing and confessing scriptures, they are able to live in total victory and control their physical and financial fate."[29]

Hagin's starting point was based on his interpretation of Gal 3:13, that Christ has redeemed believers from the curse of the law. The curse, he argued, was threefold: "poverty, sickness, and spiritual death."[30] Hagin's style is anecdotal and he does not attempt to construct a rational argument, but he does continually assert that God wants us to prosper, wants to make us rich.[31] And an integral part of this is that the believer gives first: "Actually, we haven't really given until we've paid our tithes."[32] In one of his anecdotes, Hagin recalls a preacher who demanded that people give not what they could afford but what they could not afford. This was at a kind of holy crowd-funder for air conditioning in a church, and the preacher reported how two businessmen who were on the verge of bankruptcy gave respectively $500 and $250. Within a month, both their businesses had recovered.[33]

It would be easy to mock this approach, as if God did not have more important things to think about than air conditioning. Hagin's scriptural hermeneutic is also somewhat *sui generis*, to put it kindly. But this would be to ignore the fact that there is a long tradition of finding divine justification for one's blessings, material as well as spiritual. Indeed, arguably the prosperity gospel offers a more faithful reading of the Jewish scriptural tradition. Writing on Jewish economic theology, Joseph Lifschitz argues:

> In many places [the Jewish tradition] also encourages the accumulation of wealth. Economic success is considered a worthy aim so long as one achieves it through honest means. In the Jewish view, man's obligation to exercise dominion over the world, as a function of his having been created in God's image, brings him to an affirmation of wealth. For wealth that is gained

---

29. Lee, "Prosperity Theology," 228. See also Vincent, "Formation," 34, who defines Positive Confession as "the practice of verbally declaring scriptures in support of the believer's faith for a desired outcome."

30. Hagin, *Redeemed from Poverty*, 5.

31. Hagin, *Redeemed from Poverty*, 9. God, says Hagin, does not necessarily want to make us all millionaires, but he will see to it that we have an abundant supply of what we need.

32. Hagin, *Redeemed from Poverty*, 8.

33. Hagin, *Redeemed from Poverty*, 6–8.

through hard work and honest means is, in Judaism, a positive expression of man's efforts as a godly being.³⁴

This is something to which Hagin could—and quite probably, given his literary style, would—say "Amen." For prosperity theology does not inevitably encourage dishonesty and breaking the law, however often one might find stories of preachers and evangelists who have done just that.³⁵ In fairness it should not be judged on its worst examples.

The analysis of the attitude towards wealth in the Jewish tradition can also serve as a reminder that a prosperity theology does not have to imply a causal relationship between giving and receiving, at least not in terms of the Divine-Human relationship. Wealth is gained, in Lifschitz's words, through "hard work and honest means." In itself this is not giving anything to God, but it is to act in a "godly" way, to seek to live up to the image and likeness of God in which the human being was created. So, it is important to look at some of the factors behind the undoubted success of the prosperity gospel, in both the Global South and the North. Or to put it in the words of Laclau and Mouffe, why is this such a powerful hegemonic discourse, allowing it to build a people? How does it help reinforce the political discourses of conditionalities of exclusion?³⁶

Strengths of Prosperity Theology

Paul Freston is among the leading sociologists of religion in the English-speaking world in terms of the study of evangelical movements in Africa, Asia, and Latin America. Writing on the subject of prosperity theology (and setting himself up as a kind of inverse "devil's advocate" for it, in that he wishes to show why it has been successful), he says that prosperity has proved a popular message that "does especially well where hard work and the other economic virtues produce little reward, at least for sectors of the

---

34. Joseph Isaac Lifschitz, "Jewish Economic Theology," in Schwarzkopf, *Economic Theology*, 268.

35. This is obviously a favorite trope in many films. A classic example is *Leap of Faith* (1992), starring Steve Martin and directed by Richard Pearce. This film ends up affirming the possibility of faith, whilst laughing at the manipulation of the preacher.

36. With the phrase "conditionalities of exclusion," I refer to the way in which many negative populist discourses are constructed around conditions of exclusion that will resort in an improvement for the "included." Frequently, as in the Czech Republic, this is about excluding the other: without migrants, the European Union, people whose sexual orientation is different to ours, etc., our society will be much better.

population."[37] In other words, it is precisely successful for those who find that traditional paths to material security are denied to them.

To this extent, it is also helpful to bear in mind another distinction that Freston makes, between the "sellers" and the "consumers" of theologies of prosperity.[38] This distinction is one that might help explain the cliché about liberation theology choosing the poor and the poor choosing Neo-Pentecostalism. Although somewhat tiresome, like many clichés it also contains at least an element of truth. The problem that liberation theologies have faced is similar to that faced by many non-populist politicians. Telling the truth does not always bring rewards. From the viewpoint of the addressees of the message of liberation theology, namely the poor, they do not need to hear that they are poor because of unjust structures. For them prosperity theologies have given shorter-term hope (another element Freston points to) of improvement.

Traditional Protestantism, especially Calvinism, tended to emphasize a sober approach to work and to the enjoyment of its benefits, but this is not always the case in those places where especially Pentecostalism is expanding.[39] It tends to have the greatest effect, according to Freston, in countries or regions where informal economies dominate (which is why it is so prevalent in Brazil), and where the skills and motivations needed tend to favor those who are independent with strong interpersonal skills.[40] In general, then, prosperity theology gains credence among people because it often seems to work for them—it is a successful hegemonic discourse.

It works for a number of reasons. To quote Freston:

> In Pentecostalism, the poor discover they are capable of giving and not just of receiving. In addition, it should be remembered that generous giving often replaces previous spending on medicines, drink or drugs. For many members, giving to the Church and a rationalization of overall economic behavior are inseparable.[41]

37. Freston, "Prosperity Theology," 66.
38. Freston, "Prosperity Theology," 67.
39. See Freston, "Prosperity Theology," 68.
40. Freston, "Prosperity Theology," 71.
41. Freston, "Prosperity Theology," 72. See also on this Teixeira, "The God of Prosperity," 68: "The pastors are selling salvation in heaven and enrichment on earth, but the faithful are not necessarily 'buying' a commodity, as market logic implies. They are 'giving' something; they are using their money to be involved in a 'cause.' That is different and changes everything."

Both these points are of vital importance, certainly in a Brazilian context. Old forms of *clientelismo* are still present in Brazilian society.[42] The poor receive in return for their votes, or for other benefits of the donor. Of course, in good Hegelian terms, this also creates a kind of Master-Bondsman relationship, in which the poor can expect and demand. It is this explanation that is common in discussions on prosperity theology, where God is the Master and the believer the Bondsman, to whom in fact the Master is also enslaved.

But Freston wants to argue, I think rightly, that there is another way of looking at things. Through following the prosperity gospel, most especially through giving tithes, the person with little finds that they still have something, that they too can give. This is not a new phenomenon in Brazil or in Brazilian religious life—the Fraternities, even among slaves, in the eighteenth century are another example.[43] But that does not make it any less powerful. Those who had no power now become those with power, to give, to make demands, to have expectations, to have hope of improvement, to be able to do something, however small, that makes them feel that they are more in control of their lives.

The sense of regaining control of one's life is not to be underestimated. I remember a friend of mine in Brazil who was very close to becoming, if not in fact already, an alcoholic. First through Catholic charismatics and then later through joining a Neo-Pentecostal church, his life was indeed transformed. He stopped drinking and the fact that he was not spending money on beer meant that he had more money, time, and energy to devote to work, to his family, and to the church. And money given to the church does not serve simply to make the pastor rich, but funds are also created that can be used to support people in starting their own small businesses, in something akin to micro-banking. That in turn helps businesses to grow and people in the church to be able to

---

42. See Hevia, "Relaciones," 212–13. The discussion on *clientelismo* is in the context of Lula's *Bolsa Família* program, where the poor were again primarily on the receiving end. Although the design of the program sought precisely to avoid *clientelismo*, it could be argued that it merely changed the partners in the relationship, rather than the nature of the relationship itself. On the related system of *coronelismo*, see Schwarcz and Starling, *Brazil*, 360. They describe how it functioned in the early years of the first Brazilian Republic (from 1889), noting that it "was based on the exchange of favors and loans, favoritism, repression, and negotiation."

43. See the reference in Schwarcz and Starling, *Brazil*, 126, and in more detail, Andrade, "Pretos devotos."

employ other church members. This is, in many poor neighborhoods, a genuinely virtuous circle.

The other area that prosperity theology stresses is the link between the material and spiritual. Many criticisms of prosperity theology, justified in themselves, run the risk of bringing back some form of dualism. *Askesis* is a virtue, but it is not to be identified solely with denial of the material, or with a purely spiritual attitude. Both these forms of dualism are present and need to be avoided. At its best, prosperity theology claims that the world is God's, and the world is good, and God will provide. Giving is not seen as a transaction, a deposit in an account on which the Banker God will pay high interest, but as a form of liberation and self-assertion. The giver is free to give to God. The faith that God will provide is not a consequence of the giving, rather the giving is an affirmation of the experience of receiving from God. As the offertory prayer in the Roman Catholic liturgy puts it: "Blessed are you, Lord God of all creation, for through your goodness we have received the bread we offer you: fruit of the earth and work of human hands, it will become for us the bread of life." What is received is returned and transformed, what is good becomes even better, the source of life now becomes the source of eternal life.

Problems with Prosperity Theology

Although it is important to bear this positive reading in mind, there are other ways of reading prosperity theology that are more negative in their judgements and it is to these that I now turn. For even if, as I have argued, it is not fair to judge a movement or a practice by its worst examples, neither should we ignore those examples. Theologies of prosperity can give rise to highly problematic forms of behavior, and that is a problem for them. So the question is what difficulties there are with the theologies of grace that lie behind theologies of entitlement, and in this case especially prosperity theology.

As in much theological discourse, there is an eschatological dimension to the discussion about grace. Grace is both as it were the motor of the Christian life and the fulfilment in God to which Christians are called and drawn. The eschatological dimension can be expressed in terms of promise, of what is held before the Christian as the end (as both goal and culmination) of their lives. One form of proclamation of this end would be in post-mortem terms—what will happen after we die. But there are two other forms of proclamation that are more concentrated on this-worldly rewards, namely liberation and prosperity, as a Brazilian Lutheran scholar, Júlio Cézar Adam, has noted.[44] Adam's chief interest is in preaching, which is, in itself, a form of hegemonic discourse, and in the best cases seeks to construct a people (the community that is part of the preaching event). I will return to the liberation version in the next chapter, but here I want to look at prosperity theology.

Adam characterizes the prosperity theology discourse as a fundamentally individualist discourse that offers the promise of what he terms "hedonist satisfaction"[45] in the present. Although he is using hedonism here in a more philosophical than moral sense, it is still a telling term. Prosperity theologies offer the promise of material satisfaction in a very concrete way. Even if one accepts that material satisfaction is a worthy aim, at least if pursued honestly and with attention to the other, critics of prosperity theology are concerned with the way in which such satisfaction is linked more generally to faith and more specifically to the paying of tithes and the enrichment of pastors. Faustino Teixeira, a Brazilian sociologist of religion, notes, for example, that many pastors can be tempted to become involved in a "bureaucratic salvation business."[46]

Prosperity theology, thus, "often makes the pursuit of material things and physical well-being ends in themselves."[47] It is no longer union with God that is emphasized but the health and wealth of the individual. One of the ways theologies of prosperity do this is through what one author calls "a tendentious exegesis of the Holy Scriptures."[48] The major source of texts for prosperity theology is the Old Testament, given that it frequently talks approvingly of the wealthy. However, such readings must be made in context. Chris Wright, a leading missiologist and Old Testament scholar, makes a strong case that the Old Testament does not offer a transactional reading of the relationship between God and human beings, but that all depends on the behavior of the rich person. Wealth is

---

44. Adam, "Pregação e promessa," 402–3.

45. Adam, "Pregação e promessa," 405.

46. Teixeira, "The God of Prosperity," 68. This is in the context that Teixeira is generally positive about the effect on ordinary believers of membership in Pentecostal churches, similarly to Freston.

47. Femi Adeleye, "The Prosperity Gospel and Poverty: An Overview and Assessment," in Salinas and Steuernagel, *Prosperity Theology and Gospel*, 5.

48. The phrase is a section heading of Oliveira, *Retribuição e Prosperidade*, 96.

a blessing if it is acquired in a righteous manner,⁴⁹ but for that to be the case there are, in Wright's view, a number of criteria that have to be fulfilled.⁵⁰ These criteria can perhaps be summarized as acknowledging that God comes first and that the relationship with God, as well as with the other, is one of service, marked by what Wright says is "the first principle of wisdom, namely the fear of the Lord."⁵¹

Fear of the Lord marks the very opposite of a theology of entitlement. It is a recognition of the deep inequality of the relationship between humanity and God, the divine as, in Otto's famous description, *tremendum*.⁵² God inspires awe. The dangers of what we could call an over-familiarity with God are well-summarized by a Brazilian Baptist critic of prosperity theology, Marcelo Rodrigues de Oliveira. He argues that, although there is no problem with prosperity in itself, "the problem arises when the concept is distorted and loses any sense of mercy, justice, and judgement, and is divorced from its *Sitz im Leben*, in order to be applied in preaching and submitted to bargaining, as generally happens in the Neo-Pentecostal churches."⁵³ Awe is replaced by hardnosed business principles, where nothing is for free and every transaction should lead to profit for the believer, often in fairly crass material terms.

Proponents of prosperity theology also appeal to the New Testament, but again its message is more nuanced. As the biblical scholar Craig Blomberg puts it, "the texts that impinge on economic issues in the Bible, which might be viewed as supporting one or the other system, are

---

49. It should also be remembered that the kind of economy and the nature of economic relations in the Bible are different to those today, though in precisely what ways remains a matter of ongoing debate. For a good theoretical introduction see Miller, "Cultivating Curiosity." For a more general overview of the kind of economics proposed in the Bible, see Blomberg, "Neither Capitalism nor Socialism." He begins justifying his title (the sub-title is "A Biblical Theology of Economics) in the following way: "To begin with, perhaps the most obvious reason is that capitalism and socialism as thoroughgoing systems were not the economic systems of the biblical worlds" (208).

50. Christopher Wright, "Can the Rich Be Righteous? An Old Testament Perspective," in Salinas and Steuernagel, *Prosperity Theology and the Gospel*, 23–35. The criteria are given on 33–34.

51. Wright, "Can the Rich?," 34. I return to wisdom and fear of the Lord in the conclusion.

52. That which, in Otto's words, "may become the hushed, trembling, and speechless humility of the creature in the presence of—whom or what? In the presence of that which is a *Mystery* inexpressible and above all creatures." Otto, *The Idea of the Holy*, 13.

53. Oliveira, *Retribuição e Prosperidade*, 97.

relatively evenly distributed between the two."[54] Even texts that appear to argue against prosperity theology are not quite so straightforward. A clear example is Luke 6:35: "Love your enemies, do good, and lend, expecting nothing in return. Your reward will be great, and you will be children of the Most High; for he is kind to the ungrateful and the wicked." The first part of the sentence may indeed state that the disciple should lend without hope of return, which seems to go against the fundamental tenet of prosperity preaching, that one gives precisely because one hopes for something in return. And yet, the verse does go on to claim that "your reward will be great."[55] In fact, this is a similar position to the Old Testament accounts, and if the emphasis is less on the "righteous rich" in the New Testament, there is nevertheless an expectation of blessing. Giving "is interested giving, in the sense that givers are encouraged to anticipate some return—even if it comes from God in the form of heavenly reward, and not from human recipients."[56]

This is hardly surprising. If what we do, how we behave, the attitude we adopt towards others are all entirely meaningless, it would be purely an arbitrary decision as to how to treat "the stranger, the widow, the orphan," those whom the great twentieth-century philosopher of alterity, Emmanuel Levinas, acknowledges as the "Other who dominates me in his transcendence."[57] But even the most classical Protestant theologies, with their understandable desire to avoid equating salvation with good works, have not wished to claim that our relationship to the other is entirely arbitrary. Good works are at least a subsequent sign of devotion to and faith in Christ and the saved person will be sober in their behavior because they know that their salvation depends on God alone. So the point at issue is not whether God in some way or other rewards those

54. Blomberg, "Neither Capitalism nor Socialism," 209.

55. On this, see David Downs, "Giving for a Return in the Prosperity Gospel and the New Testament," in Salinas and Steuernagel, *Prosperity Theology and the Gospel*, 40–41.

56. Downs, "Giving for a Return," 47.

57. Levinas, *Totality and Infinity*, 215. The stranger, widow and orphan are of course the classic Old Testament categories of those to whom special attention should be given; see, for example, Exod 22:21–22; Mal 3:5. Malachi adds the category of the "hired worker", whilst Isa 1:17 also speaks of rescuing the oppressed; Zech 7:10 adds the category of the "poor." The Deuterocanonical 4 Esd 2:20–21 speaks in even more detail: "Guard the rights of the widow, secure justice for the ward, give to the needy, defend the orphan, clothe the naked, care for the injured and the weak, do not ridicule the lame, protect the maimed, and let the blind have a vision of my splendor."

who do good, but rather what kind of reward and the way in which it is provided. Prosperity gospel adherents frequently seem to reduce the transaction to a very simple correlation. If you give this amount of money, you will receive this larger sum back in return.

There are a number of texts in the New Testament that seem to warn against the danger of riches, the most obvious being Jesus' assertion that "it is easier for a camel to go through the eye of a needle than for someone who is rich to enter the Kingdom of God" (Matt 19:24, with parallels in Mark 10:25 and Luke 18:25).[58] But there are also texts that are more positive about the possibilities for those who are wealthy, for example 1 Tim 6:17–19:

> As for those who in the present age are rich, command them not to be haughty, or to set their hopes on the uncertainty of riches, but rather on God who richly provides us with everything for our enjoyment. They are to do good, to be rich in good works, generous, and ready to share, thus storing up for themselves the treasure of a good foundation for the future, so that they may take hold of the life that really is life.

Of course, this text needs to be set within a slightly wider context, not least 1 Tim 6:10, "the love of money is a root of all evil things." Where the desire for money outweighs the desire for God, there will be severe problems. Needless to say, it is very unlikely that preachers would explicitly claim to love money more than God, but the reality certainly appears to be otherwise.

Against this background, then, those who are wealthy will benefit not from using their wealth for their own good and happiness, but by using it for the good of others. What makes them successful, in the long run, is not the fact that they have a lot of money or possessions, but that they use what they have acquired for the good of others.[59] In part verses like this must be read within the context of the economic reality of the

---

58. See also the related story of the Rich Young Man in Mark 10:17–22, and the subsequent discussion; Matt 6:24 ("it is not possible to serve God and Mammon"); Luke 6:24 ("Woe to you who are rich, for you have received your consolation"), or much of the Letter of James. On Matthew, see Luz, *Matthew 8–20*, 509–23.

59. On this, see Baker, "Entrepreneurship as a Sign." Although he acknowledges (84–85) that capitalism and entrepreneurship can be touched by sin, Baker's article is largely a paean of praise to capitalism, but he reads this positively in terms of contribution to economic *shalom*.

first century. Certainly money[60] in the ancient world was not like it is today—there were no stock markets to invest in, nor banks in the modern sense that would pay good rates of interest,[61] so money had to be spent on land or indeed on slaves to work the land,[62] but of course it could also be spent on doing good (feeding the poor, building aqueducts to bring water, giving employment). What is good about money is that it can be given away.

Now in itself this may not be enough to argue against prosperity theology preachers. After all, one of the things they often seem most interested in is precisely people giving away their money, but giving it away to the preachers or at least in slightly more subtle forms of the message to "the church," even if in practice that is indistinguishable from those who benefit from the enrichment of the church, which happens to be the pastors (its employees).[63] In the words of one commentator, it

> does not take long reading the literature or hearing the sermons of "health and wealth" teachers to encounter strident appeals to this kind of interested giving. Expressed by American televangelist Robert Tilton as God's "law of compensation," scriptural

---

60. The love of money in 1 Tim is expressed by a single Greek word, *philarguría*. *Arguría* is used in reference to physical money, that is, to (silver) coins.

61. See Geva, *Payment Order*, especially chapter 2, "Money and Monetary Legal Theory in Antiquity and the Middle Ages," 68–87, and on bank deposits, 596–603. On 597, Geva notes that "under the Talmud, the deposit of money, even in an open bag, was for safekeeping, so as to be returned *in specie*. The Talmud gives the depositary the right to use money on deposit only in very limited circumstances; when they occur, the depositary becomes liable for the amount so used. At the same time, the Talmud does not permit a depositary for safekeeping to mix money deposited by different depositors as well as with his own money; hence, the Talmud has not developed a parallel to the Roman irregular deposit. Thus, in principle, a depositary of money under the Talmud is treated like a bailee for safekeeping of a specific chattel."

62. The biblical record on slavery is at best mixed. But theologies of entitlement include theologies of non-entitlement, which would conclude that those who are in slavery deserve it. It is precisely this logic that makes them so dangerous and ultimately anti-Christian.

63. On this, see the comments of Dusilek, "Traços pagãos," 201: "Entrepreneurial pragmatism has led to the suppression of historic values defended by the most diverse religious streams and led to the rise of a new 'quality' of clerics and leaders, the religious manager. In this figure there is a change from being trustworthy and personable, qualities that were once unnegotiable for a religious leader, to being impersonal and a person with corporate skills. As we know, in the corporate world, the only quality and sign of trustworthiness required and practiced is what is linked to the survival of the corporation."

texts such as Mark 10:29–30, Luke 18:29–30, 2 Cor 9:6 and Gal 6:7 are invoked, promoting the idea that the more one gives—usually to the preacher or the organization requesting donations—the more God will bless the donor with material gifts.[64]

This is where the problem emerges, since a double sense of entitlement is developed. On the one hand, the preacher, who, let us accept for the sake of argument, sincerely believes in the message that is being preached, feels entitled to the rewards due to the one who works for the Kingdom (cf. Matt 19:29; Mark 10:29–30).[65] On the other hand, those who respond to the call also have a sense of entitlement, since they have responded to the call and paid their dues, and as such they assume that they have a right to the rewards promised them. This sense of entitlement is problematic, since it always ends up relegating God to the status of servant, a God who exists to keep his side of a bargain.

Prosperity Theology and Economic Models

One criticism of prosperity theology is that it ultimately serves to support various forms of late modern capitalism. As a Brazilian Baptist religious studies' scholar notes: "Prosperity Theology can be seen as a formulation of cultural adaptation, by which values extolled by the capitalist system enter into and give meaning to religious experience."[66] Liberation theology will strongly critique this economic model, as will be seen in the next chapter. Here the point to make is that economic models should serve human beings, not the other way around. In other words, what is at stake is whether prosperity theologies avoid the pitfall of idolatry. To put it starkly, do they serve God or do they ultimately serve "Mammon"?

Prosperity theologies do not have to support current forms of capitalism. Paul Freston, for example, refers to critiques of global capitalism by two bishops of the Universal Church of the Kingdom of God,[67] the

64. Downs, "Giving for a Return," in Salinas and Steuernagel, *Prosperity Theology and the Gospel*, 36.

65. The text of Mark 10:29–31 reads "Jesus said, 'Truly I tell you, there is no one who has left house or brothers or sisters or mother or father or children or fields, for my sake and for the sake of the good news, who will not receive a hundredfold now in this age—houses, brothers and sisters, mothers and children, and fields with persecutions—and in the age to come eternal life.'"

66. Dusilek, "Traços pagãos," 203.

67. Igreja Universal do Reino de Deus, founded by Edir Macedo in 1977. The comments are in Freston, "Prosperity Theology," 72.

most vociferous and probably most numerous[68] of the specifically prosperity gospel churches in Brazil, with significant presence elsewhere too. But Freston also admits that such critiques are not common in the church, and most preachers appear simply to take for granted the economic system as they find it. It is within this system that God's rewards will be given and the churches make use of the tools of contemporary capitalism to grow their own portfolios.

A Brazilian scholar, writing over twenty years ago, pointed out:

> Its pastors are business people with low or no theological formation but who have to demonstrate a strong capacity to attract the public and generate dividends for the church according to a "know-how" administered entrepreneurially by the bishops with the church already structured as a business. It is this aggressivity of the pastors that explains to a large extent the success of this religion; the expansion of the market depends a lot on the style of the offering, of its propaganda, and its language.[69]

The fact that a church is structured like a business, though it may be an example of what in a slightly different context and with a slightly different meaning John Drane has called the McDonaldization of the Church,[70] does not necessarily mean that it is idolatrous. However, as soon as the emphasis is placed on financial or at least on material success,[71] the danger of making this the guiding principle of preaching and church life is clear. Several factors contribute to making this danger even more present. The first of these is the tendency to read the Scriptures allegorically. Although such readings have a long tradition

---

68. The church claims more than eight million adherents in Brazil, though this may be an over-estimate (the last census details are already ten years old, so outdated, but they only registered 1.8 million members).

69. Prandi, "Religião paga," 66, quoted in Silva, "Mercado, sacrifício," 133. Silva quotes the article with a title in the plural (Religiões pagas), but this seems to be an error.

70. Drane, *McDonaldization of the Church*. Drane is interested in the cultural aspects. I refer rather to the way in which churches like the Universal Church of the Kingdom of God essentially establish franchises, which are expected to pay a certain amount to the main body, the rest being the property of the "manager" (pastor).

71. I am not examining here the role of healings, another important pillar of prosperity theology. But healings are clearly material and are a reward for giving money. In a country like Brazil with a very precarious system of public health, the turn to religion for healing is present in all Christian denominations, as well as in Afro-Brazilian religions such as *Umbanda* or *Candomblé*.

within Christianity (indeed parts of the New Testament are an allegorical reading of the Jewish Scriptures),[72] they can permit interpretations of scripture that lose any contact with reality.[73]

Another problem is the emphasis on victory. Sérgio Dusilek, a Brazilian writer on the theme, puts it like this: "In emphasizing the theme of victory, the possibility of control over God and the unlimited use of images and symbols, it [prosperity theology] incorporates what is most alien to the Bible and most normal to paganism."[74] This is not the place to go deeply into the meaning and reality of idolatry, in biblical times or more recently,[75] but a few comments are needed. Dusilek speaks of the problem of symbols, but at least from the viewpoint of Catholic theology, the problem may be rather a poor understanding of symbol. Sacramental theologians such as Louis-Marie Chauvet have shown that the symbol is both a presence and an absence.[76] The danger of prosperity theology is that the symbol is reduced to a presence, which means that it ceases to be symbol. There is ultimately no room for the transcendent and God is prevented from being God. And that is idolatry.

It is the refusal to open up the space for God to be other, since now God is reduced to a part of a transaction, necessary to square the balance sheet but having no other intrinsic value. God does of course need to be able to fulfil his part of the bargain, just as the bank needs to have the funds to repay me if I deposit money. This ends up with a kind of re-enchantment of the divine, God as magician. But that is not the same as transcendence. Indeed, because God—or at least that which is named as the divine—is not transcendent, there is an even stronger need for a transactional approach. God can only help those who make contributions, like getting a cup of coffee from a machine. Without putting money in, nothing will come out.

---

72. The most obvious and explicit example is Gal 4:22–31, where in v. 24 Paul uses the verbal form *allēgoroúmena* (literally, "being spoken allegorically"), but there are many other examples in Paul and elsewhere.

73. See Dusilek, "Traços pagãos," 207–11. Dusilek argues that the problem with allegory is that it "promotes the symbol of the symbol that is the fruit, in this case, of the fantasy of the preacher. And instead of this symbolism pointing to something unconditioned, this line of thought leads back to a particular reality that is expressed by discourses of overcoming and profit displayed in internal marketing campaigns" (207).

74. Dusilek, "Traços pagãos," 211.

75. See for more detail on this in terms of liberation theology, Noble, *Poor in Liberation Theology*, 43–52.

76. See Chauvet, *Symbol and Sacrament*, 404–5; Bauer, *Znovuobjevení*.

Sacrifice in Prosperity Theology

A third way in which prosperity theology runs the risk of idolatry is in the area of sacrifice. Prosperity theology is at its worst a self-enclosed world, in which the sacrifices are either successful or, if they are not, that is merely a sign that sufficient sacrifice has not been made. In one of his books Kenneth Hagin recalls—positively—the story a friend told him of a preacher demanding money from the congregation, assuring them that they would raise $10,000 that night. Hagin continues, quoting his friend:

> Then he [the pastor] said, "I don't want anybody to give anything they can afford to give. Give what you *can't* afford. If you feel you can afford to give $50 but not $100, give the $100. If you think you can afford to give $500 but not $1,000, give the $1,000. There's where the blessing is—and that's the truth."[77]

A sacrifice has to be made—to give what one can afford is easy enough,[78] but to make the sacrifice will ensure that the return is made.

It is almost a commonplace of liberation theology to point out how the language of sacrifice is an integral part of the language of modern economies.[79] This language is employed to demand from those who have little that they sacrifice even that little for the sake of those who have much. And money is the chief vehicle of sacrifice, since it is peculiar in its ability to provide the possibility of interchange.[80]

> Money constitutes a measure of value and more still of sacrifice, although linked to the degree of faith of the believer and not, for example, to the amount of work that will have to be carried out to achieve success in such a test. In reality, the value itself is in that which the person wants to obtain and that is presented as beyond money and the amount realized. The believer wants to obtain something out of their immediate reach and that is

---

77. Hagin, *Redeemed from Poverty*, 7.

78. It may seem that this coincides with Luke 21:3-4 (Mark 12:42-44), the story of the Widow's Mite. But the widow does not put in all she has in hope of reward, and Jesus does not instruct his disciples to do as she does. Generosity without hope of reward is praised, not a shrewd financial deal.

79. Liberation theology tends to apply this to capitalism or at least to the market, but the language of sacrifice was also employed by Communist regimes. In capitalism, the sacrifice is theoretically in the name of capital, in communism in the name of the revolution, but both demand bloody sacrifices.

80. See Silva, "Mercado, sacrifício," 136-37.

possible only through divine intervention. But, for this, it is necessary to demonstrate faith and to put it to the test before God.[81]

The major problem, though, with any form of sacrificial theory is that it demands victims. Theologies of prosperity do not use the language of victim, because God is seen as preventing anyone becoming a victim. However, victims are still present in two ways. The first is that there is an element of self-sacrifice. It is all very well, in the words of the prayer on generosity attributed to St. Ignatius, "to give and not to count the cost,"[82] but if the costs are real, then sacrifice is required. The person must go without, lose something that they need (especially if they are poor in the first place). Prosperity theologies teach that the sacrifice, the making a victim of oneself, is worth it, because of the rewards that will be received. But, of course, not everyone gets rich. In that case, prosperity theology has two responses. Either it can urge the individual to make themselves a bigger victim by sacrificing more, or it can doubly victimize the person by accusing them of lack of faith and in some way or other expelling them from the community.

Most churches that rely on testimonies and conversion stories focus on the positive examples. Prosperity theologies speak of those who have been cured, of those who have had financial success or at least found a stability that they never had before. Conversion stories speak of addicts and others in dire straits who have found Christ and had their lives transformed. But they do not speak of those who have not been cured, those who remain poor or in a precarious state; they do not interest themselves in those who remain addicted or subject to other outside forces. It may be true that there is greater rejoicing in heaven over one sinner repenting than over ninety-nine just people who need no repentance (Luke 15:7), so to tell stories of sinners repenting is worthwhile. But it may also be the case that there would be even greater joy in heaven if two sinners repented, so why not tell the story of the one who got away? This is not unimportant, since it should force the church to think not so much about its successes, but about its failures. These cannot be dismissed as lost and unsaved, at least not without the effort being made to do something for them rather than victimize them further.

---

81. Silva, "Mercado, sacrifício," 137.

82. The prayer actually appears to come from the late nineteenth century, perhaps from France. See Mahoney, "Mysterious Ignatian Prayer."

Tithing

The sacrifices involved in making contributions to the church, with the promise and hope of future rewards, takes us to the question of tithing, which is one of the central planks of the practice of many churches. At least in Brazil, tithing[83] is not only a part of the practice of Neo-Pentecostal churches. I remember how in the local Catholic community in which I participated in Brazil we would have frequent reminders about tithing and celebrations of those who were giving money in this way.[84] So in Brazil the practice is widespread, even if the motivations for giving are not always—officially at least—the same. But in those churches where the Prosperity Gospel holds sway there is a very clear understanding of the transactional nature of tithing.

The practice of tithing has its roots, for most Christians, in practices recommended in the Jewish Scriptures. One-tenth of a gradually diversifying range of produce was to be given to God, which in practice meant to the Temple authorities. It would appear that there is no firm evidence for the existence of the continual practice of tithing prior to the giving of the Mosaic Law, recorded in Leviticus, Numbers, and Deuteronomy.[85] The discussion over the practices in the Mosaic Law revolve around the relationship between three types of tithing, the tithe to the Levites, the festival tithe, and the "poor tithe."[86] The details are not important for my

---

83. The Portuguese "dízimo" and the Czech "desátek" mean, as does the English, a tenth part of something.

84. For a very good overview, from a Roman Catholic perspective, of the aim and motivation of the practice of tithing (*Pastoral do dízimo* in Portuguese), see Dominus, "Entenda."

85. So Köstenberger and Croteau, "'Will a Man Rob God?,'" 54–61. Köstenberger and Croteau also point out that, on the other hand, a number of texts both in early tradition and throughout the Old Testament, refer to the practice of voluntary giving. They cite the following: Exod 25:1–2; 35:4–10.21–22a; 36:5–7; Num 18:12; Deut 16:17 ("all shall give as they are able"); 1 Chr 29:9, 16; Prov 3:9–10 (this text may be more supportive of prosperity theology: "Honor the LORD with your substance and with the first fruits of all your produce; then your barns will be filled with plenty, and your vats will be bursting with wine"); 11:24–25 (a more complex text: "Some give freely, yet grow all the richer; others withhold what is due, and only suffer want. A generous person will be enriched, and one who gives water will get water."). Veliq, "Uma análise bíblica," 229, argues that the examples of Abraham and Jacob are cases of tithing before the implementation of the Law, but Köstenberger and Croteau's arguments seem more convincing to me.

86. See Köstenberger and Croteau, "'Will a Man Rob God?,'" 61–65.

argument, but what is to be noted is that none of these tithes has as its primary purpose the enrichment or prosperity of the one who pays it.

The Levite tithe and the "poor tithe"[87] are aimed at those without land, and thus without direct means of sustenance, while the Festival tithe is about setting aside produce to use in times of celebration (so perhaps more akin to saving money for a holiday or for Christmas). Whilst criticisms of the non-payment of tithes do occur, most famously in Mal 3:8, with the ringing question "Will anyone rob God?," this is not about a simple gift-reward pattern. Two Biblical scholars, Andreas Köstenberger and David Croteau, in their examination of biblical passages directly devoted to tithing, say of the passage in Malachi:

> The withholding of tithes was a sign of a larger pattern of disobedience. The tithe mentioned by the prophet is the Levitical tithe (Lev 27:30; Num 18:21). The offerings to which reference is made as well were a primary source of livelihood for the priests and were required, rather than voluntary, offerings. The invitation to test God is limited to the context of Mal 3 and should not be universalized. For this reason the promised reward, likewise, does not carry over to people who may tithe today.[88]

The New Testament passages are even fewer[89] and do not seem to demand a practice of tithing for the church. The upshot of this brief biblical excursus is that there is no obvious mandate to practice tithing in the strict sense of the word, though this does not preclude a duty of

---

87. Based on Deut 14:28–29, and so called because it was levied every third year, and was intended for the support of the Levite, the foreigner, the orphan, and the widow (that is, the landless, without means, therefore, to grow their own food). Admittedly, v. 29 ends by saying that this is to be done "so that the LORD your God may bless you in all the work that you undertake," but this is very different to saying that they will receive material rewards. Veliq, "Uma análise bíblica," 230, says of this passage that it shows "God instituting the tithe as a way of organizing a kind of social equality between all the participants of the community."

88. Köstenberger and Croteau, "'Will a Man Rob God?,'" 70.

89. Köstenberger and Croteau, "'Will a Man Rob God?,'" 71–77, mention three passages. The first is Matt 23:23 (and parallel in Luke), which condemns the Pharisees not for paying tithes, but for neglecting more important matters. Second is Luke 18:9–14, the parable of the Pharisee and Tax-Collector. The fact that the Pharisee pays tithes is not necessarily what makes him a hypocrite, nor is the tax-collector praised for not paying tithes, so the mention of tithes is not central to the story. Finally there is Heb 7:1–10, which draws on the story of Abraham paying a tithe to Melchizedek and which aims to show the superiority of Jesus as the ultimate and unique High Priest whose sacrifice is once and for all.

giving, for the support of the church and of those in need.[90] After an exhaustive examination of biblical references to tithing and New Testament teaching on giving, Köstenberger and Croteau conclude with a series of principles of giving that they derive from their reading of the New Testament, and they remark that the principles "all require one key element: a relationship with God. In the end, obedience in giving comes down to our relationship with the Father."[91] Nowhere does the practice of giving (whether or not one decides to give a strictly counted ten per cent of one's income or not) exist solely or even principally as a means of ensuring divine favor.

And yet the practices in churches do not always bear this out. As a Brazilian writer on the topic puts it:

> However, what we see in evangelical churches, principally those of a more Neo-Pentecostal form, is that the verse of Malachi [3:8] is mostly used wrongly, implying that not bringing the tithe is opening the door for curses to enter the house of the one who does not give. An enormous judgement is placed on the life of the person who does not tithe, causing the person to do so out of fear and not as a matter of principle.[92]

Both Old and New Testaments tend to stress the importance of voluntary giving[93] and of giving being, if not entirely disinterested, at least principally for the sake of the community. The charge against those who do not pay the tithe in Malachi is to be read within the context of the prophet's words of condemnation of those who do not act justly. "Robbing God" is not a question of giving more to the church, but the practice of those who are already wealthy and who seek to increase their wealth by cheating on their obligations to contribute to the well-being of those in need. Today we may prefer to speak of individuals and companies who go to great extremes to

---

90. On this see a second article by Köstenberger and Croteau, which they present as a continuation of the article already cited above: Köstenberger and Croteau, "Reconstructing." In this article they attend to the New Testament teaching on giving.

91. Köstenberger and Croteau, "Reconstructing," 258.

92. Veliq, "Uma análise bíblica," 234.

93. As Blomberg, "Neither Capitalism nor Socialism," 211, remarks, after brief comments on some New Testament passages about the economy, "Yet, at the same time a close inspection of each of these New Testament passages demonstrates that Christian giving was always voluntary, never required by any central authority. After the shift in eras with Christ's death and resurrection, no New Testament text ever mandates a tithe but rather commands generous and sacrificial giving instead."

avoid paying tax. This is a practice that seeks self-advancement against the interest of the many and in that sense it is indeed to steal from God.

The demands made in those churches that preach the gospel of prosperity are based, then, not on the Bible or any element of Christian doctrine, but purely on convenience,[94] on what is good for the church and its leadership. It is not unreasonable for the church to ask its members for help in meeting its costs[95]—that is, after all, more or less what the Levite tithe was about. But when the tithe is regarded as a down payment on future returns, and it serves to enrich the pastors or leaders of the church, it may be good business practice, but it is very hard to see that it is good or justifiable theology. Even at its most positive, there is no theological backing for these practices. From the point of view of helping people deal with poverty, a system that accumulates relatively large sums of money that can be used to support people who need small loans is arguably a good thing.[96] But the problem is when it is linked to pressure and success is seen as a sign of faith and failure as a sign of lack of faith.

Edir Macedo, founder of the Universal Church and one of the wealthiest men in Brazil, wrote in one of his books:

> Who has the right to put God to the test, to demand of him what he promised? The one who tithes. One of the main reasons why we give our tithes is this. We can and we have the right to put God to the test. He himself invites us to put him to the test in his Word and this invitation is found precisely when referring to the tithe.[97]

God must be put to the test and if he does not repay us for paying our tithes, he is ultimately not worthy of our worship. As Manuel Rodrigues de Oliveira puts it, the approach of the prosperity gospel churches transforms the order in which Jesus suggests things should work in the

---

94. I take this from Veliq, "Uma análise bíblica," 237.

95. A Brazilian Catholic website (run by a Catholic marketing agency) explains the need for the tithe in this way: "However much it is the case that spirituality has no cost in itself, liturgy, the physical space and employees—to give only a few examples—require the most diverse resources. To sum up, it is not possible for a parish to function without income." See Dominus, "Entenda."

96. This might be seen as a form of local banking. An early example of this was the *Banco da Providência*, established by Dom Hélder Câmara in Rio de Janeiro in 1959. For a brief account, see Nascimento, "A Trajetória de 50 Anos."

97. Macedo, *Nos passos*, 64, quoted in Oliveira, *Retribuição e Prosperidade*, 96.

Sermon on the Mount. He writes that, given the fact that prosperity cannot be reduced simply to a sign of blessing, as it can also be a sign of sin:

> It is better to live in accord with what is prioritized in the gospel discourse: to seek first the Kingdom of God and his righteousness and the rest, that is, all that is necessary for life, will be added (cf. Matt 6:33). But the message of the Neo-Pentecostal churches does not follow this logic. It takes another path—that of the absolutizing and power of the promises as unequivocal evidence of God's favor. Firstly, the other things (all the things that are desired) are added, and then the Kingdom of God.[98]

By doing this, God is made into at best a banker and at worst a servant, who must do what he is paid to by the believer.

Practices of Entitlement in the Czech Republic

To end this chapter, I want to return to the second of the two countries I have been focusing on and to the nature of hegemonic discourse that we saw in the previous chapter. How are practices of entitlement present in the Czech Republic? To answer this question in the Czech context, it will be necessary to go beyond the churches, since the prosperity gospel as such is not, to any notable extent, present in the Czech churches. But even in secular discourses, God can be co-opted to bolster a sense of entitlement and that is what I will turn to shortly. The other question is about the kind of discourse that practices of entitlement are based on. Here we will be able to advance the debate by acknowledging that practices of entitlement are not simply on the side of those who seek material prosperity, but also for those who seek special status for their country or their perceived way of life.

First, though, let us look at practices of entitlement, especially with regard to the Czech Republic. Though theologies of prosperity are not a part of the tradition of church life in the Czech Republic, the concept is known and satirized in films and television programs. Indeed it has been claimed that one of the problems faced by the churches, especially the Roman Catholic Church, in the early 1990s, was to do with their attitude to money.[99] The situation was complex, since the Communists had taken

---

98. Oliveira, *Retribuição e Prosperidade*, 101.

99. For a measured comment on this, see Noble, "Czech Churches in Transition," 77. See also Nešpor, *Česká a slovenská religiozita*.

property from the churches, and many of the buildings that remained in church hands were in need of restoration.[100] Even some of the schemes, especially the Credit Unions, that the church tried to initiate were not in themselves bad, but unfortunately they attracted various people who in the most charitable interpretations were not capable of carrying out the work, or more likely saw it as a good way to become rich.[101]

Allied to this was a long debate over restitution. This debate tended to center on two different aspects, to do first with the restoration of or recompense for property seized under communism, and second, future financing of the churches. At the moment, ministers of registered churches are paid by the state, but the final agreement, reached a few years back, will see this phased out and the churches receiving a lump sum from the government, and then being expected to pay the salaries of ministers themselves. The debate has been fractious and complex. On the one hand the churches felt, not altogether unreasonably, that they had the right to property that had been stolen from them. The Roman Catholic Church, especially, had been a major landowner, though already in the late eighteenth century the reforms of Joseph II had effectively nationalized church property, and something similar had happened in the First Republic as part of the agrarian reform carried out under President Masaryk. Nevertheless, at the beginning of the twentieth century the Roman Catholic Church in the Czech Lands owned something in the region of 380,000 hectares of land and even under Masaryk's agrarian reform lost only some 10 percent of this total.[102]

Legally the churches were entitled to the restitution of their property and for most people this in itself was not a problem. But it could seem to go hand in hand with what was a different sense of entitlement,

---

100. Vladimir Michálek's 1996 film *Zapomenuté světlo* (Forgotten Light) is an excellent fictional representation of this. The film takes its title from and is very loosely based on a novella by Jakub Deml written in 1934, but updated to the late 1980s.

101. Known in Czech as *kampeličky*, after František Cyril Kampelík (1805–72), the popularizer of credit unions in the Czech lands in the second half of the nineteenth century, they proved very popular in the 1990s. Although the churches were not the only, or the main player, in their establishment, church credit unions also collapsed, causing huge problems for those who had invested in them.

102. The land owned equates to roughly 5 percent of the territory of the contemporary Czech Republic. See Wikipedia, s.v. "Pozemková reforma v Československu," https://cs.wikipedia.org/wiki/Pozemkov%C3%A1_reforma_v_%C4%8Ceskoslovensku. For the pre-history, and the comparative poverty of the Catholic Church in the seventeenth and eighteenth centuries, see Petráček, *In the Maelstrom*, 34–37.

that the church was still a power in the land. Although this attitude is not dominant amongst practicing Christians in the country, some church leaders, and most especially some Roman Catholic bishops, have given the impression of having a sense of entitlement to privilege and power that has not gone down well. But these expressions of entitlement have merely mirrored other, non-religious, expressions.

My first visits to the Czech Republic date back to 1996, and when I first came there was little exclusivist nationalism present in the country.[103] Such a position has become more developed in the past decade or so, with the realization that membership of the European Union brought not only entitlements but also responsibilities. Moreover, greater exposure to the western and northern parts of Europe only served to emphasize the gap in earnings.[104] Economically the Czech Republic has done reasonably well over the past decade, with sustained growth, low unemployment, and rising wages. And yet clearly there is a sense of dissatisfaction among a section of the population that they are not getting what they are entitled to.

A strong impulse to this movement came with the arrival in 2015 and 2016 of large numbers of migrants in Europe. Under initial European Union plans, as noted in chapter 1, the Czech Republic was asked to receive twenty thousand migrants, easily absorbable even in a rather homogeneous society, such as the Czech Republic has been since the expulsion of Germans after 1945 and the murder of its Jewish population by the Nazis in the concentration camps during the Second World War. But fears of terrorism, however rationally ungrounded, and a deep distrust of the other, led to a resurgence of support for racist and xenophobic political parties, who campaigned under slogans such as No to Migrants and Czech Republic for the Czechs. This last especially is clearly a claim of entitlement, that birth or nationality entitles someone to rights over a place and over others. This is very different from a sense of attachment to place, which need not be in the least exclusive.

---

103. It was of course present. In the 1992 and 1996 general elections, the overtly racist *Sdružení pro republiku—Republikánská strana Československa* (Association for the Republic—Czechoslovak Republican Party), gained respectively fourteen and then eighteen seats in parliament under its leader Miroslav Sládek. The party has since disbanded and although it has reformed in various ways it has not been able to regain its former position, which has been taken over by the self-styled Freedom and Direct Democracy party of Tomio Okamura.

104. Of course this is partly unrealistic. Living costs are overall lower in the Czech Republic than they are in countries like Germany or France, so comparatively salaries are more competitive, but still lag behind in many professions.

Although nationalist exclusivity is not itself particularly religious, there have also been voices who have suggested that the Czech Republic is a country with Christian values (or at least more broadly that Europe is a continent with Christian values) that need to be protected against the perceived threats of Islamization. Rationally this is nonsense: the Czech Republic is not Christian and has a minimal Muslim population.[105] But as we saw in chapter 2, rationality is not really an important factor. What matters and what needs to be taken seriously is the affective dimension. People feel threatened and feel that the stability that they imagine that they had is being taken away.[106] Reactions are not really to migrants, to Muslims, to others, but to their own lives and problems. Here the feeling is not that different to the followers of prosperity gospel—by investing in a political party (rather than a church), they are seeking to ensure that they have the security to which they feel entitled.

Thus what works best is a hegemonic discourse of entitlement that provides a plan for fulfilling that sense of entitlement. What matters is not primarily some external reality, but much more a kind of sensibility, a feeling that things are not as they should be and that by following a given path (no migrants, no Muslims, no foreigners, Czech Republic for the Czechs) the peace and security that is longed for will be provided. Such a discourse also, whether knowingly or not, underpins a materialization of life, and thus fits in well with lingering feelings of economic injustice. One's country, one's way of life, is subsumed under the broader conception of ownership—this is our country, our way of life, it belongs to us and not to anyone else. And the "not to anyone else" is dependent on a model of private ownership, rather than on some competing motif, such as stewardship. So, although prosperity as such may not be the major plank of such positions, it is nevertheless included in them. Of course, no politician is going to campaign on a program of making everyone worse off. However, what is different here is that material prosperity is a result of exclusion and, fundamentally, hatred. The other can only be excluded if they can be deemed a threat, and threats are to be feared and hated. If sufficient fear and hatred is invested, prosperity is guaranteed.

---

105. Figures vary, but it is generally reckoned that there are around twenty thousand Muslims in the Czech Republic.

106. This may be one reason why there is such a complex relationship to the Communist past. On the functions and dysfunctions of memory and their theological underpinnings in the Czech Republic, see Noble, "Memory and Remembering."

But, in conclusion, how is this related to a theology of grace? Here we can turn to the idea of common grace, expounded by, among others, Abraham Kuyper,[107] and drawing on the Noachic covenant, made with all of humanity. At least from the perspective of Christian theology, the whole of creation is graced, and so what people do is implicitly either a welcoming of that grace or a rejection of it.[108] Practices or policies of entitlement are, in this respect, a way of ordering the relationship between the two "signatories" of the covenant, God and humanity. There is a beautiful scene in the Czech film *Forgotten Light*, where the main character, Father Holý (played by Bolek Polívka) recounts a dream:

> Not long ago I went into an abandoned church and I saw God there, praying. He was praying to humanity. He said: "Human being, if you exist, show yourself!" Then he saw me and said "Human being! A human revelation" I said "But you created me, why are you surprised?" And he replied "No one's been in this church for such a long time. I began to doubt, but now I can say with certainty. Humans exist. I have seen one."

This poetically sums up the change in the ordering of relationship, where God is placed after humanity. The dream presents this more kenotically, but theologies of entitlement tend to incarnate it. God exists only to oversee the entitlements that human beings consider they deserve.

Summary

In this chapter I have looked at practices and theologies of entitlement. Although there are some biblical passages that are used to justify this, it is clear that the Bible does not offer a basis for entitlement. God will indeed reward those who are generous, but that does not mean that one is entitled to such rewards. They are a product of God's goodness, not

---

107. On this, see the editorial and articles in *Journal of Markets & Morality* 18.1 (2015).

108. The echoes of Karl Rahner's position on anonymous Christians are deliberate. As did Rahner, I insist that this is a statement made from the perspective of Christian theology. It is not attempting to colonise the other or downplay their own religious beliefs, but rather, again as did Rahner, to assume that they will have to find some way of including Christianity within their beliefs. But religious beliefs, certainly Christianity, have a universalist nature, and seek to include all within their realm of interest. This is neither exclusive nor a statement of superiority. It does not have to deny either the existence or the efficacy of other faiths or worldviews, but clearly it interprets that efficacy in its own language.

human investment. The danger has been to move from a focus on God's super-abundant generosity to a focus on human entitlement and divine obligation. The restoration of *Gemüt* or *shalom* becomes dependent solely on human endeavor and "God" is the external motivating factor to encourage this endeavor.

One traditional way of talking about grace is as sanctifying. God is present at work within creation and thus within each person, so that the person can respond in faith to God.[109] Theologies of entitlement distort this picture because they begin always from humanity. Either through my activity and contributions in kind (theologies of prosperity) or because of an accident of birth (as seen in Czech practices of entitlement), there is an expectation that God (named as such or not) will respond and reward. Unlike arcade games with their element of chance, here whenever we put something in, we are guaranteed to get a winning line. And entitlement breeds entitlement rather than gratitude.

Although not all those who have recourse to theologies of entitlement are evil or even motivated by base desires, this chapter has shown that ultimately it is impossible to practice such a theology and leave space for the transformative action of God (grace) to touch the whole of creation. It rather perpetuates a division of society into winners and losers (or saints and sinners). This division sees, often simplistically, a direct correlation between success and holiness or failure and sinfulness and is thus of special value in a hegemonic discourse based on conditionalities of exclusion. I am included in the Kingdom of God and in the kingdom of the just (that is, my country) as a reward for my contributions, material or otherwise. I deserve the good that I receive and others, at least implicitly, deserve the evil they receive.

This transactional view of grace, though a common temptation throughout the history of the church, is not enough. In the end, it is God-denying, because it seeks to limit God, to make God dependent on humanity. It seeks to exclude and condemn, as well as to give hope and succor. But in doing so it will always fail to unify the individual or the society. The person ends up enslaved, because it is only by constantly giving more and more that God can be guaranteed to keep rewarding. This is why theologies of prosperity are ultimately so deeply sacrificial. And societies end up being forced to exclude, to scapegoat, to condemn, so that "our" society will prosper over "their" society. This is also God-denying,

---

109. This is what is traditionally called habitual grace.

because it depends on what Old Testament scholars sometimes call "henotheism." We have only one god and you have only one god, and they will fight it out between them and we will believe in the strongest. In the next chapter, I turn to a radically other approach, that of liberation theology, where the concern is not with the survival of the strongest but of the weakest.

4

Liberation from Dis-grace

IN THE PREVIOUS CHAPTER I looked at the danger of the kinds of theology of grace that underpin political practices of exclusive entitlement. In the following chapters I turn to a different theology of grace, underlying political practices of liberation, focusing on Latin American theologies of liberation. But, just as I used the term "theologies of entitlement" in the previous chapter, I want to broaden the debate here to include theologies of responsibility. I employ this term in two ways. The first is to show how theologies of liberation always point to a communal engagement, in which the needs of the excluded, exploited, and oppressed are placed center stage. As we saw in chapter 2, this is not to claim that such theologies are not also supportive of forms of populism and their associated hegemonic discourse. But these discourses are not theologically neutral, and in this chapter I look at an alternative approach that resists the temptation to exclusive and selfish entitlement.

This need to make a choice, to discern between what is truly of God and what is not, leads me to the second way of understanding the term "theologies of responsibility." The word can be broken down into its two elements "response" and "ability." In other words, "responsibility" is about the capacity to respond to the world around us; theologically, to respond to the world around us in faith. The only entitlement claimed here, the only fundamental human right, is to serve, and freedom is ultimately a freedom for the freedom of the other. Even, it has been suggested, such complex and often controversial texts as the permission to have dominion in Gen 1:26–28, can be read as giving permission to work the land for the benefit of the species, of all humans.[1] So, in what follows, I look at liberation theologies of grace, to see what kind of basis they can give to populist hegemonic discourses of mutual and communal service, or to put it in more scriptural terms, how are we to go about fulfilling the "greatest commandment," namely, to "love the Lord your God with all your heart, and with all your soul, and with all your mind" and the second that is like it, to "love your neighbor as yourself" (cf. Matt 22:37–39)?

Any theology of liberation has as a fundamental presupposition the need for liberation as well as the construction of a new freedom. In this chapter, then, after a very brief comment on grace, and a discussion of the grounds for a grace-filled relationship between faith and politics, I look at the notion of "dis-grace," all that refuses or turns from God's gracious self-giving. This can be summed up as sin, both personal but also social. As a response to this, I look at a grace that liberates through love that recognizes the limits of all its practices whilst never giving up on them.

Some Brief Comments on Grace

In order to embark on this journey, I turn very briefly and schematically to some of the key ways of understanding grace. In the introduction to his volume on grace, Juan Luis Segundo examines the meaning of the word "grace" (*gratia* in Latin, *charis* in Greek, *ḥen* in Hebrew), pointing out that it bears a multiplicity of meanings, with "such different connotations as charm, benevolence, mercy, gratitude."[2] Grace came to be understood, again in Segundo's words, as "the new life brought in Christ," but brought in an unexpected, transformative way.[3] Later, this kind of grace would come to be called "supernatural."[4] This term wanted to emphasize the

---

1. See Wöhrle, "*dominium terrae*." Another noted Old Testament scholar, commenting on this passage, has said: "dominion is not license to caprice and tyranny, but in its best sense, a challenge to responsibility and to make right prevail; power should be exercised in the cause of right and justice and equality, the way God exercised it in Israel's history and the way he intended that man should exercise it as his surrogate." Vawter, *On Genesis*, 59, quoted in Sharp, "A Biblical Foundation," 309.

2. Segundo, *Grace*, 5.

3. Segundo, *Grace*, 9.

4. On this, the classic twentieth-century work is Lubac, *Surnaturel*. There is still no English translation of the work, though there is a translation of a later work that

givenness, the gratuity of grace, as something, in contrast to theologies of entitlement, to which humans have no right, but that comes from the infinite goodness and generosity of God. Its problem, as Segundo points out, is that it ends up quantifying grace, which becomes in fact a kind of measure of God's favor. The task, then, for liberation theologians like Segundo, is to help to associate "the traditional word, grace . . . with another term that sums it up: [human] liberation."[5]

In an article on grace in the two-volume work *Mysterium Liberationis*, the Belgian-born liberation theologian José Comblin (1923–2011) approaches grace in two ways, "the grace of God from the point of view of being and the grace of God from the point of view of acting."[6] He goes on to say that these two different viewpoints are fundamentally equivalent to the traditional Roman Catholic distinction between habitual and actual grace. Habitual grace is, then, an ontological quality, what makes us who we are before God. It is the gratuity of which Segundo spoke. Actual grace is linked to ideas of orthopraxis, the human being-acting, as Comblin puts it, in probably deliberately Blondelian terms.[7] It is the manifestation of God through the actions of human beings, who act in, with, and from God.

These comments may seem to suggest that liberation theology would tend to place actual grace over habitual grace. But this is not really the case. Partly this is because, as Comblin puts it, "we have no words to name a 'being' that is not also an 'acting.' God's grace enters into human being-acting. Human beings exist in their action and inseparably are their action, as is the case with all living things."[8] The distinction between being and acting is a purely heuristic one. But apart from that, there is also a strong sense, as we shall see, of the gratuity of God, which directly acts against theologies of entitlement. God does not bestow gifts because of human merit, certainly not out of necessity. There is no entitlement.

Lubac wrote to try to clarify some of the passages in *Surnaturel*: Lubac, *Mystery*. Lubac's argument is that there are not two natures, but only one, God-given and graced. For a reading of the question of nature and the supernatural from a liberation theology perspective, see Miranda, *Libertados*, 38–45.

5. Segundo, *Grace*, 11.

6. Comblin, "Grace," 205; Comblin, "Gracia," 79.

7. One of Comblin's first books was *Vers une théologie de l'action*. On Blondel and his critique of *Action Française*, the proto-Fascist French Catholic organization to which social Catholicism would respond, see Portier, "Twentieth-Century," 115–19.

8. Comblin, "Grace," 211–12; Comblin, "Gracia," 88.

Liberation from Dis-grace

Rather, the gifts are bestowed, we might say, gracefully and graciously. God gives because God loves. Already it is clear that such an attitude translated into political discourse will favor a praxis that promotes service and attention to the good of the other.

Faith and Politics

The mention of political discourses leads me to the discussion in liberation theology of the relationship between faith, theology, and politics. Already when examining theologies of entitlement I pointed to their link with political practices, but now it is time to look more closely at this relationship, because it is at the heart of liberation theologians' reflections on grace. In *Liberating Grace*, one of the most extensive treatments of grace by a liberation theologian, Leonardo Boff says at one point that faith "sees as grace conscientization, that is, the action that seeks to translate growing self-awareness into a transformative praxis that aims to set in progress a process of liberation, where the oppressed and the oppressor are surpassed by a new person, more capable of love, of communion, and of social justice."[9]

It is not simply, then, that there is a relationship between faith and politics, but that transformative political engagement is in itself a manifestation of grace. As a Brazilian Jesuit, Mario de França Miranda, puts it: "a state of grace is only present where there is a life engaged with the struggle for justice, an engagement that is realized in the most diverse ways, according to the conscience and situation of each person."[10] This comment makes clear there need not be a single political program that is demanded by the presence of grace—conscience and situation can and do demand different specific options. But there are limits to this diversity, since it must be expressed in response to the "calls of the neighbor, the widow, the orphan, the poor, the one to whom injustice is done, the oppressed, the marginalized, the solitary egoist, the enemy."[11]

What this means somewhat more concretely is argued by Enrique Dussel, who examines the political import of the Pauline corpus. It is only

---

9. Boff, *Graça*, 140; Boff, *Liberating Grace*, 86. There are some differences, so the passage is not exactly identical in the two volumes. I work mainly with the Portuguese fifth edition, but where possible will point to the English translation.

10. Miranda, *Libertados*, 109.

11. Miranda, *Libertados*, 104.

fairly recently that Biblical scholars have come to focus on the political implications of Paul. As one of these scholars, Richard Horsley, has written, approaches to Paul have traditionally adopted "the unquestioned and distinctively modern Western assumptions that Paul is concerned with religion and that religion is not only separate from political-economic life, but also primarily a matter of individual faith."[12] But more recently[13] this temptation to separate religion and politics has been challenged, and as Dussel puts it, the Pauline letters "have to be situated in the economic and political context of the Roman Empire."[14] Or, in the words of Juan Luis Segundo, it "took only a glance at the New Testament to realize that Paul was the author whose situation was more like ours. So even though it was not easy to approach the thought of Paul, we found ourselves drawn closer to it *from politics*."[15] Dussel himself broadens the understanding of Paul's attack on the Law, not as simply a polemical engagement with aspects of Judaism that were now regarded as insufficient, but as an attack on the Empire itself. He points to the way in which the Law had become fetishized to such an extent that it "can even produce death. This death is suffered by all the oppressed of the system (the Totality) which is justified by the Law."[16]

Dussel's point here is an important one, because it underlines what Leonardo Boff means when he says that where there is grace, there is also "dis-grace."[17] I will return to this shortly, but at this point it is crucial to note that the gratuitous self-giving of God encounters opposition. The Law[18] in its fetishization is ultimately all that is anti-God, because

12. Horsley, "Introduction," 1.

13. An influential voice was that of Krister Stendhal. See Stendahl, "Paulus och Samvetet" (in English, "The Apostle Paul"). For more on this see also Horsley, "Introduction."

14. Dussel, "Paulo de Tarso," 16.

15. Segundo, *Humanist Christology*, 174, cited in Allen Dwight Callahan, "Paul, Ekklēsia, and Emancipation in Corinth: A Coda on Liberation Theology," in Horsley, *Paul and Politics*, 216.

16. Dussel, "Paulo de Tarso," 28.

17. The first reference to this is Boff, *Graça*, 16–17; Boff, *Liberating Grace*, 4, but the term returns frequently throughout the book. The Portuguese speaks of *"graça"* and *"des-graça,"* hence "dis-grace."

18. What is at stake is not whether or not the Jewish people of Jesus' time were faithful to the Torah. "Law" here has to be understood as an adherence to a narrow interpretation of an ideal at the cost of human lives. Pope Francis's frequent criticisms of this attitude in the Roman Catholic Church suggest that it is a universal human temptation, in any religious or other ideological system.

it is always a form of reductionism. Hegemonic discourses of populism are not neutral nor are they games that people play. Rather, they have a direct and often tragic effect on the lives of the other. The examples are numerous, as we see whenever politicians offer tacit support to racist and supremacist groups, in Europe, in the United States, in Brazil. These are the conditionalities of exclusion of which I have spoken, the way in which we make a Law out of hatred, so that by ridding ourselves of this or that group all will be well for us.[19] To this attempt to exclude, Paul responds, according to Dussel, by calling the oppressed "children of God." "For slaves, the oppressed and excluded," this, he says, "is the moment of 'rescue' (the payment that is made to liberate the slave: 'redemption')."[20]

A Personalist Grace-Filled Politics

For liberation theologians, there is a necessary link between faith and politics, because God does not restrict his gratuitous self-giving to only one narrow aspect of life (the "spiritual"). Moreover, grace is never individual, even if it is always in some sense personal. This key distinction is always present in the background of early liberation theology, not least due to the influence of Emmanuel Mounier's Personalism. Through the 1950s his work became increasingly well-known, especially to those who read French. Writing on the French influences on early liberation theology, Michel Löwy and Jésus Garcia-Ruiz suggest:

> What struck Mounier's Brazilian Catholic readers was, above all, his radical critique of capitalism as a system founded on the anonymity of the market, the negation of the personality and the "imperialism of money," an ethical and religious critique leading to the search for an alternative, personalist socialism, which he acknowledged "had enormous debts to Marxism."[21]

Also important in this respect is the influence, mostly indirect, of one of Mounier's own inspirations, the Russian religious philosopher,

---

19. This is also a clear example of what René Girard calls scapegoating. Although he uses different language, the processes that Girard has laid bare are essentially the same as what Dussel means when he talks of fetishization.

20. Dussel, "Paulo de Tarso," 18.

21. Löwy and Garcia-Ruiz, "Les Sources françaises," 21. The volume of the journal in which this article appears bears the title "Religion et politique en Amérique Latine." The quotation in the text is from Mounier, *Feu*, 52. On Mounier's influence in Europe, see the indispensable work of Horn, *Western European Liberation Theology*, 98–100.

Nikolai Berdyaev (1874–1948). Berdyaev, who had engaged enough with Marxism in his youth to be sentenced to internal exile in Tsarist Russia, remained interested, in his extremely idiosyncratic way, in politics for his whole life.[22] In exile in France he would also influence Mounier and others through his insistence on the primacy of freedom as the prefoundational basis of all existence.[23] Juan Luis Segundo, for whom freedom was always a key theme, wrote his doctorate on Berdyaev's concept of the person.[24] What Segundo takes from Berdyaev is the insistence on freedom as what shapes and gives meaning to human life, indeed to all of creation and ultimately (at least for Berdyaev) even to God.

For Mounier this came to be part of his Personalist agenda. In what proved to be his final major statement of his position, he argued:

> The person is a presence directed towards the world and other persons, mingled among them in universal space. Other persons do not limit it [i.e., the person], they enable it to be and to grow. The person only exists thus towards others (*autrui*), it only knows itself in knowing others, only finds itself in being known by them.[25]

But, if the person is only truly alive in relation, this means for Mounier that the "primary action of the person [is] to sustain, together with others, a society of persons, the structure, the customs, the sentiments, and the institutions of which are shaped by their nature as persons."[26] In order that the person can act in this way, Mounier proposes five different attitudes that must be present: going out of oneself, understanding, taking upon oneself, giving, and being faithful.[27]

---

22. As an example, in an autobiographical note to his book, Berdyaev, *Slavery and Freedom*, 14, published in English translation in 1943, he writes that he "continued to regard the social demands of Marxism as just."

23. Berdyaev even contributed an article on the "truth and lies of communism" to the first issue of the journal that Mounier founded, *Esprit*: Berdyaev, "Verité et mensonge." When Berdyaev died in March 1948, Mounier penned a short and rather beautiful tribute to him in the pages of *Esprit*: Mounier, "Nicolas Berdiaeff."

24. Segundo, *Berdiaeff*. I have dealt in much more detail with Segundo and Berdyaev in Noble, "Whose Liberation?"

25. Mounier, *Personalism*, 21. Because the English translation is not always reliable, the reference to the French text is Mounier, *Le Personnalisme*, 40.

26. Mounier, *Personalism*, 21; Mounier, *Le Personnalisme*, 41.

27. Mounier, *Personalism*, 21–22; Mounier, *Le Personnalisme*, 41–42.

It is not necessary to examine all these attitudes here, but, because grace is connected to the gratuity of God, the God who gives, the fourth attitude is important. Mounier explains it thus: "the economy of the person is an economy of gift and not of compensation or of calculation."[28] And this economy is relational, thus demanding a long-term commitment. Mounier describes this commitment as "faithfulness." This was evidently an important concept for him in the late 1940s, underlying his ongoing involvement in both the personalist agenda and in political action. Indeed, what proved to be the last editorial that he wrote for *Esprit*, in February 1950,[29] was entitled "*Fidelité*," "Faithfulness." Towards the end of it, he wrote: "The Christian does not abandon the poor, the socialist does not abandon the proletariat, or they perjure their name."[30] It is this commitment to the poor and excluded that helps explain why Mounier's writings were seized upon in Brazil in the 1950s.[31] For like Mounier these young intellectuals, among whom were also future theologians, came to see that to be human is to be a free person in relation to the other, poor, oppressed, and excluded.

What does this mean for a theology of grace? Writing some fifty years ago, Francis Colborn already pointed out that theologies of grace were moving from a more metaphysical approach to seeing that "grace is personal not only because it is a gift from person to person but because it is a relationship between persons."[32] As Mounier put it in *Personalism*, "I love, therefore being is."[33] Existence is predicated on the grace-filled loving relationship between persons and between God and humanity. Colborn sums up his survey of those he calls "personalist" theologians of grace as follows: "Although none of them rejects metaphysical analysis, they show more interest in phenomenological description of the grace

---

28. Mounier, *Personalism*, 22; Mounier, *Le Personnalisme*, 42. I have used here the French version. The idea of gift and donation used here by Mounier will return later with Jacques Derrida and Jean-Luc Marion.

29. He died, aged only 44, of a heart attack on March 22, 1950.

30. Mounier, "Fidelité," 181–82.

31. Löwy and Garcia-Ruiz, "Les Sources françaises," 22.

32. Colborn, "Theology of Grace," 694.

33. Mounier, *Personalism*, 23; Mounier, *Le Personnalisme*, 43. Again, I work with the French text, "J'aime, donc l'être est," as the English text here is somewhat inaccurate by seeking to maintain the reference to the *Cogito*.

relationship: rather than ask 'Is love an act or a habitus?' they ask 'How do human persons experience a love relationship?'"[34]

Social Sin

The move from the ontological to the phenomenological reflects what was going on elsewhere in philosophy and also in society. To understand human beings in relational terms is also to understand them in social terms. Grace is thus always also a social category. Before going on to look at this in more detail, I want first to look more closely at the absence or the exclusion of grace, that is, at sin. Although early liberation theology, especially, tended to work with the philosophical categories of modernity (with a liberal dose of Thomism), in fact it was trying to transcend those categories. For under them, ontologically all are already free and there is no room for liberation, for transformation. A more phenomenological approach affords two different possibilities. The first is a more realistic view of sin, of the breakdown of the personal and the triumph of the individual. The individual is the atomic, materialist version of what it is to be human,[35] touched by sin, not in action, but in being ultimately divorced from God. Sin is thus in behaving, in the famous phrase of Hugo Grotius, *etsi Deus non daretur* ("as if God did not exist"). The person may indeed be more sinful, because more free, expressing the transcendent element of human existence and experience. But, and this is the second possibility, the person is also capable of acting *veluti si Deus daretur* (as if there were indeed a God),[36] of doing good and of searching for liberation.

Juan Luis Segundo understands something similar when he argues against attempts to reform society by reforming individuals. "Such a statement is based," he writes, "on an erroneous conception of the human. It does not appreciate the fact that individuals can be truly liberated only in terms of their total human condition, i.e., within their *social* context."[37] In any consideration of the political and the discourses on conditionalities

---

34. Colborn, "Theology of Grace," 698. Colborn briefly discusses Rahner, Juan Alfaro, Piet Fransen, Heribert Mühlen, Jon Cowburn, Charles Meyer, James Mackey, and Gregory Baum, all of whom he includes under the broad label of personalist theologians of grace.

35. I have in mind here Jacques Maritain. On this, see Schultz, "Liberation."

36. This was a favorite trope of Emeritus Pope Benedict XVI during his pontificate. On this, see Lenehan, "*Etsi*," 35, quoting Ratzinger, *Christianity and the Crisis*, 51–52.

37. Segundo, *Grace*, 37.

of exclusion or inclusion that it employs, the relation between the individual and the social is crucial. The classic political philosophies of the seventeenth and eighteenth centuries (Hobbes, Rousseau, Locke) all work from the "fact" of the individual to determine how and why such individuals may come together to trade rights and responsibilities. In their time and subsequently these rather atomistic views of society have been extremely powerful in helping to safeguard the relationship between the needs and rights of the individual and the requirements and responsibilities of the social body that those individuals form. However, these views have also tended to present another form of dualism alongside that of mind and body. In this perspective the individual is akin to the mind, as the center and motor of social existence, and society is a kind of Cartesian extension of that mind, existing only in a secondary fashion.

But, as Segundo points out, "society is not the end result of juxtaposing already constituted individuals, [but] from the very start it is a system of human reactions and interrelationships that constitute the individual and form part of his total human condition."[38] Although all such statements are ultimately unprovable, it is clear that most of what we consider to be human life above the purely physical is social in nature. The language we speak, the norms, values, attitudes, and behavior patterns (to use Segundo's terminology: we might simply say "culture") that we adopt, all of these are learned within a social setting, first that of the family, but within the family also as part of a wider society. This is clearly not to deny that people are different: the effect that the exposure to society has on each particular member of that society can and does vary. We all have our idiolects, our own way of using our native language or some other language, and much of our political conflict comes from the varied emphases we give to different norms, values, attitudes, and behavior patterns within our societies.

These also stress sometimes more the social element, sometimes more the individual. Here we come again to forms of hegemonic discourse, which, as we saw in chapter 2, seek to justify a particular view of society, or, in other words, give voice to an ideology. For Segundo and other liberation theologians, this ideology is embedded or expressed in social structures. This is why the concept of social sin has been so central to liberation theology. José Ignacio González Faus speaks of sin

---

38. Segundo, *Grace*, 38. Pope Francis's principles, to which I turn to in the next chapter, will reinforce this point.

as "the masking of the truth with unjust egoism."[39] But this egoism is both individual and social, and in social terms it is present in social or structural sin, which González Faus defines as follows: "human beings, in sinning, create structures of sin, which in turn make human beings sin."[40] Or as Miranda puts it, in more Rahnerian terms, human concupiscence[41] is exacerbated "by the situation of sin scandalously present in a society structured in function of capital, of production, of consumption."[42]

The concept of social sin must not be regarded as simply an attempt to absolve individuals of complicity in what they do. But at the same time it does mean that human beings can only be liberated if they become aware of the "unconscious determinisms"[43] that surround them. Most contemporary examples are fraught with controversy, so let us consider what I hope is an uncontroversial case from history, namely that of slavery. In the ancient world, and then especially from the sixteenth to nineteenth centuries, economic and social systems were built on the premise of slavery, which could only function in modernity by denying full humanity to those who were enslaved. As the long campaigns for its abolition show, from Bartolomé de Las Casas,[44] to William Wilber-

---

39. González Faus, "Pecado," 97; English: González Faus, "Sin," 197.

40. González Faus, "Pecado," 99. Pope John Paul II is often said to have been opposed to the idea of structural sin, but in fact he himself spoke on a number of occasions of the structures of sin, even whilst emphasizing that sin is always a personal act. See, for example, John Paul II, *Reconciliatio et paenitentia*, 16; John Paul II, *Sollicitudo rei socialis*, 36. On this, see Breen, "John Paul II." It is also worth recalling the impact of Personalism on John Paul II: an early but pertinent article is Hellman, "John Paul II," and most recently, Hołub, *Understanding the Person*.

41. Concupiscence is a term that was rescued for Roman Catholic theology by Karl Rahner. He saw it as an integral part of human existence, describing the possibility of a tendency towards sin within us, in conflict with the inner desire for God. There is thus a constant struggle between who we are and who we desire to be. See Rahner, "Theological Concept."

42. Miranda, *Libertados*, 173.

43. The phrase is taken from Segundo, *Grace*, 39.

44. De Las Casas famously first supported the import of African slaves to spare the indigenous peoples, though it is sometimes argued that he changed his mind. On this, see Souza, "Las Casas," 25–37. Souza argues that Las Casas really only argued against the manner in which Africans had been enslaved, rather than against slavery itself. In which case, he is an excellent example of how the "unconscious determinisms" of which Segundo spoke function in daily life. Lampe, "Las Casas and African Slavery," is more positive about Las Casas's motivation, though he does conclude his chapter by saying that "more research is necessary to determine . . . the rationale of his third conversion." As he does not quote Souza, her article seems to me a convincing portrayal of that rationale.

force in the United Kingdom, abolitionists in the USA, or in Brazil,[45] this system was never universally accepted, but it remained prevalent for many centuries. Slavery is far more than an umbrella term for describing myriad acts of barbarism, cruelty, and inhumanity carried out by diverse and unrelated individuals. These acts continue to this day, though in nearly all countries they are against the law. But the system of slavery legitimated them, so that brandings, floggings, rape, and other practices were somehow "normalized."[46] But even in the exceptional cases where slave owners were not themselves cruel and sought to treat their slaves with some decency, the system was still sinful, slavery was still wrong. No amount of good behavior changes that.

Structural or social sin refers, then, to the way in which societies are structured (or choose to structure themselves, since minimally we would have to say that at some point a sufficient group of people become complicit in a way of acting). When these structures are against God, because of the way in which they exclude and dehumanize other people, abuse and destroy God's creation, and impose and support injustice in any form, they are manifestations of structural or social sin. In a Latin American context, Leonardo Boff argues that from "the perspective of faith the situation of dependency and under-development of the South American continent can only appear as a great social and structural sin."[47] Thus, conversion is never purely individual, but necessitates an engagement that "will have to fight for the conversion of the social structure, for its roots to be transformed, that is to say, for it to open itself to the grace of God."[48]

The Hiding of Sin in Plain View

This discussion should not be taken to imply that liberation theologians are not interested in or downplay the reality of sin at a personal level. They are fully aware of the human tendency to turn away from as well

---

45. Brazil was the last country in Latin America to abolish slavery, after Cuba, which had taken the final step in 1886. This occurred with the promulgation of the *Lei Áurea* (the Golden Law) on May 13, 1888; see Schwarcz and Starling, *Brazil*, 343–48. For a list of dates, see Andrews, *Afro-Latin America*, 57, and on abolition in Brazil, 83–84.

46. Schwarcz and Starling, *Brazil*, 85–93, a section entitled "Slavery is Synonymous with Violence." This foundational violence is one of the hardest legacies to escape.

47. Boff, *Graça*, 138; Boff, *Liberating Grace*, 84.

48. Boff, *Graça*, 140; Boff, *Liberating Grace*, 85.

as towards God. It is possible to become aware of the unconscious determinisms to which Segundo referred. But when people become aware of determinisms, they can either continue to let themselves be ruled by them or they can take action to change the situation, given that the determinisms are always only partial. Even if in many places the abolition of slavery happened primarily because economic realities meant that it was no longer viable, it still took certain people, who benefitted from the system, to become aware of how it functioned and its blatant injustices so that a climate for abolition existed. This also means that there are no excuses for those who, having being made aware of the injustice of the system, nevertheless continue to make use of it.

In another article on sin, González Faus draws attention to the different kinds of personal sinfulness that are found in the Bible. He draws on the story of David to show how sin can be the giving in to the logic of desire in his behavior towards Uriah and Bathsheba.[49] This logic is drawn out to its fullest extent in the work of René Girard,[50] who showed how desire is a determinism that is present nearly everywhere, be it in terms of material possessions or ultimately the desire to possess the other. Another type of personal sinfulness is to be found in the story of the reactions of the Pharisees to the healing of the man born blind (John 9:1–41). The negative reaction is caused, suggests González Faus, by another form of desire, namely that of "the preserving of their own reputation."[51] This is particularly important in political conflict, where changing one's mind is portrayed often as a sign of weakness. Governments in different countries have faced these accusations during their responses to the COVID-19 pandemic. Frequently this is caused by their own initial hubris, declaring victory over a disease that had not gone away and categorically ruling out measures that they then found that they needed to reinstate. The problem here is not in the measures themselves but in the pride that meant that they wanted to avoid losing face and thus failed to take the requisite decisions in time. It is this "fear of losing face" that is at the heart of this kind of personal and social sinfulness.

---

49. González Faus, "La realidad," 385–86. The reference is to 2 Sam 11:1—12:13.

50. See, for example, Girard, *The Scapegoat*; Girard, *Violence and the Sacred*.

51. González Faus, "La realidad," 387. Politicians who refuse to accept that they could lose an election and thus spread lies provide an excellent example of this. I leave it to the reader to provide their own contextual illustrations of this point, though efforts to trump the American case may prove hard.

More, though, than losing face, what is in play here for González Faus is the losing of sight, blindness. The key verse is John 9:39: "Jesus said, 'I came into this world for judgment so that those who do not see may see, and those who do see may become blind.'"[52] Coming immediately after the cured blind man's profession of faith (v. 38), Jesus points both to the fundamental "masking"[53] that is involved in sin, and the power of God's grace to "unmask" this sin. The problem with the Pharisees is not that they are bad people, but their awareness of how good they are becomes essentially idolatrous, because they cannot see beyond it. This is what makes them blind.[54] Sin is a masking because it is what might be termed a "mis-seeing," focusing on the intermediate as the ultimate (idolatry).

The worst kind of sin, as González Faus goes on to argue, is that which does not recognize itself as sinful. This kind of blindness is in many ways incurable. In John 9:40–41 we read "Some of the Pharisees near him heard this and said to him, 'Surely we are not blind, are we?' Jesus said to them, 'If you were blind, you would not have sin. But now that you say, "We see," your sin remains.'" The problem for the Pharisees is that they do not see that they are blind. Many of the criticisms of the Pharisees in the gospels are at this level, as is expressed most clearly in Matthew 23:2–3: "The scribes and the Pharisees sit on Moses' seat; therefore, do whatever they teach you and follow it; but do not do as they do, for they do not practice what they teach." They have the ability and knowledge to act differently but do not see the gulf between what they proclaim and what they practice.[55]

Grace then enables the unmasking or unveiling of states of sinfulness. This is always more than determining whether a given action is right

---

52. A reading of this text from a speech-act perspective can be found in Ito, "Story." On John 9:38, see 422–31. For a symbolic narrative reading, see Lee, *Symbolic Narratives*, especially 161–87.

53. González Faus, "La realidad," 388. In this article and in his related article in *Mysterium Liberationis* he uses the metaphor of "masking" (*enmascaramiento*) or conversely of "unmasking" (*desenmascaramiento*) to refer to the nature of sin and how it is revealed and thus overcome. Another of René Girard's books, referring to Matt 13:35, is entitled *Things Hidden since the Foundation of the World*. For Girard, Jesus unmasks the reality of mimesis.

54. On this, see Noble, "What To Do," where I work with Jean-Luc Marion to point to the problem of becoming fixated with one particular (if excellent) idea at the cost of all others.

55. Again, this has obviously a much broader reference than the historical attitude of the Pharisees at the time of Jesus.

or wrong, good or evil. Here the Pauline distinction between sin (*hamartia*) and sins (either *hamartia* in the plural, or transgression, *parabasis* or *paraptōma*) is relevant. Although there is debate over the relative weight to be attached to this division,[56] there are two separate, though clearly related categories. Sin is not some kind of Manichean reality supposing a battle between the forces of good and evil, but is perhaps best understood as a descriptive term for the human tendency to turn away from God. This applies to both social and personal sin, since the blindness, the masking of the truth, is a temptation and a reality in both spheres (or to be more precise, along with Segundo, in the one sphere with its differently experienced dimensions). The status quo, the way things are and appear immutably to be, is the location of structural sin, since the structures are always imperfect. Politically this is why there is always conflict, since any hegemonic discourse makes claims that are true and good and claims that mask the truth. This is not to say that any act of violence or attempt to destroy a hegemonic discourse is positive from a Christian point of view. But it does mean that we always need to be humble before our beliefs, recognizing that they are weak in some areas, even while they are strong in others.

Structural sin is not an excuse for behaving badly, claiming that "society is to blame!" The status quo always needs to be seen critically, and most especially critically as we search for the advantages that we obtain from it. This is why racist and anti-migrant rhetoric is sinful, since it essentially aims to exclude the other so that I can continue to enjoy my privileges. But the same is true for other conditionalities of exclusion, since the reason for excluding the other is to prevent access to what I regard as mine or as ours. That society affords me such privileges does not mean that this is some kind of state of nature or that it is right. Thus the need to see and unmask the way in which structures act is important. It is also why theologies of entitlement are always anti-theologies, the discourses of what the Old Testament calls "the false prophets."[57]

And, it goes without saying, structures exist because people support them and work within them. Most empires ultimately fail because sufficient people stop believing in them. This is the basis of Václav Havel's

---

56. See Gathercole, "'Sins' in Paul." Gathercole's aim is to redress the balance, in order to give more weight to the importance of "sins" as individual actions in Paul. However to do so, he helpfully summarizes the debate that has tended to place more weight on the more abstract power of Sin.

57. I return to this in chapter 7.

story of the greengrocer, to which I referred above. As long as he continues to connive with the structures by placing the message in which he does not believe among his vegetables, the greengrocer is sinning. But when he and sufficient others like him refuse to play along, as was indeed shown with the Velvet Revolution in Czechoslovakia in 1989, the structures fall apart very fast. So structural sin always involves also individual acts that bolster the structures or at least prevent it from breaking down. Needless to say, in concrete cases, there are all sorts of reasons (fear often being a leading one) why people collude with a system that they know is evil. But at least objectively such behavior can only be classed as sinful. To understand is not to condone.

How Societies Should Behave

Alongside this there are also the individual actions of people. Much modern religious and indeed political controversy suffers from the tendency to focus on sexual matters. Churches debate (and divide) over what kind of relationships people can enter into, and attempts are made to enshrine the outcomes of these debates in laws, usually to the exclusion of minorities. But far less energy is spent on decrying those who manage to avoid paying taxes or on those who seek to deprive others of their rights or even of their lives. This is a relatively modern phenomenon. Patristic and Medieval writers on ethics and morality did not wholly ignore sexual ethics, but it was not their primary concern. A French writer on moral theology, in the course of an overview of Patristic ethics, and in particular the contribution of Augustine, makes the following comment:

> St. Augustine teaches us a great lesson: theology must always remain humble before the mystery of God present in the least of believers. It must be lovingly aware of the imperfection of all its theories and systems in the face of the divine reality. Far from causing discouragement, this should spur us on to further research, so that we may advance toward the light, which illumines and attracts us through the darkness of faith. Like St. Paul, forgetting the past we should strain forward with our whole being to the goal of all our journeying (see *De trinitate*, 8.1.1). Consequently, no theological or moral system should be viewed as absolutely complete or definitive, to the point of

supplanting others or rendering them useless. Nor should any one system be seen as the center and measure of all others.[58]

I have used this rather lengthy quotation because it is an excellent reminder of the kind of sin that we saw attributed to the Pharisees. The assumption of our own rightness (and indeed righteousness) in ethics, or in any other field of human endeavor, is always a failure of vision. One of the systemic or hegemonic factors that the Church Fathers sought to counter was the undervaluing of the material.[59] This is arguably a temptation that has never gone away and lies behind attempts to divorce faith and politics. A well-known Methodist ethicist Philip Wogaman suggests that if the material and spiritual are separated, "political questions, preoccupied as they generally are with distribution of resources, protection of property, and regulation of the material circumstances of a society, would lose moral relevance."[60] But this did not happen, or at least not in full as we saw when I discussed prosperity theology. There I pointed to the way in which the Church Fathers were very attentive to the temptations of riches and the problem of poverty.

This is not to say that sexual ethics were unimportant in the early church. We already have indications of this in First Corinthians, and there is no absence in the Fathers of condemnation of what they considered unacceptable practices. But it is not the only area of interest, and in general, the emphasis is as much on the positive aspects of Christian morality, as shown in the well-known quotation from the second-century Letter to Diognetus:

> They live in their own countries, but only as aliens (*paroikoi*). They have a share in everything as citizens (*politai*), and endure everything as foreigners (*xenoi*). Every foreign land is their fatherland, and yet for them every fatherland is a foreign land. They marry, like everyone else, and they beget children, but they do not cast out their offspring. They share their board with each other, but not their marriage bed. It is true that they are "in the flesh," but they do not live "according to the flesh." They busy themselves on earth, but their citizenship is in heaven (*en ouranō politeuontai*). They obey the established laws, but in their

---

58. Pinckaers, *Sources*, 212. As we will see in chapter 6, Pope Francis makes a similar comment in *Fratelli tutti*, 214.

59. On this temptation see Wogaman, *Christian Ethics*, 28–29.

60. Wogaman, *Christian Ethics*, 28.

own lives they go far beyond what the laws require. They love all, and by all are persecuted.⁶¹

Like many such summaries this is no doubt at least partly prescriptive rather than descriptive, but it at least indicates the aims of Christian morality, which is partly an identity-building exercise.⁶² Although this could be read as a condition of exclusion, it seems to me that it is rather an invitation to inclusion, a presentation of a different way of life, which we could call a life of grace. It is, moreover, also a political statement, since what they enjoy is *politeia*, citizenship, which is linked to belonging to a particular place. The Letter expands this, not denying the political but placing it in the context of the church. It also emphasizes the importance of being "a migrant," "a foreigner."

The respective roles of the church and the state continued to occupy Christians in the intervening centuries, not least at the time of the Reformation when several tendencies appeared, the Lutheran, the Calvinist, and the Radical Reformation (Anabaptist). The classic expression of the Lutheran position is in the doctrine of the Two Kingdoms. This is based on a fundamentally negative view of humanity, serving as an "expression of his [Luther's] underlying conception of a fallen humanity requiring the stern governance of the kingdom of the world."⁶³ This decisive break between world and church is one of the most profound consequences of the Reformation. Although John Calvin opted in practice for the theocracy of Geneva, in principle he held a similar position to Luther, distinguishing between the realms of the church and of the state and recognizing the need of the state to deal with the base evil of humanity.

Anabaptists were different (and thus gained the dubious distinction of being persecuted as heretics by Lutherans and Calvinists as well as by Roman Catholics) in that many of them rejected the use of violence. The sixteenth-century Anabaptists were not uniform in their approach and a number of different strands existed, mostly advocating a very strong separation of church and state, which, in its rejection of participation in the state, challenged governments of all persuasions. One of the most famous founding documents was the Schleitheim Confession, written by

---

61. Epistle to Diognetus, 5:5-11, quoted in Wogaman, *Christian Ethics*, 38. *Paroikoi* and *xenoi* are used in Eph 2:19 to describe the Christian experience; see also 1 Pet 1:1, 17; 2:11.

62. On this aspect of the Epistle to Diognetus, see also Lieu, *Neither Jew nor Greek?*, 185-203.

63. Wogaman, *Christian Ethics*, 120.

Michael Sattler in 1527 on behalf of a group of early Swiss Anabaptists. In it there is a firm rejection of civil authority as part of the evil world from which true Christians should be separated.[64] Whilst clearly dividing the world into "good" and "evil," the Confession also refuses to accept any use of violence, so that arms should not be taken up nor should there be physical resistance to evil. At the same time, however, it categorically rules out Christians serving in positions of authority in the state.[65]

It was only with the Enlightenment and the growth of secularism that the trend became for ethical positions to focus more on personal morality. Roman Catholic teaching continued to take a—mainly negative—view of political developments. Both Pope Gregory XVI and Pope Pius IX used their first encyclicals to attack what they saw as wrongful forms of government. In *Mirari Vos*, published in 1832, Gregory XVI attacked a number of social developments pointing out that "[e]xperience shows, even from earliest times, that cities renowned for wealth, dominion, and glory perished as a result of this single evil, namely immoderate freedom of opinion, license of free speech, and desire for novelty." So he desires that church leaders should encourage fidelity to monarchic structures, since it would not be possible to

> predict happier times for religion and government from the plans of those who desire vehemently to separate the Church from the state, and to break the mutual concord between temporal authority and the priesthood. It is certain that that concord which always was favorable and beneficial for the sacred and the civil order is feared by the shameless lovers of liberty.[66]

Shortly after his election to the pontificate in 1846, Gregory's successor Pius IX issued his first encyclical, *Qui Pluribus*, in which he speaks of "the unspeakable doctrine of Communism, as it is called, a doctrine most opposed to the very natural law. For if this doctrine were accepted, the

---

64. Sattler, *Brüderlich vereinigung*, 12–13.

65. For much more on this, see Noble, "Nowhere," which looks at Thomas More's *Utopia* and the early Anabaptists and their search for a better world. See also on the Radical Reformation and Christian ethics, Wogaman, *Christian Ethics*, 144–53.

66. Gregory XVI, *Mirari Vos*, quotations here taken from paragraphs 14 and 20. It is only fair to note that Gregory XVI was also responsible for one of the most clear and complete denunciations of the institution of slavery that was made in the period, contained in his Apostolic Constitution, *In supremo apostolatus*, issued on December 3, 1839.

complete destruction of everyone's laws, government, property, and even of human society itself would follow."[67]

Elsewhere though there was a gradual turn to the personal, but the social was never completely neglected. Starting with the Social Gospel movement, the twentieth century could even be said to have seen increased Christian engagement with society, both positively and negatively, or approvingly and disapprovingly. Most obviously there was the radical divide between people like Dietrich Bonhoeffer, Karl Barth, and others connected with the Barmen Declaration on the one hand, and the German Christians on the other. This Christianity of social engagement and transformation was one of the roots of liberation theology. But despite these important counter-examples, there were also many Christians who reduced their interest in engagement with the state to questions such as abortion rights, or the ways in which different relationships (both heterosexual and homosexual) should be recognized by the state, and other types of broadly sexual or reproductive ethics.

The important point here is not who is right or wrong in these matters, nor indeed whether they are valid issues for political engagement. There can in some of these cases be legitimate debate and coherent opposing interpretations of the scriptures, given that, as David Tracy has noted, we all have partial readings of the Scriptures.[68] But the problem has been when they have become exclusive, so that, for example, people who claim to be Christians would vote for candidates based on their professed views on abortion, whilst ignoring other aspects of those candidates' policies that are clearly destructive of human life. Certainly, in these cases as in others, choices have to be made and conflicting claims balanced out, but Christian witness is severely damaged, since, in Pauline terms, God's grace is placed under the law, not this time of the state, but of a supposed Christian morality.

A Liberating Grace

Over against this dependence on a law that ultimately kills can be juxtaposed a vision of liberating grace. Grace is not some kind of bonus or added extra that comes with baptism. Rather as Juan Luis Segundo puts it, "in the concrete order of human history as we know it there does not

67. Pius IX, *Qui pluribus*, 16.
68. See Woodward, "Interview with David Tracy."

exist any human being who is totally alien to God's grace."[69] In somewhat similar vein, in the Preface to the Portuguese language fifth edition of *Grace and Human Experience,* his major work on grace, Leonardo Boff presents a parable, of a group of people travelling on a train. Though it is lengthy, I quote it in full:

> A train is moving at speed towards it destination. It cuts through the fields like an arrow. It clings to the sides of mountains. It passes over the rivers. It snakes along like a moving wire. Within, the whole drama of human existence plays out. People from all nations. People who talk, people who are silent, people who work on their computers, business people with their concerns, people who calmly contemplate the countryside, people who have committed crimes, good people, people who think ill of everyone, sunny people who are happy with the minimum of light that they encounter in each person, people who love travelling by train, people who for ecological reasons are against trains, people who have caught the wrong train, people who do not doubt, knowing they are on the right track and when they will arrive in their city, anxious people who run to the front coaches hoping to arrive earlier than the rest, people who are stressed and who want to arrive as late as possible, and who sit in the rear coaches. And absurdly people who try to escape from the train walking in the opposite direction to the way it is going. And the impassive train follows its fate, traced by the tracks. Unbothered, it carries everybody. No one escapes. It serves all and offers to all a journey that can be splendid and happy. And it guarantees to leave all at the destination written on their itinerary. In this train, as in life, all travel for free. Once it sets off, there is no escaping, getting off, or getting out. You can be mad at it or rejoice. But the train does not stop heading towards its predetermined destination, carrying all with courtesy. The grace of God—the presence, mercy, goodness, and love of God—is like a train. The destination of the journey is God. The way is also God because the way is nothing else than the destination being realized meter by meter. The way only exists because of the destination to be reached.[70]

At a fundamental level, for Boff, grace is both means, end, and way, because the grace of God is not other than God—in Orthodox theological

---

69. Segundo, *Grace,* 14.

70. Boff, *Graça,* 10. A similar but slightly longer and different version of this is contained in Boff, *Liberating Grace,* xiii–viv.

language, grace can indeed be understood as the uncreated energy of God.[71] All of creation is caught up in this grace, suffused with the creative and sustaining presence of God, and in one way or another moving towards God.

But, as Boff's parable indicates, there are a number of human reactions to being enclosed within the grace of God, ranging from welcome, through acceptance, to indifference, or attempted rejection. Segundo puts it less poetically but perhaps more clearly: "There is a profound tension within human beings between that which they desire and decide within themselves and that which they end up doing externally."[72] As we have already examined the reality of sin, I want to concentrate now on what human beings desire and decide within themselves, on the inclination to God that is within and without every human being. To put it in those terms is already to suggest that the search for human fulfilment is not and cannot be separated from the human search for God, a search that starts and ends and takes place within God—as Paul is reported to have said in Acts 17:28, quoting Epimenides, "in him we live and move and have our being."

Grace and Freedom

For grace, this transformative presence of God, to be genuinely transformative and liberative, requires, first of all, freedom. As already briefly noted, this is something that Juan Luis Segundo in particular took from Nikolai Berdyaev, for whom freedom precedes all else. God, for Berdyaev, creates out of freedom. The "nihil" of creation *ex nihilo* is the *Ungrund*, a term he borrowed from the seventeenth-century Pietist mystic Jakob Boehme (1575–1624). As Berdyaev puts it in one of his early works, even before he had begun to work with Boehme, "Freedom is the baseless foundation of being."[73] Berdyaev's insistence on freedom as the starting

71. See, for example, Lossky, *Mystical Theology*, 88–89.

72. Segundo, *Grace*, 15.

73. Berdyaev, *Meaning*, 145. The original was published in 1916 as *Smysl tvorchestva. Opyt opravdanija cheloveka*, which translates as "The Meaning of Creativity: An Essay on the Justification of Humankind." The French translation, used by Segundo, speaks of freedom as *"le fondement sans fond de l'être"* (Berdiaeff, *Le sens de la création*, 191), whilst Berdyaev's original Russian speaks of *"bezosnovnaja osnova bytija."* To keep the wordplay, "a baseless basis," or "a foundationless foundation," would probably be the best English translations. Berdyaev seems to have begun to engage more with Boehme in the 1920s. See also on this, Siljak, "Personalism of Nikolai Berdyaev," 313.

point of all existence is allied to his recognition of the limitations placed on freedom by sin and thus on the fundamentally liberative impact of the life, death, and resurrection of Jesus.

The relation of freedom and grace is, for Berdyaev and for Segundo, of prime importance. The two are not to be placed in opposition, but are rather seen as two ways of talking about the same thing. Berdyaev sees the development of the opposition as going back to the fifth-century debate between Augustine and the Pelagians concerning what it means to talk of free will. In one of his books, he writes:

> Pelagius, the fanatical upholder of a natural and invariable free will, was a rationalist quite incapable of understanding the mystery of freedom. The very antithesis between freedom and grace is false and vicious, because it involves a rationalization of freedom which subjects it to the natural world order. This false antithesis of freedom and grace was the precursor of the division between Protestantism and Catholicism.[74]

Segundo reads Berdyaev as arguing that grace can be understood as "the putting into action of the designs of God, and these designs aim above all at the freedom of humanity."[75] The question that arises for Segundo is the following: "Does grace actually come to help *liberty* or to help the *law*? In other words, does it make the human being more free or less a sinner?"[76] In the end, the roles of freedom and the law are reversed, so that "The law moves from being an end to a means; freedom, from means to end."[77] So, ultimately, grace is, or grace gives us, the ability to live out the freedom in which we are created over against concupiscence.[78] Grace is the recognition that freedom "is not ready-made. It is not some liberated, spiritual, numinal zone wherein human beings are able to construct their own existence. Liberty is a *possibility* given and a value to be won by handling an ever-increasing number of determinisms."[79]

---

74. Berdyaev, *Freedom and the Spirit*, 117–18, cited in Segundo, *Berdiaeff*, 104–5, with reference to Berdyaev, *Esprit et la liberté*, 126. Segundo himself discusses Pelagius in *Grace*, 17–19.

75. Segundo, *Berdiaeff*, 113.

76. Segundo, *Grace*, 19.

77. Segundo, *Berdiaeff*, 110. Segundo would return to this in Segundo, *Grace*, 21–28.

78. Here he works with Karl Rahner, also influential for the development of his theology.

79. Segundo, *Grace*, 33.

José Comblin, writing in the late 1990s, suggested that liberation theology had a tendency to downplay the importance of liberty or freedom in relation to the role of liberation.[80] Liberty is not easy to define, partly because, from one perspective, to put limits on (that is, to define) freedom would be to negate it. But certainly freedom is connected to human relationships, which are fundamentally transformed in and through Jesus. This is most famously illustrated in Gal 3:28, where Paul argues that in Christ all distinctions based on ethnicity, social status, or gender are overcome.[81] Although Comblin agrees with Berdyaev on the fundamental nature of freedom—"humankind's very reason for being, the depth, the core of all human existence"—there is for him something even more basic, because "human freedom comes from God's love."[82]

A Gracious Love

Love, in Comblin's thought-provoking interpretation, is always in some sense disruptive. Frequently political positions emerging from liberation theology are dismissed as utopian, with "utopian" understood to imply something naively impossible. But in their own way utopias, going back to Thomas More's original, are always disquieting and disruptive. They question the way things are, they provoke, they frighten and challenge by presenting a possible world that is not acted on. They suggest what might happen if love was truly present, and, says Comblin, "love shatters every structure of order. Love is the basis for freedom, and hence for disorder."[83] As José Ignacio González Faus points out, there is an also "an identity between the concepts of liberty and love. Both have as their antithesis egoism, which is at the same time the falsification of liberty and the destruction of love."[84]

Both González Faus and Comblin understand that love and freedom are always in what Comblin calls a "process of self-construction."[85]

---

80. See Comblin, *Called for Freedom*. The title of the original Portuguese is very different: *Cristãos Rumo ao Século XXI: Nova Caminhada de Libertação*, which can be translated as *Christians on the Way to the Twenty-First Century: A New Path of Liberation*.

81. Comblin, *Called for Freedom*, 22.

82. Comblin, *Called for Freedom*, 28.

83. Comblin, *Called for Freedom*, 28.

84. González Faus, "Antropología," 77.

85. Comblin, *Called for Freedom*, 29; González Faus, "Antropología," 77. See also

This journey is one that is always taken with others. "Freedom is a social reality; there is no freedom in solitude. Freedom is always such in relation to others. In Christianity this relation is that of love (*agape*, that is, charity, love, solidarity)."[86] The concrete political implications of this claim were seen frequently in relation to reactions to the COVID-19 pandemic, in relation to mandates to wear masks or invitations to be vaccinated. In many countries there were (sadly vociferous) minorities, who objected to government interventions and mandates in the name of their freedom. Here freedom is reduced to the level of individual desire, where what I want is the ultimate criterion for any decision, regardless of its impact on the other. This is more than about competing freedoms—my freedom to wear or not wear a mask against my freedom to infect or seek not to infect others, for example. It is fundamentally about reactions to the other, and the willingness to place solidarity above narrow self-interest (in Mouffe's words, the egalitarian above the libertarian). So, Comblin says, "Freedom consists in opening dialogue with 'other' persons, even those who are not included in common social life."[87] There is no freedom without relationship, and there are no relationships without freedom.

This relational emphasis, the broadly personalist approach mentioned above, explains why liberation theologians often end up by emphasizing the centrality of love as the defining category of a grace-filled Christian existence lived in gratuity and gratitude. Love here is the actual way in which a person acts towards their neighbor, the concrete response to the hungry, sick, naked, imprisoned, to all those, in other words, who have been placed on the edges of society or excluded from it altogether.[88] But the question of love is always related to the question of freedom, and more specifically of free will. Even in our political choices and commitments, do we act freely, so that it is fair to ask if someone is acting in a way that clearly demonstrates love for neighbor? As Segundo acknowledges, the experience or reality that Paul deals with in Romans 7, the struggle

---

Miranda, *Libertados*, 73: "the human is a being who has to self-determine in history by his or her free acts. . . . Being created in Christ to participate in the very life of God implies the free construction, by the person, of what we call freedom."

86. Comblin, *Called for Freedom*, 37. See also González Faus, "Antropología," 70–77, where he argues for the need to overcome two conflicting threats. One is Western individualism, the other is "Marxist" collectivism.

87. Comblin, *Called for Freedom*, 43.

88. See Segundo, *Grace*, 140–41.

between the desire to be "a slave to the law of God" and the reality of being "a slave to the law of sin," are an integral part of human life.

For Paul, of course, slavery to the law of God, a life lived under obedience to the law of Christ, is paradoxically the path to the fullest freedom: "Bear one another's burdens, and in this way you will fulfil the law of Christ" (Gal 6:2). And yet slavery to the law of sin is never far away, as Paul goes on to say in verse 8 of the same chapter.[89] For Segundo, this division, or this inability to fully realize what we desire, is a quintessential part of what it is to be human.[90] The pull to self, to act in my own interests for myself alone, is always present and always threatening my freedom, and the only way to move beyond it is to "continually seek to fashion and recover the nearness of others as neighbors."[91] And that attempt is, as we saw, something that can be called "love."

The emphasis on love also brings us to what Jon Sobrino has called "the centrality of the Kingdom of God" for liberation theology.[92] Sobrino offers three paths to understanding the Kingdom,[93] which he calls the notional way, the way of Jesus' praxis, and the way of the addressee. He dismisses the first, which concentrates on trying to outline what Jesus thought the Kingdom was, as too general, but the second and third he sees as both linked and important. The third, the way of the addressee, is, he suggests, "the most specific methodological contribution of liberation theology."[94] The addressees par excellence are the poor, who are

> an economic and social reality: those for whom life is a hard burden because of the difficulty of living and of marginalization. The poor are a collective reality: poor peoples or poor as a people. The poor are a historical reality: they exist not principally because of natural reasons but historical ones, because of injustice. The poor are a dialectical reality: they exist because there are rich people, and vice-versa. The poor are a political

---

89. The text of Gal 6:8 reads: "If you sow to your own flesh, you will reap corruption from the flesh; but if you sow to the Spirit, you will reap eternal life from the Spirit."

90. See Segundo, *Grace*, 145.

91. Segundo, *Grace*, 147.

92. Sobrino, "Centralidad"; English, Sobrino, "Central Concept."

93. The Kingdom of God is in some senses a key Christian Master Signifier. The parables refuse to define it, because it is a call to a new way of life rather than a concept to be possessed and owned (defined).

94. Sobrino, "Centralidad," 488; Sobrino, "Central Concept," 54. See also on this, Aguirre and Vitoria Cormenzana, "Justicia," 553.

reality: in their very reality they possess at least a conflictive and transformative potential for society.[95]

In other words, we might say that they are the actually disentitled, those whom the dominant part of any given society seeks to exclude from participation.

Liberating grace is then the transformative love of God in action, through and with the cooperation of humanity. In Acts 10:38, Peter, speaking to Cornelius and his household, tells how Jesus went about "doing good" or more literally, "working well" (*eúergetōn*). This "doing good" was, said Peter, manifested in healing all those who were oppressed by or under the power of the devil. Sobrino frequently uses the expression "anti-Kingdom," but the meaning is much the same, since oppression is not accidental, but deliberate, an active "doing bad" or "working evilly," "dis-grace." The healing, the making whole (*shalom*, *Gemüt*), the reintegration of the psychical and spiritual reality of human existence, is one way of describing grace and it is also always necessarily political, since everywhere human beings exist in concrete societies and in particular experiences of disintegration and incompleteness.

Because it is political, it will also demand taking sides. Here we come back to Laclau and Mouffe, and the competing ideological discourses, the different hegemonies that seek to impose themselves to contribute to the building up of a people. Christians are generally loathe to speak of their beliefs as a hegemonic discourse, but it may be time to embrace the description rather than run from it. For if there is no Christian hegemonic discourse, there is no Christian vision for how to live one's life in communion with others, and that means ultimately that grace is removed from the equation. It is to suggest that God is not active in the world, God does not have a plan for the world, the Holy Spirit is rendered powerless, life in Christ and obedience to the law of Christ are either rejected or at best regarded as practically meaningless. The question is not whether there is a hegemonic Christian discourse, but over which one is the most faithful to the Good News.

Grace and Eschatology

Fidelity to the Good News always includes an eschatological dimension. The theology of grace underlying theologies of entitlement that we

---

95. Sobrino, "Centralidad," 489; Sobrino, "Central Concept," 55.

examined in the previous chapter suffered most of all from its reduction of grace to a tangible reward (in terms of material well-being, power, social status, or position). Over against this, a liberative theology of grace always pushes beyond the here and now, even whilst firmly rooted within history. That is what it means to talk of the supernatural, as Segundo points out.[96] "Grace," says Segundo, "is that which enables us to journey forward as human beings . . . from the natural human condition to the creative liberty of the [children] of God."[97] This dynamic understanding of grace is a somewhat more systematic way of stating what Boff expressed in the parable of the moving train and its diverse passengers, the journey with God, in God, to God.

It is for a similar reason that Segundo and others engage in the question of the dimensions or spread of grace. In a letter written in 1902 to his French confrere Henri Brémond (1865–1933), the Anglo-Irish Jesuit and Modernist George Tyrrell (1861–1909) said "The idea of *grace* as a special favour—a piece of Divine favouritism—is to me utterly repulsive. I would not accept salvation on such iniquitous terms. If the *massa* is to be *damnata*, be my soul with the masses and not the Saints!"[98] Tyrrell's argument is against any attempt to reduce the effects of grace to a few chosen people, and it touches on what has arguably been the major theological challenge of the past half-century or so. How do people of other religious faiths, beliefs, or practices, or indeed those who hold to none, fit into a Christian understanding of the salvific impact of God's grace at work in the world? Or to put it in terms of the search for integration and wholeness, the task is to see whether grace can be something that can bring all of humankind and all of creation together and not just serve as rewards for holders of a Christian loyalty card.

Segundo points out that in practice such people, despite claiming to be Christian, can effectively be pagan:

> A person may have listened to the message of Jesus and believed
> in it as a message coming from God—in other words, he may

---

96. Segundo, *Grace*, 64. He does this in the course of what is essentially a discussion of the relationship between grace and nature, or the "supernatural" and the "natural", which he understands in Rahnerian terms as a *"Restbegriff,"* a necessary but empty concept, or perhaps better a kind of counter-factual—what things would have been like if we did not have the gift of grace.

97. Segundo, *Grace*, 70.

98. George Tyrrell, Letter to Henri Brémond, August 2, 1902, cited in Sagovsky, *"On God's Side"*, 150.

have *faith* in the sense of a bloc-commitment to the person and doctrine of the Word—and he may nevertheless not possess the faith which is identified with the salvific outlook that relates us to God. He can be materially a Christian without having comprehended his own religious alienation, the alienation which is denounced by Christianity and from which grace liberates us in the true outlook of faith.[99]

This is at least one of the ways in which, it seems to me, that Segundo would have responded to theologies of entitlement. Genuine claims about belief have to be backed up by genuine practice (relational, transformative, liberative, de-alienating). In the language of liberation theology, orthodoxy also requires orthopraxis.

Liberating grace, then, is present in all who act in a way that seeks the restoration of the wholeness of human existence and the wholeness of creation. Everyone is touched by grace, everyone can respond to it. Grace, Segundo suggests, "also liberates [people] from religious alienation in order to launch [them] into the fashioning of the total body of Christ: the new humanity."[100] Or, as George Tyrrell put it, reflecting on the story of the Last Judgement in Matthew 25:

> Do we forget that natural kindness is a God-given instinct; that it is God within us crying out to us, and to whom we may either hearken or turn a deaf ear? . . . Whence comes this devil's doctrine which gives us a God of nature, and a God of grace at enmity with one another? Many millions who have never heard the name of Christ, will hear: "I was hungry and you fed Me;" and they will say, "Who are Thou, Lord?" and He will say, "I am Jesus."[101]

The political implications of this are many. To quote another part of Matthew (7:21), "Not everyone who says to me, 'Lord, Lord,' will enter the kingdom of heaven, but only the one who does the will of my Father in heaven." Those who claim to be acting according to Christian values and support parties that deny the rights of significant sections of the population, because of their gender, ethnic background, or social status,[102] may, as Segundo suggests, "have faith", as a genuine commit-

99. Segundo, *Grace*, 111.
100. Segundo, *Grace*, 114.
101. Tyrrell, *Nova et vetera*, 162–63.

102. This seems to me a bare minimum, building as was mentioned above on the Pauline categories in Gal 3:28. It should also be noted that denying rights refers here to

ment to the "person and doctrine of the Word." Those who cry "Lord, Lord" are those who possess such a faith. But if it is not enacted, if it does not lead in some way to what the story of the Final Judgement sums up in categories such as feeding the hungry, clothing the naked, visiting the sick and the imprisoned, then it is not a participation in the salvific faith in Jesus Christ.

This does not mean that there cannot be genuine differences in political opinion and legitimate arguments about how to carry out concretely the task of transforming the life of the other, which is also a way of transforming one's own life. But it does mean that in some way all political engagement and action can be read in these terms and that only those courses of action that visibly and actually seek to serve the interest of the other can be legitimized. Again, one need not oversimplify this and there are arguments to be made from different places on the political spectrum. But to choose policies that in fact lead to economic injustice, to increased poverty, to imprisonment based on ethnic origin or skin tones rather than on justice, to ill-health caused by poverty and inadequate health provisions, and the list could go on, is to act, as Leonardo Boff might put it, according to the presence of dis-grace rather than grace.[103]

To say this, though, is not to solve the problem, but simply to move the focus of the argument to a different plane. In this chapter I have examined the problem of sin, as both social and structural. Sin is ultimately an attempt to act against the grace of God. It is, in the term I have borrowed from Leonardo Boff, a dis-grace, a lack of gratitude and gratuitousness. As such, it is also an act against the freedom from which the human person stems and to which, in God, they are called. Thus, I looked at the question of freedom as a correlative of the integrative transformative grace of God. As sin is always both personal and social, so is freedom, and so is love, as the active engagement with and for the other. To see, though, what this liberative grace may look like, I turn now to Pope Francis, as someone who has both pronounced the need for reconciliation and the need for an active engagement on behalf of the poor.

---

actual systemic behavior rather than theoretical claims a society makes. Many societies, in their laws and constitutions, do not permit discrimination on these grounds, but the actual experience is very different, and political parties that, through their rhetoric and actions, support this actual discrimination are what I am referring to here.

103. See Boff, *Graça*, 107; Boff, *Liberating Grace*, 65.

5

A Liberating Theology of Service

On March 13, 2013, Jorge Mario Bergoglio, SJ,[1] the Cardinal Archbishop of Buenos Aires, was elected as Bishop of Rome. In this chapter, I want to examine the theology of this pope "from the ends of the earth," as he described himself to the crowd gathered that evening in St. Peter's Square. How does Francis's approach help give more substance to a liberating theology of grace? To answer this question, I will first situate Francis's theology within the Argentinean and broader Latin American context. Then I will look at the four principles that underlie his theological vision, all of which go against theologies of entitlement and support theologies of responsibility and service. This will emerge even more clearly in the following chapter where I concentrate on his encyclical *Fratelli tutti*, since in it he engages with precisely the issues that are preoccupying me in these pages. What does it mean for all to be sisters and brothers? The pope gives no simplistic answer either, but he does set out a program for action that deserves to be taken seriously.

Pope Francis and Liberation Theology

When Pope Francis remarked that the cardinal electors had to go to the end of the earth to find a pope, he was referring both to Acts 1:8 and to

---

1. There are many biographies of Pope Francis. By far the best that I have read in English is Ivereigh, *The Great Reformer*.

his native country of Argentina. The country is always something of an anomaly in Latin America, including its version of liberation theology. At the time of his election, it is probably fair to say that liberation theologians were not entirely convinced by Bergoglio.[2] When I was studying in the Jesuit Center for Higher Studies (now the Jesuit Faculty of Philosophy and Theology) in Belo Horizonte, Brazil, in the early 1990s, a number of our teachers would go off for some months to teach in the Jesuit theologate in Argentina. The way we heard the story (also from some Argentinean Jesuits who passed through) was that there was more or less a civil war between two factions among Jesuits in Argentina, one of which was portrayed as "liberationist" and the other as "conservative." Bergoglio was seen as the leader of the conservative faction.[3]

This impression was not improved by the final document of the Fifth Conference of CELAM, the Latin American Council of Bishops, which took place at the National Shrine of Aparecida, in the Brazilian state of São Paulo, in May 2007. Bergoglio was tasked with chairing the committee that was responsible for drafting the Conference's final document. The Fourth Conference had taken place fifteen years previously in 1992 in Santo Domingo in the Dominican Republic, to mark the five-hundredth anniversary of the arrival of Europeans in the Americas and had been seen as a threat to liberation theology.[4] Thus when the Fifth Conference decided to abandon the See—Judge—Act methodology, there were grave fears that this was another attack on liberation theology.[5]

Despite this, there were also some signs of hope. Bergoglio's pastoral practice and obvious simplicity of lifestyle were welcomed and even before he spoke, his choice of the name Francis was an indication of change. As he himself recorded, when it became clear that he had been elected, his friend, Dom Claudio Hummes, then the Cardinal Archbishop of São

---

2. See Magister, "Quando Bergoglio," for one account of how this distrust was expressed.

3. For what actually happened, I can best refer the reader to Ivereigh, *The Great Reformer*, especially chapter 5, "The Leader Expelled," and within it, 191–97. He is admittedly very sympathetic to Francis, but his reading of the situation seems to me fair and not at odds with the few facts that I heard.

4. Cabestrero, "Santo Domingo."

5. On this, see Libanio, "Conferencia de Aparecida." But see also Brighenti, "Documento de Aparecida," which compares the original final document produced at the CELAM conference in Aparecida, under the leadership of Cardinal Bergoglio, with that passed by those Brighenti calls "the censors" in Rome, and shows how Pope Francis has reaffirmed the original text in his writings as pope.

Paulo, had urged him "Don't forget the poor." From his very first encounter with the press, a couple of days after his election, it became clear that Francis was in fact speaking the same language as liberation theologians. He too desired, he said, "a church that is poor and for the poor."[6] Since then, his acceptance of the theology of liberation and more importantly of theologians of liberation has been notable. He has worked with Leonardo Boff on the text of his encyclical *Laudato Si'*, he has greeted and rehabilitated Gustavo Gutiérrez and Jon Sobrino, both victims of attacks by the Vatican in the past. He also lifted the canonical suspension imposed on Ernesto Cardenal by Pope John Paul II. The cases of Gutiérrez and Sobrino both reveal a lot about how Francis acts.

As Pope, Francis first met with Gutiérrez in private in 2013, and again more publicly in 2014, as well as a brief meeting during the papal visit to Peru in January 2018. Later that year, on June 8, 2018, Gutiérrez celebrated his ninetieth birthday. Pope Francis sent him a letter in which he thanked him for his service to the church, continuing:

> I join with your thanksgiving to God and I thank you for how much you have contributed to the Church and to humanity by your theological service and your preferential love for the poor and the discarded of society. Thank you for all your efforts and for the way you have challenged the conscience of each one, so that no one can remain indifferent to the drama of poverty and exclusion.[7]

With Sobrino, who, unlike Gutiérrez, was the subject of an official notification from the Vatican's Congregation for the Doctrine of Faith, there was also a brief but telling encounter. In October 2018 the canonization of Archbishop Oscar Romero took place in Rome. This in itself was a demonstration of Francis's commitments and vision, the process having been stalled under his predecessors. After the canonization, there was a meeting in the Audience Hall for the more than 6,000 Salvadorans who had come to Rome for the event. A Salvadoran Jesuit prison

---

6. On this, see Sedmak, *Church of the Poor*. He quotes this remark and that of Cardinal Hummes on p. ix. See also Ilo, *Poor and Merciful Church*.

7. There are numerous sources of the text of the letter. See, for example, "Father Gustavo Gutiérrez." The Spanish text reads: ""Me uno a tu acción de gracias a Dios, y también a ti te agradezco por cuanto has contribuido a la Iglesia y a la humanidad, a través de tu servicio teológico y de tu amor preferencial por los pobres y los descartados de la sociedad. Gracias por todos tus esfuerzos y por tu forma de interpelar la conciencia de cada uno, para que nadie quede indiferente ante el drama de la pobreza y la exclusión."

chaplain, Javier Sánchez, recounted what happened as he, Sobrino, and another Salvadoran Jesuit stood in the hall:

> When [Francis] was passing by and was already turning to people on the other side of the aisle, the [other] Salvadoran Jesuit said to the Pope: "Your Holiness, Jon Sobrino is here." Francis's face lit up and he smiled broadly, turned and gave the Jesuit theologian a warm embrace. This was the little dialogue between the two: "Ah, Jon" [said the pope. Sobrino replied]: "I've left a copy of the last book I published, called 'Conversations.' I guess they will give it to you" [The pope then said] "Thank you, Jon, for the book, but thank you most of all for your witness." At this point other hands tugged at the Pope's cassock and he moved on, but not without giving another sincere and grateful smile to the theologian. [8]

I mention both these stories, not only because they are beautiful in themselves, but because they sum up the kind of approach the pope has constantly favored. Inasmuch as it is an action-based demonstration of who God is for Francis, it is not impossible to speak of this as one element of his theology, which always focuses on what people do or do not do, rather than on what they say, and whether they tick the right boxes.[9] Following his own four principles that I will examine shortly, he responds first to people and not to ideas, which is to say that he acts "graciously." The gratuity of the embrace, the repeated use of the word "gracias,"[10] none of these are accidental. This is not to say that they are carefully planned gestures designed to be noticed approvingly. It is simply that grace encounters grace and the recognition of goodness in others, of how people have sought to live their lives in fidelity first to God, second to God's people, and especially to the loved of God, the poor and excluded, and finally, though not therefore least, in fidelity to the body of Christ, the people of God, namely the church.

To this end, Francis himself picks up on the words of his predecessor, Pope Benedict XVI, who said "Being a Christian is not the result

---

8. The story is contained in a report by Vidal, "El Papa."

9. The Czech theologian and religious commentator Tomáš Halík speaks of what he calls "Pseudoreligion F," where F stands for fundamentalism, fanaticism, and Pharisaism (which in Czech also begins with F—*farizejství*). These latter are the kind of people who insist on the box-ticking approach to faith, and who are amongst the strongest opponents of Pope Francis within the Roman Catholic Church. See Halík, "Pseudonáboženství F."

10. Meaning "thank you," of course, but also "graces."

of an ethical choice or a lofty idea, but the encounter with an event, a person, which gives life a new horizon and a decisive direction."[11] And this leads on to a particular theological perspective, to which I now turn.

The Theology of Francis

One of the features of Francis that the "box-tickers" have sometimes picked up on is the fact that he does not have a doctorate in theology. This, they imply, means that he is not competent to pass judgement on theological issues and that therefore anything he says that is even remotely theological can be safely ignored. But to say that there are various levels at which theology occurs is a commonplace and the task of the pope is not primarily to produce academic theology. Moreover, as a Brazilian writer on Francis's theological method says: "There is no doubt that the teaching of the magisterium constitutes a theological teaching, given that it occurs through a discourse that thinks faith."[12] Or as another author puts it, drawing on a distinction made by Thomas Aquinas between two *magisteria*, or two "*cathedrae*" within the church, the *cathedra pastoralis* and the *cathedra magistralis*: "Pope Francis . . . exercises the pastoral *cathedra*. . . . His engagement is not that of a professional academic theologian, but of a pastor who seeks above all else the spiritual well-being of the people of God."[13]

None of this implies that his theology is therefore any less "theological" or less important. Indeed it could be argued that the opposite is true, that a theology that seeks to express the grace of God, the active and transformative presence of God at work in the world, based on the experience of that activity, is what is most central to the proclamation of the Christian gospel. It would also be unwise, and inaccurate, to write off Francis as theologically uneducated. Rather he draws on a rich tradition of European and Latin American theology, even if his "engagement with European Catholic theology was by no means an uncritical repetition of the thought of others, but a creative and inspired appropriation grounded in pastoral praxis, spiritual discernment, theological reflection, and an

---

11. Pope Francis, "Papal Foreword," in Lee and Knoebel, *Discovering Pope Francis*, xiv. The Spanish original is also printed on the preceding pages, and the quotation is at xii. The reference is to Pope Benedict XVI, *Deus caritas est*, 1.

12. Passos, *Método Teológico*, 9.

13. Codina, *Teologia do Papa Francisco*, 8.

acute awareness of the concrete life of societies and the church."[14] This engagement with both Latin American and European theology provides key insights on the mutual relationship between Francis's theology and ministry, in which each shapes the other.

Theology of the People

I want to begin by considering briefly some of the intellectual roots of that theology. The pastoral roots are both the most obvious and the hardest to capture in writing. In Francis's case, these roots can be found especially in the parish that he established in the region around the Argentinian Jesuit study center, the Colegio Máximo. This vast parish[15] was home to new internal migrants and as much as any books it was from these people that Francis also learned his theology. But in his contact with them, he also brought to bear his reading, both narrowly theological and, as has become clear in his pontificate, more broadly cultural.[16]

The first crucial influence on Francis in terms of the shape it gives to his theological thinking is the theology of the people (*teología del pueblo*). In one of the most acute analyses of Francis's thought, the Argentinean theologian Emilce Cuda, says that "The first questions that arise in anyone who reads Francis are: 'from which theology does he take the categorical *corpus* that is found as the basis of his discourse? Is his theology the Theology of Liberation? . . . Is the Argentinean version, called Theology of the People, part of liberation theology?"[17] We will come to her answer to this question later, but first we need to look at the theology of

---

14. Bryan Lee and Thomas Knoebel, "The Story of a Symposium: Why We Need a Theological Understanding of Pope Francis's Thought," in Lee and Knoebel, *Discovering Pope Francis*, 7.

15. Containing some forty thousand people, spread over seven *barrios*, it continues to be a place where Jesuits in formation gain pastoral experience. See Austen Ivereigh, "Close and Concrete: Bergoglio's Life Evangelizing a World in Flux," in Lee and Knoebel, *Discovering Pope Francis*, 28. The size is not unusual. The community I participated in Brazil, in the area of Justinópolis, part of the municipality of Ribeirão das Neves on the outskirts of Belo Horizonte was at that time part of a parish that contained something like one hundred thousand people, with sixteen different church communities (and a couple of additional churches). It is now a separate parish, but the parishes remain very large.

16. The fact that Francis does not entirely distinguish between the two is an integral part of his theological method. See, for example, Passos, *Método Teológico*, 103.

17. Cuda, *Para leer*, 26.

the people,[18] which prior to Francis tended to be largely ignored outside of Argentina.[19]

There were several important contributors to the foundation and development of the theology of the people. Among the most influential was the Argentinean priest Lucio Gera (1924–2012).[20] Like Bergoglio, his family was Italian, though, unlike the pope, he was himself born in Italy, moving to Argentina at the age of five. Ordained to the priesthood in 1947, he taught theology for over fifty years. He was present at the final session of the Second Vatican Council.[21] After the Council he was an important member of the Episcopal Pastoral Commission (COEPAL), established by the Argentinean bishops to implement the pastoral insights of Vatican II. He was joined in this enterprise by others, such as Rafael Tello (1917–2002)[22] and the Jesuit Juan Carlos Scannone (1931–2019). As a young theologian Scannone began his teaching career at the Jesuit theologate in Argentina at the same time as Jorge Mario Bergoglio was beginning his theological studies there, and he is often credited with having stimulated Bergoglio's interest in the nascent theology of the people, both then and later after Bergoglio's ordination, including when he was rector of the theologate.[23]

The theology of the people was born, then, in the aftermath of the Second Vatican Council, and was a specifically Argentinean contribution to the attempt to contextualize the Council for Latin America, both contributing to, and later drawing on insights from, the CELAM conference in Medellín.[24] The designator "theology of the people" refers to two elements, one of which is theology, the other being the people. Leaving aside, for now, what is meant by "theology," the first question to ask is

---

18. I will use the English translation, but I think there are overtones to the word "pueblo" or "povo" that can be lost in the English word "people," as I explain below.

19. There were some exceptions. One of its principal claims, about the centrality of the people, was examined, for example, by Fernández Beret, *El Pueblo*. But the literature outside of Argentina is very scarce before the election of Francis.

20. On Gera, see briefly Albado, "La Teología del Pueblo," 39–46; Scannone, *Teología del pueblo*, 41–56. Further references to Gera's work are given below.

21. Scannone, *Teología del pueblo*, 16. See also the entry on the website Cardijn Priests, that notes that Gera was there as an invitee, not a *peritus*; see "Gera, Lucio."

22. For an introduction to Tello, see Albado, "La pastoral popular."

23. See Lemna and Delaney, "Three Pathways," 31.

24. Scannone, *La teología del pueblo*, 16–20.

what is meant by the word "*pueblo*," "people." In a lecture that he gave on popular religion, Lucio Gera asked:

> What is the historical condition in which the people (*pueblo*) of Latin America, considered in relation to their religiosity, were and are with respect to the Christian faith? Considered in their particular religious behavior, are they a Christian people or not? We are interested in directly capturing the contemporary situation of these peoples (*pueblos*); nevertheless their current situation can only be understood if we know the process of the formation of these peoples (*pueblos*).[25]

The first point to note is the sudden and unexplained move between "Latin American people" and "these peoples." The use of the word "people" or "peoples" obviously takes us back to Laclau and Mouffe, both in their understanding of the centrality of the theme and in their recognition that a people is constructed rather than simply existing. Given a shared background, especially in regard to Peronism, this is not at all surprising.[26] But the differentiation between people and peoples points to a key element of the theology of the people, namely its insistence on the cultural setting. In this sense, of course, it is possible to speak of Latin American people and peoples,[27] though this already introduces an unresolved and generally unresolvable tension into the debate about culture and indeed religiosity.

Gera himself already understood this tension. In the article quoted above, he goes on to offer a brief definition of what he understands by "people." For him, "a people is a collective subject, that is a specific form of community. It is, then, a plurality of individuals, a reduced multitude and a unity: unified and (relatively) totalized."[28] The reference to the people as a "collective subject" immediately raises the question of the relationship to Marxism. Proponents of the theology of the people would

25. Gera, "Pueblo," 102–3.

26. See Cuda, "Latinoamérica en el siglo XXI," 60; Azcuy, "Introducción," in Gera, *La teología argentina*, 10: "Above all it is necessary to mention the phenomenon of Peronism, with its populist roots, its political viewpoint and the strong antagonisms that this produced in the country, but also the 'emerging of the popular' that was perceived in this political movement by the representatives of the nascent theological-pastoral vision."

27. On what "Latin American" means in liberation theologies, see Noble, "Singing."

28. Lucio Gera, "Pueblo, religión del pueblo e Iglesia (1976)," 723, cited in Albado, "La Teología del Pueblo," 41. Gera's article, quoted above, was originally a lecture and first published as Gera, "Pueblo."

argue that their theology is not Marxist in the way that they think liberation theology is.[29] A former rector of the Pontifical Argentinean Catholic University and now Archbishop of La Plata, Víctor Manuel Fernández, said that "the Theology of the People distinguishes itself from both Marxist analysis and from liberal visions. For this reason it does not fit well into either of these two perspectives, which it considers *populist*."[30] In part, this may be to do with a struggle present within Marxism itself. As Emilce Cuda points out:

> In the 1960s the Marxists in Argentina became post-Marxists and placed themselves under the title of national and popular thought. They justified this, criticizing the category of *class* and putting in its place that of *people*. In this way, the Argentinean critical thinking that defends the demands of the popular sectors for the basics of life is not called *Marxist* in Argentina but *populist*, and public opinion terms it "the left."[31]

The theology of the people belongs more to what two Israeli authors have called a synthetic Marxist postmodernism, whose proponents

> espouse a "dual perspective" that recognizes the simultaneous workings of two heuristically separate chains of hierarchy, namely, a hierarchy of classes and a hierarchy of identities. The first one creates material exploitation and inequality; the second one, symbolic underestimation or disrespect. The main point is that material and cultural inequalities cannot be reduced to each other, even if in real-life situations they are always intermingled.[32]

This refusal to reduce the cultural to the material is a central point of theology of the people and for Pope Francis, though both also recognise that the two are not entirely separate. But theology of the people is also influenced by post-Marxists, such as Ernesto Laclau, and his reading is, like that of Gera, Tello, Scannone, and others, influenced by his experiences in Argentina. Classic liberation theology would probably be best classified, in these terms, as drawing on a Marxist Postmodernism,[33]

---

29. For example, Guzmán Carriquiry Lecour, "The 'Theology of the People' in the Pastoral Theology of Jorge Mario Bergoglio," in Lee and Knoebel, *Discovering Pope Francis*, 42–69; Scannone, *Teología del pueblo*, 27.

30. Fernández, *El programa*, 76, cited in Cuda, *Para leer a Francisco*, 52.

31. Cuda, "Latinoamérica en el siglo XXI," 59.

32. Filc and Ram "Marxism after postmodernism," 300.

33. Filc and Ram, "Marxism after postmodernism," 299–300.

recognizing the validity of some aspects of post-modern thought, but insisting on the continuing centrality of the material (or for liberation theology more specifically the economic).

In other words, when it comes to distinguishing classic liberation theology and theology of the people, the use of language may frequently conceal as much as it reveals and, though there are clear differences, there is without doubt a kind of Wittgensteinian "family resemblance." The degree, then, to which theology of the people differs from liberation theology elsewhere on the continent depends often on the context in which the distinction is being made and why. For my purposes here it is enough to say that, whilst recognizing differences in emphasis and even in methodology, there is a broadly shared focus,[34] especially, as is clear in Pope Francis, in making the poor a privileged *locus theologicus*.[35]

The People in the Theology of the People

The importance of the theology of the people for Pope Francis is not measurable in terms of direct references to it.[36] Rather, it serves as a kind of theological *Sitz im Leben* for his theological approach, giving it a foundation and a context. It is therefore worth returning to look in more detail at how this theological tradition understands the "people," given the importance of this term in understanding populism. In attempting to define who the "people" are, Juan Carlos Scannone is one of a number who have turned to Ernesto Laclau, to compare and contrast his understanding of the "popular,"[37] of the people, and of populism.

Scannone wants to distinguish the concept of "people" in Laclau and in the theology of the people, but he does say that Laclau's use of the "empty signifier" could be analogically used to understand the unity

---

34. On this, see also Scannone, *Teología del pueblo*, 88–94.

35. See Cuda, *Para leer a Francisco*, 161–62. Scannone, "Situación," 263–64, argues that the poor are not a *locus theologicus* in the way Melchior Cano used the term, but that they can be understood as a "hermeneutical locus."

36. See Albado, "Teología del Pueblo," 53–55, showing how Francis utilizes themes from the theology of the people, even if there are no direct references to Gera, Scannone, or Tello.

37. "Popular" in Spanish and Portuguese is most fundamentally the adjectival form of "pueblo" or "povo" and is perhaps best rendered in English as "people's." However to avoid excessive feats of grammatical gymnastics, I will translate it as "popular." The problem of how to translate "pueblo" was noted by Scannone in an interview, as reported in San Martin, "Pope's Late Teacher."

of the people, even if he admits that his way of using this term is against Laclau. The example he uses is "justice": "the signifier 'justice' is the same, even if not univocally so, but rather analogically, according to the type of injustice (economic, political, racial, gender, religious discrimination . . .) that is being fought against and what justice is claimed."[38] However, despite Scannone's own disclaimer, there are some overlaps between his thought and that of Laclau that can help us go deeper into the understanding of the "people." For, as Emilce Cuda notes, "Ernesto Laclau . . . enables us to understand a little more the position of the theologians of the people towards the social problem."[39]

Scannone is one of a number of authors to speak of a "theology of the people or of culture."[40] This relationship is developed by Rafael Tello:

> The Church as People of God has to be incarnated in a temporal people. . . . And given that the people is constituted as a culture, it has to incarnate itself in a culture. The Church as People of God does not exist as a separate entity, but always—and this is its particular mission—becomes incarnate, and in becoming incarnate the People of God is realized in a concrete fashion, whilst transcending all particular ways. This leads to the people of God incarnated in diverse cultures being also diverse—whilst maintaining its unity—as the People of God. . . . That is to say, culture gives it an incarnated modality and the universal values of the people of God and thus multiplies it in space and time, without ever exhausting it.[41]

The emphasis and reminder that the theology of the people refers always to the people as culturally rooted is key, and explains, for example, the emphasis on popular religiosity.[42] But culture is also a political reality,

38. Scannone, *Teología del pueblo*, 90. This may be closer to Laclau's concept of the equivalential relationship.

39. Cuda, *Para leer a Francisco*, 142.

40. Sometimes, they speak of theology of the people and of culture (Scannone, *Teología del pueblo*, chapter 1, 15–40), sometimes as here of theology of the people or theology of the culture (see, for example, Cuda, *Para leer a Francisco*, 131), or sometimes of theology of culture or theology of the people (see, for example, Cuda, *Para leer a Francisco*, 67), or even theology of culture or of the people (Cuda, "Latinoamérica en el siglo XXI," 61).

41. Rafael Tello, tape recording of the *Segundo encuentro de reflexión y diálogo sobre pastoral popular*, cited in this way in Fernández, "Con los pobres," 188.

42. As just one example, see the article cited above, Gera, "Pueblo, religión del pueblo e Iglesia." See also the story recounted in Albado, "Teología del Pueblo," 34, on how observing people making the Stations of the Cross outside in a park inspired Gera in his reflections.

expressive of the way in which groups of people understand their place in a wider society, in what Laclau referred to as the "*populus*." Culture is the self-understanding of a particular group. For theology of the people and Laclau, the particular interest is in the poor, the excluded, the oppressed, those Laclau terms the "plebs." What happens, as we saw in chapter 2, is that there is a tension between "cultures," between different totalizing hegemonic discourses. Cuda describes the roots of "the crisis that threatens the current global system" as lying "in an egoistic hegemonic culture, rather than in the social relations of production, since the latter are merely the effect of the former."[43] Not all cultures are good, and not all cultures help construct a people that is good. That is the problem with theologies of entitlement, in Brazil, the Czech Republic, and elsewhere.

Rather than a clash of civilizations or a clash of economic models, then, what lies at the heart of most forms of current social malaise, according to this reading, is a hegemonic struggle between two cultures, which in the traditional language of liberation theology might be called cultures of death and cultures of life. For Cuda, at least, the theology of the people seeks to view this clash from a post-Marxist perspective, in that Marxist readings have tended to focus too strongly on the global economic context at the expense of a more focused reading of particular groups.[44] The struggle is how to allow for a focused engagement with the life of the community.

Francis takes this emphasis on the people from the theology of the people, but "the people" is not simply a synonym for everyone. To understand more of what the pope understands by the term, we can turn to his Apostolic Exhortation *Evangelii gaudium*. In the second and third sections of this document (paras. 186–238) he looks at the inclusion of the poor in society and then at the common good and peace in society. As is suggested by the genre of the document (Exhortation), such publications are meant to encourage, and in this case specifically to encourage people to a re-orientation or, more theologically, to conversion. But for Francis and for theologians more generally in Latin America this conversion is never individual (although it will be personal, in the sense we saw in the previous chapter). The task is to include the excluded (the poor) in society, and to speak of the common good is already necessarily to turn to society.

---

43. Cuda, "Latinoamérica en el siglo XXI," 61.
44. Cuda, "Latinoamérica en el siglo XXI," 61–63.

Notably, Francis begins with the place of the poor. A people can only be fully constructed if the poor are part of that people. The realization that this is the case is, says Francis, "born of the liberating action of grace within each of us" (EG, 188).[45] Liberating grace is what makes it possible in the first place to hear with the ears of God, to hear the cry of the poor and to respond. It enables solidarity, something that "presumes the creation of a new mindset which thinks in terms of community and the priority of the life of all over the appropriation of goods by a few" (EG, 188). Here already we see one of the four central pillars of Francis's approach, to which I will return soon, namely the superiority of the whole over the parts.

For Francis, too, the option for the poor[46] remains crucial. It is "primarily a theological category" (EG, 198), since in the first place it says something about God. This is important to recognize. It is not an economic, cultural, or political choice, and in this sense, at least in principle, it refuses to engage in the establishment of a hegemonic discourse. In practice, of course, the option for the poor also includes concrete choices about the way in which society should be structured that have a clear and necessary political dimension. But such choices are a secondary element of the option for the poor. Primarily it is a theological statement, and the socio-political engagement is secondary both chronologically and in the hierarchy of truths. "Secondary" does not mean that political choices are unimportant, but it is a reminder that they are at the service of faith.

---

45. Numbers refer to paragraph numbers of *Evangelii gaudium* (EG). The Spanish and Italian versions speak of the "liberating work of grace" (*obra liberadora, opera liberatrice*). See also Boff, *Liberating Grace*, 101: "[People] may choose to love and unite themselves with an oppressed class.... Such an encounter gives the lie to a different kind of encounter that is glorified in societies that are wrapped up in their own egoism.... They would evade the demands of Christian praxis as a love committed to the liberation of other human beings from inhuman and unjust conditions." In other words, liberating grace is utterly different to the grace underlying theologies of entitlement, which are always egoistical.

46. Unlike his predecessors, Francis speaks not only of the "preferential option for the poor," but also of "the option for the poor." The difference/similarity between the two terms has given rise to much debate, with some claiming that "preferential option" marks a watering down of the original. Perhaps a more helpful approach is suggested by Rohan Curnow, who argues that there are two different and ultimately competing interpretations, one favored by liberation theology (and I would argue Pope Francis), the other by the Vatican, especially John Paul II and Cardinal Joseph Ratzinger, later Benedict XVI. The liberation approach focuses, as does Francis, on the importance of conversion. See Curnow, "Which Preferential Option." See also Sedmak, *Church of the Poor*, 89–97.

A Theology of, with, and for the Poor

There can be a danger in both the theology of the people and in other forms of liberation theology of a reductionist language about the poor or the people, who often seem to end up as an indiscriminate "they." Pope Francis appears sometimes to give into this temptation too.[47] It is a challenge going back to the Medellín conference. The bishops at Medellín desired to serve the poor, but they could not claim to be poor, materially, educationally, or in terms of social status. However, even if the bishops or the pope cannot claim to be literally poor, Francis also realizes that this is not an excuse not to stand with the poor, in all their diversity. This is not because the poor are necessarily morally superior. Rather, as Gustavo Gutiérrez put it, "the option [for the poor] is not made because the poor are good, but because God is good. If the poor are not good, then it's still the same. Many people became disappointed with the commitment [to the poor] because they believed the poor were good. If they had committed themselves because God is good, they would still be committed."[48] Again we see that the option for the poor is a theological option, because of who God is and how God interacts with the world.

Nevertheless, neither Gutiérrez nor Pope Francis want to imply that there is no need to take concrete steps to change things. In *Evangelii gaudium* and, as we shall see, in *Fratelli tutti* Francis is clear that there also needs to be systemic change. It is one of the key claims of liberation theology that the poor are not poor because of some natural law or because God wants them to be poor: the poor are poor because they are made poor.[49] In other words, and here we cannot avoid hegemonic language, systems are set up in such a way that some are rich and many more are poor, and these same systems lead to the dehumanization of the poor (and ultimately of the rich).

The task of the church, then, for Francis, is to be with and of the poor. To do this is to reject the existing status quo. In the second chapter of *Evangelii gaudium* there are a series of rejections of what the pope calls

---

47. For example, in EG, 200, he writes: "The great majority of the poor have a special openness to the faith; they need God and we must not fail to offer them his friendship, his blessing, his word, the celebration of the sacraments and a journey of growth and maturity in the faith." But precisely because he is talking about faith and the role of the church, it may be argued that the division is, if not justified, at least understandable.

48. Carrero, "Entrevista."

49. See, for example, Gutiérrez, "The Liberation of the Poor: The Puebla Perspective," in *The Power of the Poor*, 125–65; Zaffaroni, "Processos."

"some challenges of today's world." These are outlined in four sections: "No to an economy of exclusion" (EG, 53–54); "No to the new idolatry of money" (EG, 55–56); "No to a financial system which rules rather than serves" (EG, 57–58); "No to the inequality which spawns violence" (EG, 59–60). Apart from the content, in full agreement with the language of liberation theology (the attack on unjust systems that kill), what is important to note here is that the pope is making a systemic point. The problem is not with individuals, or at least not primarily with individuals, even if it is true that systems function with the collaboration of people. But the systems create the parameters within which people act, and it is these parameters that need to change. The problem is structural sin.

These comments are predominantly theological. With liberation theology and the theology of the people, he wants to make a claim about who God is and how God acts (grace) and therefore who human beings, created in the image and likeness of God, are called to be. Thus at an important level the rejection of the current *modus operandi* of the markets is not a political one, a battle between "right" and "left." The struggle is not only between two political hegemonic discourses, but between what is in agreement with the will of God for his people and what is against it. The task of the church, "faced by a society that suffers so much and is so unjust, so lacking in meaning and values," is "to manifest the *merciful face of God* . . . to be a place of welcome so that it can lead our contemporaries to an encounter with God in Jesus Christ."[50] The system is one that prevents this encounter, and thus it needs to be changed.

The precise relationship between those who are called "the poor" and the "people" is not made clear, either in Francis or in the theology of the people. Essentially, we can see the poor as "political and cultural subjects in the process of liberation."[51] The recognition of the poor as "subjects" is a complex and contested part of liberation theology. First emphasized in the early days of liberation theology by people like Hugo Assmann, the claim that the poor were subjects of their own liberation sought to highlight the fact that the poor were not simply a problem for other people to talk about, but that they themselves were the fashioners of their own future—hence the claim that the poor were "subjects of their own history."[52] The

---

50. Miranda, *Reforma de Francisco*, 91.

51. Passos, *Método Teológico*, 70. Passos uses this description in relation to the theology of the people.

52. One of the leading proponents in the first wave of liberation theology of the idea of the poor as subject of their own history was the Brazilian theologian Hugo

problem has always lain in the clash between desire and reality, since the poor are also those who are excluded and denied their subjectivity. Again Francis's approach is a theological one, recognizing that each person is a child of God, and that therefore, the status of poor people needs to be constantly reaffirmed, since the system denies it.[53]

The emphasis on the poor as subjects comes also from the way in which, whatever the differences, they are also seen as part of the "people." As Juan Carlos Scannone explains, theology of the people "understands the people as the communal subject (*sujeto comunitario*) of a history and a culture."[54] There are links to the idea of a "nation," but as *ethnos* rather than as state.[55] A people shares a common experience of life and most importantly they share in the search for the common good. It is therefore the poor and the working class who "constitute the structuring axis of the people-nation."[56] Those who do not search for the common good exclude themselves and are the "anti-people."[57]

Theology of liberation and of the people see in the people a particular expression of faithfulness.[58] This must be understood with care. Gutiérrez's warning needs to ring in our ears, for the claim is not that

---

Assmann. See, for example, Assmann, *Pueblo oprimido*. He would later come to criticize this emphasis. See Assmann, "Apuntes." For a brief but nuanced reading, see Bingemer, *Latin American Theology*, 55, 100.

53. In this, the argument would be similar to that of movements such as Black Lives Matter. The lives of the poor (and of course in Brazil and many other Latin American countries the poor are also those with African or indigenous forebears) cannot be objectified, but have to be recognized as having value simply as human lives

54. Scannone, *Teología del pueblo*, 83 in a chapter entitled, in translation, "'People' and 'Popular' in the Social Reality, in Pastoral Activity, and in Theological Reflection."

55. For a consideration of the biblical background of the term, and especially the concurrent use of all three "people" words in 1 Pet 2:9–10, see Horrell, "'Race,' 'Nation,' 'People.'" All three senses are present, it seems to me, in theology of the people, without sufficient distinction always being made.

56. Scannone, *Teología del pueblo*, 84. Scannone refers to the "poor and workers' sectors" (*los sectores pobres y trabajadores*), so my translation is misleading if it seems that he ends up introducing classist language, which theology of the people wants to avoid because of its Marxist overtones.

57. Scannone, *Teología del pueblo*, 84–85.

58. Scannone, *Teología del pueblo*, 205–7. Scannone refers to EG, 95 and 96. The English version only has the phrase in the first of these paragraphs, which in Spanish speaks of the *Pueblo fiel de Dios*, "God's faithful people" in the English version. Paragraph 96 in Spanish speaks of the *la realidad sofrida de nuestro pueblo fiel*, which the English renders as "the real lives and difficulties of our people." The phrase is also not translated in paragraphs 120, 125, and 142.

simply by belonging to a particular group, there is a moral superiority to given individuals. Because the people is a construction, the way of life, the ethical attitude, the understanding of history come first, and it is those who are committed to this way of life who are the people. A clear sign of belonging to this group is faith, and faithfulness to God, which reminds us yet again that the people are in the first place a theological and not a socio-economic or even socio-cultural category. The references to the faithful people (of God) in *Evangelii gaudium* underline the way in which, despite the challenges and difficulties of life, the people do not give up on God, because they know that God does not give up on them.[59]

The Four Theological Criteria of Pope Francis

None of this, however, can be taken for granted, which is why Pope Francis develops his famous four criteria, which he introduces in EG, 221:

> Progress in building a people in peace, justice, and fraternity depends on four principles related to constant tensions present in every social reality. These derive from the pillars of the Church's social doctrine, which serve as "primary and fundamental parameters of reference for interpreting and evaluating social phenomena." In their light I would now like to set forth these four specific principles which can guide the development of life in society and the building of a people where differences are harmonized within a shared pursuit. I do so out of the conviction that their application can be a genuine path to peace within each nation and in the entire world.[60]

Although introduced into the magisterium of the Catholic Church at this point, the principles themselves date from much earlier.[61] They state that: i) time is superior to space; ii) unity prevails over conflict; iii) the reality is more important than the idea; iv) the whole is superior to the part.[62]

---

59. See, apart from the references in the previous footnote, for example, EG, 14, 119, 130, 135, 144, 274.

60. The citation within the quotation is from the Pontifical Council for Justice and Peace, *Compendium of the Social Doctrine of the Church*, 161. The paragraph in question constitutes the preamble to the fourth chapter on the principles of the church's social doctrine.

61. Scannone, *Teología del pueblo*, 256–57. See also Ivereigh, *The Great Reformer*, 142–43.

62. This is the order in which they appear in *Evangelii gaudium*. In order of

Romano Guardini and the Need for Opposites

Before moving on to the principles themselves, I turn to a brief consideration of a key source for Francis's thinking here, namely Romano Guardini, on whose thought he had at one stage planned to write a doctoral dissertation. Guardini worked with a theory of polar opposites[63] and it is on this that Bergoglio drew, rather than on Hegelian dialectics.[64] What is meant by this theory is the necessary coexistence of two opposites, two poles of behavior or of existence that can neither be reduced one to the other or superseded by a synthesis.[65] Guardini sought in his teaching on opposites (*Gegensatzlehre*) to bring together distinct realities (life and faith, reflection and action, for example).[66] The provisional title of Bergoglio's proposed doctoral thesis, "Polar Opposition as Structure of Daily Thought and of Christian Proclamation," showed how he had planned to focus on precisely this aspect of Guardini's thinking.[67]

Even though he barely managed to start, let alone complete, his doctoral thesis, he never lost interest in Guardini, nor in the theme, and it continued to inspire him. Indeed, as he himself noted, the section on the four principles was inspired by the work from the thesis.[68] For my

---

development in Bergoglio's thinking, however, the order is somewhat different: unity prevails over conflict, the whole is superior to the parts and time is superior to space, were the first three, with the principle of reality being superior to ideas coming only later. Apart from Scannone quoted in the previous footnote, see the (somewhat confusing) account in Borghesi, *Mind of Pope Francis*, 57–60.

63. On polarity in Guardini, see Ghia, "'La verità è polifônica.'" The musical imagery Ghia employs is suggestive, since it reinforces the need to maintain difference as constitutive of harmony. Ghia does not make this point, but it is also of course true that not all difference is harmonious and polyphony has its rules and structures too.

64. How present Hegel is in Latin American liberation theology is a debatable point. Certainly there are hints of a Hegelian approach in some Latin American philosophy, including among those linked to liberation theology such as Ignacio Ellacuría. On Ellacuría, see Schulz, "La presencia," 302–4.

65. Bergoglio's dialectics are discussed in more detail in Borghesi, *Mind of Pope Francis*, 65–68. Borghesi offers a clear distinction between Bergoglio and Hegel. For a critical reading of the dialectical background of the four principles, pointing also to some of their problems, see Regan, "The Bergoglian Principles."

66. See Gorevan, "Only Connect." It is perhaps worth noting that Guardini speaks of *Gegensatz* and not *Widerspruch*. That is, opposition is something that is placed over against something else, rather than an opposition that sees some kind of resistance (speaking against); see Mikulášek, "'I Dream,'" 66.

67. Borghesi, *Mind of Pope Francis*, 104.

68. Borghesi, *Mind of Pope Francis*, 103.

purposes, it is helpful to consider the approach adopted by Pope Francis in relation to that of Laclau and Mouffe, when they talk of antagonisms. These, it will be recalled, are incompatible and ultimately inimical positions, especially political positions. In this sense, they too are polar opposites, just as are the theologies of grace behind theologies and practices of entitlement on the one hand, and theologies of grace behind theologies and practices of liberation on the other. Guardini's oppositions as read by Francis are, however, very different, perhaps more akin to what Chantal Mouffe calls "agonistics." The approaches of both Francis and Mouffe reject compromise or a synthesis of the opposing views, to find some kind of "centrist" position. But Mouffe still sees agonistics as adversarial. Her view would be, I think, closer to what in the first principle Francis calls "space," the struggle for possession of (or hegemony over) the political.

On the other hand, the position of Francis is one that allows for the coexistence of both poles, because both are necessary. The obvious example is how political change often ends up only bringing the same problems (of oppression, of corruption, of neglect for the poor) that were there before, only under different slogans. In the Czech Republic the post-1989 politicians have generally not been able to escape the practices of the Communist period, whatever party they belong to, whatever apparent beliefs they hold. The practices of the Communists, and going further back of other powers, such as the Nazis or the Habsburgs, in their different ways have produced a way of doing politics that is agonistic, but whose shared ground allows no growth. For Francis, if the ground shifts, then the poles need be neither antagonistic nor even simply agonistic. They can also be complementary.[69]

Time Is Superior to Space

The first of the principles, that time is superior to space, sounds at first in contradiction with a strong strand in contemporary theology and philosophy that has sought to emphasize the importance of place.[70]

---

69. Complementary is not the same as a synthesis. The positions remain different (sweet and sour flavours in a sauce), but they complement each other, rather than destroy each other. This is in other words agonistics rather than antagonism, though Mouffe would hesitate to use a word like "complementary."

70. Because he would influence Pope Francis, we can take as one example the French Jesuit philosopher, Michel de Certeau (1925–86). See, for example, his influential essay "Walking in the City," in Certeau, *Practice*, 91–110. In fact, as Borghesi,

However, it is necessary first to distinguish carefully between "space" and "place." Although the use of these two terms is complex and not always consistent,[71] broadly speaking "space" is a more abstract term, the setting within which places are located. Thus Pope Francis is not diminishing the importance of place or of the local. Indeed his insistence on synodality as a form of ecclesial governance suggests that he wants to strengthen the role of place, which would fit in with the emphasis on culture in theology of the people. This, though, points to what is meant by space and time. A culture and a people can only be constructed over time. In the words of *Evangelii gaudium*, it is only thus that it becomes possible to "generate new processes in society and engage other persons and groups who can develop them to the point where they bear fruit in significant historical events" (EG, 223).

Francis draws also on the polarity between fullness and limit or, in Guardini's expression, *Fülle-Form*. The theological emphasis here is on time understood in a broadly eschatological sense, as *pleroma*, the fullness of existence in God. Although the pope does not use the language of *theosis* (deification), his claim on the superiority of time can be understood as the journey of encounter in which God descends to humanity (the incarnation) and humanity ascends to God in Christ through the Spirit. Time is, then, about processes, or, in the language I am using in this book, about the ongoing experience of grace. *Evangelii gaudium* introduces this principle in the following way:

> "time" has to do with fullness as an expression of the horizon which constantly opens before us, while each individual moment has to do with limitation as an expression of enclosure. People live poised between each individual moment and the greater, brighter horizon of the utopian future as the final cause which draws us to itself. (EG, 222)

There is a tension (for Guardini, and, following him, Francis, it is an inevitable tension) between time and space or moment. Time is the movement, the dynamic progress of humanity towards God. What he terms "space" is the moment, the pinpoints on the map of the journey. But, as

---

Mind of Pope Francis, 238–43, makes clear, Certeau's major influence on Francis was through his work on Peter Faber (Pierre Favre), one of the founding members of the Society of Jesus, and one of the first saints to be canonized by Francis (in December 2013). For the influence of Certeau on the distinction between time and space, see Mikulášek, "'I Dream,'" 68–69.

71. On this, see Agnew, "Space and Place."

Certeau argues in "Walking in the City," these pinpoints are always records of what is not there.[72] Spaces are about power and immediacy and we could say that, if allowed to dominate, they are always ultimately idolatrous, since they reduce to this moment and this space the fullness towards which we journey. In a document he produced when he was Archbishop of Buenos Aires, Francis had already spoken of what he calls, echoing Guardini, "the bipolar tensions," and he reflects that "one of the sins that sometimes occurs in socio-political activity is to privilege the spaces of power over the times of processes."[73] Grace, in other words, becomes an entitlement to be seized now rather than a gift unveiled over time.

Unity Prevails over Conflict

The second principle referred to in *Evangelii gaudium* is that unity prevails over conflict. The use of words like "prevail" or "superior to" are clear reminders of the "bipolar tensions." Because time is superior to space does not mean that space is unimportant, as we have just seen. And because unity prevails over conflict is not to say that conflict is unnecessary. Indeed Pope Francis begins this section of *Evangelii gaudium* by affirming that "conflict cannot be ignored or concealed. It has to be faced" (EG, 226). This is important to remember. Conflict will occur.[74] Francis lived through the most brutal years of the military dictatorship in Argentina, and is only too well aware of the reality of conflict. But conflict cannot be responded to, either, simply by being conflictual or by being, as he puts it "its prisoners" (EG, 227). The call instead is to be peacemakers, creating a people and a place of peace. Francis does not himself use the word "*shalom*," but it is about being constructors or agents of *shalom*, in which conflict is not allowed to be the final word.

Acting in such a way,

72. Certeau, *Practice*, 97.

73. Bergoglio, *Nosotros como ciudadanos*, 4.1.1. The phrase "bipolar tensions" (*tensiones bipolares*) occurs for the first time on p. 13. "Bipolar" here is obviously not a medical reference, but a reference to two poles, two contradictory points, which have to coincide, something that Bergoglio, following the Orthodox tradition, tends to call antinomy; see the reference in Borghesi, *Mind of Pope Francis*, 66–67.

74. In a fascinating essay "The Grace of Conflict," Bradford Hinze draws on both Pope Francis's account in *Evangelii gaudium* and on Michel de Certeau, to argue that in situations of conflict the "offer of God's grace . . . can elicit an examination of conscience and a repudiation of prejudice and behavior that provide the conditions for conversion and transformation, repentance and healing" (42).

> it becomes possible to build communion amid disagreement, but this can only be achieved by those great persons who are willing to go beyond the surface of the conflict and to see others in their deepest dignity. This requires acknowledging a principle indispensable to the building of friendship in society: namely, that unity is greater than conflict. Solidarity, in its deepest and most challenging sense, thus becomes a way of making history in a life setting where conflicts, tensions, and oppositions can achieve a diversified and life-giving unity. This is not to opt for a kind of syncretism, or for the absorption of one into the other, but rather for a resolution which takes place on a higher plane and preserves what is valid and useful on both sides. (EG, 228)

I quote this paragraph more or less in full, because it seems to me to sum up very well the thought behind all of the principles. First, Pope Francis is realistic. It is possible to build communion amid disagreement, and it is possible because it has been done. But this does require special qualities in those who try to carry out this task, and even great people may not always succeed. An example would be the trip of Francis of Assisi to visit the Sultan,[75] where Francis succeeded neither in his initial desire of being martyred (something that the pope would, I think, consider as a temptation to prioritize space over time) nor in bringing the peace he wanted. But even those who are able to take the necessary steps must enter into solidarity, which involves making history, that is, entering into a constructive process that allows for opposites to bring life. The tensions are not resolved but the strengths of both are allowed to coexist, for the common good.

Francis is clear that what is needed is neither pure conflict—diversity without unity—nor pure unity without diversity.[76] In *Evangelii gaudium* he speaks of a reconciled diversity,[77] in which the differences are not destroyed but neither do they dominate. In fact, in EG, 230, he

---

75. For an engrossing account, see Moses, *The Saint and the Sultan*. Pope Francis comments on this story in *Fratelli tutti*, 3, though principally as a story of going out to the other.

76. See a sermon he gave on the Feast of Pentecost in 2017, cited in Massimo Borghesi, "The Polarity Model: The Influences of Gaston Fessard and Romano Guardini on Jorge Mario Bergoglio," in Lee and Knoebel, *Discovering Pope Francis*, 112.

77. The phrase is used in EG, 230, in quotation marks. The concept of reconciled diversity, or more specifically "unity in reconciled diversity," first entered the ecumenical dialogue in 1974 in a report prepared by the World Council of Churches after two meetings in Geneva. On this, see Meyer, "'Einheit in versöhnter Verschiedenheit,'" especially 99–100. See also Chapman, "Ecumenism and the Visible Unity of the Church."

does speak of "a new and promising synthesis" that occurs because "the unity brought by the Spirit can harmonize every diversity." Diversity and conflict are not synonyms and conflict must be overcome but not at the expense of a diversity that is, as the final principle will remind us, part of a greater whole.

The Reality Is More Important Than the Idea

But before turning to that principle, the third principle, as enunciated in *Evangelii gaudium*, is that the reality is more important than the idea.[78] "Reality," he writes, "simply is, the idea is elaborated" (EG, 231).[79] The emphasis on "reality" is a clear hint of the liberation theology influence on Pope Francis.[80] In this setting, there is an immediacy to reality that goes beyond discussions on competing hegemonies, be they antagonistic or agonistic. This is because God is both perceived and therefore understood as active in the world, the grace of God present in attempts to transform the reality as lived and experienced by the "people," those who are poor, excluded, oppressed, be it materially, because of their gender, their beliefs, their sexual orientation, and so on.

Francis uses here a comparative adjective, "more important," or elsewhere "superior" or, in the English translation, "greater."[81] It is not that the pope does not realize or appreciate the power of ideas, something that would be incongruous in a written document or indeed in the enunciation of sets of principles. Elsewhere the pope has expressed the same thought by saying that people concentrate too much on adjectives rather than on substantives. Although, as is often the case with Francis when he hits on a good line, he has returned to this on several occasions, he seems

78. In the Spanish of *Evangelii gaudium*, Francis always refers to the singular, *realidad*, reality, and mostly *idea*, idea, whereas the English translation favors the plural. The distinction is small but not insignificant, since, as the previous principle made clear, there are not ultimately conflicting realities, but one reality, one time, one eschatological *pleroma*. In terms of English style, the translation may be understandable, but it needs to be read with care.

79. This is an example of where the English text uses the plural: "Realities simply are, ideas are elaborated." The Spanish reads: "La realidad simplemente es, la idea se elabora." And where the Spanish refers to "una tensión bipolar," the English text speaks of "a constant tension."

80. See Regan, "The Bergoglian Principles," 11.

81. EG, 231: "la realidad es superior a la idea;" "realities are greater than ideas." This is also the form used in Bergoglio, *Nosotros como ciudadanos*, 4.2.1.

to have first made the remark in an address to the Vatican's Dicastery of Communication when he visited it in 2019. He said:

> The third thing I take from what I said earlier, which I am slightly allergic to: "This is something *authentically* Christian", "this is *truly* so". We have fallen into the culture of adjectives and adverbs, and we have forgotten the strength of nouns. The communicator must make people understand the weight of the reality of nouns that reflect the reality of people. And this is a mission of communication: to communicate with reality, without sweetening with adjectives or adverbs. "This is a Christian thing": why say authentically Christian? It is Christian! The mere fact of the noun "Christian", "I am of Christ", is strong: it is an adjectival noun, yes, but it is a noun. To pass from the culture of the adjective to the theology of the noun. And you must communicate in this way.... Your communication should be austere but beautiful: beauty is not rococo art, beauty does not need these rococo things; beauty manifests itself from the noun itself, without strawberries on the cake! I think we need to learn this.[82]

This passing "from the culture of the adjective to the theology of the noun" is what lies behind the claim that reality is superior to idea. Ideas are abstract and like adjectives they ultimately hide or obfuscate reality. In the Spanish text of EG, 231, the pope lists many "-isms,"[83] which prevent engagement with the person, with reality.

---

82. On the visit, the first official visit of the Pope to the Dicastery, which had been formed in 2015, there was a formal address that the pope encouraged people to read, and a more informal set of comments, from which this is taken. He also made a similar comment to a gay British comedian Stephen Amos, who in a private audience with the pope asked why people like him were excluded from the church. Pope Francis replied: "Giving more importance to the adjective than the noun. That is not good. We are all human beings and have dignity. It does not matter who you are or how you live your life, you do not lose your dignity. There are people that prefer to select or discard people, because of the adjective. These people don't have a human heart." See a report on Siedlecka, "Stephen K. Amos Meets Pope Francis."

83. The English translation retains some of these words, but not all really work in English, so some are changed. The Spanish text speaks of *"los purismos angélicos, los totalitarismos de lo relativo, los nominalismos declaracionistas, los proyectos más formales que reales, los fundamentalismos ahistóricos, los eticismos sin bondad, los intelectualismos sin sabiduría,"* which the English renders as "angelic forms of purity, dictatorships of relativism, empty rhetoric, objectives more ideal than real, brands of ahistorical fundamentalism, ethical systems bereft of kindness, intellectual discourse bereft of wisdom."

At the heart of liberation theology and indeed of theology of the people has been an emphasis on the primacy of praxis. In what remains the most influential work on methodology in liberation theology, Clodovis Boff, after a lengthy discussion of the relation between the two poles of theory and praxis, essentially argues for a priority of praxis.[84] In arguing for the superiority of reality, the pope is following a similar line. Ideas must be incarnated, must be practiced, or else they remain what at the beginning of his book Boff criticizes as "slogans,"[85] words that look good on a banner but that change nothing. Grace, in this perspective, is not a scheme or a program or a list of ideas, but something that is revealed in God's ongoing action in the world and interaction with creation. It is this reality that is more important than the adherence to the law, as we saw in the previous chapter. Indeed, we could paraphrase this principle as "Grace is, the law is elaborated."

The Whole Is Greater Than the Part

The final principle is that the whole is greater than the part, or as Scannone puts it, "the whole is greater than the part (and the mere sum of the parts)."[86] In many ways this principle ends up as a kind of summary of the others, offering "a practical implication of solidarity and subsidiarity."[87] Throughout his teaching, Francis repeatedly refers to the classic principle of Catholic Social Teaching, the common good, and the common good is always precisely that, common, for all together. The same attention to the search for fullness exists as in the other principles, here expressed as a "bipolar tension" between globalization and localization (EG, 234).[88] The danger, as Bergoglio expressed it, is that people feel themselves caught between "a globalizing universalism [and] a folkloric or anarchic localism."[89] The positive tension is one that is modelled on a polyhedron,[90] "which is the union of all the partialities that in that

---

84. See, for example, Boff, *Teologia e Pratica*, 328; Boff, *Theology and Praxis*, 190.

85. See Boff, *Teologia e Pratica*, 22–23; Boff, *Theology and Praxis*, xxii.

86. Scannone, *Teología del pueblo*, 267. Again, "greater" translates "*superior.*"

87. Turner, "*Pacis Progressio,*" 123.

88. See also Bergoglio, *Nosotros como ciudadanos*, 4.3.

89. Bergoglio, *Nosotros como ciudadanos*, 4.3.

90. For those like me who need to picture something to understand mathematical shapes, an obvious example of polyhedrons would be dice.

unity conserve the originality of their partiality. It is, for example, the union of the peoples (*pueblos*) who, in the universal order, retain their particularity as people (*pueblo*); it is the union of persons in a society who seek the common good."[91]

As with the other principles, here too it is necessary to avoid an exclusivist interpretation. It is not saying that the parts do not matter or do not exist. The people, as the quotation above makes clear, continue to exist, as do individual persons within the people. But the persons form a union to make a people, and the people unite with other people to make peoples. The polyhedron can only be such if it consists of multiple and diverse sides, but the two-dimensional sides only become three-dimensional (complete) when assembled into the polyhedron. The tension between the individual parts and the whole is not simply about the parts trying to break away from the whole, but the whole exists because of the tension.

Theology of Grace and the Four Principles

Before I turn to see how these principles are reflected in *Fratelli tutti*, it is worth reflecting on the theology of grace that underlies them. They stand first as an implicit critique of all theologies of entitlement, even if, because the polar tensions are not allowed to be reduced to one pole, they can accommodate the thought that such theologies may have something to contribute. As Francis says in EG, 236, "Even those who can be questioned because of their errors have something to offer that should not be lost."[92] But theologies of entitlement are always more interested in the immediate, in the gaining of goods now, rather than working towards the fullness of the Kingdom for all. God's grace is reduced to the moment, to the space that can be captured. Similarly they over-emphasize conflict, against the devil, against the other who is different, even against God, who is to be berated if he does not keep his side of the bargain. Grace is here weaponized, as a means of gaining a foothold and of getting rid of the other. The idea of reward and of entitlement is also the driving force, rather than the reality of people's lives. And finally the partial, the I, is at the center, as the donator and thus the recipient. Because these are polar tensions, these are

---

91. Bergoglio, *Nosotros como ciudadanos*, 4.3. He returns to the polyhedron in EG, 236, and in *Fratelli tutti*, 145, 215, as we will see in the next chapter.

92. I translate here from the Spanish: the English reads "Even people who can be considered dubious on account of their errors have something to offer which must not be overlooked."

not always simply bad behaviors, and it may be that there are situations where they are even necessary, as a protest against pushing God too far to an eschatological justification for violence. But they are in tension with something that is "more important," "greater," "superior."

Although theologies of grace cannot simply be reduced to word-count, it is nevertheless noteworthy that in *Evangelii gaudium* Francis uses the word "grace" twenty-six times.[93] With reference to Thomas Aquinas, he writes that "Works of love directed to one's neighbor are the most perfect external manifestation of the interior grace of the Spirit: 'The foundation of the New Law is in the grace of the Holy Spirit, who is manifested in the faith which works through love'" (EG, 37).[94] Grace is manifest, not in what God gives to us, but in what each person does in love for their neighbor. Because grace is of God, it is not up to the church to be its controller or arbiter, but rather its facilitator (EG, 47, and see also EG, 94).[95] The divine origin of grace gives it a primacy in all that the church does, including evangelizing: "The salvation which God offers us is the work of his mercy. No human efforts, however good they may be, can enable us to merit so great a gift. God, by his sheer grace, draws us to himself and makes us one with him" (EG, 112). This insistence on the primacy of grace is a reminder of the liberating power of grace that comes from God, the "ambience" in which we live, the train, in Boff's parable, on which we travel.

The pope also notes that "Grace supposes culture, and God's gift becomes flesh in the culture of those who receive it" (EG, 115), a fundamental claim, as we have seen, of the theology of the people. Grace is manifest somewhere specific, in a given culture, and the giftedness of God is received and practiced in particular settings. The theme of culture has long been important for Bergoglio.[96] Already in 1985, as rector of the Colegio Máximo, the Jesuit study center outside of Buenos Aires, he convened a conference on the evangelization of culture and the inculturation

---

93. The number of times the word is used is roughly similar to the count for words like "sin(s)," "salvation," or "hope", but much less than the words "joy" or "love."

94. The citation in the text is from *Summa Theologiae*, I-II.108.1.

95. See also Austen Ivereigh, "Close and Concrete: Bergoglio's Life Evangelizing a World in Flux," in Lee and Knoebel, *Discovering Pope Francis*, 39–40, where he speaks of the task of the church as "helping people open to the workings of grace in their lives."

96. Guzmán Carriquiry Lecour, "The 'Theology of the People' in the Pastoral Theology of Jorge Mario Bergoglio," in Lee and Knoebel, *Discovering Pope Francis*, 56.

of the gospel. Bergoglio gave a brief opening address to the conference in which he affirmed that "the diverse cultures, in their movement of ascent, are a reflection of the creative and perfective Wisdom of God. Cultures are the place where creation becomes aware of itself at the highest level."[97] To see culture as "the privileged place for the mediation between the Gospel and human beings"[98] is to recognize that culture is the setting within which God's grace is active.

But if that is the more general truth, it is not some abstract culture (the idea) that is most important. Rather it is specifically the reality, the "diverse cultures." In EG, 116, Francis puts it like this: "In the diversity of peoples who experience the gift of God, each in accordance with its own culture, the Church expresses her genuine catholicity and shows forth the 'beauty of her varied face.'"[99] The danger that underlies every turn to culture and inculturation is that the ambiguities of culture are ignored. The specific culture is never for Francis the yardstick by which to measure the gospel, but rather it is in the culture that the presence of God's grace is found, it is "in the gestures and simplest [*más sencillos*] cultural values that the profound wisdom of the peoples [*pueblos*] is hidden."[100] The hermeneutical key that is used to read culture and the gospel is a prophetic one,[101] that seeks to discern what each culture contains and reveals of the gracious presence of God. As a Brazilian writer on Francis's theology of culture has put it, "the task of a Theology of Culture according to Francis implies the recognition of the signs of the presence of grace, as the presence of the Kingdom in a globalized world, read in a Christological key."[102]

Grace, the liberating work of grace,[103] is thus a key element or even pre-supposition of Francis's theology. Grace is connected with mercy, with justice, and with the possibility of change and transformation. It

---

97. Bergoglio, "Discurso inaugural," 16. A version of this text and Bergoglio's concluding remarks to the conference can also be found in Bergoglio, "Fe en Cristo," 23.

98. Bergoglio, "Discurso inaugural," 17 = Bergoglio, "Fe en Cristo," 23.

99. The reference is to John Paul II's Apostolic Letter marking the beginning of the new millennium and the end of the Great Jubilee: John Paul II, *Novo millenio ineunte*, 40.

100. Bergoglio, "Discurso inaugural," 17 = Bergoglio, "Fe en Cristo," 23.

101. See Luciani, "La opción," 83.

102. Villas Boas, "Francisco e Teologia da Cultura," 781.

103. EG, 188. The Spanish "obra liberadora de la gracia" brings to mind the original title of Boff's work on grace, *A graça libertadora*, though in fact the Spanish title from the beginning was *Gracia y experiencia humana*.

is what unites, what helps restore the inner union within people that both becomes and accompanies the inner union of the people, marked as they are by a shared world or culture, which necessarily includes the political and the social and the economic, but is not reduced to any single element, for indeed in culture as elsewhere the whole is greater than the parts or the mere sum of the parts. In looking at *Evangelii gaudium*, I have investigated what is generally seen as the programmatic statement of Pope Francis's vision for the church. Many of the themes are present in documents such as *Laudato si'*, *Amoris Laetitia*,[104] *Querida Amazonia*, and others. But now I turn to the 2020 encyclical *Fratelli tutti*, since in it the Pope considers whether and how unity might prevail over conflict.

---

104. This title is obviously very reminiscent of *Evangelii gaudium*. Both Spanish and English translations begin with the same words: "La alegría," "The joy."

6

Fratelli tutti
The Grace-Filled Path to Liberation

On October 3, 2020, Pope Francis issued his third encyclical,[1] entitled *Fratelli tutti*.[2] Most papal documents of this type end with a date and location, a phrase beginning "Given at . . ." Normally the place is Rome,[3] and the date is often a feast day that is somehow relevant to the encyclical's theme. But in this case Pope Francis travelled to Assisi, on the Vigil of the Feast of St. Francis,[4] to celebrate a mass and then sign the document at the tomb of the saint. This unusual step served to emphasize the extent to which Francis wanted to draw on the saint whose name he had taken as pontiff[5] as an example of how to engage with division. In what follows I will examine the encyclical to see how it suggests a liberating theology of grace can inform a hegemonic discourse that seeks to transcend its own limitations.

---

1. The first, *Lumen Fidei*, issued in 2013, was started by Benedict XVI, and finished by Francis. Thus, the two encyclicals that Francis himself has written are *Fratelli tutti* and his landmark ecological document *Laudato Si'* (2015).

2. References in the text will be marked FT and paragraph number.

3. The last encyclical to be signed outside Rome was Pius VII's *Il Trionfo* in 1814, on his return to Rome after his imprisonment in France. The title of the encyclical (*The Triumph*) is self-explanatory.

4. The feast day is October 4.

5. The Minister General of the Order of Friars Minor (the Franciscans), Michael Perry, OFM, reflects on Pope Francis and his relationship to St. Francis of Assisi in Michael Perry, OFM, "Saint Francis," in Wooden and McElwee, *Pope Francis Lexicon*, 160–66.

The opening words of the encyclical are from a phrase used by St. Francis of Assisi to address his fellow Franciscans, in a work called *Admonitions*. These words of advice invite all members of the order to attend "to the Good Shepherd who to save his sheep bore the sufferings of the cross."[6] Specifically the Pope draws on the following Admonition: "Blessed is the servant who would love and fear his brother as much when he was far from him, as when he were next to him, and would say nothing behind his back that he would not say with love in his presence."[7] The encyclical seeks to complement the previous encyclical, *Laudato Si'*, which had encouraged a closer attention (with St. Francis) to the world around us.[8] *Fratelli tutti* focuses on "the poor, the abandoned, the infirm and the outcast, the least of his brothers and sisters" (FT, 2).

The introduction already points to the re-emergence of Francis's four principles, even if not yet stated explicitly. Especially he seeks to show how unity can prevail over conflict and time over space, through a recognition that the reality is more than the idea. Even the quotation from St. Francis can be read as another way of stating the claim that time is greater than space, since fullness of love is found in being present to those who are near or far, rather than concentrating only on those who immediately impinge on our existence. *Fratelli tutti* is a document that not only speaks of "human fraternity and social friendship," but grows out of its practice[9] and aims to encourage the practice (for reality is greater than idea). Francis writes:

> The following pages do not claim to offer a complete teaching on fraternal love, but rather to consider its universal scope, its openness to every man and woman. I offer this social Encyclical as a modest contribution to continued reflection, in the hope that in the face of present-day attempts to eliminate or ignore others, we may prove capable of responding with a new vision of

---

6. The Italian text reads: "Guardiamo con attenzione, fratelli tutti, il buon pastore che per salvare le sue pecore sostenne la passione della croce."

7. This is Admonition 25, one of a series of "Beatitudes," running from Admonition 13 to 26. On some of the background or parallels to this, see Karris, "St. Francis." Karris is also responsible for the most recent English-language edition of the Admonitions: Karris, *Admonitions*.

8. The Spanish for "environment", *medio ambiente* (Portuguese: *meio ambiente*) has as its literal meaning "the ambient medium," that is, the world around us.

9. It is particularly significant that he mentions by name the Ecumenical Patriarch Bartholomew, but also the Grand Imam Ahmad Al-Tayyeb, whom he had met in Abu Dhabi (FT, 5).

fraternity and social friendship that will not remain at the level of words. Although I have written it from the Christian convictions that inspire and sustain me, I have sought to make this reflection an invitation to dialogue among all people of good will. (FT, 6)

In terms of the language of hegemonic discourse, or the language of entitlement, the pope is trying to engage in an exercise of seeking for unity that does not deny or lament difference (conflict). In this sense, he is engaging in an agonistic enterprise, something that will become even clearer as he condemns in unequivocal terms certain behaviors and discourses. But for him all are capable of turning to the other, of welcoming and loving every brother and sister, far or near. The pope does not for a moment think that this is a description of life as it is everywhere, but it is part of the utopia towards which we need to journey in eschatological hope.[10] This utopic dimension of culture is important for Francis and for the theology of the people, as a Brazilian theologian, Alex Villas Boas, points out:

> In this sense we can name two signs of the presence of grace in popular culture. There is faith as giver and sustainer of the sense of utopia and of struggle, and there is the living and wounded conscience of the poor, that is, the conscience of needing others, because the *people* is the crowd of poor people who have nothing in which to trust except in God.[11]

In *Fratelli tutti*, the pope speaks concretely of dreams, of the dream of the whole of humanity, but those dreams are ultimately a form of utopia, of an end towards which we aspire.

Seeing the World

The first section of the encyclical is essentially the "See" part of the traditional "See–Judge–Act" method of liberation theology, "the perspective" in which "the Pope thinks and speaks."[12] Francis is aware that this part of the methodology of liberation theology is never intended to be

---

10. On this, see Borghesi, *Mind of Pope Francis*, 113, linking utopia to the polar tension of fullness and limit, where utopia is, in Francis's words, "journey towards." Borghesi refers to Bergoglio, *Nosotros como cuidadanos*, 4.1.

11. Villas Boas, "Francisco e Teologia da Cultura," 783.

12. Brighenti, "Documento de Aparecida," 691.

exhaustive, but always takes place from a particular standpoint and with a particular aim. His intention in the encyclical is to examine what hinders the development of greater fraternity.[13] The title of this chapter—"Shadows of a World Closed In on Itself"[14]—also points towards the Jesuit pope's emphasis on discernment. As Emilce Cuda, a leading commentator on Pope Francis, points out, his writings frequently aim at "desacralizing false gods,"[15] and that is only possible through the exercise of discernment.

Discernment always occurs from a particular hermeneutical standpoint, which in the case of Francis is that of the poor. Cuda indeed changes "See–Judge–Act" to "Discern–Judge–Act,"[16] since it is precisely the rejection of violence and the place of mercy that are stressed as Francis "sees" the world. Thus, in all that he writes, and clearly drawing heavily on his Ignatian background,[17] "The aim is not to produce a doctrine, but to discern about how to change the world."[18] To change the world for Francis is necessarily political.[19] However, the starting point for the political is the discernment of the transformative presence of God's liberating grace.[20] Ignatius begins his Spiritual Exercises with a period of coming to understand both one's own sinfulness and one's participation in the sinfulness of the world, in order that one might seek and recognize the merciful forgiveness of the Father, so that one is able to follow his Son with a more open and joyful heart. Similarly, in order to find a way to

---

13. In English, fraternity is a problematic word. Apart from the fact that there are no easy gender-neutral variants, it can, as many Latinate words in English, appear rather abstract. However, in the absence of a simple alternative, I will reluctantly stick with "fraternity," as the English translation of *Fratelli tutti* does.

14. The English title is "Dark Clouds over a Closed World," whilst the Spanish reads "Las sombras de un mundo cerrado."

15. Cuda, "Francisco y la teología," 591.

16. Cuda, "Francisco y la teología," 601. On the importance of mercy for Francis, see Ivereigh, "Offering a Precious Stone," who notes (326) that in the face of our current technocratic paradigm (see *Laudato si'*, 112) "mercy is ... countercultural."

17. See, for example, James Martin, SJ, "Discernment," in Wooden and McElwee, *A Pope Francis Lexicon*, 48–52; McEvoy, "Time of Choosing"; Rixon, "Dwelling," especially 306–8 on the importance, for Francis, of the First Principle and Foundation of the Spiritual Exercises of St. Ignatius.

18. Verstraeten, "Entering Fully," 105.

19. See "Necesidad de una antropología política: un problema pastoral," in Bergoglio, *Reflexiones*, 274–99, especially 276–81.

20. Ivereigh, "Offering a Precious Stone," 325.

establish or to grow universal fraternity, social friendship, it is necessary to see clearly what stands in its way.

It is not necessary to look in detail at all the shadows that Francis sees present in the world, since many of them are well-known and endlessly debated. The strength of *Fratelli tutti* is in naming them and showing succinctly and clearly what the problem is. Globalism, he writes, for example, leaves us "more alone than ever in an increasingly massified world that promotes individual interests and weakens the communitarian dimension of life" (FT, 12). When we talk about "opening up the world," it is only for the more powerful, so that there are fewer or no obstacles in their becoming richer and still more powerful. In general, this does not lead, as we saw in the first chapter, to the poor becoming better off, as the gap between the richest and poorest expands rather than contracts.

The pope also refers to what he calls the loss of historical consciousness (FT, 13–14). This is an almost Marxist plea for conscientization. Most nationalist and exclusivist political movements appeal strongly to an imagined history,[21] in which certain events are read as entitling a nation or a group to something that others cannot or should not have access to.[22] "Certain words like democracy, freedom, justice, or unity" have essentially lost their meaning. "They have been bent and shaped to serve as tools for domination, as meaningless tags that can be used to justify any action" (FT, 14). Consider, for example, how "freedom of speech" has been assimilated or abused by those who wish to lie and denigrate the other and remove their right to a voice.[23] This abusive disregard for lan-

---

21. For example, much of the Brexit debate in the UK about recovering control of our laws and our sovereignty was based on a reading of history that appealed to a rosy-eyed view of an English (not British) past that never existed. The Czech Republic hankers after a history that it does not really have. The centenary of the establishment of the first Czechoslovak Republic in 2018 was hardly celebrated at all in Slovakia, but was in the Czech Republic. This in itself shows why the Czechoslovak Republic was "the state that failed." Bolsonaro in Brazil harks after the dictatorship, despite its being a failure politically, economically, and above all morally.

22. Another example of this are the legends of great figures or armies of the past who will return to save the country. King Arthur and the Knights of the Round Table is an example from England (somewhat oddly, as Arthur was purportedly fighting against the Anglo-Saxon invaders), or the Knights who are said to rest in Blaník mountain in the Czech Republic. This is where the Europhobic former prime minister and president Václav Klaus said he would take himself when the Czech Republic joined the EU in 2004. The Knights were obviously far more relaxed about the idea, as they made no appearance.

23. See the remarks of the CEO of Index on Censorship, Jodie Ginsberg, "The

guage is one of the signs of those who seek to promote exclusion and hate (FT, 15–17). Such an approach ends up acting against the grace of God, because it seeks to limit, to exclude, to sow confusion, lies, and hatred, frequently in the name of some supposed entitlement. The superiority of time over space necessitates attention to history, to the ongoing story of God's liberating work in the world (grace).

The pope also condemns what he calls "the 'throwaway' world" (in Spanish, *el descarte mundial*). This worldwide discarding includes both material goods and even more cruelly people, the unborn, the elderly, the poor. All are surplus to the requirements of those who have. In keeping with liberation theologians, Francis believes that God is the God of life. As the head of the Roman Catholic Church, he is certainly not supporting abortion, as FT, 18, makes clear, but the right to life does not end with birth. Life is God's gift, the setting for the irruption of God's grace, and to restrict it to only the unborn is ultimately to make a mockery of God.

Thus Francis is very clear on the ongoing reality of poverty. As he says:

> the claim that the modern world has reduced poverty is made by measuring poverty with criteria from the past that do not correspond to present-day realities. In other times, for example, lack of access to electric energy was not considered a sign of poverty, nor was it a source of hardship. Poverty must always be understood and gauged in the context of the actual opportunities available in each concrete historical period. (FT, 21)

As we saw in the first chapter, poverty in absolute terms may have fallen in parts of Latin America, but relative poverty first of all still exists, and indeed in many settings it has recently grown worse. And even when people slowly have some of the basic necessities of life—a slow and highly unstable process—the gap between the poor and the rich or even the poor and the middle increases.

Human Rights

Alongside the deprivation of means for material existence, the pope also criticizes all other forms of deprivation of rights, decrying the abuse of

---

Far-Right," 66: "The far-right are not in favour of free speech. The far-right . . . are in favour of protecting the speech of their own interest group, not the speech of those who oppose them, nor those whose human rights—and very existence—they openly challenge."

human rights in many places across the world. The strong language used by Pope Francis in this context is a further significant development in the long and contested history of the Catholic Church's relationship to human rights, which has been described as including both "a historical convergence and the persistence of tension."[24] The underlying rationale for human rights is based on the dignity of the human person and the striving for the common good (cf. FT, 22). This at least places Francis in tension with appeals to human rights that focus solely on the individual or that more commonly are expressions of forms of entitlement, what we deserve, usually more than "them."

Support for human rights was already very strong under Pope John Paul II,[25] whose thinking was informed by his experience of the lack of human rights in his native Poland under the Communist government. But Francis has given even greater impulse, with even more pointed interventions.[26] For Francis this no doubt goes back to his experiences as Jesuit provincial in Argentina between 1976 and 1983 at the start of the military dictatorship in the country, when he was witness to abuses visited not only on those under his care, but on all sorts of people across the country. He had seen what happens when the dignity of the human person is denied and the good that is sought is of a small and criminal minority, who can even abuse the language of rights to defend their inhumanity.

The Rights of Women

A notable aspect of rights that the pope mentions in *Fratelli tutti* is to do with the rights of women. Repeating what he had written in *Evangelii gaudium* he notes that women are doubly poor, or in the words of the

---

24. Carozza and Philpott, "The Catholic Church," 16. For a fascinating account of some of the pre-history, much more positive towards human rights than is often recognized, see Lehner, *Catholic Enlightenment*. Lehner shows how both popes and Catholic thinkers were open to or promoted racial equality, women's rights, and other human rights in the seventeenth and eighteenth centuries.

25. See Hehir, "Modern Catholic Church," 125, and more generally on John Paul II, at 125–31.

26. For a fascinating piece of research on the measurable effects of papal visits on human rights' records, see Endrich and Gutmann, "*Pacem in Terris*." If I have understood the data correctly, Francis's visits have marginally more effect than those of John Paul II. Pope Benedict XVI was generally less directly politicized than his predecessor and successor, but he did not neglect human rights, and his visits also had a significantly positive effect on human rights' records in countries he visited.

Puebla conference, "doubly oppressed and marginalized."[27] It is open to question as to how far the Roman Catholic Church has genuinely moved when it comes to the role and place of women. The situation has changed under Pope Francis, though not enough for some (and needless to say too much for others). Male entitlement may prove one of the hardest of entitlements to shift. There is, however, a growing awareness in liberation theology, not least as an increasing number of women study and teach theology, that women's voices need to be heard ever more strongly.

This had begun already in the 1970s, with a particular attention to what was called the "feminization of poverty."[28] This attention to poverty has marked Latin American feminist liberation theology,[29] but it is a slow process and much of Latin American feminist theology is still deeply rooted in North American and European debates. These are not irrelevant but the inculturation of this theology is an ongoing endeavor.[30] At the very least it has to be said that by drawing attention to the double oppression of women—as poor and as women—the pope has provided ammunition for those who feel that he has not gone far enough in the church in recognizing the place of women.

Here too the title of the encyclical has not exactly won him any favors. Whilst St. Francis was writing to his fellow Franciscans who were all men, the title does sound exclusive. So it was not insignificant that on his way to sign the encyclical in Assisi, Francis lunched with the Poor Clares in their nearby convent and made an unscheduled stop at the Basilica of St. Clare before going to the Basilica of St. Francis. The

---

27. The reference is to a note added to paragraph 1135 of the Puebla document, the concluding document of the Third General Conference of the Latin American Episcopate, held in Puebla, Mexico, in January and February 1979. See also Gutiérrez, *Theology of Liberation*, xx (either he was working with a slightly different version of Puebla, or there is a misquotation as he refers to paragraph 1134), and xxii and xxiii (these references are to the Introduction to the Revised Edition of his book). It is also now common to refer to a triple oppression, experienced by those who are excluded as women, as poor, and as of African or indigenous descent.

28. See Tepedino and Brandão, "Teología de la mujer," 296. On Ana Maria Tepedino, Maria Clara Bingemer, and Tereza Maria Cavalcanti, three of the leading lights of early feminist-inspired liberation theology, see Furlin, "Trajetória e pensamento intelectual."

29. See also Bingemer, *Latin American Theology*, 69–85, in a chapter headed "Gender and Human Rights in Latin America." The chapter actually focuses on feminist theology, partly because human rights' abuses are even more prevalent in relation to women in the region.

30. See, for example, Azcuy, "Indicios."

Pope's understandable desire to reference St. Francis has its advantages, but given the very different context of St. Francis's words, and the suspicion concerning the Roman Catholic Church in terms of its treatment of women, the title and even more the content of the document is not without problems.

Unity, Conflict, and Migration

In "scrutinizing the signs of the times,"[31] Francis is well aware of the wounds of the world, which give rise to and reinforce different forms of populism, especially right populism, in a vicious circle. He offers a powerful description of the way in which the fear of the "other," the "barbarian," leads to the building of walls, which themselves become a sign of the danger we face and a means of imprisonment (see FT, 27). He thus takes aim at all those who seek to use fear of the other as a means of gaining power. I noted in the previous chapter that the early Christians also regarded themselves as *paroikoi*, as immigrants and foreigners. Thus to reject the "outsider" is also a rejection of what it is to be Christian, despite the claims made by church leaders and others who desire to keep migrants out of their countries.[32] The pope is here developing a strong hegemonic discourse against all forms of exclusive and destructive right populisms (cf. FT, 28).

In the previous chapter we saw how one of the four planks of Francis's thinking is the principle that unity prevails over conflict. In the opening part of *Fratelli tutti* he presents the conflicts and their sources that act against unity. We saw in chapter 4 how José Ignacio González Faus described sin as "the masking of the truth with unjust egoism."[33] To read the signs of the times, then, is to unmask the truth, calling out sin—acting against God—for what it is. The presence of disunity is a sin

---

31. Second Vatican Council, *Gaudium et spes*, 4. On Francis as an interpreter of *Gaudium et spes*, see Faggioli, *Catholicism and Citizenship*, 99–100; Malone, "From *Gaudium et spes*."

32. In Brazil, the Bishops' Conference has condemned such attacks on the other and sought to support migrants. See, for example, the report at "Espaço cedido pela CNBB." At the time of revision of this text at the end of July 2021, more voices are being heard in the Czech Roman Catholic church condemning these attacks. They include people who previously had been silent and whose contributions are a pleasant surprise.

33. González Faus, "Pecado," 97; González Faus, "Sin," 197.

but also a symptom or sign of the failure to work for unity. As the pope describes it, we lack a shared destination or pathway.[34] Unity is difficult to achieve if there is no shared vision of what unity consists in. Space, the fighting for immediate advantage, would seem to have become more important than time. There were, indeed, as Pope Francis points out, possible signs of hope at the beginning of the COVID-19 crisis, but as many countries around the world have entered successive waves and people's willingness to make any sacrifices for others grows less and less, it is not obvious that there will be long-term change for the better. Francis writes:

> God willing, after all this, we will think no longer in terms of "them" and "those," but only "us."[35] If only this may prove not to be just another tragedy of history from which we learned nothing. If only we might keep in mind all those elderly persons who died for lack of respirators, partly as a result of the dismantling, year after year, of healthcare systems.[36] If only this immense sorrow may not prove useless, but enable us to take a step forward towards a new style of life. If only we might rediscover once for all that we need one another, and that in this way our human family can experience a rebirth, with all its faces, all its hands and all its voices, beyond the walls that we have erected. (FT, 35)

The challenge is to allow this experience to be one that enables a coming together of peoples, rather than further division, as the richer nations have access to medicines that the poorer nations cannot afford, so that

---

34. The English translation (FT, 31) speaks of a "shared roadmap," but the Spanish speaks of a *"rumbo comun."* *"Rumbo"* means something like "course," or "direction," so the problem is that we do not have a sense either of our shared destination or of the course we are taking—recalling Boff's parable, we do not know where the train is going.

35. The phrase translated here as "God willing," and in subsequent sentences as "if only," is in Spanish *"ojalá,"* derived probably from an Arabic expression meaning "if God (*alá* = Allah) were so to wish." The words "them" and "those" translate the Spanish *"los otros,"* literally "the others," which is in contradistinction to the Spanish for "we," *nosotros*. So, the Spanish reads: "Ojalá que al final ya no estén 'los otros,' sino sólo un 'nosotros.'" The original speaks not of a step but of a *"salto,"* a leap, something rather more dynamic. And the Spanish "nos necesitamos y nos debemos los unos a los otros" is translated in English simply as "we need one another," which leaves out "nos debemos". This could perhaps be translated here as "we need and are indebted to one another."

36. This is a good place to remember my friend from Brazil, Margareth, who died in 2018 because she was not given the medicine she needed for the disease she was suffering from, despite a court order instructing the health system to provide it for her. The minister of health at the time is now facing an inquiry for corruption. See Alvim, "'Se eu morrer, denunciem.'" Margareth was a good woman who died because of sin, structural even more than individual.

places where sanitation, food, access to healthcare are all limited become poorer, less healthy, and more prone to all sorts of disease.[37]

The call to international unity is, in the pope's eyes, juxtaposed with the negative attitude towards migration. Pope Francis, the son of migrants, has always had a particular concern for migrants. In *Fratelli tutti* he makes two points. One is that people should also have a right to remain at home (FT, 38), which may sound rather redundant, but actually is fundamental, since migration mostly occurs when the conditions at home are simply untenable.[38] A more just distribution of resources would enable those tempted to migrate in search of a sustainable life for themselves and their families to remain at home.

The second major point is that anti-migrant policies are fundamentally at least xenophobic (in the literal sense of the word, which is fear of the foreigner, or of the foreign), if not often racist or, to coin a word, misoxenist, that is, displaying hatred of the foreign or of foreigners. Examples of this abound, from the rhetoric of Brexit Britain to Salvini in Italy, and including Trump's America, Tomio Okamura in the Czech Republic, and Bolsonaro in Brazil. Pope Francis is very clear that such people do not defend Christian or human values:

> No one will ever openly deny that [migrants] are human beings, yet in practice, by our decisions and the way we treat them, we can show that we consider them less worthy, less important, less human. For Christians, this way of thinking and acting is unacceptable, since it sets certain political preferences above deep convictions of our faith: the inalienable dignity of each human person regardless of origin, race, or religion, and the supreme law of fraternal love. (FT, 39)

Christian values can never be defended by behavior that runs contrary to fundamental Christian beliefs.

---

37. On the great inequality of vaccine distribution across the world, see, for example, Dyer, "COVID-19." Despite vague promises from richer countries, the prediction that most poor countries will not receive vaccines is being borne out only too evidently at the time of writing.

38. See also FT, 51–53. These paragraphs point to the way in which the cultures of poor countries are challenged to become more like those of rich countries, rather than being allowed to develop their own way of life. The critique here is a central one of the theology of the people, which works with the indigenous culture as the place of revelation.

One of the correlatives of the growth in hatred of the other has been the power of what the encyclical calls digital communication. These forms of communication

> lack the physical gestures, facial expressions, moments of silence, body language and even the smells, the trembling of hands, the blushes and perspiration that speak to us and are a part of human communication. Digital relationships, which do not demand the slow and gradual cultivation of friendships, stable interaction or the building of a consensus that matures over time, have the appearance of sociability. Yet they do not really build community; instead, they tend to disguise and expand the very individualism that finds expression in xenophobia and in contempt for the vulnerable. (FT, 43)

Admittedly during the coronavirus pandemic digital media have served well in maintaining already established relationships. But the pope's words are a reminder of the dangers inherent in contact that is not personal. The current spreading of lies about COVID-19 vaccinations, or about the results of the 2020 American presidential elections, to name but two examples, are a vivid demonstration of how "realities" are created that are unconnected with the non-digital world. When a people is constructed around demands based on lies, there can be no restoration of the "Gemüt," the heart of the world that unites within us, as individuals and communities, what it is to be most fully human.

The Good Samaritan

With its focus on the parable of the Good Samaritan (Luke 10:25–37), *Fratelli tutti* moves to the "judge" part of the liberation methodology, bringing into conversation the situation and the Word of God. This parable, with its message of disinterested practical love and care of the poor, has long been a favorite among liberation theologians.[39] The call to love for the other is present from the story of Cain and Abel onwards, including the frequent exhortations to look after the stranger (the resident alien or *gēr*).[40] The Spanish version of the encyclical translates this

---

39. For more on this and references to liberation theologians who work with this parable, see Noble, *Poor in Liberation Theology*, 17–19.

40. See Noble, *Mission*, 17–23.

not as "*extranjero*" or "*forastero*,"[41] but as "*migrante*" (FT, 61). A similar translation of the verse was used already by Pope Francis in *Gaudete et Exultate* 103, where the word "*emigrante*" is employed. The "stranger," the one who draws near from outside of where I am, is always therefore also a migrant. The response of the Samaritan to the man in need thus doubly subverts the perspective, since the one who does good is, from a Jewish perspective, an outsider, but now the reader is forced to see things from the perspective of this "outsider," this Samaritan. What unites us is that we are all strangers, all "outsiders" somewhere.

For Francis one of the most important things that the Samaritan offers to the wounded other is his time. Indeed, it would be hard to find a better illustration of his principle that time is more important than space. Space in the story is what prevents people drawing close to each other, the fear of being contaminated or threatened, the worry of one's own time being compromised. For the pope, the Samaritan can "re-place" his plans for the day, to give of his time (cf. FT, 63); he recognizes that "life is not simply time that passes; life is a time for interactions."[42] Much of the time, many of us, the Pope observes, do walk by on the other side. The fact that the first two people who pass by are religious people illustrates that

> belief in God and the worship of God are not enough to ensure that we are actually living in a way pleasing to God. A believer may be untrue to everything that his faith demands of him, and yet think he is close to God and better than others. . . . Paradoxically, those who claim to be unbelievers can sometimes put God's will into practice better than believers. (FT, 74)

Allowing oneself to be interrogated by the face of the other is painful and demanding and "religious" people are as capable of anyone else of putting off the pain and the demands.

But, because "the whole is greater than the part, but it is also greater than the sum of its parts" (the Pope repeats this principle in FT, 78), there is a way of responding that can change the world. The Samaritan stops, the innkeeper takes the injured man in, health can be restored, hope can return in a broken world, if each and all combine to do what they can. The call is to overcome a world based on division and hatred

---

41. The first is used by the *Reina-Valera Actualizada* translation and by the *Biblia Latinoamericana*, the second by the Spanish version of the Jerusalem Bible.

42. FT, 66, quoting the Pope's *Video Message to the TED Conference in Vancouver* (26 April 2017), also in *L'Osservatore Romano*, 27 April, 2017, 7.

of the other for being different. Francis ends this section of *Fratelli tutti* with a confession:

> I sometimes wonder why, in light of this, it took so long for the Church unequivocally to condemn slavery and various forms of violence. Today, with our developed spirituality and theology, we have no excuses. Still, there are those who appear to feel encouraged or at least permitted by their faith to support varieties of narrow and violent nationalism, xenophobia and contempt, and even the mistreatment of those who are different. Faith, and the humanism it inspires, must maintain a critical sense in the face of these tendencies, and prompt an immediate response whenever they rear their head. For this reason, it is important that catechesis and preaching speak more directly and clearly about the social meaning of existence, the fraternal dimension of spirituality, our conviction of the inalienable dignity of each person, and our reasons for loving and accepting all our brothers and sisters. (FT, 86)

Of course, there are those who would argue that the Roman Catholic Church and other churches too still foster forms of exclusion (based on gender or sexuality, for example). But that might be to miss the point. The emphasis on the inalienable dignity of each person and the need to love and accept all our brothers and sisters can be taken at face-value. However, love of all is not agreement with all, and those who use their faith to justify xenophobia, violent and narrow nationalisms, mistreatment of those who are different, stand condemned. It is not a case of understanding the Bible differently. Evil is evil, perhaps especially when carried out by those who claim to be Christian.[43]

The Importance of the Community

Over against this conditionality of exclusion, *Fratelli tutti* posits the value of the communal. All theologies of entitlement are ultimately self-serving and thus individualist, even nationalist ones such as those present in the

---

43. *Fratelli tutti* was written in 2020 against the background, amongst other things, of the American presidential election campaign. But in condemning Christians who claimed to support exclusionary and hateful policies as Christians, the rejection of the abuse of Christianity has a wider reach than just Trump and America. The pope does not use the language of entitlement here, but his words are a critique of it, in Europe and in Latin America as well. The fundamental entitlement or privilege of being human is the ability to love God and one's sister and brother, wherever one encounters them.

Czech Republic. What "we," as the inhabitants of this particular segment of the earth's surface, are entitled to by that simple fact is also what I am entitled to over against someone born elsewhere.[44] But Pope Francis argues for the necessary inter-relation of all humanity. Human beings cannot "fully know themselves apart from encounters with others" (FT, 87).[45] That encounter should be in love, even if "some believers think that it [love] consists in the imposition of their own ideologies upon everyone else, or in a violent defense of the truth, or in impressive demonstrations of strength" (FT, 92). Hegemonic discourses that claim that acts of exclusion, of hatred, of violence (even, note, of violence in defense of the truth), are manifestations of Christian love are condemned, because they are intentionally destructive of the other. There is a strong critical element in the kind of love that Pope Francis proclaims, much as Jon Sobrino has noted is present in the love of Jesus for those whom he encounters. Jesus may indeed love all, both the poor, the oppressed, and the excluded, as well as the rich, the oppressors, and those who exclude, but his attitude to them, Sobrino insists, is not identical.[46]

A chief characteristic of love for Francis is its inclusivity, especially of those on the margins. There are two ways of reading the document in this respect. More positively, it focuses on the need to include those on what the pope calls the "existential" margins, those who are often neglected in our societies. He mentions the curse of racism and the marginalization of the disabled and the elderly. These latter groups are indeed marginalized and excluded and relegated to second-class status much of the time. However, there are other excluded groups who are not mentioned. Even the critique of racism (FT, 97), still a major blight in much

---

44. As the pope puts its, "Closed groups and self-absorbed couples that define themselves in opposition to others tend to be expressions of selfishness and mere self-preservation" (FT, 89).

45. As an aside, it is interesting that this claim is supported with a quotation from Gabriel Marcel (1889–1973), the French Catholic philosopher who after the war hosted fortnightly evenings at his home, attended by people such as Nikolai Berdyaev, Jean Wahl, and younger philosophers such as Emmanuel Levinas and Paul Ricoeur. The discussions about otherness continued in these philosophers in diverging directions, but Marcel was one important catalyst in bringing the topic to the fore in mid-twentieth-century French philosophy; see Swetman, *Vision of Gabriel Marcel*, 54.

46. See Sobrino, *Jesus the Liberator*, 79: "In order to grasp what it means for the Kingdom of God to have specific addressees and so to be essentially partial, we need to remember that Jesus offered God's love to all, but not in the same way."

of the world,⁴⁷ seems almost an afterthought, and there is no mention of those marginalized because of sexual identity or indeed of women who are still practically marginalized in many countries. It is true that a reading of the paragraphs of the encyclical on what universal love means allows for inclusion of a far wider range of the excluded than the examples the pope gives. Quoting an address he gave to young people in Tokyo, Francis writes: "'the future is not monochrome; if we are courageous, we can contemplate it in all the variety and diversity of what each individual person has to offer. How much our human family needs to learn to live together in harmony and peace, without all of us having to be the same!'" (FT, 100).⁴⁸ Too often people are still treated, in Francis's telling image, as adjectives and not nouns.

The problem, as the pope sees it, is that many have forgotten how to be neighbors, because each is so focused on their own narrow interests. We live, he says, "in a world that constantly witnesses the emergence and growth of social groups clinging to an identity that separates them from others" (FT, 102). This leads to a breakdown in the ability to be neighbors, to be alongside the abandoned, excluded other, to be vehicles of God's grace.⁴⁹ The balancing act that the pope is trying to perform here is to allow both for the variety of human existence, which will find expression in different groups (*pueblos*), and for the unity of humanity (*pueblo*). We are all, the encyclical wants to say, sisters and brothers, but we are not all identical twins. The danger he sees and wants to avoid is a kind of closed club with its signed-up members (*socios*), who can go behind concrete walls, enjoying the swimming pool and grounds, whilst outside, like Lazarus (Luke 16:19–31), people starve, because they are of no interest to those within.⁵⁰

---

47. Predominantly in Europe and the United States, but not only—racism remains rife in Brazil, for example.

48. The Spanish text uses the diminutive form "*igualitos*" for what in English is translated "the same": a more colloquial translation might be something like "spitting images of each other."

49. Here the word translated (correctly) as "neighbor" is in the Spanish text "*prójimo*," rather than the more normal "*vecino*." "*Prójimo*" is the more biblical term, referring not simply to the person who happens to live next door, but to the relationship between any two people who encounter each other. It is the word used in the gospel translations of the story of Good Samaritan, for example.

50. I have in mind a number of concrete (both literally and metaphorically) examples of such places in Brazil. Presumably similar places exist in Argentina too.

To put it in the terms of Laclau and Mouffe, the hegemonic discourses against which the pope speaks here have been readily apparent during the time of the coronavirus pandemic. Most bizarrely this has come about frequently in a refusal to wear masks, or be vaccinated, since this is considered an infringement of the freedom of the individual. Francis reminds us, however:

> Individualism does not make us more free, more equal, more fraternal. The mere sum of individual interests is not capable of generating a better world for the whole human family. Nor can it save us from the many ills that are now increasingly globalized. Radical individualism is a virus that is extremely difficult to eliminate, for it is clever. It makes us believe that everything consists in giving free rein to our own ambitions, as if by pursuing ever greater ambitions and creating safety nets we would somehow be serving the common good. (FT, 105)

Here too we see that "the whole is greater than the part." Freedom is not self-serving, and the story of Lazarus and the rich man is a permanent reminder that there is no inherent freedom to harm one's neighbor, the "other" who is alongside us. Freedom of speech is not the freedom to lie and to spread hatred and suspicion of the other, because they are of a different race, gender, sexual orientation, or whatever other feature of human existence is used to make fundamentally false distinctions. As we saw Nikolai Berdyaev argue in chapter 4, freedom is the creative impulse that drives us, and to turn it against itself is ultimately destructive.

But the reference to "*socios*" is a reminder that there is also something akin to a group individualism, in which the privileged parts of society combine to exclude those who do not contribute economically. So-called market freedom and efficiency are not enough to guarantee the well-being of all in a society, and indeed are frequently weaponized to attack those who are less immediately able to contribute to the aims of the market (cf. FT, 108–10). Here too there is an implicit condemnation of all theologies of entitlement that seek to emphasize the benefits for the individual over against others and the sinfulness of those who have nothing. The liberating grace of God works in building up a more just society, one in which people can live as sisters and brothers with a sense of common belonging. In *Laudato si'*, Francis laid out the arguments for belonging to the Common Home, and now he focuses on human participation in this Common Home, which necessarily includes a sense of commonality of existence. Because this is "other"-focused, aliocentric, it rejects any sense of self-entitlement.

Ethics as First Theology

Engagement with the other happens within the ethical sphere. As Emmanuel Levinas insisted, ethics is the first philosophy, preceding ontology. Both a theology of the people and Francis's own four principles reinforce the importance of the relationship to the other as fundamental for theology too. The need to escape from individualist tendencies is paramount (FT, 111). Rather, we are because we strive for good (the encyclical refers to the Greek word *agathosyne*, used in Gal 5:22 to describe one of the fruits of the Spirit).[51] The pope urges his readers to "return to promoting the good, for ourselves and for the whole human family, and thus advance together towards an authentic and integral growth" (FT, 113). The message of *Fratelli tutti* is both simple, radical, and practical. Either we destroy the world, and human relationships in it, step-by-step, or we set about restoring the world, and human relationships in it, step-by-step. Rather than seeing the encyclical as a top-down encouragement of grassroots change, it is better to see it as an example in action of what the pope envisages. This is his particular contribution[52] to building a better world, and he encourages each of his readers to take their own steps. Not all will write encyclicals, not all will be as widely heard, but that is unimportant, if each takes an appropriate step, because "the whole is greater than the part or the sum of the parts."

In order for this approach to work, there is a need for solidarity (FT, 114–17). Solidarity is the practical expression of a view of human existence that focuses on service to the other, and thus it also serves as a reminder of the secondary nature of the right to property (FT, 120, 123).[53] For Francis, solidarity is not a geographically limited concept,

---

51. The reference is found in FT, 112, which is linked to the Latin *benevolentia*, much stronger than the English "benevolence."

52. "A modest contribution," "*un humilde aporte*," as he terms it in FT, 6.

53. This is a restatement of a long-held Roman Catholic teaching. The right to private property is "a secondary natural right, derived from the principle of the universal destination of created goods" (FT, 120). This is not the place to go into the complex history of Roman Catholic teaching on private property, but this right never outweighs other, more fundamental, rights. For more, see Scarnecchia, "Property Law"; Oliynyk, "St. John Chrysostom and St. Thomas Aquinas"; Astier and Disselkamp, "Pauvreté et

either, since rights are rights, inalienable for all human beings, whoever they are and wherever they live. "As it is unacceptable that some have fewer rights by virtue of being women, it is likewise unacceptable that the mere place of one's birth or residence should result in his or her possessing fewer opportunities for a developed and dignified life" (FT, 121). I noted above that there is not a great deal in the encyclical specifically on women, which makes this sentence important. What is unacceptable is simply unacceptable, and discrimination because of gender is wrong, and this does not need to be demonstrated or proved.

The pope continues to develop the idea of a global solidarity, emphasizing the universality of humanity. This is particularly pressing in terms of response to migrants, implicitly at least including those who come (as the pope's parents had done) as economic migrants. Thus, the encyclical argues, "Seen from the standpoint not only of the legitimacy of private property and the rights of its citizens, but also of the first principle of the common destination of goods, we can then say that each country also belongs to the foreigner, inasmuch as a territory's goods must not be denied to a needy person coming from elsewhere" (FT, 124). Or, in the next paragraph, "If every human being possesses an inalienable dignity, if all people are my brothers and sisters, and if the world truly belongs to everyone, then it matters little whether my neighbour was born in my country or elsewhere. My own country also shares responsibility for his or her development, although it can fulfil that responsibility in a variety of ways" (FT, 125).

It is true that this may all appear "wildly unrealistic" (FT, 127, "*fantasia*" in the Spanish text), but this is in a way precisely the point. The critique is of the current system and the way in which it operates to exclude, to impoverish, to kill. From within, the system does not view it itself in this way and thus any other way appears unrealistic. But from a theological viewpoint, this is not the way to build *shalom*, and practically the system manifestly has not worked. *Shalom* requires a very different logic that seeks to improve life for all. This does not exclude either

---

propriété privée"; Hirschfeld, "Standard of Living." The first gives a good overview of Catholic teaching on property rights, linking it to developments in American property law, the second looks at the tradition of St. John Chrysostom and St. Thomas Aquinas (each of whom is quoted twice in *Fratelli tutti*), whilst the third and fourth both point to ways in which the teaching has developed and appropriated both John Locke and more recent economic theories.

business (for which we could read capitalism) or the ownership of private property, but always subsumed under the common destination of goods.

The construction of a society based on the realization of *shalom*[54] has profound implications for how human societies deal with the excluded, particularly again migrants. In an ideal world, he acknowledges, there would be no need for migration (FT, 129). Although the encyclical sees as the end result of migration a process of integration (FT, 129), it is important to see that this is not a one-way process, especially as the language of integration is often problematic.[55] At least as envisaged by Pope Francis, integration is sharing of gifts, a reciprocal process in which a new culture is formed (FT, 133–36). Rooted in the theology of the people, the pope does not want to see cultures destroyed—"A country that moves forward while remaining solidly grounded in its original cultural substratum is a treasure for the whole of humanity" (FT, 137)—but to serve as the basis for growth. Cultures are neither dispensable nor static.

For the pope, in order, however, for cultures to continue to grow and develop, they need to have an element of what he calls "gratuitousness" (*gratuidad*).[56] In a world that has been increasingly marked by a rather crude utilitarianism (cf. FT, 139), the encyclical suggests another way, where societies and nations do not do things because of hoped-for kickbacks, but because it is the right thing to do: it is "the ability to do some things simply because they are good in themselves, without concern for personal gain or recompense"(FT, 139). The degree to which subconsciously the language of utilitarianism has taken over is evident to the extent that the pope's deontological approach sounds novel. The only arguments against his suggestion that nations should welcome the other simply because it is the right thing to do are utilitarian ones: "they" could be a danger, "they" could use up "our" resources, "they" could threaten "our" culture, "our" religion. This way of arguing may accept that in an

---

54. For more on this concept, see Noble, "Who Do You Say," on *shalom* especially 358–60. In the chapter I use *shalom* to talk about the aim of encounter with the migrant other, which has much in common with the approach favored by Pope Francis.

55. See, for example, Sunier, "Religious Newcomers." See also the *Journal of International Migration and Integration*, which has been publishing articles on this topic since 2000.

56. In English the word "gratuitous" often has the rather pejorative sense of "uncalled for" (as in phrases like "gratuitous violence" or a "gratuitous insult"). That is why in its first use in FT, 139, the English translation places the word in quotation marks. In Spanish and Portuguese the adjective "gratuito" can also mean "free", as in of no cost, and the meaning here is that; to give freely of what we have received.

ideal universe it would be right to welcome all, but it suggests that the benefits of not doing so bring greater happiness to the greater number.

It also implies a sense of entitlement, which I indicated above by repeated use of the word "our." We have rights that are peculiar in this place to us, and others should not be allowed to enjoy them. The linguistic relation between grace and gratuitousness is not accidental, however. The pope's theology of grace insists that God breaks through all barriers and is at work everywhere. In opposition to a theology of grace that supports positions of entitlement, this grace is liberating and transformative. Grace is not utilitarian and therefore ethics is always fundamentally social. As one writer, offering a summary of the novelty of the pope's development of Catholic ethical teaching puts it, "For Francis, it is not simply that individuals make choices in a social context. It is that the *individuals themselves are essentially social*—thoroughly enculturated in the way that they perceive the world, grasp their own flourishing, understand their obligations, and make their choices."[57] This social dimension is moreover a universal social dimension, one that sees people as being interrelated not only within cultures but across cultures too.

The encyclical develops this latter point by criticizing a kind of cultural parochialism that cannot see the good elsewhere. Of course, the pope's insistence on the importance of local cultures means that he does not subscribe to the opposite danger, of disparaging one's own culture (FT, 145, where once again he returns to the image of the polyhedron and the whole being greater than the parts). The insistence on this particular polarity is found most clearly expressed in FT, 149, where Francis writes:

> For a healthy relationship between love of one's native land and a sound sense of belonging to our larger human family, it is helpful to keep in mind that global society is not the sum total of different countries, but rather the communion that exists among them. The mutual sense of belonging is prior to the emergence of individual groups. Each particular group becomes part of the fabric of universal communion and there discovers its own beauty. All individuals, whatever their origin, know that they are part of the greater human family, without which they will not be able to understand themselves fully.

This is a fundamental presupposition of his beliefs, the guiding language of his hegemonic discourse. In this sense the pope is expressing what the

---

57. Kaveny, "Catholic Healthcare Ethics," 192.

very descriptor "Roman Catholic" suggests, the necessary interrelation and "bipolar tension" between the particular (Roman) and the universal (Catholic). The antinomy becomes creative and life-giving in a way that concentration on either pole cannot be.

It is also a theology of grace. A heart open to all is a grace-filled heart, a liberating heart. This theology of grace is radically opposed to the theology of grace implicated in theologies of entitlement, since it is an outward-looking approach. *Shalom*, *Gemüt*, cannot happen through concentrating only on self and building up conditionalities of exclusion. For there to be peace, for there to be wholeness, the heart must be inclusive, building up from what it has and is to include the good of the whole of creation.

A Better Politics

To restore this wholeness we need, the pope suggests, a better politics.[58] This section of the encyclical deals with the issues I looked at in the first two chapters, namely the problems, both actual and theoretical, of populism. The pope begins by noting, as we saw earlier, that "populism" is a term that has been reduced more or less to a form of insult. For him, not surprisingly given his inspiration by the theology of the people, "people" is an important concept, what he calls "a mythic category" (FT, 158). Francis also concedes that there can be good "popular" leaders. He may be thinking of Juan Perón in Argentina, but there are others, such as, arguably, Lula in Brazil, or Václav Havel in the Czech Republic, or perhaps even less debatably Nelson Mandela.

At their best, the "service they provide by their efforts to unite and lead can become the basis of an enduring vision of transformation and growth that would also include making room for others in the pursuit of the common good" (FT, 159). But of course too often this is not what happens, as again can be seen in politicians like Jair Bolsonaro in Brazil or the Czech President, Miloš Zeman, who "seek popularity by appealing to the basest and most selfish inclinations of certain sectors of the population. This becomes all the more serious when, whether in cruder or more subtle forms, it leads to the usurpation of institutions and laws" (FT, 159).

---

58. The English title is "A Better Kind of Politics"; the Spanish is "La mejor política."

Again, in the language of Laclau and Mouffe, these are competing hegemonic discourses that appeal to the people, who are always constructed around a need. But the kind of need is important. It can be good or evil. In most cases motives will be mixed and there are no perfect leaders (and by extension no wholly imperfect ones either).[59] But either doing what the people want or articulating for and to the people what it is that they want is not in itself proof that what the people want is good and the best "populist" leaders are those who can draw people beyond themselves to a wider vision. In this sense, at least, Pope Francis is a populist leader, in a similar way that I have argued that liberation theologies are frequently populist. This is not, as Laclau and Mouffe argue, necessarily a bad thing.

However, populist or not, it would be wrong to dismiss (or indeed praise) Francis as simply "liberal." Indeed he criticizes what he calls liberal political visions, though he uses "liberal" in the Latin American sense, which is linked to forms of nineteenth-century economic liberalism, rather than to attitudes to morality.[60] Thus the pope points out that liberalism cannot create the kind of social unity (*shalom*) that he favors, because liberalism classically focuses on the individual (FT, 163). Freedom is an individual quality and set against the needs of the "people."

The encyclical, not surprisingly given the pope's insistence on the importance of each culture, does not propose a one-size-fits-all political approach. This is a kind of anti-hegemonic hegemonic discourse, one that insists (hegemony) on the need for both unity and difference (and thus anti-hegemonic). It certainly excludes those positions that would seek to limit charity (see FT, 164–65) to self or those who are like us. But the pope also seeks to lay out a vision of the playing field in which fundamental opposition can take place. Specifically, there is a need to decide that something needs to be solved. Here Pope Francis goes beyond what has often been seen as the tendency in Catholic social teaching to opt for social transformation.[61] There is a profound need, instead, for a systemic change in how societies interrelate:

59. Admittedly there are leaders (the usual suspects such as Hitler or Stalin), about whose leadership it would be extremely hard to find anything good to say. But the question then becomes about the meaning of "perfection" or "imperfection," a topic I will leave for now.

60. On liberalism in mid-twentieth-century Argentina, see Nallim, *Transformations*.

61. For a historic overview of the development of Catholic Social Teaching, see the essays by Aubert, *Catholic Social Teaching*, especially "The Great Themes of the Social Teaching of the Popes from Leo XIII to Paul VI," 205–39.

> Everything, then, depends on our ability to see the need for a change of heart, attitudes, and lifestyles. Otherwise, political propaganda, the media, and the shapers of public opinion will continue to promote an individualistic and uncritical culture subservient to unregulated economic interests and societal institutions at the service of those who already enjoy too much power. My criticism of the technocratic paradigm involves more than simply thinking that if we control its excesses everything will be fine. (FT, 166)

It is not enough to tweak the way in which technology (especially social media) are used, but a profound revolution is called for in how human beings relate to one another. It is, as we may expect from Francis, a change of culture that is called for. The term that he uses to describe the problem is concupiscence, a concept that goes back to Augustine, was developed by Thomas Aquinas, and returned to the twentieth-century theological debate through the writings of Karl Rahner.[62] This tendency (what St. Ignatius in his *Spiritual Exercises* would call disordered attachment) prevents seeing the other as sister or brother, and thus inhibits the development of the fraternity that the pope sees as fundamental for the creation of a suitable political engagement.

Against those who would decry this as naïve utopianism, Francis points out that there are community-based responses to late modern forms of capitalism that have been tried and have worked. Moreover, one thing that has been abundantly clear during the coronavirus pandemic is the inflexibility of capitalism, and indeed the tacit recognition that in such circumstances it fails (FT, 168). In modern capitalist economies "there seems to be no place for popular movements that unite the unemployed, temporary and informal workers, and many others who do not easily find a place in existing structures. Yet those movements manage various forms of popular economy and of community production" (FT, 169).

Something similar can be observed, in the encyclical's view, in terms of international relations. Here the pope notes the way in which nation-states really no longer function as purely independent realities, because human coexistence is in fact largely transnational. This can be seen in the arguments in England[63] at the time of the Brexit referendum about regaining sovereignty. Apart from the fact that the United Kingdom had

---

62. As noted previously, especially his early essay from 1941, Rahner, "The Theological Concept." On this, see, for example, Ferrugia, "Karl Rahner"; Jowers, "Conflict."

63. I deliberately write "England," and not the United Kingdom, because the other nations of the United Kingdom were largely ignored.

never lost its sovereignty, it has become increasingly clear that the cost of any trade agreement is always a partial giving up of sovereignty. But the pope is referring to a wider reality. This requires, for him, the strengthening of international bodies (such as the United Nations), where leadership will be at the service of the international community itself rather than of jockeying for position among individual countries. Here again he notes that there are alternatives, often in the form of non-governmental organizations that work internationally. Such groups[64] are one way of showing how an aliocentric politics might work. Politics is indeed necessary, especially to prevent the domination of the narrowly economic, which at least in its current form always and necessarily excludes. In this respect, the pope is fully in agreement with the long tradition of liberation theology's critique of the market. But the critique in itself is not an alternative, nor a program.

The Transformative Power of Social Love

We saw already in chapter 4 how liberation theology has stressed the transformative power of love. As the reference to different international non-governmental organizations already begins to suggest, the underlying thrust of the pope's political vision is the same, the transformative power of social love. In terms of my argument in this book, this is the inbreaking presence of grace at work in the world. Again this has to be understood with its full force. It is easy to dismiss the pope's call as unrealistic and unrealizable, but, as is often the case in such situations, the question of where the burden of proof lies is important. In his inimitable way, Francis gives some examples, which are versions of the approach that claims "If you give a man a fish, you feed him for a day. If you teach him to fish, you feed him for a lifetime." The encyclical puts it like this:

> It is an act of charity to assist someone suffering, but it is also an act of charity, even if we do not know that person, to work to change the social conditions that caused his or her[65] suffering. If someone helps an elderly person cross a river, that is a fine act of charity. The politician, on the other hand, builds a bridge, and

---

64. None are named, but one might think of the Red Cross/Red Crescent or Médecins Sans Frontières.

65. The more inclusive formulation is in the official translation on the Vatican website. The presence of such inclusive language is both a pleasant surprise and a small but important symbol of what the pope is getting at in the encyclical.

that too is an act of charity. While one person can help another by providing something to eat, the politician creates a job for that other person, and thus practices a lofty form of charity that ennobles his or her political activity. (FT, 186)

These examples serve to show that it is indeed possible to make changes that are expressions of social love. These have nothing to do with sentimentality, but are very clear demonstrations of how lives can be changed for the better. Although the pope does not stress the other side of the coin, that too should be noted. There are acts of social hatred, acts that seek to exclude the other, as migrant, as being of different race, as woman, as of different sexual orientation, as poor, as unemployed, and the list could continue. These expressions of short-term populism (cf. FT, 161) may of course provide brief satisfaction to certain segments of the population—those who feel they benefit most from them—but they cannot bring lasting change for the better. Such behavior is an example of what René Girard calls "scapegoating,"[66] and as Girard pointed out, this form of sacrifice always eventually demands new victims.

That is to say that theologies of entitlement, ones that seek to appropriate God's grace for their own ends and to make God subservient to the demands of the human, will always end up with dissatisfaction. Like the gambler confident that their big win is sure to come with the next bet, people can of course keep giving more and more in the hope that their return from God will be even greater and that faith may prove enough satisfaction for them for a while. But it is not liberating and in the end what comes will not be of God. However, this does not mean that the pope is siding with one particular political party against another. To a large extent, no doubt bolstered by his Jesuit experiences in Argentina, he is deeply suspicious of all arguments that deal with too many abstractions. The reality, as one of his principles insists, is more important than the idea. As he puts it: "Often, as we carry on our semantic or ideological disputes, we allow our brothers and sisters to die of hunger and thirst, without shelter or access to health care" (FT, 189).

This is reminiscent of the criticisms that were made by some of Mother Teresa.[67] It was claimed that in taking the poor from the street and caring for them she was applying a kind of Band-Aid approach, or

---

66. Girard, *Scapegoat*.

67. On some of these criticisms and a response to them, see Doino, "Mother Teresa and Her Critics."

what is called in Portuguese "*assistencialismo*."⁶⁸ That is to say, she was solving a short-term problem but doing nothing to protest the fact that people were dying on the street in the first place. The pope's point is that it is not a question of "either–or," but of "both–and." One needs both to care for those who are dying of hunger now and to work to change the system, so that in the future no one will die of hunger.

This multi-faceted response explains why we encounter the pope's favored "polyhedron" again. "Through sacrifice and patience, they [politicians] can help to create a beautiful polyhedral reality in which everyone has a place. Here, economic negotiations do not work. Something else is required: an exchange of gifts for the common good. It may seem naïve and utopian, yet we cannot renounce this lofty aim" (FT, 190). As noted above, again here the question is about where the burden of proof lies. Does the pope have to demonstrate that his suggestions would work, or do those who claim that they are "naïve and utopian" have to justify why they cannot work?

The pope wants to encourage the vocation of politics, but precisely as vocation, as a way of expressing service to the other. It is noticeable that the pope does not appeal to narrowly Christian arguments in this section, since clearly not all politicians are Christian, even in countries that are in some loose sense still Christian. Rather he appeals to what one might call a common humanity. Summing up his thoughts on politics, he suggests:

> At times, in thinking of the future, we do well to ask ourselves, "Why I am doing this?," "What is my real aim?" For as time goes on, reflecting on the past, the questions will not be: "How many people endorsed me?," "How many voted for me?," "How many had a positive image of me?" The real, and potentially painful, questions will be, "How much love did I put into my work?," "What did I do for the progress of our people?," "What mark did I leave on the life of society?," "What real bonds did I create?," "What positive forces did I unleash?," "How much social peace did I sow?," "What good did I achieve in the position that was entrusted to me?" (FT, 197)⁶⁹

---

68. The Aurélio dictionary defines *assistencialismo* as follows: "a doctrine, system, or practice that advocates and/or organizes and offers assistance to deprived or needy members of a national or even international community, to the detriment of policies that would take them out of the condition of being deprived or needy" (quoted in Fialho, "Assistência social"). See also Adriance, *Opting for the Poor*, 17–18.

69. This calls to mind the classic questions of the Ignatian *Spiritual Exercises*:

It is this eschatological perspective (therefore the perspective of the Kingdom of God) that matters most. What positive difference have I made? This is not the question for the political memoirs, but for the innermost part of the politician's heart and it may be a question that only God can answer. But if it is not asked, and if actions do not take place in the light of these questions, the politics will be lacking its most important element, that of constructing a new people, a new unity between peoples.

Social Friendship in Dialogue

Though politics is of fundamental importance, there is also a need for the fruits of a "good" politics to be implemented more widely, and this, the encyclical goes on to suggest, will happen through "Dialogue and Friendship in Society."[70] Dialogue is understood as "[a]pproaching, speaking, listening, looking at, coming to know and understand one another, and to find common ground: . . . If we want to encounter and help one another, we have to dialogue" (FT, 198). The British Jesuit, Michael Barnes, the most insightful contemporary theologian of dialogue, has argued that dialogue is not just necessary for theology and for encounter, but that the act of dialogue is itself theological.[71] Although Francis is not so explicit, his comments on the nature of true dialogue suggest that he would agree. Dialogue is, for him, about constructing a better world.

Quoting his words to Brazilian political, economic, and cultural leaders in Rio de Janeiro in 2013,[72] he says that a "country flourishes when constructive dialogue occurs between its many rich cultural components: popular culture, university culture, youth culture, artistic culture, technological culture, economic culture, family culture, and media culture" (FT, 199). Here we see the impact of the theology of the people, both stressing the importance of culture and recognizing that culture is a multivalent

---

"What have I done for Christ, what am I doing for Christ, what ought I do for Christ?" These questions form part of the colloquy with Christ on the cross.

70. The Spanish text speaks of "amistad social," social friendship, which I presume the translator changes because it is a somewhat unusual English expression. However, I am not convinced that "social friendship" and "friendship in society" are quite as synonymous as the translation implies.

71. See Barnes, *Waiting on Grace*.

72. The actual document referred to in the footnote is addressed to the "leaders of society," which in Portuguese is *a classe dirigente* (*la clase dirigente* in Spanish, the language in which Francis spoke).

reality in the lives of people. Indeed he referred in the speech from which this quotation is taken to one of the founding myths of Brazilian identity, the integration of cultural diversity.[73] However accurate a representation of history this particular myth is, what the pope is stressing is the need for encounter within as well as between groups of people. Dialogue is not, he says, a meeting of monologues, which it so often seems to be (FT, 200, 202). It requires a genuine turn to the other, a willingness to listen deeply. True dialogue has to be attentive to both the said and the unsaid.[74]

The need for coming together, working together, communicating together, runs through the whole of the encyclical. The document recognizes both the possibilities and dangers inherent in today's world. It points to the need for interdisciplinary engagement, so that one particular approach is not taken reductively as the only one. Media should also be used to bring people together, not to push them apart. The struggles for which way the internet and (often anti-) social media will go is another key area. Here the problem is often precisely the lack of social engagement. The bile that is produced by some commenters on the internet is very rarely the kind of language that people would use in face-to-face discussions. There is a kind of functional anonymity that prevents people from engaging with the other in a human way. Disagreement is important, and some people do behave in ways that are wrong and damaging to others, but finding constructive ways to communicate that disagreement is far more complicated.

"The solution," the pope argues, "is not relativism. Under the guise of tolerance, relativism ultimately leaves the interpretation of moral values to those in power, to be defined as they see fit" (FT, 206). It is important to be careful about what we label relativism. There is a huge difference between saying that truth is always relative,[75] and saying that we do not have final and complete access to the whole truth in any

---

73. The text is available at Francis, "Meeting." See section 1 of the speech: "It is only right, first of all, to esteem the dynamic and distinctive character of Brazilian culture, with its extraordinary ability to integrate a variety of elements."

74. Apart from hermeneutical insights from Gadamer and Heidegger, this relationship is also discussed by other writers. In his essay, "The Eloquence of Silence," in Illich, *Celebration*, 39–46, Ivan Illich argues that languages are only truly learned when the silences are understood, the gaps between the words, as much as the words themselves.

75. Of course, strictly speaking relativism can only ever make relative claims. It would be self-contradictory to claim that truth is always relative, though the claim is made anyway.

concrete situation. What the pope is arguing against here, though, is genuine relativism, where the argument is about who has the power to define a situation—whether COVID-19 vaccines are safe, who won the 2020 US elections, and so on. The fact that some people refuse to accept the truth does not render it untrue and attempts to replace it with alternative "truths" are purest relativism.

Francis illustrates what he means with an example. "Murder is not wrong simply because it is socially unacceptable and punished by law, but because of a deeper conviction. This is a non-negotiable truth attained by the use of reason and accepted in conscience. A society is noble and decent not least for its support of the pursuit of truth and its adherence to the most basic of truths" (FT, 207). Murder is wrong because it is wrong, not because it is against the law.[76] The serial abuse of truth is one of the most serious threats to human societies at the moment. It is not universal, nor is it present necessarily all the time in those places where it is prevalent. But it is depressingly common, in dictatorships like Putin's Russia, but in alleged democracies like Britain, Brazil, or the Czech Republic too, to name just a few examples. At the very least, it is incumbent on those who call themselves Christian and who support these regimes to call out and criticize their cavalier attitude to the truth. For without it society simply cannot function.[77]

The importance of this search for truth is repeatedly underlined:

> The dignity of others is to be respected in all circumstances, not because that dignity is something we have invented or imagined, but because human beings possess an intrinsic worth superior to that of material objects and contingent situations. This requires that they be treated differently. That every human being possesses an inalienable dignity is a truth that corresponds to human nature apart from all cultural change. (FT, 213)

Human dignity is not a social construct or a utopian dream, but it is, for the pope, the truth. It is not something that is up for discussion. All else must serve human dignity. So, economic choices or political engagement can only be justified if they lead to the maintaining and building up of human dignity. And human dignity is something that is shared by all,

---

76. Normally, murder is simply defined as unlawful killing, so what Francis points to is the way in which all taking of life is profoundly troubling, which is why he rejects the possibility of "just war."

77. On this, see FT, 206–10, on the basis of consensus (the Spanish speaks of "*El fundamento de los consensos*, so perhaps "agreements" would be better).

believers or not, and it is especially necessary to safeguard it for those who are excluded and whose dignity is threatened.

Nevertheless, Christians

> are convinced that human nature, as the source of ethical principles, was created by God, and that ultimately it is he who gives those principles their solid foundation. This does not result in an ethical rigidity nor does it lead to the imposition of any one moral system, since fundamental and universally valid moral principles can be embodied in different practical rules. Thus, room for dialogue will always exist. (FT, 214)

This is an important recognition. Christians have their beliefs and in thinking of the dignity of humankind, our reference point as Christian believers must always be God. But this does not mean the imposition of a single moral system. This is perhaps a surprising statement from a Roman Catholic church leader. But, as the pope argues, an insistence on "fundamental and universally valid moral principles" does not necessitate a single set of rules for embodying those principles. Francis does not give examples, but I would suggest that one fundamental and universally valid moral principle might be that economic systems should be at the service of human beings and not human beings at the service of economic systems. However, this does not tell us which economic system to choose, and dialogue can be undertaken as to how best to embody that principle.

Giving attention to dialogue will mean the fashioning of a new culture. Pope Francis quotes the great Brazilian poet and *Bossa nova* singer and songwriter, Vinicius de Moraes (1913–80). In one of his songs, *Samba da bênção* (Samba of Blessing), Vinicius writes, in the official English translation "'Life, for all its confrontations, is the art of encounter'" (FT, 215).[78] The quotation comes from a section of the poem that speaks of the

78. The Portuguese is more poetic: "A vida é a arte do encontro, embora haja tanto desencontro na vida." The whole poem is worth reading; the Portuguese text and music can be found at "Samba da Bênção." Perhaps one attraction for Pope Francis is that Vinicius was a pupil at the Jesuit high school in Rio. His Portuguese-language Wikipedia page also describes him as "an inveterate Bohemian, smoker, and appreciator of whisky." See Wikipedia, s.v. "Vinicius de Moraes," https://pt.wikipedia.org/wiki/Vinicius_de_Moraes. The entry also reports that he was married nine times, which may explain another quotation from his Sonnet on Fidelity (*Soneto de Fidelidade*), much-loved by one of my teachers in Brazil, where Vinicius says of love that "it may not be immortal, given that it is a flame / But it is infinite for as long as it lasts" (Que não seja imortal, posto que é chama / Mas que seja infinito enquanto dure). In *Querida Amazonia*, 46, Pope Francis also quotes Vinicius, from a poem that turns on its head Isa 2:4, noting how the good of the Amazon region has been transformed into weapons.

value of life. The poet says that he has proof, "a certificate that has been through the notary's office in heaven, signed below: God. The signature is notarized. Life is no joke, my friend, life is the art of encounter, although there are so many failures of encounter (*desencontros*) in life." For Pope Francis, too, life is this art of encounter, of knowing how to meet with the other in their difference and to find it not a threat, but a blessing. For the second time in this encyclical he draws on the image of the polyhedron, which "can represent a society where differences coexist, complementing, enriching, and reciprocally illuminating one another, even amid disagreements and reservations. Each of us can learn something from others. No one is useless and no one is expendable" (FT, 215).

To say that no one is expendable is to recognize the value of the encounter with those on the margins, who "see aspects of reality that are invisible to the centers of power where weighty decisions are made" (FT, 215). Ultimately, though, *shalom* can only be established through the practice of humility. In this respect, the encyclical says that social peace (*shalom*)

> demands the realization that some things may have to be renounced for the common good. No one can possess the whole truth or satisfy his or her every desire, since that pretension would lead to nullifying others by denying their rights. A false notion of tolerance has to give way to a dialogic realism on the part of men and women who remain faithful to their own principles while recognizing that others also have the right to do likewise. This is the genuine acknowledgment of the other that is made possible by love alone. We have to stand in the place of others, if we are to discover what is genuine, or at least understandable, in their motivations and concerns. (FT, 221)

Dialogue is not simply acceptance of all that the other says as true. It is to remain faithful to what one believes, whilst having the humility and the grace to acknowledge that our view of the world is necessarily always limited and incomplete. Clodovis Boff once noted that there is an inherent temptation for theologians to think that because they talk about the absolute, what they themselves say is absolute.[79]

---

79. See Boff, *Teologia e Prática*, 102: "In brief, theology is not absolute discourse. It is discourse of the Absolute" (Boff, *Theology and Praxis*, 45); "when theology undertakes to express the absolute of faith, it can do so only by means of human language—that is, something relative" (Boff, *Teologia e Prática*, 103; Boff, *Theology and Praxis*, 46).

The challenge is to build a new culture that will be an expression of what Mario de França Miranda calls "an authentic humanism," expressed in "care for others, true fraternal love, commitment to the lives of others, responsibility for justice and social coexistence, concern with the happiness of the other."[80] This call to cultural renewal can be read in light of the principle that time is superior to space. For a "cultural covenant eschews a monolithic understanding of the identity of a particular place; it entails respect for diversity by offering opportunities for advancement and social integration to all" (FT, 220). It is only the patient recognition of the good of the other that allows for the liberating grace of God to transform us.

For this to happen, the pope suggests, we need to rediscover kindness (*amabilidad*). Referring to St. Paul, who names kindness as a fruit of the Holy Spirit (Gal 5:22), Francis notes that the apostle uses "the Greek word *chrestótes*, which describes an attitude that is gentle, pleasant, and supportive, not rude or coarse. Individuals who possess this quality help make other people's lives more bearable, especially by sharing the weight of their problems, needs, and fears" (FT, 223). The "fruits of the Spirit" are in contrast to "the works of the flesh" (Gal 5:19). For my purposes, "the works of the flesh" are the rewards expected in theologies of entitlement (what I give, and more specifically, what I give materially, I deserve to receive back materially), whilst the fruit is gift.[81] In Galatians, kindness is linked to patience, thus suggesting again the importance of time, of the slow practice of daily attentiveness to the other (cf. FT, 224).

Paths towards *Shalom*

The practice of kindness, of loving attentiveness to the other, is one way to engage in what *Fratelli tutti* calls "Paths of Renewed Encounter." Perhaps reflecting on his own experiences under the Argentinean military dictatorship, Francis begins by arguing for the need of something akin to Truth and Reconciliation processes.[82]

---

80. Miranda, *A reforma de Francisco*, 162.

81. See Deidun, *New Covenant Morality*, 81, cited in Longenecker, *Galatians*, 259.

82. He mentions these specifically in FT, 231, where he insists that it "is always helpful to incorporate into our peace processes the experience of those sectors that have often been overlooked, so that communities themselves can influence the development of a collective memory."

> Those who were fierce enemies have to speak from the stark and clear truth. They have to learn how to cultivate a penitential memory, one that can accept the past in order not to cloud the future with their own regrets, problems, and plans. Only by basing themselves on the historical truth of events will they be able to make a broad and persevering effort to understand one another and to strive for a new synthesis for the good of all. (FT, 226)

The decision by Václav Havel not to establish such a commission in Czechoslovakia or later the Czech Republic has been regarded as one of his biggest failures, since it did not allow for the public unveiling of the injustices of the Communist regime. As noted in chapter 2, Havel's justification was that so many people were at least passively involved in the perpetration and perpetuation of injustice that nothing would be served by such a commission. But this left open the possibility of recreating memories,[83] and of people being able to ignore their own role. Arguably the results of this are still being felt in the Czech Republic. By failing to allow for any attempt to understand what happened, space was left for people to avoid telling the truth to themselves, or to others, and thus the possibility of encounter in truth is lessened. As the pope makes clear, truth is not always pleasant, but it is necessary. If the truth is told, then there is hope. For, says Francis, quoting his message for World Peace Day in 2020, "'We should never confine others to what they may have said or done, but value them for the promise that they embody'" (FT, 228). Again we see Francis's eschatological vision, focusing on the promise rather than the past failures. This is not to deny that people have done wrong. As we have seen, he is not supporting relativism, and he acknowledges that they may have acted badly. But that cannot be the endpoint of the discussion. Virtuous as well as vicious circles can be created.

Stressing again the superiority of time over space, the encyclical acknowledges that *shalom* is an ongoing process: "There is no end to the building of a country's social peace" (FT, 232). The starting point for this is the inclusion of the excluded, the poor, marginalized, oppressed. The pope is under no allusion that, without this, peace is not possible. In its early days liberation theology was often accused of supporting violence. But this was never really the case.[84] As with Pope Francis (and indeed the Old Testament prophets, or even Jesus himself), there was a

---

83. This is vividly conveyed by Noble, "Memory and Remembering."
84. On this, see Villaseñor, "Teología de la Liberación."

recognition that violence done to others was likely to engender violence and that there could be no peace built on injustice. Nevertheless, "Violence perpetrated by the state, using its structures and power, is not on the same level as that perpetrated by particular groups" (FT, 253). *Shalom* requires the building up of a new culture of peace, which in turn implies the dismantling of structures of exclusion and the incorporation of all into society. This incorporation is not itself an act of violence, if it allows for all to belong in their diverse ways.

The problem with *shalom* is that not everyone wants to contribute to it. There are no simple ways to deal with this, and in the gospels Jesus suggests that where *shalom* is missing the disciples on mission should abandon the place and go elsewhere (Matt 10:13–14; cf. Luke 10:10–11). What we are called to work towards, as far as *Fratelli tutti* is concerned, is a kind of "herd immunity" to acts against *shalom*. If enough people want it, it will be able to cope with the contrarians. The establishment of full *shalom* may be an eschatological event, but precisely for this reason it can and must be worked for already. The fullness may be still to come, but that does not preclude its manifestation in the here and now.

Forgiveness

It is this problem that occupies the pope in his discussion of forgiveness. Forgiveness is not the same as overlooking or denying that something happened. To forgive entails also to demand justice (FT, 241). The question is not whether we do this, but how. The construction of *shalom* requires a commitment to justice and a refusal to be overwhelmed by anger. It is not that conflict should be avoided. Indeed, in agreement with Mouffe and Laclau, the pope says that "Authentic reconciliation does not flee from conflict, but is achieved *in* conflict, resolving it through dialogue and open, honest, and patient negotiation" (FT, 244). That is, agonistics is the place for the encounter of competing hegemonies. These hegemonies are ultimately irreconcilable, but authentic reconciliation does not mean finding some kind of compromise position. Authentic reconciliation necessitates a refusal to define the other or self by a single characteristic (as victim or perpetrator, for example), whilst acknowledging the evil that was done as evil. It requires living with the tension.

To forgive is most definitely, however, not to forget (FT, 250–54), and the encyclical is very clear about the importance of memory. In this respect, the pope says that there can be no social forgiving, no imposition of a kind of "blanket reconciliation" (FT, 246). Again this is the problem that has been faced in the Czech Republic, but also elsewhere, where amnesty laws have prevented justice being seen to be done. And, says the pope, "In any case, forgetting is never the answer" (FT, 246). He lists a number of things that should never be forgotten, beginning with the Shoah (FT, 247), and also mentioning the nuclear bombs dropped on Hiroshima and Nagasaki, as well as "the persecutions, the slave trade, and the ethnic killings that continue in various countries, as well as the many other historical events that make us ashamed of our humanity" (FT, 248). These cannot be swept under the carpet, and need to be always before us, just as the memory of the good done, even amidst some of these horrors, also needs to be remembered (FT, 249).

Remembering what has gone before may help to prevent the resurgence of failed attempts to deal with problems. The chief among these is war. Francis is clear in this encyclical that recourse to the doctrine of just war is something that is almost inconceivable today. "We can no longer think of war as a solution, because its risks will probably always be greater than its supposed benefits. In view of this, it is very difficult nowadays to invoke the rational criteria elaborated in earlier centuries to speak of the possibility of a "just war." Never again war!" (FT, 258). War is always a failure of imagination, ultimately a failure of humanity (FT, 261). To avoid it requires a strengthening of the mandate of the United Nations and the active promotion of a fund to help poorer countries, so that war is not seen as a necessary option for gaining land, water, or food (FT, 257, 262).

War is social violence writ large, but the pope also speaks out against more individual forms of state violence, especially the death sentence, which, he says, "is inadmissible" (FT, 263). This is a challenge to all those who claim to be Christian and support regimes and governments that allow the death penalty. This leads to the absurdity of people claiming to be pro-life, because they are opposed to abortion, and yet supporting parties who favor the use of the death penalty. Indeed, the pope goes even further, arguing that whole life tariffs are really a secret form of death penalty (FT, 268). This is not because people are innocent or good, but because there is always the possibility of conversion and change. In practice, the pope might accept that, for their own good and that of society, some people will have to spend their whole lives in jail, but the sentencing of someone for the whole of their life without possibility of release is, he argues, inhuman and unjust.

The Role of the Religion in the Construction of *Shalom*

Much of *Fratelli tutti* is not particularly dependent on people having a shared Christian or even religious belief. The pope's arguments are trenchant and clear and the solutions he proposes, while necessarily somewhat sketchy, offer ways forward for the reconstruction of cultures of *shalom* that go against the inward-looking demands of theologies of entitlement. But in the final section of the encyclical Francis turns to the specific contributions of the world's religions to the construction of this *shalom*. Though the kind of religious language adopted in this section is more applicable to the monotheistic religions, Judaism, Christianity, and Islam,[85] there is no evidence the pope wants to exclude other religions. So it may be better to take at face value the pope's desire to include all religions, recognizing that this is not a text book on interreligious encounter. What is important, anyway, is the very fact of dialogue. Citing the Bishops of India, Francis says that "'the goal of dialogue is to establish friendship, peace, and harmony, and to share spiritual and moral values and experiences in a spirit of truth and love'" (FT, 271). As Michael Barnes points out,[86] dialogue is already a theological endeavor, an act of constructing *shalom*.

The pope insists that the world's religions and religious believers have something to contribute:

> From our faith experience and from the wisdom accumulated over centuries, but also from lessons learned from our many weaknesses and failures, we, the believers of the different religions, know that our witness to God benefits our societies. The effort to seek God with a sincere heart, provided it is never sullied by ideological or self-serving aims, helps us recognize one another as travelling companions, truly brothers and sisters. (FT, 274)

---

85. This final chapter begins with this affirmation: "The different religions, based on their respect for each human person as a creature called to be a child of God, contribute significantly to building fraternity and defending justice in society" (FT, 271). As phrased, this would rather seem to exclude at least Buddhism, though I suspect that was not Francis's intent.

86. Barnes, *Waiting for Grace*.

The world's religions and their classic texts are a repository of wisdom that can serve for the construction of the new culture of *shalom* that the pope envisages. He does not claim that religions have always acted well, but he does suggest that they have had the time to reflect on their mistakes and learn from them (time is superior to space). Moreover, in searching for the transcendent (God), there is a willingness to recognize as fellow-travelers all those whose search is the same, even if they name the goal of their journey very differently.

Drawing on the wisdom accrued over the centuries and millennia, religious believers, and in this case particularly Christians, have both the right and the duty to engage in politics. To some extent, the pope also justifies his own engagement, in this encyclical and elsewhere, in political questions. "It is true that religious ministers must not engage in the party politics that are the proper domain of the laity, but neither can they renounce the political dimension of life itself, which involves a constant attention to the common good and a concern for integral human development" (FT, 276). To refuse to side with a particular political party is not to be non-political, though in practice to engage in favor of the political dimension of life means making choices, always incarnated in specific parties. This has been the challenge of liberation theology in Brazil. It is also more negatively a problem in the Czech Republic, where there are no obvious parties to choose that would place a moral vision such as that of Francis at their core. That is a challenge, as we saw above, to a better politics.

Religion and politics also collide when it comes to the freedom to practice religion. Here Francis pleads for religious freedom for all, both for Christians where they are a religious minority, and for religious minorities in predominantly Christian countries (FT, 279). He also makes a special plea for increased effort to promote unity among Christians themselves, since, if even Christians cannot create *shalom* among themselves, it is hard to work for it in the broader world (FT, 280). At the end of the document, the pope recalls that "In these pages of reflection on universal fraternity, I felt inspired particularly by Saint Francis of Assisi, but also by others of our brothers and sisters who are not Catholics: Martin Luther King, Desmond Tutu, Mahatma Gandhi, and many more" (FT, 286). Those who have worked for peace are not just Catholics, not just Christians, but people from all sorts of faith traditions and none. Notably those he mentions by name are those who eschewed violence, for forms of direct non-violent action, agonistics, the confrontation of evil with good, of violence with a peace that is active and transformative.

Religion can promote violence (FT, 284), but that is a debased religion that goes against the God it claims to serve.[87] The aim of religion and religious belief is unity and peace.

The document finishes with two prayers, but the final paragraph refers to Charles de Foucauld (1858–1916), the French hermit who lived among the Tuareg in the Algerian desert and was the inspiration for the Little Brothers of Jesus (known in Italian as the *Piccoli Fratelli di Gesù*). No doubt he was fresh in the pope's mind, as in May 2020 Francis had approved a miracle that opened the way for his canonization (he was beatified in 2005). Of de Foucauld the pope has this to say:

> Blessed Charles directed his ideal of total surrender to God towards an identification with the poor, abandoned in the depths of the African desert. In that setting, he expressed his desire to feel himself a brother to every human being, and asked a friend to "pray to God that I truly be the brother of all." He wanted to be, in the end, "the universal brother." Yet only by identifying with the least did he come at last to be the brother of all. May God inspire that dream in each one of us. Amen.

To be brother or sister of all means first to become brother or sister to the least. The universal is always incarnated in the particular.

---

87. See the statement issued with the Grand Imam Ahmad Al-Tayyeb, cited in FT, 285.

7

Transformation through the Spirit

IN THIS CONCLUDING CHAPTER I want to take what we have seen in the study of Pope Francis and his encyclical *Fratelli tutti* and return to Brazil and the Czech Republic. I do this through the lens of a consideration of the role of the Holy Spirit as the giver or maker of life,[1] because grace is, at one level, the possibility of the construction of a new life in the Spirit, leading through Christ to the fullness of being in the Father. The Spirit is not, as in theologies of entitlement, a cashier who hands over our dues, but the one who enables change to take place, who opens the way for life for those under the threat of death, frequently literally, through conditionalities of exclusion.

The Holy Spirit, Giver of Life and Justice

The Second Vatican Council led to an increased attention in Roman Catholic theology to the Holy Spirit.[2] With the principal exception of José

---

1. The Greek text of the Nicene creed calls the Spirit *Zōopoion*, or in Latin *vivificator* or *vivificans*. The English translation (Czech and Portuguese are similar) speaks of the giver of life, which is obviously not inaccurate, but always seems to me to separate the Spirit from the creative initiation of life that are contained in the Greek and Latin references to making (*poion* and—*ficator* or *ficans*).

2. On this, see, for example, Balthasar, "Konzil des Heiligen Geistes," in *Spiritus Creator*, 218–36. As the title suggests, this volume of von Balthasar's works focuses on the Holy Spirit. Among the important chapters are "Das Unbekannte jenseits des

Comblin,³ this was, however, picked up in the Latin American church only in the twenty-first century. In the past decade a number of books have appeared,⁴ and a major liberation theology conference was devoted to the theme of the Holy Spirit.⁵ This is not the place to investigate this pneumatological turn in detail.⁶ Rather, I want to reflect on how a more Trinitarian—and thus pneumatological—theology can encourage not so much the overcoming of hegemonic agonistics, which is not possible, but the construction of a people, whose hegemonic discourse is one that consistently and constantly aims at the re-establishment of *Gemüt* and of *shalom*. That is to say, it proffers a discourse that does not claim entitlements but seeks to restore harmony and wholeness.

The desire for harmony and wholeness is precisely a desire, not an entitlement. Not all expectations that we have of God are about entitlements, at least as I am using the term in this book. Those who are poor, excluded, oppressed, may well have expectations that God will be with them, that the one whom Victor Codina calls "the Spirit of justice"⁷ will act on their behalf. But this will not be for something they have done. It will be because they are God's children and God rejects injustice because it is antithetical to him. As we saw with Pope Francis, for peace and harmony to exist, what is opposed to them must be excised. Although justice and *shalom* are not the same, the fulfilment of God's plan for the world will see justice and peace⁸ embrace (Ps 85:10). As Codina puts it, "since the Old Testament the Spirit acts in favor of justice between human beings as an anticipation of the eschatological justice of the Kingdom of God."⁹ This justice is both universal and at the same time focused on those who

---

Wortes," 95–105, and "Geist als Liebe," 106–22. The defining work of Roman Catholic pneumatology of the later twentieth century is Congar, *I Believe*.

3. Especially Comblin, *Holy Spirit and Liberation*.

4. Among the most important is the posthumous and unfinished work by Comblin, *O Espírito Santo*; Codina *"Não extingais o Espírito"*; Codina, *O Espírito do Senhor*; Boff, *O Espírito Santo*; Boff, *Come, Holy Spirit!*

5. The conference was the second pan-continental conference of Amerindia, a network of liberation theologians, and was held in Belo Horizonte, Brazil in October 2015. The main papers are published in Prada et al., *Iglesia que camina*. The title of the book was also the title of the conference.

6. See also Noble, "Holy Spirit and Reform."

7. Codina, *O Espírito do Senhor*, 47–53.

8. The Hebrew text uses the word *shalom*.

9. Codina, *O Espírito do Senhor*, 53.

are excluded.[10] The claims of those in Brazil or the Czech Republic who seek to reserve justice for a particular segment of society are at odds with the work of the Spirit, and for that reason alone it is necessary for the church to stand against them.

Political choices must be about life, not death. The Holy Spirit is the source of life, the Vivifier. As Leonardo Boff puts it, "To say that 'the Spirit is life' means that the spirit is continually creating and sustaining life, and that the Spirit is constantly beside and within the people whose life is diminished."[11] In chapter 3, we saw that ultimately theologies of grace that underlie and support a sense of entitlement are always essentially idolatrous, and idolatry is anti-Spirit: it is that which takes life away, denies the fullness of life by offering something less, but this less precisely as the absolute. This may be one way of trying to understand the saying in the Synoptic gospels (Matt 12:31; Mark 3:28; Luke 12:10) that blasphemy against the Spirit cannot be forgiven.[12] For it is to assume that life is not a gift but a right and that the Spirit exists not as the maker and giver of life but as a kind of genie who will fulfil our commands.

There may be more than one way of choosing life, but not all hegemonic discourses that make claims about supporting life are trustworthy. The burden of proof rests with those whose policies include any form of exclusion based on race, gender, sexual orientation, social status, place of birth, to name some of the major ways in which one group of human beings seeks to demean and dehumanize another group. They must, for Christians to support them, seek to show how the grace of God is being allowed to work in the world through their positions and demonstrate that they are not guilty of the sin against the Spirit, a sin of a sense of self-entitlement to well-being only at the expense of the other.

In his work on liberating grace, Leonardo Boff wrote:

> In the light of reflection on the Person of the Holy Spirit it was understood that divine grace, its experience, its salvific force that runs through history, the impulses of creation towards its final destination, ultimately divine life itself, are nothing but manifestations of the Holy Spirit, making himself present and acting in all parts.[13]

10. Jonathan Sacks speaks of the "universality of justice and the particularity of love." This is the chapter heading of Sacks, *Not in God's Name*, 189–206.

11. Boff, *Come, Holy Spirit!*, 162.

12. On this, see Luz, *Matthew 8–20*, 206–10; Lammé, "Blasphemy," especially 20–29 on the history of interpretation.

13. Boff, *Graça*, 313; Boff, *Liberating Grace*, 196.

Grace is the presence of the Holy Spirit, the working of the Spirit in history to transform history. This attitude is shared by Pope Francis. A commentary on his theology of the Holy Spirit notes that for Francis, the Spirit is "the principle of life in the faithful, in the Church, and in society." The commentary continues: "For Francis, the Spirit is the motor and dynamism that calls us to a reform of the Church."[14] Discernment requires listening to the voice of the Spirit, to choose the political path that offers greatest protection of life for all, born and unborn, from wherever they come.

Speaking against the False Prophets

The Spirit transforms history through the actions of human beings who are inspired by the Spirit to speak out against those who are false prophets. Writing in the context of what would turn out to be the last days of Judah before defeat by the Babylonians, the destruction of the temple, and the taking off into exile of its leading citizens, Ezekiel 13 denounces these false prophets. The chapter begins with the Lord ordering Ezekiel to prophesy against those who have "envisioned falsehood and lying divination," saying "'Says the Lord,' when the Lord has not sent them, and yet they wait for the fulfillment of their word!" (Ezek 13:6). Such prophets are not to be registered amongst the people of Israel "because they have misled my people, saying, 'Peace,' when there is no peace" (v. 10). Ezekiel also speaks out against those who have ganged up on the innocent:

> Will you hunt down lives among my people, and maintain your own lives? You have profaned me among my people for handfuls of barley and for pieces of bread, putting to death persons who should not die and keeping alive persons who should not live, by your lies to my people, who listen to lies. Therefore thus says the Lord God: I am against your bands with which you hunt lives; I will tear them from your arms, and let the lives go free, the lives that you hunt down like birds. (Ezek 13:18–20)

These three categories, those who lie, those who proclaim peace when there is no peace, and those who spare the guilty and punish the innocent, are also those who live with a sense of entitlement and make political choices based on it. They think that what they speak from their own hearts must be the word of the Lord, they aim to please and proclaim

---

14. Codina, *Espírito Santo*, 9.

peace for themselves when all around there is no peace, and they seek to serve their own interests ("handfuls of barley and pieces of bread") at the cost of the lives of those who are the special ones of God, the poor, the excluded, those to whom injustice is done. In turning against the Spirit, in seeking to maintain society in its injustice and exclusion, they are rejected by God. Those who follow a politics and a theology of entitlement either are or follow the false prophets, seeking an echo of their own idolatrous desires.

The Spirit of Unity and Diversity

False prophecy supports the disharmony and the fracturing of society beloved by all who are keen to profit from their sense of entitlement. But the Holy Spirit is always a Spirit of unity in diversity.[15] The body of which Paul speaks in First Corinthians is necessarily made up of many members: "If all were a single member, where would the body be?," Paul asks sarcastically in 1 Cor 12:19. It is only because there are many members (hands, feet, eyes, etc.) that there can be a body, but it is the body that gives meaning and function to the members. The great threat of any position of entitlement is to be totalitarian, both politically but even more anti-ethically.[16] All is to be seen from the position of the "I," whether that I is individual or communal, the Pharisee who is greater than the tax-collector (Luke 18:9–14), or the nation that considers itself and its needs as superior to those of any other. Jonathan Sacks points out that the great sin of the builders of the Tower of Babel is precisely the desire to reduce all to their own image and likeness by forcing all to speak their own language.[17] Sacks refers to the Qur'an 49:13, which in English translation reads: "O humanity! Indeed, We created you from a male and a female, and made you into peoples and tribes so that you may 'get to' know one another. Surely the most noble of you in the sight of Allah is the most righteous among you. Allah is truly All-Knowing, All-Aware."[18]

    15. See Boff, *Come, Holy Spirit!*, 138–39.

    16. Here I have in mind Emmanuel Levinas, in works such as *Totality and Infinity*.

    17. Sacks, *Not in God's Name*, 192.

    18. The quotation is in Sacks, *Not in God's Name*, 193–94. I have taken the full verse translation from Khattab, *Quran*. In a footnote, this translation refers to one of the *hadith*: "The Prophet is reported in a ḥadîth collected by Imâm Aḥmed to have said, 'O humanity! Your Lord is one, and your ancestry is one. No Arab is superior to a non-Arab, nor is any non-Arab superior to any Arab. No white is superior to any black, nor is any black superior to any white except on account of their righteousness.'"

Righteousness is imputed here to those who recognize that the other is not a reason for hatred or division, but for unity, for enrichment (unity prevails over conflict). Neither the Qur'an in this instance, nor the Bible, claim that there is any superiority to being part of one nation or another. As Jonathan Sacks also points out, Israel as the chosen nation is not made superior, but rather is made into a servant of God, and in the call of Abraham charged with being a blessing to all nations.[19] This is clearly not to say that there are not different languages, different cultures, different religions, different ways of seeing the world. But difference is simply that. It does not require evaluating and placing on a scale from least to most, from worst to best. This, I stress again, is a vital point to recall in making concrete political choices and goes against those in power in Brazil and the Czech Republic who seek to exclude. There is nothing wrong (indeed a lot that is very good) about being Czech, for example, but that does not depend on getting rid of anyone who is different.

The Spirit is also the one who gives life not just to individuals but to communities, and in a special way to the church. Because the Spirit that enables and leads the church, "the sacrament of the Holy Spirit,"[20] is also the Spirit of justice, there is a duty for the church to be a place of justice and a voice that cries out for justice. This is how Pope Francis has understood his role. The seeking for justice in the church is always a work in progress, and many times, both historically and now, Christian churches have not behaved and do not behave justly. But as one of the Roman Catholic Eucharistic prayers used in Brazil puts it, the church in its concrete manifestation is made up of us, "a holy and sinful people."[21] It is precisely as such that we ask for the "strength to build together [God's] Kingdom that is also ours," to work for the establishment of *shalom*. And this Kingdom, which is always one of justice and mercy and love, will not be built only outside of history, outside of the world in which we live, but within it, and that means, therefore, also having to engage with politics, with the way our societies are structured.

---

19. Sacks, *Not in God's Name*, 198.

20. Boff, *Come, Holy Spirit!*, 141–58 (the phrase is the title of chapter 11 of his book).

21. The phrase (in Portuguese, "somos povo santo e pecador") is taken from the Fifth Eucharistic Prayer, first authorized for use at the Eucharistic Congress in Manaus in 1975 and then permitted for use in the Roman Catholic liturgy in Brazil. For both the text and a commentary on this prayer, see Taborda, "Uma anáfora brasileira."

The Gifts of the Holy Spirit

Traditionally, the presence of the Spirit in the world has been named, though never exclusively, in terms of seven gifts. Drawing on the biblical text of Isa 11:1–2,[22] these gifts are listed in the *Catechism of the Catholic Church* as "wisdom, understanding, counsel, fortitude, knowledge, piety, and fear of the Lord."[23] But for my purposes we can group them together, first as "wisdom, understanding, counsel, and knowledge," which are only possible if based on "piety and fear of the Lord," and which can only be implemented through "fortitude."

Piety and Fear of the Lord

Piety and fear of God[24] are the most fundamental gifts, because without them the others run the risk of serving only to support our own prejudices and convictions, leading to an ongoing cycle of conflicting entitlements. These two related gifts are about one's attitude before God. It is the recognition that we stand on holy ground in the presence of God and the Spirit of God. In this sense it is the ultimate antidote to entitlement, because it is the recognition that we deserve nothing before God, and yet all the same God loves us and is with us (Emmanuel) and showers us with gifts. These gifts are not to be possessed, for then they cease to be gifts. The classic biblical image is the gift of manna (Exod 16). There is sufficient for the day, but when some of the people try to keep it, it goes off. And the gift remains finally unknown: the folk etymology in the bible is that the name comes from the question "*man hu?*", what is it? We know what we are entitled to and thus diminish it, but the gift, the fullness of grace, is always beyond us. As Louis-Marie Chauvet, discussing this passage, puts it: "Grace as a question, grace as a non-thing, grace as a non-value."[25]

---

22. On the Spirit in Isaiah, see Ma, *Until the Spirit Comes*, especially on these verses 180–84.

23. I use the formulation of the *Catechism of the Catholic Church*, §1831.

24. These essentially translate one word in the Hebrew version of Isa 11:2. Hebrew uses the same word in v. 3, whilst the Septuagint and Vulgate translate the phrase "fear of God" as respectively *eusebeia* and *pietas*, in v. 2, and as *pneuma phobou Theou* and *spiritus timoris Domini* (the spirit of the fear of the Lord) in v. 3.

25. Chauvet, *Symbol and Sacrament*, 45. I am grateful to my wife, Ivana Noble, for this reference.

The word "piety" itself is not an appealing one in most languages today. But drawing on the Roman concept of *pietas*, Leonardo Boff describes piety as "a filial relationship of familiarity and intimacy towards God, the Father/Mother who cares lovingly for God's sons and daughters."[26] The Greek word used in the Septuagint is *eusebeia*, the root word *sebas* meaning awe or reverence.[27] And it is this awe and reverence, this recognition of the closeness of the transcendent otherness of God who comes to us, that is captured in English by the expression "fear of God," which I already considered above in chapter 3.

Without this attitude, no other gifts will suffice. For the danger will always be of succumbing to the temptation to entitlement, to seeing God as a divine broker whose task is to maximize benefits for the individual or the chosen community, and to punish those who are outside. Fear of God is, then, ultimately liberating, since it allows us to recognize God as God and to accept our dependence on God. An old adage attributed (without evidence) to St. Ignatius of Loyola (and also to St. Augustine) suggested that we should pray as if everything depended on God and work as if everything depended on us. But Ignatius's actual words are more pertinent, since his stress is on trusting completely in God and his gifts and then acting. Writing to Francis Borgia (1510–72), the nobleman who would become the third Father General of the Society of Jesus, Ignatius remarked:

> I consider it an error to trust and hope in any means or efforts in themselves alone; nor do I consider it a safe path to trust the whole matter to God our Lord without desiring to help myself by what he has given me; so that it seems to me in our Lord that I ought to make use of both parts, desiring in all things his greater praise and glory (*mayor alabança y gloria*), and nothing else.[28]

As always with Ignatius, there is a search for what is greater (*magis* in Latin, *mayor* in the Spanish text), but a recognition that to leave all to

---

26. Boff, *Come, Holy Spirit!*, 178.

27. Barclay, *New Testament Words*, 106–7, says in relation to *eusebeia* and cognate words that "the root meaning of all of them is awe in the presence of that which is more than human, reverence in the presence of that which is majestic and divine . . . they also imply a worship which befits that awe and a life of active obedience which befits that reverence."

28. Cited in Walsh, "'Work,'" 128. The reference is to *Monumenta Ignatiana I.9*, 626. The letter is dated September 17, 1555. The article by Walsh offers a careful consideration of how Ignatius understood trust in the Lord.

God and do nothing, or to do everything as if there were no God are equally problematic. There is a need to use the gifts of the Spirit.

Wisdom, Understanding, Counsel, Knowledge

Leonardo Boff writes that "in the midst of conflicting messages, [wisdom] helps us recognize which ones make sense; it gives us a sense of measure and balance, which is characteristic of wisdom."[29] The Spirit provides us with wisdom, first of all to acknowledge that there are conflicting messages, and that not all of them are correct. Political engagement requires the wisdom to discern, to find the truth and follow it. Wisdom also requires, says Boff, measure and balance. This suggests that any kind of single-issue politics is not an expression of wisdom. Too often, the loudest Christian voice in politics is heard on such single issues, be it opposition to abortion, or to same-sex marriages, or to some other form of sexual or relational ethics. One of the imbalances of such approaches is that they end up in self-contradiction. In Brazil, for example, Bolsonaro has, on the one hand, suggested opposition to abortion, but has also praised the death squads of the dictatorship and ridiculed those who have died from COVID-19. Inevitably, as already noted, choices will have to be made, and often they will be complex and painful. But if they do not work for the poor, the excluded, the oppressed (including, but not exclusively, the unborn), then it is the wrong choice from a Christian perspective.

But measure and balance will also require speaking out against wrong-doing by those whom one supports. This has arguably been a weakness of liberation theologians in Brazil, at least until recently. There is a need to critique any form of corruption, even corruption that seeks to do good.[30] All forms of injustice, from the smallest to the largest, are destructive of the task of building the Kingdom. This means that support will always be dependent on discernment. This requires wisdom, which is not a question of being cleverer than someone else, but of seeking for God at work, for the transformative power of the Spirit. The gifts of the Spirit are those that enable us to perceive the presence of the Spirit.

---

29. Boff, *Come, Holy Spirit!*, 175–76.

30. For example, some of the Workers' Party politicians, who created fictitious posts that brought in salaries, used the money from the salaries for funding projects in poor neighborhoods.

Measure and balance does not mean that sides cannot and should not be taken. And it also does not mean that all sides in a political debate are equally good and equally acceptable. On occasions this may be the case, with the proviso that they are critiqued when they fail to do what they set out to do. But in many cases in modern politics, in the Czech Republic or in Brazil, there are political parties that are inimical to Christianity and to those who wish to declare themselves followers of Christ. This has nothing to do with apparent attitudes to religion; indeed it is frequently the opposite. The more a political party seeks to draw on the language of religion or morality, the more suspect it should be, since it often desires to impose its hateful (or hate-filled) message on all. Wisdom in this case is needed not to discern between approaches, but to recognize how best to respond.

Wisdom is the starting point for any process of discernment, but it is not enough. There is also the need for understanding. Leonardo Boff remarks that "intelligence grasps the whole beyond the parts, and moves from the parts to the whole."[31] This ties in closely with the principle of Pope Francis, that the whole is superior to the parts and the mere sum of the parts. Fraternity is the ability to understand "familiarity" as an all-embracing term, in which the family is extended to all creation. And this is liberating, for it unshackles us from the reliance only on the known and familiar and extends our universe, extends our existence. Understanding also requires recognizing that time is greater than space, because it takes time to understand, patience, the ability to wait, look, listen, and learn.

The Holy Spirit, then, allows us to appreciate diversity as a basis for unity. The problem with theologies of entitlement is that they see grace as emphasizing uniformity of the individual or group. This excludes others who are different, so that there is no room for understanding, no room for welcoming diversity as a basis for unity. And yet understanding and the gift of counsel are needed in making the effort to construct a picture of the world that makes sense to other people. The desire for familiarity is not to be dismissed and many people turn to positions of entitlement precisely as a result of experiences of being disentitled. This is the case in the Czech Republic and was the case with the election of Bolsonaro too. Understanding and counsel require, then, not simply an intellectual

---

31. Boff, *Come, Holy Spirit!*, 176. The translator of Boff's books uses "intelligence." I do not have access to the Portuguese version, but assume he must use the word "inteligência." The official Portuguese translation of the Catechism of the Catholic Church translates as "entendimento."

appreciation of what is going on, but some form of empathy that will enable or at least make available the opportunity for dialogue.

But dialogue in itself is not enough. As Mouffe insists, there is an agonistic encounter between two hegemonies that cannot be reconciled. There is no need for relativism, for suggesting that all opinions carry the same weight. Wisdom is needed to know which is the correct or better opinion and understanding to recognize that some opinions are dangerous, destructive, and ultimately opposed to God's plan for creation. Counsel requires engaging with those who are tempted to believe the lies, helping them to see that this is, in Ignatius's words, the work of "an angel of light," and that "if the course of the thoughts suggested to us leads us finally to something bad . . . all this is a clear sign of the bad spirit, the enemy of our progress and eternal well-being."[32]

The three gifts of wisdom, understanding, and counsel are all gifts of the Spirit for an agonistic church, one that attends to the "joy and the hope, the grief and the anxiety of the people of this age, especially those who are poor or in any way afflicted," because "these are the joys and hopes, the griefs and anxieties of the followers of Christ."[33] One of the many tasks of the church is to offer political counsel, because all humans are involved in politics, inasmuch as all humans are members of different societies that seek to utilise forms of governance. Because the joy of one may well be the sorrow of another, there will be disagreement, both within the church and outside. But wisdom and understanding show that it is not a matter of indifference as to which side the church walks on.

In rejecting certain positions (that are life-denying, exclusionary, based on hate) as at odds with being a follower of Jesus Christ, we return, however, once again to how far we should support the opponents of those who go around doing ill. If they bring less evil, (if they are more life-giving), the answer, at least in traditional Catholic moral theology, is that they can be supported. The criteria for judging whether something is more life-giving are, for Pope Francis, more deontological than utilitarian. It is not that this policy saves or enhances x lives, and this x+y lives, so the second is better. Rather, it is to do with who seeks to do good because it is good. Those who seek to build up society, to care for those who are excluded, to welcome the other, migrant or not, are those who

---

32. Ignatius of Loyola, *Spiritual Exercises* 333, cited in Munitiz and Endean, *Saint Ignatius*, 352.

33. The famous opening words of Vatican II's Pastoral Constitution on the Church and the Modern World, *Gaudium et spes*, 1 (slightly modified).

seek to do good. Those who reject the other, use language to demean and exclude, are not doing good.

Nevertheless, support cannot be unconditional. This was the problem that many proponents of liberation theology discovered in Brazil with their support for the PT. By assuming that the election of Lula had resolved all the challenges of corruption in Brazilian politics or that those who were elected for the party were all going to be somehow morally admirable, the party was allowed to act in ways that were wrong.[34] Not all its members and not all of the time, of course, but enough for it to become problematic and make itself the target of a still powerful opposition. To this extent, the agonistic church is one that is always against any political hegemonic discourse, since it presents its own discourse, one that is indeed hegemonic but whose hegemony is eschatologically tempered. The Christian discourse will speak against all parties, in different ways and with different severity perhaps, but it will claim that all positions are penultimate and incapable of giving true meaning to life, and that the fullness of the meaning of life can only be found in union with Christ (*theosis*). Political hegemonic discourses will ultimately be judged according to how far they enable or hinder the journey towards that union.

This raises the crucial question of how we can know what helps or prevents this journey. Here we need the gift of knowledge. It is now over forty years since Jean-François Lyotard published his ground-breaking report for the Council of Universities of the Quebec government on "the problems of knowledge in the most-developed industrial society," later published as *The Postmodern Condition*. The sub-title of the book is "a report on knowledge," and in it Lyotard distinguishes two kinds of knowledge, which he terms "narrative knowledge" and "scientific knowledge." Lyotard argues that science seeks to provide a discourse of legitimation (a hegemonic discourse), and that this discourse in modernity is based on a grand narrative that seeks to encompass the whole. As an alternative, he proposes narrative or postmodern knowledge, which is "not simply a tool of the authorities; it refines our sensitivity to differences and reinforces our ability to tolerate the incommensurable."[35] Postmodern knowledge is constructed through "small stories," which do not seek or need external legitimation. A story is a story and that is enough.

---

34. On this, see Bakker, "O 'mensalão/petrolão,'" 841, who suggests that the problem was that the PT moved away from its "religious roots." But arguably this was because its supporters in the churches also forgot their religious roots.

35. Lyotard, *Postmodern Condition*, xxv.

The scientific approach has been dominant and, in many spheres of life, this continues to be the case. The knowledge that comes from the Spirit is, however, closer to a form of narrative knowledge, discerning the presence of God in the world. This knowledge, along with wisdom, understanding, and counsel, allows us to tell the story of our world within the framework of faith. We do not have to legitimate the knowledge of what a good society is by reference to an overarching discourse that is susceptible to proof or falsification, but the common good is self-legitimating, through a series of small stories that build up the good of all. With understanding and wisdom this can be known, and it is why we can accept at least provisionally some political approaches and reject others. In this sense, to be a Christian is not to be ensnared in a grand narrative, because the narrative of the bible is about learning, about changing, about getting it wrong time and time again and still trying, still moving towards union with God in Christ through the Spirit. Revelation is precisely that, the gradual unveiling of the fullness of the mystery of God, something that will continue even after we see face to face (1 Cor 13:12), when we know fully that God is unknowable.

Fortitude

The major challenge facing any attempt to name positions of entitlement is to avoid replacing one entitlement with another. All hegemonic discourses have at least the inbuilt tendency to this sense of entitlement, to claiming the right of possession of what is perceived as "ours," or "mine." Conflict is, as Mouffe makes clear, inevitable. The false prophets, because they announce the entitlement to which the powerful and those who seek to latch on to them lay claim, will find a welcome and those who speak against them will be subject to ridicule and worse. In Ezekiel the false prophets are condemned because they claim that there is *shalom* when none is present. But the true prophets, who point to the absence of *shalom*, will suffer. We can recall Jeremiah being thrown into the well (Jer 38:6). The court officials urged King Zedekiah: "'This man ought to be put to death, because he is discouraging the soldiers who are left in this city, and all the people, by speaking such words to them. For this man is not seeking the welfare of this people, but their harm'" (Jer 38:4).

To speak the truth, against the interests of those in power, from whichever political party or position they are, will bring hatred, violence, untruth. The ubiquitous presence of different forms of online propaganda has only allowed more people to join in with the mob violence. So to speak truth requires strength and fortitude, the courage to believe in the rightness of what one does, regardless of the consequences. This is not about provoking for the sake of provoking. The incident of Jeremiah in the well continues with him being released and led to a secret meeting with the king, who instructs him to give what is essentially a false account of their meeting if anyone should ask. Jeremiah does this, and thus saves his life (Jer 38:20–27). Fortitude is also to be combined with wisdom, understanding, and counsel. It requires knowing when to be silent as well as when to speak.

There is also a need for the courage to be wrong and to admit it. Whenever Christians (or anyone else for that matter) make political choices, they will have to choose between imperfections. This means that there will have to be an ongoing re-evaluation and what Leonardo Boff calls resilience, "the art of bouncing back, learning from failure, rising above disappointment."[36] Here too prophets such as Isaiah, Jeremiah, or Ezekiel, to name just three, are exemplary. The truth does not cease to be true because it is rejected. The need to stand by what is true is arguably greater than ever, with claims to "truth" being made on the basis of who has the most followers on different "social media" platforms and who can tell lies loudest. It is of course not easy to find the courage and strength to stand against hegemonic discourses of hatred and destruction, without falling prey to the same values. But this is what the church is called to do.

The Gifts of the Spirit in Context

As I come to a conclusion, it is now time to ask what these gifts mean more concretely in the contexts of Brazil and the Czech Republic. As I noted in the Introduction, the "church does not have a political party, but it does have 'a side.'"[37] But it is always more than just taking sides, because to take sides is to align oneself, in a given situation, with one—admittedly always imperfect—manifestation of political will and practice. The church may not have a political party, but Christians have to vote for someone representing something, and in nearly all more or less democratic political systems that person is at least nominally a member of a

---

36. Boff, *Come, Holy Spirit!*, 177.
37. Bakker, "O 'mensalão/petrolão,'" 841.

political party or political grouping. But what does a spirit of piety and fear of the Lord that receives and uses the gifts of wisdom, understanding, counsel, knowledge, and fortitude bring that will enable us to make these concrete choices?

One place to start is to acknowledge that we need the courage to criticize that which is closest to one's own heart. Both in Brazil and in the Czech Republic there is a need for the church (and of course the wider society of which the church is part) to engage both with those who support positions of entitlement, but also with their own positions. I have already noted how frequently the liberation support for the PT ended up being too uncritical, and thus ultimately did not help the party in carrying out its aims. Because much of what is being done is admirable, it does not mean that the penultimate hegemonic discourse of the political party is sufficient. As I noted in chapter 1, for example, Lula's first government started by essentially continuing many of the neoliberal policies of his predecessor. There were good political reasons for doing this, and it would be possible to admit this whilst still arguing that in the long run it is (and was) unsustainable. Like the classic school report, a church and a Christian community that acknowledges the presence of liberating grace will always evaluate any political engagement with the phrase "could do better."

The opposite may also be true. Sometimes, political parties that are normally in opposition to the common good can act well. In the Czech Republic, movements like "A Million Moments for Democracy," with their admirable non-acceptance of much of what the Babiš government did, ran the danger of being almost a self-parody, opposing whatever was done simply for the sake of opposing. Even the worst governments, through accident or design, usually manage to do some things that are right in the given circumstances. It does not weaken one's arguments to admit this, but it does take courage and fortitude.

Courage will also be needed to stand against those in power in both settings. In Brazil there are many Christians, both Roman Catholic and Evangelicals, who reject the hatred preached by Bolsonaro and his allies. Especially amongst the Evangelicals this requires a great deal of courage, since many of their fellow-believers think that Bolsonaro is blessed, as his discourse of entitlement and its concomitant disentitlement of the majority chimes in with their own discourse. To introduce a constructive hegemonic discourse that seeks to build up a people of truth, of justice, of love is not easy in these circumstances, and the political choices it entails will have to be constantly re-negotiated, but it is necessary. No one politician can change things forever, and it is not good to pin hopes solely on, for example, the re-election of Lula in Brazil. The stories of the great moral political exemplars of the last century, people like Mahatma Gandhi, Martin Luther King, Nelson Mandela, or, in a Czech context, Václav Havel are reminders that such people cannot change everything for good for all time. But they can offer hope and the possibility to advance a few steps towards a better possible world, even if it is a case of two steps forward and one step back.

In the Czech Republic the political alternatives are not for the most part encouraging. Political parties are mostly only popular when they are not in power, and range from the extremists of the left (the Communists, who have never fully apologized for the evil carried out between 1948 and 1989) and the far-right (currently represented by the Freedom and Direct Democracy party), to amorphous centrist parties, such as the party of the current government, ANO. The major opposition now comes from a coalition of two parties, the Pirate Party[38] and the Mayors and Independents Party. But, as in Brazil, founding political parties is now a kind of vanity project for the rich or would-be rich, and mostly not matched by any sense of creating a common good. Entitlement speaks louder than liberation.

This suggests that the Czech context calls for an openness to hope, and to engagement. There are good people involved in politics in the country, in different parties, both right and left. Most of them are more active in local politics, genuinely striving to do their best for their communities. Such people need support, for if there is one thing liberation theology teaches us, it is that change comes from the roots, not from being imposed. Moreover, Christians in the Czech Republic have to have the courage to become involved in politics, as a calling of service.[39] It will be hard, because there is always a conflict between the need to gain power and position in a party and the need to stand up for what is good, at times against one's own party. There is a need to work with all those who are trying to construct a better country, one that does not seek entitlements,

---

38. Despite its rather infantile name, so far this party, which is centrist, appears to be trying to change the way politics is done. It has roused the ire (or fear) of current prime minister Andrej Babiš, which seems to suggest it is doing something right, but past experience leads to a fairly strong hermeneutic of suspicion.

39. An excellent example is Hayato Okamura, brother of Tomio Okamura, who entered politics for the Christian Democrat party in protest against his brother's racist policies.

be it money or benefits without costs from the European Union, or exclusive rights to land or nation against the needs of refugees and migrants from elsewhere. It will involve speaking out against some members of the church hierarchy, who side with the message of xenophobia and hatred of Islam. These church leaders, a minority, do not represent Christianity. Neither do those who claim to be Christians at the same time as they proclaim a refusal to accept the presence of others in the country.

Many Czech Christians are engaged in speaking out against these positions, but again this must be done in a constructive way that builds something better. This will have to start at local level and build up, rather than imposing a new hegemony from above that will alienate as many as it attracts. Theology must recognize its limits. The ways in which it is possible to move from very successful and more participative forms of local democracy to similar expressions at a national level is a question for political scientists and politicians. As long as we are stuck with the problem of the nation-state, these changes may prove very difficult, but if theology cannot provide the best answers, it can at least say that the churches have a duty to participate in the debate, to press for moving forwards towards a just world, where the poor and excluded are reintegrated into a society that is worth living in and for.

This also suggests that the response in the Czech Republic or Brazil is not to try to develop alternatives that are simply reliant on the same parameters as the current politics. Replacing one form of grand narrative with another is not enough. In the Czech Republic this has become increasingly clear over the past thirty years, since the fall of communism at the end of 1989. The kind of communism that existed in the countries under the sway of the Soviet Union after the Second World War was almost a parody of scientific knowledge, but the idolatrous worship of capitalism that replaced it has been little better. Much of the narrative about the European Union and subsequent disappointment with it was based on a similar approach, with benefits (and losses) expressed in monetary and quantifiable terms, rather than in more intangible cultural terms or in relation to the possibility for increased empathy with others. Reactions are often based on a desire for a better narrative, one that will honor and respect what people hold to be important. So the most important task is to proclaim the narrative that includes the gospel as liberating, that tells of God's grace at work in the world. Whether this is done in directly religious terms or in other narrative forms will depend on the context and the situation, but the same story can be told in different words to different audiences. It may thus become a different small story, but small stories can be part of a larger story without becoming a grand narrative themselves.

All this is true for engagement in politics in order to restore *shalom*, to find the inner harmony and peace, the *Gemüt*, that has been lost. This is not some kind of restore point on a computer, to go back to an earlier world, because that is not possible. We live when we live, after all that has happened. As I have noted on numerous occasions, this will inevitably involve making mistakes and the choices that have to be made will have to be constantly revised. But that is not a reason not to make choices. We have been given the gifts we need to engage in the world, to work to transform it, so that God's liberating grace is experienced against all sense of entitlement and exclusion. This liberating grace will break through all our attempts to define it. It will push and question and leave us permanently dissatisfied, because all our attempts will be inadequate. This is not always a comfortable position to be in, but it is the only one that can even begin to guarantee that any discourse that we adopt will be open to the Spirit and able to contribute to a new and better world.

Bibliography

Adam, Júlio Cézar. "Pregação e promessa: a prédica escatológica da libertação, da prosperidade e da cultura pop." *Perspectiva Teológica* 49 (2017) 399–419.

Adriance, Madeleine. *Opting for the Poor: Brazilian Catholicism in Transition*. Kansas City, MO: Sheed & Ward, 1986.

Agnew, John. "Space and Place." In *Handbook of Geographical Knowledge*, edited by John Agnew and David Livingstone, 316–30. London: Sage, 2011.

Aguirre, Rafael, and Francisco Javier Vitoria Cormenzana. "Justicia." In *Mysterium Liberationis. Conceptos fundamentales de la liberación*, edited by Ignacio Ellacuría and Jon Sobrino. 2:539–77. 2nd ed. San Salvador: UCA, 1992.

Ahlert, Alvori. "Fé e ideologia na teologia da libertação: inter-relações na obra de Juan Luis Segundo." *Theologia Xaveriana* 58 (2008) 317–46.

Albado, Omar César. "La pastoral popular en el pensamiento del padre Rafael Tello. Una contribución desde Argentina a la teología latinoamericana." *Franciscanum* 55 (2013) 219–45.

———. "La Teología del Pueblo: su contexto latinoamericano y su influencia en el Papa Francisco." *Revista de Cultura Teológica* 26 (2018) 31–57.

Althusser, Louis. *For Marx*. London: Verso, 2005.

Alves, José Eustáquio Diniz. "O voto evangélico garantiu a eleição de Jair Bolsonaro." https://www.ecodebate.com.br/2018/10/31/o-voto-evangelico-garantiu-a-eleicao-de-jair-bolsonaro-artigo-de-jose-eustaquio-diniz-alves/.

Alvim, Mariana. "'Se eu morrer, denunciem': a mulher que faleceu à espera de remédio no ministério de Ricardo Barros, alvo de CPI." *Terra*, July 9, 2021. https://www.terra.com.br/noticias/brasil/se-eu-morrer-denunciem-a-mulher-que-faleceu-a-espera-de-remedio-no-ministerio-de-ricardo-barros-alvo-de-cpi,76cb2d973bc1fdc98f01bd615a93f0226kplean5.html.

Anderson, Perry. *Brazil Apart: 1964–2019*. London: Verso, 2019.

Andrade, Francisco Eduardo de. "Os pretos devotos do Rosário no espaço público da paróquia, Vila Rica, nas Minas Gerais." *Varia Historia* 32 (2016) 401–35.

Andrews, George Reid. *Afro-Latin America: 1800–2000.* Oxford: Oxford University Press, 2004.
Arato, Andrew. "Political Theology and Populism." *Social Research* 80 (2013) 143–72.
Assmann, Hugo. "Apuntes sobre el tema del sujeto." In *Perfiles Teológicos para un Nuevo Milenio,* edited by José Duque, 115–46. 2nd ed. San José: DEI, 2004.
———. *Pueblo oprimido, señor de la historia.* Montevideo: Tierra Nueva, 1972.
Astier, Isabelle, and Annette Disselkamp. "Pauvreté et propriété privée dans l'encyclique *Rerum novarum.*" *Cahiers d'économie politique* 59 (2010) 205–24.
Aubert, Roger. *Catholic Social Teaching: An Historical Perspective.* Edited by David Boileau. Milwaukee: Marquette University Press, 2003.
Azcuy, Virginia Raquel. "Indicios para una reforma de la iglesia en clave inclusiva: anhelos de igualdad y aportes eclesiológicos que buscan florecer." In *Iglesia que camina con Espíritu y desde los pobres,* edited by Óscar Elizalde Prada et al., 333–70. Montevideo: Fundación Amerindia, 2016.
Baker, Bruce. "Entrepreneurship as a Sign of Common Grace." *Journal of Markets & Morality* 18 (2015) 81–98.
Baker, Peter. "'We the People': The Battle to Define Populism." *The Guardian,* January 10, 2019. www.theguardian.com/news/2019/jan/10/we-the-people-the-battle-to-define-populism.
Bakker, Nicolau João. "O 'mensalão/petrolão' e a teologia pública no Brasil." *Revista Eclesiástica Brasileira* 76 (2016) 820–43.
Balík, Stanislav, and Jiří Hanuš. *Katolická církev v Československu: 1945–1989.* Brno: CDK, 2013.
Balthasar, Hans Urs von. *Spiritus Creator. Skizzen zur Theologie III.* Einsiedeln: Johannes, 1967.
Barbosa, Imerson Alves. "A Esquerda Católica na Formação do PT." MSS thesis, Universidade Estadual Paulista, Faculdade de Filosofia e Ciências, 2007.
Barclay, William. *New Testament Words.* Louisville: Westminster John Knox, 1976.
Barnes, Michael. *Waiting on Grace: A Theology of Dialogue.* Oxford: Oxford University Press, 2020.
Basset, Yann, and Stephen Launay. "Latin American Populism: A Polemic." In *Contemporary Populism: A Controversial Concept and Its Diverse Forms,* edited by Sergiu Gherghina et al., 143–66. Newcastle-upon-Tyne: Cambridge Scholars, 2013.
Bastos, Pedro Paulo Zahluth. "Ascensão e crise do governo Dilma Rousseff e o golpe de 2016: poder estrutural, contradição e ideologia." *Revista de Economia Contemporânea* 21 (2017) 1–63.
Bauer, Kateřina. *Znovuobjevení symbolu u Louise-Marie Chauveta.* Brno: CDK, 2010.
Bautista, Juan José. *¿Que significa pensar desde la América Latina? Hacia una racionalidad transmoderna y postoccidental.* Madrid: Akal, 2014.
BBC. "O que é o movimento 'Somos 70%' e outras iniciativas contra o governo Bolsonaro?" *UOL,* Feruary 6, 2020. https://noticias.uol.com.br/ultimas-noticias/bbc/2020/06/02/o-que-e-o-movimento-somos-70-e-outras-iniciativas-contra-o-governo-bolsonaro.htm?cmpid=copiaecola.
———. "STF anula condenações contra Lula: o que acontece agora." *BBC,* March 8, 2021.https://www.bbc.com/portuguese/brasil-56327483.
Benedict XVI, Pope. *Deus caritas est.* http://www.vatican.va/content/benedict-xvi/en/encyclicals/documents/hf_ben-xvi_enc_20051225_deus-caritas-est.html.

Bibliography

Berdiaeff, Nicolas. *Le sens de la création. Un essai de justification de l'homme.* Paris: Desclée de Brouwer, 1955.
Berdyaev, Nicolas. *Esprit et la liberté.* Paris: Je sers, 1933.
———. *Freedom and the Spirit.* New York: Scribner's and Sons, 1935.
———. *Slavery and Freedom.* London: Bles, the Centenary, 1943.
———. "Verité et mensonge du communisme." *Esprit* 1 (1932) 104–38.
Berdyaev, Nikolai. *The Meaning of the Creative Act.* London: Gollancz, 1955.
Berglund, Bruce. *Castle and Cathedral: Longing for the Sacred in a Skeptical Age.* Budapest: Central European University Press, 2017.
Bergoglio, Jorge Mario. "Discurso inaugural." In *Evangelización de la Cultura e Inculturación del Evangelio,* 15–19. Buenos Aires: Guadalupe, 1988.
———. "Fe en Cristo y humanismo." *Razón y Fe* 273 (2016) 21–26.
———. *Nosotros como ciudadanos, nosotros como pueblo.* https://pastoralsocialbue.org.ar/documento/nosotros-como-ciudadanos-nosotros-como-pueblo/.
———. *Reflexiones en Esperanza.* Buenos Aires: Ediciones de Universidad del Salvador, 1992.
Bingemer, Maria Clara. *Latin American Theology: Roots and Branches.* Maryknoll, NY: Orbis, 2016.
Bitrus, Ibrahim S. "'Give Us Today Our Daily Bread': Martin Luther's Theology of Prosperity." *Journal of Theology for Southern Africa* 160 (2018) 21–39.
Blažek, Václav. "Čech." https://www.czechency.org/slovnik/%C4%8CECH.
Blomberg, Craig. "Neither Capitalism nor Socialism: A Biblical Theology of Economics." *Journal of Markets & Morality* 15 (2012) 207–25.
Blühdorn, Ingolfur, and Felix Butzlaff. "Rethinking Populism: Peak Democracy, Liquid Identity, and the Performance of Sovereignty." *European Journal of Social Theory* 22 (2019) 191–211.
Boff, Clodovis. *Teologia e Prática: Teologia do Político e suas Mediações.* 2nd ed. Petrópolis: Vozes, 1982.
———. *Theology and Praxis: Epistemological Foundations.* Translated by Robert Barr. Maryknoll, NY: Orbis, 1987.
Boff, Leonardo. *Come, Holy Spirit! Inner Fire, Giver of Life, and Comforter of the Poor.* Maryknoll, NY: Orbis, 2015.
———. *Graça e experiência humana.* 5th ed. Petrópolis: Vozes, 1998.
———. *Liberating Grace.* Translated by John Drury. Eugene, OR: Wipf and Stock, 2005.
———. *O Espírito Santo: fogo interior, doador de vida e Pai dos pobres.* Petrópolis: Vozes, 2013.
Bohn, Simone. "Contexto político-eleitoral, minorias religiosas e voto em pleitos eleitorais." *Opinião Pública* 13 (2007) 366–87.
Borghesi, Massimo. *The Mind of Pope Francis: Jorge Mario Bergoglio's Intellectual Journey.* Translated by Barry Hudock. Collegeville, MN: Liturgical, 2018.
Breen, John. "John Paul II, the Structures of Sin, and the Limits of Law." *St. Louis University Law Journal* 52 (2008) 317–73.
Brighenti, Agenor. "Documento de Aparecida: O texto original, o texto oficial e o Papa Francisco." *Revista Pistis & Praxis* 8 (2016) 673–713.
Buttigieg, Joseph. "Antonio Gramsci: Liberation Begins with Critical Thinking." In *Political Philosophy in the Twentieth Century: Authors and Arguments,* edited by Catherine Zuckert, 44–57. Cambridge: Cambridge University Press, 2011.
Cabestrero, Teófilo. "Santo Domingo, un año después. La recepción del documento." https://servicioskoinonia.org/relat/012.htm.

Cairus, Brigitte Grossmann. "De Alemão a Cigano: a construção da identidade de Juscelino Kubitscheck como fator legitimador das políticas étnicas ciganas no Brasil Contemporâneo." http://www.snh2015.anpuh.org/resources/anais/39/1427677224_ARQUIVO_Cairus,BrigitteANPUHFloripa2015.pdf.

Čapková, Kateřina. *Czechs, Germans, Jews? National Identity and the Jews of Bohemia*. New York: Berghahn, 2012.

Carozza, Paolo, and Daniel Philpott. "The Catholic Church, Human Rights, and Democracy: Convergence and Conflict with the Modern State." *Logos* 15 (2012) 15–43.

Carrero, Angel Dario. "Entrevista exclusiva al padre de la teología de la liberación, Gustavo Gutiérrez, en su 80 aniversario: La teología como carta de amor." http://www.redescristianas.net/entrevista-exclusiva-al-padre-de-la-teologia-de-la-liberacion-gustavo-gutierrez-en-su-80-aniversarioangel-dario-carrero-ofm/.

Catechism of the Catholic Church. https://www.vatican.va/archive/ENG0015/_INDEX.HTM.

Cerman, Ivo. "Název ANO je narážkou na fašistickou organizaci." https://ivocerman.blog.idnes.cz/blog.aspx?c=371816.

Certeau, Michel de. *The Practice of Everyday Life*. Berkeley: University of California Press, 1988.

Chapman, David. "Ecumenism and the Visible Unity of the Church: 'Organic Union' or 'Reconciled Diversity'?" *Ecclesiology* 11 (2015) 350–69.

Chauvet, Louis-Marie. *Symbol and Sacrament: A Sacramental Reinterpretation of Christian Existence*. Translated by Patrick Madigan and Madeleine Beaumont. Collegeville, MN: Liturgical, 1995.

Chodor, Tom. *Neoliberal Hegemony and the Pink Tide in Latin America: Breaking Up with TINA?* New York: Palgrave Macmillan, 2015.

"Cizinci celkem podle státního občanství k 31. 12. 2018." https://www.czso.cz/documents/10180/91605941/290027190101.pdf/22106831-6bd2-4cf2-86b0-4c7bc79fd052?version=1.0.

Clevenger, Samuel M. "Sport History, Modernity and the Logic of Coloniality: A Case for Decoloniality." *Rethinking History* 21 (2017) 586–605.

Codina, Victor. *O Espírito do Senhor: força dos fracos*. São Paulo: Paulinas, 2019.

———. *Espírito Santo*. Coleção Teologia do Papa Francisco. São Paulo: Paulinas, 2018.

———. "Não extingais o Espírito" *(1Ts 5,19): Iniciação à pneumatologia*. São Paulo: Paulinas, 2010.

Colborn, Francis. "Theology of Grace: Present Trends and Future Directions." *Theological Studies* 31 (1970) 692–711.

Comblin, José. *Called for Freedom: The Changing Context of Liberation Theology*. Maryknoll, NY: Orbis, 1998.

———. *O Espírito Santo e a Tradição de Jesus*. São Bernardo do Campo: Nhanduti, 2012.

———. "Grace." In *Systematic Theology: Perspectives from Liberation Theology*, edited by Jon Sobrino and Ignacio Ellacuría, 205–15. London: SCM, 1996.

———. "Gracia." In *Mysterium Liberationis. Conceptos fundamentales de la liberación*, edited by Ignacio Ellacuría and Jon Sobrino, 2:79–92. 2nd ed. San Salvador: UCA, 1992.

———. *The Holy Spirit and Liberation*. Translated by Paul Burns. Eugene, OR: Wipf & Stock, 2004.

———. *Vers une théologie de l'action*. Brussels: La Pensée Catholique, 1964.

Congar, Yves. *I Believe in the Holy Spirit*. London: Chapman, 1983.
Conniff, Michael, ed. *Populism in Latin America*. 2nd ed. Tuscaloosa, AL: University of Alabama Press, 2012.
Cuda, Emilce. "Francisco y la teología de la cultura: Discernimiento sobre violencia-misericordia en la modernidad postsecular." *Perspectiva Teológica* 49 (2017) 589–609.
———. "Latinoamérica en el siglo XXI: posmarxismo, populismo y teología del pueblo." *Cuadernos de Filosofía Latinoamericana* 40 (2019) 57–75.
———. *Para leer a Francisco. Teología, ética y política*. Buenos Aires: Manantial, 2016.
Čulo, Ivan, and Ivan Šestak. "Recepcija Emmanuela Mouniera u Hrvatskoj i bivšoj Jugoslaviji od sredine 60-ih godina do kraja 20. Stoljeća." *Diacovensia* 26 (2018) 359–81.
Cunha, Christina Vital da, and Ana Carolina Evangelista. "Electoral Strategies in 2018: The Case of Evangelical Candidates Running for Brazilian Legislatures." *SUR* 16 (2019) 83–96.
Curnow, Rohan. "Which Preferential Option for the Poor? A History of the Doctrine's Bifurcation." *Modem Theology* 31 (2015) 27–59.
Dahrendorf, Ralf. "Acht Anmerkungen zum Populismus." *Transit. Europäische Revue* 25 (2003) 156–63.
———. "Acht Anmerkungen zum Populismus / Eight Remarks on Populism." https://shop.freiheit.org/#!/Publikation/798.
"Decree 4: 'Our Mission and Culture,' General Congregation 34 (1995)." https://jesuitportal.bc.edu/research/documents/1995_decree4gc34/.
Deidun, Thomas. *New Covenant Morality in Paul*. Analecta Biblica 89. Rome: Biblical Institute Press, 1981.
Deifelt, Wanda. "Teologia luterana como desafio ao fundamentalismo religioso e à teologia da prosperidade." *Estudos Teológicos* 57 (2017) 333–49.
Diamanti, Jeff, et al., eds. *The Bloomsbury Companion to Marx*. London: Bloomsbury Academic, 2019.
Dixon, Thomas. *Weeping Britannia: A History of Britain in Tears*. Oxford: Oxford University Press, 2015.
Doino, William. "Mother Teresa and Her Critics." *First Things*, January 4, 2013. https://www.firstthings.com/web-exclusives/2013/04/mother-teresa-and-her-critics.
Domezi, Maria Cecilia. "A Devoção nas CEBS: Entre o Catolicismo Popular Tradicional e a Teologia da Libertação." PhD diss., Pontifícia Universidade Católica de São Paulo, 2006.
Domingues, José Maurício. "Crise da república e possibilidades de futuro." *Ciência e Saúde Coletiva* 22 (2017) 1747–58.
Dominus. "Entenda o que é a Pastoral do Dízimo e sua importância." https://www.dominuscomunicacao.com/o-que-e-a-pastoral-do-dizimo/.
Dornelles, João Ricardo. "Direitos humanos em tempos sombrios: barbárie, autoritarismo e fascismo do século XXI." *Revista Interdisciplinar de Direitos Humanos* 5 (2017) 153–68.
Drane, John. *The McDonaldization of the Church: Spirituality, Creativity, and the Future of the Church*. London: Darton, Longman & Todd, 2000.
Duden. "Geist." https://www.duden.de/rechtschreibung/Geist_Verstand_Destillat#Bedeutung-1.
———. "Gemüt." https://www.duden.de/rechtschreibung/Gemuet.

Dusilek, Sérgio Ricardo Gonçalves. "Traços pagãos no discurso da Teologia da Prosperidade." *Revista Pistis & Praxis—Teologia Pastoral* 10 (2018) 199–220.

Dussel, Enrique. "Paulo de Tarso na filosofia política atual." In *Paulo de Tarso na filosofia atual e outros ensaios*, 9–94. São Paulo: Paulus, 2016.

Dvorník, František. *Byzantine Missions among the Slavs: SS. Constantine-Cyril and Methodius*. New Brunswick, NJ: Rutgers University Press, 1970.

———. *Byzantské misie u Slovanů*. Prague: Vyšehrad, 1970.

———. *The Photian Schism: History and Legend*. Cambridge: Cambridge University Press, 1948.

———. *Zrod střední a východní Evropy: Mezi Byzancí a Římem*. Prague: Prostor, 1999.

Dyer, Owen. "COVID-19: Many Poor Countries Will See Almost No Vaccine Next Year, Aid Groups Warn." *British Medical Journal* 371 (2020). https://www.bmj.com/content/bmj/371/bmj.m4809.full.pdf.

Endrich, Marek, and Jerg Gutmann. *Pacem in Terris: Are Papal Visits Good News for Human Rights?* ILE Working Paper Series 37. University of Hamburg, Institute of Law and Economics, 2020.

Errejón, Iñigo, and Chantal Mouffe. *Podemos: In the Name of the People*. London: Lawrence and Wishart, 2016.

"Espaço cedido pela CNBB acolherá migrantes venezuelanos em Brasília." *Notícias*, January 29, 2021. https://noticias.cancaonova.com/igreja/espaco-cedido-pela-cnbb-acolhera-migrantes-venezuelanos-em-brasilia/.

Eurostat. "Asylum in the EU Member States." https://ec.europa.eu/eurostat/documents/2995521/7203832/3-04032016-AP-EN.pdf/790eba01-381c-4163-bcd2-a54959b99ed6.

———. "Gini Coefficient of Equivalised Disposable Income - EU-SILC Survey." https://ec.europa.eu/eurostat/databrowser/view/ILC_DI12/default/table?lang=en.

Faggioli, Massimo. *Catholicism and Citizenship: Political Cultures of the Church in the Twenty-First Century*. Collegeville, MN: Liturgical, 2017.

"Father Gustavo Gutiérrez Thanks Greeting from Pope Francis." https://www.servindi.org/actualidad-noticias/09/06/2018/padre-gustavo-gutierrez-agradece-saludo-del-papa-francisco.

Fernández Beret, Guillermo. *El Pueblo en la Teología de la Liberación: Consecuencias de un concepto ambiguo para la eclesiología y la pastoral latinoamericanas*. Frankfurt–Madrid: Vervuert–Iberoamericana, 1996.

Fernández, Víctor Manuel. "Con los pobres hasta el fondo: el pensamiento teológico de Rafael Tello." *Revista Proyecto* 12 (2000) 187–205.

———. *El programa del papa Francisco*. Buenos Aires: San Pablo, 2014.

Ferrugia, Mario. "Karl Rahner on Concupiscence: Between Aquinas and Heidegger." *Gregorianum* 86 (2005) 330–56.

Fialho, Juliana. "Assistência social x Assistencialismo." www.gesuas.com.br/blog/assistencia-social-x-assistencialismo/.

Figueiredo, Marcelo. "Os mais relevantes problemas político-eleitorais no Brasil (o sistema proporcional) e a luta contra a corrupção: do 'Mensalão' à 'Operação Lava Jato.'" *Revista de Direito Administrativo* 277 (2018) 399–435.

Filc, Dani, and Uri Ram. "Marxism after Postmodernism: Rethinking the Emancipatory Political Subject." *Current Sociology* 62 (2014) 295–313.

Fishlow, Albert. *Starting Over: Brazil Since 1985*. Washington, DC: Brookings Institution, 2011.

Bibliography

Fitzi, Gregor, et al., eds. *Populism and the Crisis of Democracy*. London: Routledge, 2019.

Foroohar, Manzar. "Liberation Theology: The Response of Latin American Catholics to Socioeconomic Problems." *Latin American Perspectives* 13 (1986) 37–58.

Francis, Pope. "Address to Employees of the Dicastery." https://www.vatican.va/content/francesco/en/speeches/2019/september/documents/papa-francesco_20190923_dicastero-comunicazione.html.

———. *Evangelii gaudium*. http://www.vatican.va/content/francesco/en/apost_exhortations/documents/papa-francesco_esortazione-ap_20131124_evangelii-gaudium.html.

———. *Fratelli tutti*. fhttp://www.vatican.va/content/francesco/en/encyclicals/documents/papa-francesco_20201003_enciclica-fratelli-tutti.html#_ftnref2. Spanish translation: http://www.vatican.va/content/francesco/es/encyclicals/documents/papa-francesco_20201003_enciclica-fratelli-tutti.html.

———. "Meeting with the Brazil's Leaders of Society." https://www.vatican.va/content/francesco/en/speeches/2013/july/documents/papa-francesco_20130727_gmg-classe-dirigente-rio.html.

———. *Querida Amazonia*. https://www.vatican.va/content/francesco/en/apost_exhortations/documents/papa-francesco_esortazione-ap_20200202_querida-amazonia.html.

Francis of Assisi. "Admonitions, Rules, Etc." https://www.sacred-texts.com/chr/wosf/wosf03.htm#fr_81. Italian: http://www.icamminidifrancesco.it/le_ammonizioni.

Freston, Paul. "Prosperity Theology: A (Largely) Sociological Assessment." In *Prosperity Theology and the Gospel: Good News or Bad News for the Poor?*, edited by Daniel Salinas and Valdir Steuernagel, 66–76. Peabody, MA: Hendrickson, 2017.

Freyre, Gilberto. *Casa-grande & senzala: formação da família brasileira sob o regime da economia Patriarcal*. 48th ed. São Paulo: Global, 2003.

———. *The Masters and the Slaves*. Translated by Samuel Putnam. New York: Knopf, 1946.

Furlin, Neiva. "Trajetória e pensamento intelectual de professoras da PUC-RIO: Representantes de uma geração de Teólogas Feministas." *Revista Eclesiástica Brasileira* 74 (2014) 624–52.

Gabatz, Celso, and Rudolf von Sinner. "Populismo e 'povo': precariedades e polarizações como desafio para os direitos humanos na perspectiva de uma teologia pública na contemporaneidade." *Estudos Teológicos* 60 (2020) 188–205.

Gathercole, Simon. "'Sins' in Paul." *New Testament Studies* 64 (2018) 143–61.

Gavras, Douglas and Érika Motada. "Cresce número de trabalhadores que ganham no máximo um salário mínimo." *Economia*, March 2, 2020. https://economia.uol.com.br/noticias/estadao-conteudo/2020/02/03/cresce-numero-de-trabalhadores-que-ganham-no-maximo-um-salario-minimo.htm?cmpid=copiaecola.

Gera, Lucio. "Pueblo, religión del pueblo e Iglesia." *Teología* 27–28 (1976) 99–123.

———. *La teología argentina del pueblo*. Edited by Virginia Azcuy. Santiago de Chile: Ediciones Universidad Alberto Hurtado, 2015.

"Gera, Lucio." https://sites.google.com/a/josephcardijn.com/cardijn-priests/gera-lucio.

Geva, Benjamin. *The Payment Order of Antiquity and the Middle Ages: A Legal History*. Oxford: Hart, 2011.

Ghia, Guido. "'La verità è polifônica.' Rapsodia dell'opposizione polare e dottrina del metodo in Romano Guardini." *Humanitas* 74 (2019) 215–26.

Ginsberg, Jodie. "The Far-Right Are Not in Favour of Free Speech." *Index on Censorship* 46 (2017) 66–67.

Girard, René. *The Scapegoat*. Translated by Yvonne Freccero. London: Athlone, 1986.

———. *Things Hidden Since the Foundation of the World*. Translated by Michael Metteer and Stephen Bann. Stanford: Stanford University Press, 1987.

———. *Violence and the Sacred*. Translated by Patrick Gregory. Baltimore: Johns Hopkins University Press, 1977.

Gonçalves, Eduardo. "O mais fiel dos eleitores." *Veja*, May 3, 2019. https://veja.abril.com.br/politica/o-mais-fiel-dos-eleitores/.

Gonçalves, Vinícius Batista, and Daniela Meirelles Andrade. "A corrupção na perspectiva durkheimiana: um estudo de caso da Operação Lava Jato." *Revista de Administração Pública* 53 (2019) 271–90.

González Faus, José Ignacio. "Antropología." In *Mysterium Liberationis. Conceptos fundamentales de la liberación*, edited by Ignacio Ellacuría and Jon Sobrino, 2:49–78. 2nd ed. San Salvador: UCA, 1992.

———. "Pecado." In *Mysterium Liberationis. Conceptos fundamentales de la liberación*, edited by Ignacio Ellacuría and Jon Sobrino, 2:93–106. 2nd ed. San Salvador: UCA, 1992.

———. "Sin." In *Systematic Theology: Perspectives from Liberation Theology*, edited by Jon Sobrino and Ignacio Ellacuría, 194–204. London: SCM, 1996.

———. "La realidad del pecado." *Revista Catalana de Teologia* 10 (1985) 383–433.

Gorevan, Patrick. "Only Connect: Romano Guardini, *Gaudium et Spes*, and the Unity of Christian Existence." *New Blackfriars* 100 (2019) 425–33.

Grebe, Eduard. "Contingency, Contestation, and Hegemony. The Possibility of a Non-essentialist Politics for the Left." *Philosophy & Social Criticism* 35 (2009) 589–611.

Gregory XVI, Pope. *In supremo apostolatus*. https://www.papalencyclicals.net/Greg16/g16sup.htm.

———. *Mirari Vos*, 1832. https://www.papalencyclicals.net/Greg16/g16mirar.htm.

Guadalupe, José Luis Pérez, and Brenda Carranza, eds. *Novo ativismo político no Brasil: os evangélicos do século XXI*. Rio de Janeiro: Konrad Adenauer Stiftung, 2020.

Gutiérrez, Gustavo. *The Power of the Poor in History*. London: SCM, 1983.

———. *A Theology of Liberation*. Rev. ed. London: SCM, 1988.

———. *The Truth Shall Make You Free: Confrontations*. Maryknoll, NY: Orbis, 1990.

Hagin, Kenneth. *Redeemed from Poverty, Sickness, and Spiritual Death*. 2nd ed. Tulsa, OK: Kenneth Hagin Ministries, 1995.

Halík, Tomáš. "Pseudonáboženství F—příklad náboženské patologie." http://blog.aktualne.cz/blogy/tomas-halik.php?itemid=38176.

Hamplová, Dana, and Zdeněk Nešpor. "Invisible Religion in a 'Non-believing' Country: The Case of the Czech Republic." *Social Compass* 56 (2009) 581–97.

Havel, Václav. "Moc bezmocných." http://scriptum.cz/cs/periodika/havel-moc-bezmocnych.

———. *Prosím stručně*. Prague: Gallery, 2006.

———. *To The Castle and Back*. London: Portobello, 2008.

Havlíček, Jakub. "'Měřítko vytváří jev': K pojetí obsahů a funkcí náboženství ve výzkumech religiosity v současné české společnosti." *Religio* 27 (2019) 117–41.

Hawkins, Kirk, and Cristóbal Rovira Kaltwasser. "The Ideational Approach to Populism." *Latin American Research Review* 52 (2017) 513–28.

Hawkins, Kirk, et al., eds. *The Ideational Approach to Populism: Concept, Theory, and Analysis*. Abingdon: Routledge, 2019.

Hehir, J. Bryan. "The Modern Catholic Church and Human Rights: The Impact of the Second Vatican Council." In *Christianity and Human Rights: An Introduction*, edited by Frank Alexander and John Witte, 113–34. Cambridge: Cambridge University Press, 2010.

Heimann, Mary. *Czechoslovakia: The State That Failed*. New Haven: Yale University Press, 2009.

Hellman, John. "John Paul II and the Personalist Movement." *Cross Currents* 30 (1980–81) 409–19.

Herrero, Montserrat. "Laclau's Revolutionary Political Theology and Its Backdrop." *Síntesis* 11 (2019) 9–25.

Hevia, Felipe. "Relaciones sociedad-estado, participación ciudadana y clientelismo político en programas contra la pobreza. El caso de 'bolsa familia' en Brasil." *América Latina Hoy* 57 (2011) 205–38.

Hill, Patrick. "Emmanuel Mounier: Total Christianity and Practical Marxism." *Cross Currents* 18 (1968) 77–104.

Hinze, Bradford. "The Grace of Conflict." *Theological Studies* 81 (2020) 40–64.

Hirschfeld, Mary. "Standard of Living and Economic Virtue: Forging a Link between St Thomas Aquinas and the Twenty-First Century." *Journal of the Society of Christian Ethics* 26 (2006) 61–77.

Hołub, Grzegorz. *Understanding the Person: Essays on the Personalism of Karol Wojtyła*. Bern: Lang, 2021.

Hook, Derek, and Stijn Vanheule. "Revisiting the Master-Signifier, or, Mandela and Repression." *Frontiers in Psychology* 6 (2016). https://www.frontiersin.org/articles/10.3389/fpsyg.2015.02028/full.

Horn Gerd-Rainer. *Western European Liberation Theology, 1924–1959*. Oxford: Oxford University Press, 2015.

Horrell, David. "'Race,' 'Nation,' 'People': Ethnic Identity-Construction in 1 Peter 2.9." *New Testament Studies* 58 (2011) 123–43.

Horsley, Richard. "Introduction: Krister Stendahl's Challenge to Pauline Studies." In *Paul and Politics: Ekklesia, Israel, Imperium, Interpretation*, edited by Richard Horsley, 1–16. London: Bloomsbury Academic, 2000.

———, ed. *Paul and the Roman Imperial Order*. London: Bloomsbury Academic, 2004.

Hošek, Pavel. "Discerning the Signs of the Times in the Post-Communist Czech Republic: A Historical, Sociological, and Missiological Analysis of Contemporary Czech Culture." In *A Czech Perspective on Faith in a Secular Age*, edited by Tomáš Halík and Pavel Hošek, 13–42. Washington, DC: Council for Research in Values and Philosophy, 2015.

Howard, Damian. "St Ignatius: The Dark Side of Entitlement." https://www.jesuit.org.uk/st-ignatius-dark-side-entitlement.

Hus, Mistr Jan. *Řeč o míru*. Edited and translated by František Dobiáš and Amadeo Molnár. Prague: Kalich, 1963.

Hutchinson, Dawn. "New Thought's Prosperity Theology and Its Influence on American Ideas of Success." *Nova Religio* 18 (2014) 28–44.

Illich, Ivan. *Celebration of Awareness: A Call for Institutional Revolution*. Harmondsworth: Penguin, 1980.

Ilo, Stan Chu. *A Poor and Merciful Church: The Illuminative Ecclesiology of Pope Francis*. Maryknoll, NY: Orbis, 2018.

Inácio, Magna. "Presidential Leadership in a Robust Presidency: The Brazilian Case." In *Presidents and Democracy in Latin America*, edited by Manuel Alcántara et al., 167–203. New York: Routledge, 2018.

Indralak, Laura, and John Giordano. "Chantal Mouffe and Religious Pluralism: Agonistic Experiments in Non-Western Societies." *Prajñā Vihāra* 18 (2017) 84–93.

Innes, Abby. "The Political Economy of State Capture in Central Europe." *Journal of Common Market Studies* 52 (2014) 88–104.

Ito, Hisa. "The Story of Jesus and the Blind Man: A Speech Act Reading of John 9." *Acta Theologica* Supplement 21 (2015) 1–538.

Ivereigh, Austen. *The Great Reformer: Francis and the Making of a Radical Pope*. New York: Picador, 2015.

———. "Offering a Precious Stone: The Communication of Pope Francis's Jubilee of Mercy." *Church, Communication, and Culture* 2 (2017) 322–43.

Jandourek, Jan. "Jak to Marx myslel s tím náboženstvím jako opiem lidstva. Ještě na okraj Marxova výročí." *Christnet*, May 21, 2018. http://www.christnet.eu/clanky/6067/jak_to_marx_myslel_s_tim_nabozenstvim_jako_opiem_lidstva.url.

John Paul II, Pope. *Novo millenio ineunte*. http://www.vatican.va/content/john-paul-ii/en/apost_letters/2001/documents/hf_jp-ii_apl_20010106_novo-millennio-ineunte.html.

———. *Reconciliatio et paenitentia*. http://www.vatican.va/content/john-paul-ii/en/apost_exhortations/documents/hf_jp-ii_exh_02121984_reconciliatio-et-paenitentia.html.

———. *Sollicitudo rei socialis*. http://www.vatican.va/content/john-paul-ii/en/encyclicals/documents/hf_jp-ii_enc_30121987_sollicitudo-rei-socialis.html.

Johnston, Raymond. "Czech Republic Ranks Last on European Anti-corruption Index; Ignored Warnings." *Expats.cz*, March 6, 2020. https://www.expats.cz/czech-news/article/czech-republic-ranks-last-on-european-anti-corruption-index-ignored-warnings.

Jowers, Dennis. "The Conflict of Freedom and Concupiscence: A Difficulty for Karl Rahner's Theological Anthropology." *Heythrop Journal* 53 (2012) 624–36.

Junge, Benjamin. "'Our Brazil Has Become a Mess': Nostalgic Narratives of Disorder and Disinterest as a 'Once-Rising Poor' Family from Recife, Brazil, Anticipates the 2018 Elections." *Journal of Latin American and Caribbean Anthropology* 24 (2019) 914–31.

Jurok, Jiří. "Mírová a propagační poselstva krále Jiřího z Poděbrad v letech 1461–1467." *Historica Olomucensia* 53 (2017) 47–86.

Karris, Robert J. *The Admonitions of St. Francis: Sources and Meanings*. Rev. ed. St. Bonaventure, NY: Franciscan Institute, 2015.

———. "St. Francis of Assisi's Admonitions in New Ecclesiastical and Secular Contexts." *Franciscan Studies* 74 (2016) 207–30.

Katz, Andrea Scoseria. "Making Brazil Work: Brazilian Coalitional Presidentialism at 30 and Its Post-Lava Jato Prospects." *Revista de Investigações Constitucionais* 5 (2018) 77–102.

Kaveny, Cathleen. "Pope Francis and Catholic Healthcare Ethics." *Theological Studies* 80 (2019) 186–201.

Khattab, Mustafa, trans. *The Quran*. https://quran.com/49.

King, C. Richard, and Jorge Moraga. "Postcolonialism and Sport." In *The Blackwell Encyclopedia of Sociology*, edited by George Ritze, 3547–48. Chichester: John Wiley, 2015.

Klimentová, Monika. "Prohlášení předsedy ČBK k některým kandidaturám do poslanecké sněmovny." *CBK*, July 27, 2021. https://www.cirkev.cz/cs/aktuality/210727prohlaseni-predsedy-cbk-k-nekterym-kandidaturam-do-poslanecke-snemovny.

"Kompletní spis spolupracovníka StB Andreje Babiše." https://zpravy.aktualne.cz/domaci/kompletni-spis-spolupracovnika-stb-andreje-babise/r~i:gallery:31547/r~i:photo:571922/.

Kopczyk, Michał. "Those Problematic Slavs: Silesia in the Eyes of a German Traveler (Case Study)." *Annales–Anali za Istrske in Mediteranske Studije* 27 (2017) 53–60.

Kopeček, Lubomír, and Miloš Brunclík. "How Strong Is the President in Government Formation? A New Classification and the Czech Case." *East European Politics and Societies* 33 (2019) 109–34.

Köstenberger, Andreas, and David Croteau. "Reconstructing a Biblical Model for Giving: A Discussion of Relevant Systematic Issues and New Testament Principles." *Bulletin for Biblical Research* 16 (2006) 237–60.

———. "'Will a Man Rob God?' (Malachi 3:8): A Study of Tithing in the Old and New Testaments." *Bulletin for Biblical Research* 16 (2006) 53–77.

Kratochvíl, Petr. "Analýza role římskokatolické církve při spoluutváření české zahraniční politiky." *Mezinárodní vztahy* 2 (2011) 20–34.

Kyrilo, James, and Drick Boyd. *Paulo Freire: His Faith, Spirituality, and Theology*. Rotterdam: Sense, 2017.

Lacan, Jacques. *The Psychoses: The Seminar of Jacques Lacan: Book III, 1955–1956*. Edited by Jacques-Alain Miller. Translated by Russell Grigg. London: Routledge, 1993.

Laclau, Ernesto. "The Defender of Contingency: An Interview with Ernesto Laclau." *Eurozine*, February 10, 2010. https://www.eurozine.com/the-defender-of-contingency/.

———. "The Impossibility of Society." *Canadian Journal of Political and Social Theory* 7 (1983) 21–24. Republished in *The Discourse Studies Reader: Main Currents in Theory and Analysis*, edited by Johannes Angermuller et al., 122–26. Amsterdam: Benjamins, 2014.

———. *Misticismo, retórica y política*. Buenos Aires: Fondo de Cultura Económica, 2002.

———. "On the Names of God." In *Political Theologies: Public Religions in a Post-Secular World*, edited by Hent de Vries and Lawrence Sullivan, 137–47. New York: Fordham University Press, 2006.

———. *On Populist Reason*. London: Verso, 2007.

———. "Populism: What's in a Name?" In *Populisms and the Mirror of Democracy*, edited by Francisco Panizzi, 32–49. London: Verso, 2005.

———. "Why Constructing a People Is the Main Task of Radical Politics." *Critical Inquiry* 32 (2006) 646–80.

———. "Why Do Empty Signifiers Matter to Politics?" In *Ernesto Laclau: Post-Marxism, Populism, and Critique*, edited by David Howarth, 66–74. Abingdon: Routledge, 2015.

Laclau, Ernesto, and Chantal Mouffe. *Hegemony and Socialist Strategy: Towards a Radical Democratic Politics*. 2nd ed. London: Verso, 2001.

Lammé, Nicholas. "The Blasphemy against the Holy Spirit: The Unpardonable Sin in Matthew 12:22–32." *Mid-America Journal of Theology* 23 (2012) 19–51.

Lamounier, Bárbara, and Rosiene Guerra. "Eleições no Brasil 2018: Instabilidade institucional e a onda da extrema direita." *Iberoamericana America Latina-Espana-Portugal* 18 (2019) 254–59.

Lampe, Armando. "Las Casas and African Slavery in the Caribbean: A Third Conversion." In *Bartolomé de las Casas, O.P.: History, Philosophy, and Theology in the Age of European Expansion*, edited by David Thomas Orique and Rady Roldán-Figueroa, 421–36. Leiden: Brill, 2019.

Laudátová, Marie, and Roman Vido. "Současná česká religiozita v generační perspektivě." *Sociální studia* 4 (2010) 37–61.

Lee, Brian, and Thomas Knoebel, eds. *Discovering Pope Francis: The Roots of Jorge Mario Bergoglio's Thinking*. Collegeville, MN: Liturgical Academic, 2019.

Lee, Dorothy. *The Symbolic Narratives of the Fourth Gospel: The Interplay of Form and Meaning*. Journal for the Study of the New Testament Supplement Series 95. Sheffield: JSOT, 1994.

Lee, Shayne. "Prosperity Theology: T. D. Jakes and the Gospel of the Almighty Dollar." *CrossCurrents* 57 (2007) 227–36.

Le Goff, Jacques. *The Birth of Purgatory*. Chicago: University of Chicago Press, 1986.

Lehner, Ulrich. *The Catholic Englightenment: The Forgotten History of a Global Movement*. Oxford: Oxford University Press, 2016.

Lellis, Nelson. "O Presidente pode misturar política e religião? O sistema político-teológico do Messias a partir da série João 8:32." *Protestantismo em Revista* 46 (2020) 19–33.

Lemna, Keith, and David Delaney. "Three Pathways into the Theological Mind of Pope Francis." *Nova et Vetera* 12 (2014) 25–56.

Lenehan, Kevin. "*Etsi Deus Non Daretur*: Bonhoeffer's Useful Misuse of Grotius' Maxim and Its Implications for Evangelisation in the World Come of Age." *Bonhoeffer Legacy* 1 (2013) 34–60.

Levinas, Emmanuel. *De Dieu qui vient à l' idée*. 2nd ed. Paris: Vrin, 2004.

———. *Totality and Infinity*. Translated by Alphonso Lingis. Pittsburgh: Duquesne University Press, 1969.

Libanio, João Batista. "Conferencia de Aparecida. Documento final." *Revista Iberoamericana de Teología* 6 (2008) 23–46.

Libanio, João Batista, and Francisco Taborda. "Ideología." In *Mysterium Liberationis: conceptos fundamentales de la teología de la liberación*, edited by Jon Sobrino and Ignacio Ellacuría, 2:579–600. 2nd ed. San Salvador: UCA, 1992.

Lieu, Judith. *Neither Jew nor Greek? Constructing Early Christianity*. London: T. & T. Clark, 2016.

Longenecker, Richard. *Galatians*. Word Biblical Commentary 41. Dallas: Word, 1990.

Lossky, Vladimir. *The Mystical Theology of the Eastern Church*. Cambridge: Clarke & Co., 2005.

Löwy, Michaël, and Jésus Garcia-Ruiz. "Les sources françaises du christianisme de la libération au Brésil." *Archives de sciences sociales des religions* 97 (1997) 9–32.

Lubac, Henri de. *The Mystery of the Supernatural*. Translated by Rosemary Sheed. London: Chapman, 1967.

———. *Surnaturel: Etudes Historiques*. Edited by Michel Sales. Paris: Desclée de Brouwer, 1991.

Luciani, Rafael. "La opción teológico-pastoral del Papa Francisco." *Perspectiva Teológica* 48 (2016) 81–115.

Luther, Martin. *Commentary on the Sermon on the Mount*. Translated by Charles A. Hay. Philadelphia: Lutheran Publication Society, 1892.
Luz, Ulrich. *Matthew 8–20*. Minneapolis: Fortress, 2001.
Lyotard, Jean-François. *The Postmodern Condition: A Report on Knowledge*. Manchester: Manchester University Press, 1994.
Ma, Wonsuk. *Until the Spirit Comes: The Spirit of God in the Book of Isaiah*. London: Bloomsbury, 2009.
Macedo, Edir. *Nos passos de Jesus*. Rio de Janeiro: Universal Produções, 2001.
Magister, Sandro. "Quando Bergoglio derrotou os teólogos da libertação." *Instituto Humanitas Unisinos*, October 5, 2013. http://www.ihu.unisinos.br/noticias/524393-quando-bergoglio-derrotou-os-teologos-da-libertacao.
Mahoney, Jack. "A Mysterious Ignatian Prayer." *Thinking Faith*, February 17, 2012. https://www.thinkingfaith.org/articles/20120217_1.htm.
Malone, Philip. "From *Gaudium et Spes* to *Evangelii Gaudium*: From Proclamation to Pastoral Response." *Compass* 50 (2016) 3–5.
Mansfeldová, Zdenka, and Tomáš Lacina. "Czech Republic: Declining Bipolarity and New Patterns of Conflict." In *Coalition Governance in Central Eastern Europe*, edited by Torbjörn Bergman et al., 129–69. Oxford: Oxford University Press, 2019.
Maragnoa, Lucas Martins Dias, et al. "Corrupção, lavagem de dinheiro e conluio no Brasil: evidências empíricas dos vínculos entre fraudadores e cofraudadores no caso Lava Jato." *Revista de Contabilidade e Organizações* 13 (2019) 5–18.
Martin, Gabriela. *Pré-história do Nordeste do Brasil*. 5th ed. Recife: Editora Universitária UFPE, 2008.
Marx, Karl. *A Contribution to the Critique of Hegel's "Philosophy of Right."* https://www.marxists.org/archive/marx/works/1843/critique-hpr/intro.htm.
———. *Critique of Hegel's "Philosophy of Right."* Edited by Joseph O'Malley. Translated by Annette Jolin and Joseph O'Malley. Cambridge Studies in the History and Theory of Politics. Cambridge: Cambridge University Press, 1970.
———. "Zur Kritik der Hegel'schen Rechts-philosophie." In *Deutsch-Französische Jahrbücher*, edited by Arnold Ruge and Karl Marx, 71–85. Paris: Bureau der Jahrbücher, 1844.
McClendon, James W., and James Smith. *Convictions: Defusing Religious Relativism*. Rev. ed. Eugene, OR: Wipf & Stock, 2002.
McCormick, William. "The Populist Pope? Politics, Religion, and Pope Francis." *Politics and Religion* 14 (2021) 159–81.
McEvoy, Tim. "A Time of Choosing: Conversion and Discernment in the Mind of Pope Francis." *The Way* 59 (2020) 7–12.
Medeiros, Cintia Rodrigues de Oliveira, and Rafael Alcadipani da Silveira. "A Petrobrás nas teias da corrupção: mecanismos discursivos da mídia brasileira na cobertura da Operação Lava Jato." *Revista de Contabilidade e Organizações* 31 (2017) 11–20.
Mejía Carrillo, Martín. "Populism and Religion as in the Theory of Logics as a Unit of Explanation." *Revista Científica MQR Investigar* 2 (2018) 3–14.
Melo, Victor Andrade de, and Coriolano Pereira da Rocha Junior. "Esporte, pós-colonialismo, neocolonialismo: um debate a partir de *Fintar o destino* (1998)." *Revista Brasileira de Ciências do Esporte* 34 (2012) 235–51.
Metz, Johannes Baptist. *Theology of the World*. Translated W. Glen-Doepel. New York: Herder, 1971.

Meyer, Harding. "'Einheit in versöhnter Verschiedenheit.' Eine ökumenische Zielvorstellung. Ihre Absicht, Entstehung und Bedeutung." *Kerygma und Dogma* 61 (2015) 83–106.

Mikulášek, Josef. "'I Dream of a Church . . . ': Certain Principles from Pope Francis on the Development of the Church." *AUC Theologica* 9 (2019) 63–81.

Miller, Daniel. "Political Theory after the 'Return of Religion': Radical Democracy as Religious Affirmation." PhD diss., Syracuse University, 2010.

Miller, Marvin Lloyd. "Cultivating Curiosity: Methods and Models for Understanding Ancient Economies." In *The Economy of Ancient Judah in Its Historical Context*, edited by Marvin Lloyd Miller et al., 3–23. Winona Lake, IN: Eisenbrauns, 2015.

Min, Anselm. "The Vatican, Marxism, and Liberation Theology." *Cross Currents* 34 (1984–85) 439–55.

Miranda, Mario de França. *Libertados para a Práxis da Justiça. A Teologia da Graça no Atual Contexto Latino-Americano*. São Paulo: Edições Loyola, 1991.

———. *A Reforma de Francisco. Fundamentos teológicos*. São Paulo: Paulinas, 2017.

Monumenta Ignatiana I.9. Madrid: Gabriel Lopez del Horno, 1909.

Moore, David Chioni. "Is the Post- in Postcolonial the Post- in Post-Soviet? Toward a Global Postcolonial Critique." In *Baltic Postcolonialism*, edited by Violeta Kerletas, 11–43. Amsterdam: Rodopi, 2006.

Moraes, Vinicius de. "Samba da Bênção." https://www.vagalume.com.br/vinicius-de-moraes/samba-da-bencao.html.

Moreira, Alberto da Silva. "Esquerda Católica, Pentecostais e eleições no Brasil: um conflito entre projetos antagônicos." *Caminhos* 17 (2019) 96–119.

Moreira, Eduardo. "Porta-voz do #somos70porcento, Eduardo Moreira é capa no jornal Valor Econômico." https://edumoreira.com.br/porta-voz-do-somos70porcento-eduardo-moreira-e-capa-no-jornal-valor-economico/.

Morelock, Jeremiah, ed. *Critical Theory and Authoritarian Populism*. London: University of Westminster Press, 2018.

Moses, Paul. *The Saint and the Sultan: The Crusades, Islam, and Francis of Assisi's Mission of Peace*. New York: Doubleday, 2009.

Motta, Luiz Eduardo, and Carlos Henrique Aguiar Serra. "A ideologia em Althusser e Laclau: diálogos (im)pertinentes." *Revista de Sociologia e Política* 22 (2014) 125–47.

Mouffe, Chantal. *Agonistics: Thinking the World Politically*. London: Verso, 2013.

———. *The Democratic Paradox*. London: Verso, 2000.

———. *For a Left Populism*. London: Verso, 2018.

———. "Religion, Liberal Democracy, and Citizenship." In *Political Theologies: Public Religions in a Post-Secular World*, edited by Hent de Vries and Lawrence Sullivan, 318–26. New York: Fordham University Press, 2006.

Mounier, Emmanuel. *Feu la chrétienté*. Paris: Seuil, 1950.

———. "Fidelité." *Esprit* 164 (1950) 177–82.

———. "Nicolas Berdiaeff." *Esprit* 144 (1948) 661–63.

———. *Personalism*. Notre Dame: University of Notre Dame Press, 2010.

———. *Le Personnalisme*. Paris: Presses Universitaires de Paris, 1949.

Mudde, Cas. "The Populist Zeitgeist." *Government and Opposition* 39 (2004) 541–63.

Mudde, Cas, and Cristóbal Rovira Kaltwasser, eds. *Populism in Europe and the Americas: Threat or Corrective for Democracy?* Cambridge: Cambridge University Press, 2012.

Munitiz, Joseph, and Philip Endean, eds. and trans. *Saint Ignatius of Loyola: Personal Writings*. London: Penguin, 1996.
Nallim, Jorge A. *Transformations and Crisis of Liberalism in Argentina, 1930–1955*. Pittsburgh: University of Pittsburgh Press, 2012.
Nascimento, Terezinha. "A Trajetória de 50 Anos do Banco da Providência Legado de Dom Helder Camara para a Cidade do Rio de Janeiro." http://nucleodememoria.vrac.puc-rio.br/primeiro_site/dhc/textos/terezinhanascimento.pdf.
Nash, Robert J. *Religious Pluralism in the Academy: Opening the Dialogue*. New York: Lang, 2001.
Nayar, Pramod K. *Postcolonialism: A Guide for the Perplexed*. London: Continuum, 2010.
Nešpor, Zdeněk. *Česká a slovenská religiozita po rozpadu společného státu: Náboženství Dioskúrů*. Prague: Karolinum, 2020.
Neto, Rodolfo Gaede. "Teologia de Prosperidade e diaconia." *Ensaios e monografias* 17 (1998) 5–20.
Noble, Ivana. "Czech Churches in Transition." In *Die Kirchen und das Erbe des Kommunismus*, edited by Katharina Kunter and Jens Holger Schjørring, 67–81. Erlangen: Luther, 2007.
———. "Memory and Remembering in the Post-Communist Context." *Political Theology* 4 (2008) 455–75.
———. "Various Christian Traditions within One Ecclesial Body." *Baptistic Theologies* 5 (2013) 68–83.
Noble, Ivana, and Tim Noble. "A Non-synthetic Dialectics between the Christian East and West: A Starting Point for Renewed Communication." In *Kommunikation ist Möglich. Theologische, ökumenische und interreligiöse Lernprozesse. Festschrift für Bernd Jochen Hilberath*, edited by Christine Büchner et al., 273–81. Ostfildern: Grünewald, 2013.
Noble, Ivana, et al. *Wrestling with the Mind of the Fathers*. Yonkers, NY: St. Vladimir's Seminary Press, 2015.
Noble, Tim. "The Holy Spirit and Reform in Liberation Theology." In *"Ecclesia semper reformanda": Renewal and Reform beyond Polemics*, edited by Peter De Mey and Wim François, 361–75. BETL 306. Leuven: Peeters, 2020.
———. "Kirche und Zivilgesellschaft / Theologie und Zivilreligion." *Ökumenische Rundschau* 66 (2017) 222–36.
———. "Living in the Truth in the Past and the Present in the Czech Republic." *Forum Mission* 10 (2014) 151–68.
———. *Mission from the Perspective of the Other: Drawing Together on Holy Ground*. Eugene, OR: Wipf & Stock, 2018.
———. "Nowhere Is Better than Here: The Strengths and Weaknesses of Early Sixteenth Century Utopias." *Perichoresis* 16 (2018) 3–20.
———. *The Poor in Liberation Theology: Pathway to God or Ideological Construct?* London: Routledge, 2014.
———. "Singing for the Unity of Latin America: Liberation Theology and the Struggle against Nationalisms." In *On Nations and the Churches: Ecumenical Responses to Nationalisms and Migration*, edited by Jelle Creemers and Ulrike Link-Wieczorek, 158–69. Beiheft zur Ökumenischen Rundschau 129. Leipzig: Evangelische Verlagsanstalt, 2020.

———. "Teologie osvobození v době politických a církevních proměn." *Studia Theologica* 23:3 (2021) 39–60.

———. "What to Do When Your Best Ideas Are Too Good." *Baptistic Theologies* 3 (2011) 31–44.

———. "Who Do You Say I Am? Recognising and Receiving the Other." In *Just Do It?! Recognition and Reception in Ecumenical Relations*, edited by Dagmar Heller and Minna Hietamäki, 357–68. Beiheft zur Ökumenischen Rundschau 117. Leipzig: Evangelische Verlagsanstalt, 2018.

———. "Whose Liberation? Whose Freedom? Nikolai Berdyaev and Juan Luis Segundo on Freedom as the Key to Human Identity." In *Identitary Temptations: Identity Negotiations between Emancipation and Hegemony*, edited by Judith Gruber et al., 357–66. Concordia: Reihe Monographen Band 73. Aachen: Verlag Mainz, 2019.

Nunes, Felipe, and Carlos Ranulfo Melo. "Impeachment, Political Crisis, and Democracy in Brazil." *Revista de Ciencia Política* 37 (2017) 281–304.

"O mercado de aplicativos de transporte no Brasil." https://machine.global/o-mercado-de-corrida-por-apps-no-brasil/.

Oliveira, Gustavo Moura de, and Marília Veríssimo Veronese. "Brasil y el 'fenómeno Bolsonaro': un análisis preliminar." *Revista Mexicana de Ciencias Políticas y Sociales* 64 (2019) 245–68.

Oliveira, Marcelo Rodrigues de. *Retribuição e Prosperidade. Gênese, percurso histórico e confronto com a Teologia da Graça*. Campinas: Editora Saber Criativo, 2018.

Oliynyk, Andriy. "St. John Chrysostom and St. Thomas Aquinas on Private Property." *Biblica et Patristica Thoruniensia* 12 (2019) 243–54.

Otto, Rudolf. *The Idea of the Holy*. Translated by John Harvey. London: Oxford University Press, 1936.

Padula, Ana Julia Akaishi, and Pedro Henrique Melo Albuquerque. "Corrupção governamental no mercado de capitais: um estudo acerca da Operação Lava Jato." *Revista de Administração de Empresas* 58 (2018) 405–17.

Pakosta, Petr, and Ladislav Rabušic. "Postoje k příčinám chudoby v České republice v letech 1991 až 2008." *Sociální studia* 4 (2010) 101–20.

Pagnelli, Pia. "Gramsci y el factor religioso: su relación con la teología de la liberación latinoamericana." *Ciencias Sociales y Religión* 18 (2016) 72–84.

Panotto, Nicolas. "La dimensión política de la espiritualidad como mística: alteridad, lenguaje y hospitalidad radical en la construcción de lo público." *Hojas y Hablas* 20 (2020) 13–28.

Passos, João Décio. *Teologia do Papa Francisco. Método Teológico*. São Paulo: Paulinas, 2018.

Pernes. Jiří. "Kolektivizace zemědělství v Československu v letech 1948–1960." *Forum Historiae* 10 (2016) 5–34.

Perry, Michael. "Saint Francis." In *A Pope Francis Lexicon*, edited by Cindy Wooden and Joshua J. McElwee, 160–66. Collegeville, MN: Liturgical, 2018.

Peruzzotti, Enrique. "El populismo como ejercicio de poder gubernamental y la amenaza de hibridación de la democracia liberal." *Revista SAAP* 11 (2017) 213–25.

Petráček, Tomáš. *In the Maelstrom of Secularization, Collaboration, and Persecution: Roman Catholicism in Modern Czech Society and the State*. Translated by Derek and Marzia Paton. Lublin: EL, 2014.

Pinckaers, Servais. *The Sources of Christian Ethics*. Translated by Mary Thomas Noble. Washington, DC: Catholic University of America Press, 1995.

Pinto, Michele de Lavro. "Meanings of Poverty: An Ethnography of Bolsa Família Beneficiaries in Rio de Janeiro/Brazil." In *The Social Life of Economic Inequalities in Contemporary Latin America: Decades of Change*, edited by Margit Ystanes and Iselin Åsedotter Strønen, 129–49. London: Palgrave Macmillan, 2018.

Pius IX, Pope. *Qui pluribus*. https://www.papalencyclicals.net/pius09/p9quiplu.htm.

Pixová, Michaela. "The Empowering Potential of Reformist Urban Activism in Czech Cities." *Voluntas* 29 (2018) 670–82.

Pontifical Council for Justice and Peace. *Compendium of the Social Doctrine of the Church*. http://www.vatican.va/roman_curia/pontifical_councils/justpeace/documents/rc_pc_justpeace_doc_20060526_compendio-dott-soc_en.html.

Portier, William L. "Twentieth-Century Catholic Theology and the Triumph of Maurice Blondel." *Communio* 38 (2011) 103–37.

Prada, Óscar Elizalde, et al., eds. *Iglesia que camina con Espíritu y desde los pobres*. Montevideo: Fundación Amerindia, 2016.

Prandi, Reginaldo. "Religião paga, conversão e serviço." *Novos Estudos* 45 (1996) 65–77.

Prior, Hélder. "Escândalo Político e Narratologia: tecendo os fios narrativos dos casos Face Oculta e Lava Jato." *Revista Famecos* 25 (2018) 1–25. https://revistaseletronicas.pucrs.br/ojs/index.php/revistafamecos/article/view/28191/16240.

Rahner, Karl. "The Theological Concept of Concupiscentia." In *Theological Investigations*, 1:347–82. London: Darton, Longman and Todd, 1961.

Ratzinger. Joseph (Benedict XVI). *Christianity and the Crisis of Cultures*. Translated by Brian McNeil. San Francisco: Ignatius, 2006.

Regan, Ethna. "The Bergoglian Principles: Pope Francis' Dialectical Approach to Political Theology." *Religions* 10 (2019) 1–16. https://doi.org/10.3390/rel10120670.

Richardson, Charles. *Early Christian Fathers*. Philadelphia: Westminster, 1953.

Rixon, Gordon. "Dwelling on the Way: Pope Francis and Bernard Lonergan on Discernment." *Irish Theological Quarterly* 84 (2019) 305–18.

Ryan, Alan. *On Politics*. London: Penguin, 2012.

Rychlík, Jan. "Collectivization in Czechoslovakia in Comparative Perspective, 1949–1960." In *The Collectivization of Agriculture in Communist Eastern Europe: Comparison and Entanglements*, edited by Arnd Bauerkämper and Constantin Iordachi, 181–210. Budapest: Central European University Press, 2014.

Sacks, Jonathan. *Not in God's Name: Confronting Religious Violence*. London: Hodder and Stoughton, 2015.

Safarik, Bradley. "When the Melting Pot Spills Over: The Contemporary Populist Backlash of Perceived Immigration Pressures in Brazil and the United States." *Diálogos* 24 (2020) 227–57.

Sagovsky, Nicholas. *"On God's Side": A Life of George Tyrrell*. Oxford: Oxford University Press, 1990.

Salinas, Daniel, and Valdir Steuernagel, eds. *Prosperity Theology and the Gospel: Good News or Bad News for the Poor?* Peabody, MA: Hendrickson, 2017.

San Martin, Inés. "Pope's Late Teacher Says His Concept of 'People' Just Doesn't Work in English." *Crux*, November 29, 2019. https://cruxnow.com/interviews/2019/11/popes-late-teacher-says-his-concept-of-people-just-doesnt-work-in-english/.

Sandes-Freitas, Vitor Eduardo Veras de, and Diarlison Lucas Silva da Costa. "Partidos políticos importam na definição de carreiras políticas no Brasil?" *Política e Sociedade* 18 (2019) 117–50.

Sattler, Michael. *Brüderlich vereinigung etlicher Kinder Gottes / sieben artikel betreffend*. https://www.museum-schleitheim.ch/geschichte/taeuferbekenntnis_4.htm.

Scannone, Juan Carlos. "Situación de la Problemática del Método Teológico en América Latina." *Medellín* 78 (1994) 255–85.

———. *La teología del pueblo. Raíces teológicas del papa Francisco*. Maliaño: Sal Terrae, 2018.

Scarnecchia, D. Brian. "Property Law." In *American Law from a Catholic Perspective: Through a Clearer Lens*, edited by Ronald Rychlak, 197–212. Lanham, MD: Rowland and Littlefield, 2011.

Schmitt, Gustavo. "Levantamento aponta Temer como presidente mais rejeitado do mundo." *O Globo*, October 26, 2017. https://oglobo.globo.com/politica/levantamento-aponta-temer-como-presidente-mais-rejeitado-do-mundo-21994959.

Schneider, Ronald. *Brazil: Culture and Politics in a New Industrial Powerhouse*. Boulder, CO: Westbrook, 1996.

Schultz, Walter. "Liberation, Postmodernism, and Jacques Maritain: Confronting Individualism and Collectivism in the Twenty-First Century." *Toronto Journal of Theology* 32 (2017) 247–58.

Schulz, Michael. "La presencia de G.W.F. Hegel en representantes de la filosofía latinoamericana. (L. Zea, A. Roig, E. Dussel, I. Ellacuría)." *Contrastes* 19 (2014) 285–309.

Schwarcz, Lilia, and Heloisa Starling. *Brazil: A Biography*. London: Penguin, 2018.

Schwarzkopf, Stefan, ed. *The Routledge Handbook of Economic Theology*. London: Routledge, 2020.

Scott, Peter. *Theology, Ideology, and Liberation*. Cambridge: Cambridge University Press, 1994.

Second Vatican Council. *Gaudium et spes*. https://www.vatican.va/archive/hist_councils/ii_vatican_council/documents/vat-ii_const_19651207_gaudium-et-spes_en.html.

Sedmak, Clemens. *A Church of the Poor: Pope Francis and the Transformation of Orthodoxy*. Maryknoll, NY: Orbis, 2016.

Segala, Dioner. "O grande desenvolvimento do Brasil entre 2003 e 2015: teria este sido tão grande?" *Terraço Econômico*, September 4, 2018. https://terracoeconomico.com.br/o-grande-desenvolvimento-do-brasil-entre-2003-e-2015-teria-este-sido-tao-grande/.

Segundo, Jean-Louis. *Berdiaeff: Une réflexion chrétienne sur la personne*. Paris: Aubier, 1963.

———. *Grace and the Human Condition: A Theology for Artisans of a New Humanity*. Vol. 2. Eugene, OR: Wipf & Stock, 2011.

———. *The Humanist Christology of Paul*. Maryknoll, NY: Orbis, 1986.

———. *The Liberation of Theology*. Maryknoll, NY: Orbis, 1976.

Sharp, Donald B. "A Biblical Foundation for an Environmental Theology: A New Perspective on Genesis 1:26–28 and 6:11–13." *Science et Esprit* 47 (1995) 305–13.

Sherman, Howard. "Marx and Determinism." *Journal of Economic Issues* 15 (1981) 61–71.

Sibieta, Luke. "The Crisis in Lost Learning Calls for a Massive National Policy Response." *Institute for Fiscal Studies*, February 1, 2021. https://ifs.org.uk/publications/15291.

Siedlecka, Jo. "Stephen K. Amos Meets Pope Francis." *ICN*, April 23, 2019. https://www.indcatholicnews.com/news/36967.

Sierra Bravo, Restituto. *Doctrina Social y Economica de los Padres de la Iglesia*. Madrid: Compañía Bibliografica Española, 1967.

Siljak, Ana. "The Personalism of Nikolai Berdyaev." In *The Oxford Handbook of Russian Religious Thought*, edited by Caryl Emerson et al., 309–26. Oxford: Oxford University Press, 2020.

Silva, Drance Elias da. "Mercado, sacrifício e consumo religioso." *Estudos Teológicos* 50 (2010) 131–43.

Silva, Fabricio Pereira da. "O Fim da Onda Rosa e o Neogolpismo na América Latina." *Revista Sul-Americana de Ciência Política* 4 (2018) 165–78.

Simeoni, Monica, and Francesco Vespasiano. "The Primacy of Reality: The People First of All." In vol. 30 of *Research in the Social Scientific Study of Religion*, edited by Ralph W. Hood Jr. and Sariya Cheruvallil-Contractor, 275–94. Leiden: Brill, 2020.

Sire, James. *Václav Havel: The Intellectual Conscience of International Politics: An Introduction, Appreciation, and Critique*. Downers Grove, IL: InterVarsity, 2007.

Smith, Anne Marie. *Laclau and Mouffe: The Radical Democratic Imaginary*. London: Routledge, 1998.

Sobreiro Filho, José, et al. "Beyond the Agrarian Reform Policies in Brazil: An Empirical Study of Brazilian States from 1995 through 2011." *Social Indicators Research* 129 (2016) 1093–114.

Sobrino, Jon. "Centralidad del Reino de Dios en la Teología de la Liberación." In *Mysterium Liberationis. Conceptos fundamentales de la liberación*, edited by Ignacio Ellacuría and Jon Sobrino, 1:467–510. 2nd ed. San Salvador: UCA, 1992.

———. "Central Concept of the Reign of God in Liberation Theology." In *Systematic Theology: Perspectives from Liberation Theology*, edited by Jon Sobrino and Ignacio Ellacuría, 38–74. London: SCM, 1996.

———. *Jesus the Liberator: A Historical-Theological Reading of Jesus of Nazareth*. Translated by Paul Burns and Francis McDonagh. Tunbridge Wells: Burns and Oates, 1993.

Souza, Juliana Beatriz Almeida de. "Las Casas, Alonso de Sandoval e a defesa da escravidão negra." *Topoi* 7 (2006) 25–59.

Souza, Pedro H. G. Ferreira de, et al. *Os Efeitos do Programa Bolsa Família sobre a Pobreza e a Desigualdade: Um Balanço dos Primeiros Quinze Anos*. Texto para Discussão 2499. Rio de Janeiro: IPEA, 2019.

Spal, Jaromír, and Václav Machek. "Původ jména Čech." *Naše řeč* 36 (1953) 263–67.

Spencer, Nick. "From Thatcher to Corbyn, Why Are Politicians So Fond of the Good Samaritan Parable?" *Prospect*, November 7, 2017. https://www.prospectmagazine.co.uk/politics/from-thatcher-to-corbyn-why-are-politicians-so-fond-of-the-good-samaritan-parable.

Springs, Jason. "On Giving Religious Intolerance Its Due: Prospects for Transforming Conflict in a Post-secular Society." *The Journal of Religion* 92 (2012) 1–30.

Stallybrass, Peter. "Marx and Heterogeneity: Thinking the Lumpenproletariat." *Representations* 31 (1990) 69–95.

"Statistics on Income and Living Conditions." https://www.czso.cz/documents/10180/125571069/1600212019.pdf/dc590e1c-a42f-495c-a7cd-59a7a42b076f?version=1.0.

Stavvrakis, Yannis. "Antinomies of Formalism: Laclau's Theory of Populism and the Lessons from Religious Populism in Greece." *Journal of Political Ideologies* 9 (2004) 253–67.

———. "Religion and Populism: Reflections on the 'Politicized' Discourse of the Greek Church." http://eprints.lse.ac.uk/5709/1/StavrakakisPaper7.pdf.

Stendahl, Kirster. "The Apostle Paul and the Introspective Conscience of the West." *Harvard Theological Review* 56 (1963) 199–215. Reprinted in *Paul among Jews and Gentiles and Other Essays*, 78–96. Philadelphia: Fortress, 1976.

———. "Paulus och Samvetet." *Svensk Exegetisk Arsbok* 25 (1960) 62–77.

Stoddart, Eric. "Spirituality and Citizenship: Sacramentality in a Parable." *Theological Studies* 68 (2007) 761–79.

Sunier, Thijl. "Religious Newcomers and the Nation-State: Flows and Closures." In *Paths of Integration: Migrants in Western Europe (1880–2004)*, edited by Leo Lucassen et al., 239–61. Amsterdam: Amsterdam University Press, 2006.

Švandrlík, Richard. *Historie Židů v Mariánských Lázních*. Mariánské Lázně: Art Gallery Nataly–Městské muzeum Mariánské Lázně, 2009.

Švepešová, Alena. "Československá hokejová reprezentace v letech 1945–1969." Master's thesis, Charles University, 2015.

Swetman, Brian. *The Vision of Gabriel Marcel: Epistemology, Human Person, the Transcendent*. Amsterdam: Rodopi, 2008.

Szent-Iványi, Balázs, and Simon Lightfoot. "Determinants of Civil Society Influence: The Case of International Development and Humanitarian NGOs in the Czech Republic and Hungary." *Comparative European Politics* 14 (2016) 761–80.

Taborda, Francisco. *Cristianismo e Ideologia: Ensaios Teológicos*. São Paulo: Loyola, 1984.

———. "Uma anáfora brasileira: a Oração Eucarística V." *Perspectiva Teológica* 38 (2006) 35–63.

Teixeira, Faustino. "The God of Prosperity: Deconstructing Images." *Concilium* 4 (2014) 65–74.

"Temer bate próprio recorde e é o presidente mais rejeitado da história." *Veja*, June 10, 2018. https://veja.abril.com.br/politica/temer-bate-proprio-recorde-e-e-o-presidente-mais-rejeitado-da-historia/.

Tepedino, Ana Maria, and Margarida Ribeiro Brandão. "Teología de la mujer en teologia de la liberación." In *Mysterium Liberationis. Conceptos fundamentales de la liberación*, edited by Ignacio Ellacuría and Jon Sobrino, 1:287–98. 2nd ed. San Salvador: UCA, 1992.

Thatcher, Margaret. "Interview for *Woman's Own*." https://www.margaretthatcher.org/document/106689.

Third General Conference of the Latin American Bishops. "The Puebla Document." https://www.celam.org/conferencias_puebla.php.

Third Lausanne Conference. *The Cape Town Commitment*. https://lausanne.org/wp-content/uploads/2021/10/The-Cape-Town-Commitment-%E2%80%93-Pages-20-09-2021.pdf.

Tížik, Miroslav. "Struggles for the Character of the Roman Catholic Church in Czechoslovakia, 1948–1989." *Eurostudia* 10 (2015) 51–73.

Torre, Carlos de la, ed. *Routledge Handbook of Global Populism*. London: Routledge, 2019.

TSE. "TSE indefere pedido de registro de candidatura de Lula à Presidência da República." *TSE*, March 9, 2018. https://www.tse.jus.br/imprensa/noticias-tse/2018/Setembro/tse-indefere-pedido-de-registro-de-candidatura-de-lula-a-presidencia-da-republica.

Turner, Barrett. "*Pacis Progressio*: How Francis' Four New Principles Develop Catholic Social Teaching into Catholic Social Praxis." *Journal of Moral Theology* 6 (2017) 112–29.

Tyrrell, George. *Nova et vetera: Informal Meditations for Time of Spiritual Exercises*. 3rd ed. London: Longmans, Green and Co., 1909.

Vaněček, Václav, and Jiří Kejř, eds. *Všeobecná mírová organizace podle návrhu českého krále Jiřího z let 1462/1464*. Prague: Nakladatelství Československé akademie věd, 1964.

Varnam, Laura. *The Church as Sacred Space in Middle English Literature and Culture*. Manchester: Manchester University Press, 2018.

Vawter, Bruce. *On Genesis: A New Reading*. Garden City, NY: Doubleday, 1977.

Veliq, Fabiano. "Uma análise bíblica da questão do dízimo e a sua apropriação pelas igrejas neopentecostais." *Protestantismo em Revista* 45 (2019) 228–35.

Verstraeten, Johan. "Entering Fully into the Fabric of Society: Pope Francis and the Future of Catholic Social Discernment." *Concilium* 52 (2016) 104–12.

Vidal, José Maria. "El Papa, a Jon Sobrino: 'Gracias por tu testimonio.'" http://propapafrancisco.com/posts-detalle.php?id=536.

Vido, Roman, et al. "Czech Republic: Promised Land for Atheists?" In *Annual Review of the Sociology of Religion*. Vol. 7, *Sociology of Atheism*, edited by Roberto Cipriani and Franco Garelli, 201–32. Leiden: Brill, 2016.

Vieira, Rafaela. "O *transformismo* petista: considerações acerca das transformações históricas do Partido dos Trabalhadores no Brasil." *Memorias* 17 (2012) 1–58.

Vigil, José María. "A opção pelos pobres é opção pela justiça, e não é preferencial. Para um reenquadramento teológico-sistemático da opção pelos pobres." *Perspectiva Teológica* 36 (2004) 241–52.

Villas Boas, Alex. "Francisco e Teologia da Cultura." *Revista Pistis & Praxis* 8 (2016) 761–88.

Villaseñor, Pastor Bedolla. "La Teología de la Liberación: pastoral y violencia revolucionaria." *Latinoamérica* 64 (2017) 185–221.

Vincent, Michael. "The Formation of a Prosperity Theology That Takes Full Account of an 'Ideal' Considered Hermeneutical Strategy in the Light of the Strengths and Weaknesses of the Hermeneutics of Word-Faith and Non-Word-Faith Prosperity Teaching." PhD diss., Middlesex University, 2017.

Wagner, Elke. "'Und jetzt, Frau Mouffe?': Interview mit Chantal Mouffe." In *Und jetzt? Politik, Protest, und Propaganda*, edited by Heinrich Geiselberger, 105–27. Berlin: Suhrkamp, 2007.

Walsh, James. "'Work as If Everything Depends On—Who?'" *The Way Supplement* 70 (1991) 125–36.

Ward, James Mace. *Priest, Politician, Collaborator: Jozef Tiso and the Making of Fascist Slovakia*. Ithaca, NY: Cornell University Press, 2013.

Weiss, Hilda. "A Cross-national Comparison of Nationalism in Austria, the Czech and Slovac Republics, Hungary, and Poland." *Political Psychology* 24 (2003) 377–401.

Whitehead, Laurence. "Fernando Henrique Cardoso: The Astuzia Fortunata of Brazil's Sociologist-President." *Journal of Politics in Latin America* 1 (2009) 111–29.

Wogaman, Philip. *Christian Ethics: A Historical Introduction*. 2nd ed. Louisville: Westminster John Knox, 2007.

Wöhrle, Jakob. "*Dominium terrae*. Exegetische und religionsgeschichtliche Überlegungen zum Herrschaftsauftrag in Gen 1,26-28." *Zeitschrift für die Alttestamentliche Wissenschaft* 121 (2009) 171–88.

Wooden, Cindy, and Joshua J. McElwee, eds. *A Pope Francis Lexicon*. Collegeville, MN: Liturgical, 2018.

Woodward, Kenneth. "In Praise of Fragments: An Interview with David Tracy." https://danclend.medium.com/in-praise-of-fragments-an-interview-with-david-tracy-743719f18ec9.

World Bank. "Gini Index (World Bank Estimate)—Brazil." https://data.worldbank.org/indicator/SI.POV.GINI?locations=BR.

Worldometer. "Countries in the World by Population (2022)." https://www.worldometers.info/world-population/population-by-country/.

Zaffaroni, Cecilia. "Processos do empobrecimento na América Latina." In *Caminhos da Igreja na América Latina e no Caribe. Novos Desafios*, edited by Pablo Bonavia, 65–78. São Paulo: Paulinas, 2006.

Index

Adam, Júlio Cézar, 95
affects, affective, 76–78, 112
Afro-Brazilian religions, 31
agonistic, agonistics, 6, 71–73, 81, 164, 177, 209, 224, 225
almsgiving, 85
Althusser, Louis, 58
Anabaptists, 133–34
"angel of light," 7, 224
ANO (*Akce národní obrody*—Action for National Revival), 43
ANO 2011 (*Akce nespokojených občanů*), 43, 71, 229
Anselm, 86
antagonistic, antagonisms, 6, 9, 54, 64, 68, 71–73, 153, 164, 168
Aparecida, CELAM conference in, 147
apatheism, apatheistic, 47
Arato, Andrew, 56
Argentina, 17, 147, 166, 181, 197, 207
askesis, 94
Assmann, Hugo, 160–61
atheism, atheist, 47
Augustine, Saint, 131, 138, 198

Babiš, Andrej, 6, 42–44, 45, 61, 62, 64, 69, 71, 228
Baker, Peter, 63
Barnes, SJ, Michael, 202, 211

Base Ecclesial Communities. *See* CEBs, *Comunidades Eclesiais de Base*.
Belo Horizonte, 15
  Jesuit Faculty of Theology and Philosophy in, *ix*, 147
Benedict XVI, Pope. *See* Ratzinger, Joseph.
Beneš, Edvard, 36–37
Berdyaev, Nikolai, 122, 137–38, 191
Bergoglio, SJ, Jorge Mario. *See* Francis, Pope.
Bingemer, Maria Clara, 161, 182
Bitrus, Ibrahim, 87
Black Lives Matter, 76, 78
Blomberg, Craig, 96–97
Boehme, Jakob, 137
Boff, Clodovis, 5, 16, 58, 75, 170, 206
Boff, Leonardo, 13, 119, 136, 137, 143, 145, 148, 158, 172, 216, 219, 220, 221, 222, 223, 227
Bohemia. *See also* Czech Republic, Czechoslovakia.
  history, 33
  National Revival, 34
  re-catholicization, 34
Bohn, Simone, 29
Bolsa Família, 22–24
Bolsonaro, Jair, President, 3, 26–28, 59, 60, 71, 179, 185, 196

Brazil, 19, 93, 203, 228
  attitudes to democracy in, 29
  basic salary (*salário mínimo*), 22
  elections 2018, *vii*, 3
  hegemonic discourses about, 59–60, 228
  history of, 11,
  military coup in, 19
  religion in. *See also* Evangelicals, Brazilian; neo-pentecostalism; pentecostals. 29, 31, 228
  restoration of democracy in, 19
Brentano, Franz, 35
Brexit, 3, 70, 76, 179, 185, 198
Byzantium, 33

Cabral, Pedro Álvares, 17
Calvin, John, Calvinism, 92, 133
Cape Town Commitment, 84
capital, capitalism, 59, 85, 96, 98, 100, 121, 198, 230
Cardoso, Fernando Henrique, 19, 25
CEBs (*Comunidades eclesiais de base*, Base Ecclesial Communities), 20, 78
Certeau, Michel de, 164–65, 166
Chamberlain, Neville, 36
Charles IV (Holy Roman Emperor), 33
Charter 77, 38
Chavez, Hugo, 16
Chauvet, Louis-Marie, 102, 220
Christian, Christians, 2, 6, 81, 130, 140, 149–50, 201, 205, 219, 226
  anonymous, 113, 143
  discourses of entitlement, 83, 84
  and division, 4, 5, 82
  early, 183
  false claims to be, 143–44, 185, 188, 204, 210, 223
  hegemonic discourse. *See* hegemonic discourse, Christianity as.
  justice, 10
  meaning of grace for, 94, 135, 140
  noun not adjective, 169
  people as, 153
  and political choices, 6, 8, 9, 212, 216, 227
  relationship to the poor, 123
  social engagement of, 135
  task of, 14
Christ. *See* Jesus (Christ).
Christianity, 2, 33, 57, 83, 84, 223
Church Fathers, 82, 85, 132
church, churches, 82, 88, 104, 131, 133, 149, 150, 156, 162, 172, 173, 188, 215, 216, 217, 219, 225, 228
  Eastern and Western, 33, 41
  economy and, 87
  liberation and, 20
  medieval, 86–87
  of the poor, 148, 159
  and state, 134
  task of, 159, 160, 172, 224
  taking sides, 8–10, 227
clientelismo, 93
Codina, Victor, 150, 215, 217
Colborn, Francis, 123
collectivization, 74
Collor de Mello, Fernando, President, 19, 25
Comblin, José, 118, 139, 140, 215
common good, 157, 161, 167, 170, 171, 181, 191, 196, 201, 206, 212, 226, 228, 229
Common Home, 191
concupiscence, 198
conditionalities of exclusion, 114, 121, 124–25, 130, 214
conflict, conflicting, conflictual, 5, 52, 59, 71, 72, 81, 125, 128, 130, 166–68, 171, 177, 183–86, 209, 220, 226, 229
Constantine (Cyril) and Methodius, Saints, 33, 41
conversion, 127, 157, 210
convictions, convictional theology, 78
corruption, 49
  in Brazil, 21, 24, 25, 30
  in Czech Republic, 43, 71
counsel as gift of Spirit, 223–24
COVID-19, coronavirus, 4, 15, 18, 28, 43, 45, 73, 128, 140, 184, 186, 191, 198, 204, 222
Credit Unions, 110
Croteau, David, 106, 107
Cuda, Emilce, 64, 80, 151, 154, 156, 157, 178

Index   257

culture, 125, 151, 153, 156, 157, 165,
     172–73, 177, 198, 202–3
Czech Republic. *See also*
     Czechoslovakia, Bohemia. 4, 32,
     164, 179, 208, 228, 229–30
  civil society in, 45
  hegemonic discourses about, 60–62
  history of modern, 31, 38
  identity, 44, 49, 77
  origins of country name, 31
  postcolonialism, 39–40
  practices of entitlement in, 109–13,
     188–89
  religion and churches in, 46–48,
     110–12, 229–30
Czechoslovak Hussite Church
     (Czechoslovak Church), 46–47
Czechoslovakia. *See also* Bohemia,
     Czech Republic.
  Communist Party in, 37, 61
  democracy, 36
  declaration of independence, 34
  end of communism in, 19, 38, 131
  First Republic, 35, 110
  invasion in 1968, 37
  sport in, 41
  Sudeten Germans and, 35

da Silva, Luiz Inácio Lula. *See* Lula.
de Foucauld, Charles, 213
de Las Casas, Bartolomé, 126
democracy, 69, 73
dependency, theory of, 19, 20, 127
desire, logic of, 128
determinism, 70
dialogue, 202–7, 211, 224
difference, relations of, 65–66
digital media. *See* social media.
Dilma Rousseff, 17, 24, 26
Diognetus, Letter to, 132–33
Dirceu, José, 21
discernment, 18, 116, 178, 222
dis-grace, 13, 120, 142, 145
diversity, 167–68
division, vii, 4, 15, 31, 48, 50, 52, 56,
     175, 190
Dornelles, João Ricardo, 27, 28
Drane, John, 101

Duka, Dominik, Cardinal Archbishop, 48
Dusilek, Sérgio, 102
Dussel, Enrique, 119–20

ecology, 74
Eddy, Mary Baker, 89
Empty Signifier, 65–67, 76, 141, 155–56
entitlement, 10, 50, 82–83, 86, 88, 100,
     112, 113, 177, 182, 195, 217,
     218, 220, 223
  theologies of, 3, 5, 83–84, 88, 114,
     130, 142–43, 157, 171, 188, 200,
     214, 216
Ephesians, Letter to the, 4, 14
equivalence, equivalential, 56
  chain, 75, 80
  relations, 66, 68, 75
Errejón, Iñigo, 72
ethics, 131–33, 205
  as first theology, 192–96
  sexual, 132, 135
eschatology, eschatological, 57, 94,
     142–45, 177, 202, 208
European Union, 32, 38, 43, 111, 230
Evangelicals, Brazilian, 28, 228
Evangelii Gaudium, 157–59, 160, 165,
     166, 168, 171, 172, 181
Extinction Rebellion, 76
Ezekiel, 217

faith, 2, 3, 55, 84, 86, 94, 108, 114, 116,
     129, 131, 144–45, 158, 172, 177
  justification by, 87–88
  liberation theology and, 80
  perspective of, 127, 226
  and politics, 10, 13, 117, 119–21,
     132, 185
  the poor and, 159
  theology as articulation of, 73, 150
faithfulness, 122–23, 161–62, 206
false prophets, 130, 217–18, 226
Fascism, 27–28
Fernández, Víctor Manuel, 154
Forgotten Light (*Zapomenuté světlo*),
     110, 113
fortitude as gift of the Spirit, 226–27
Francis of Assisi, Saint, 167, 178, 182–
     83, 185

Francis, Pope, *vii*, 48, 146, 147, 151, 152, 157, 164, 168, 170, 172–73, 175, 181, 207, 224
　"bipolar tensions," 166, 168, 171, 196
　four theological principles. *See also* reality over idea, time superior to space, unity over conflict, whole superior to part. 3, 13, 149, 158, 162–71, 176
　Holy Spirit, 172, 217
　model of polyhedron, 18, 170–71, 195, 201, 206
　and the poor, 158
　theology of, 149, 150–51, 159–60, 195
Franks, Frankish Empire, 4, 33, 41
Fratelli Tutti, *vii*, 5, 175, 176
　community, communal, 188–92
　death penalty, 210
　forgiveness, 209–11
　fraternity, 176, 223
　Good Samaritan, 186–88
　human dignity, 181, 188–92, 193, 204–5
　gratuitousness, 194
　kindness, 207
　politics, political theology, 178, 185, 196–99, 212
　role of religion, 211–13
　shadows in the world, 178–79
　social love, social friendship, 177, 178, 199–207
　systemic change, 193, 197–98
　throwaway world, 180
　truth, 204, 208
　war, 210
Fraternities, 93
Frederick V, Elector Palatine, 34
freedom, 116, 137–38, 139, 140, 191, 197
Freedom and Direct Democracy Party (SPD), 44, 48, 62
Freston, Paul, 91–92, 93, 100
Freud, Sigmund, 58, 59
Freyre, Gilberto, 17

Galilea, Segundo, 78
Gaudium et spes, 224

Gemüt, Gemüth, 1, 2, 7, 14, 113, 142, 196, 215, 231
Gera, Lucio, 152, 153
Gini coefficient, 23
　Brazil, 23
　Czech Republic, 45
Girard, René, 128, 200
God (Father),
　love of (objective and subjective), 13–14, 83, 119, 139, 149, 188, 220
　of Justice, 9
　of life, 180
　piety and fear of, 96, 220–22
González Faus, José Ignacio, 125–26, 128, 129, 139, 183
Gottwald, Klement, President, 37
Globalism, 171, 191
Gramsci, Antonio, 57
grace, 83, 88, 94, 114, 117–19, 129, 135, 143, 149, 150, 165, 168, 170, 180, 199, 214, 217, 220
　actual, 118
　and eschatology, 142–45
　and four theological criteria of Pope Francis, 171–74
　common, 113
　freedom and, 137–39
　gratuitousness of, 118, 123
　habitual, 118
　liberating, 135–37, 138, 142, 158, 172, 173, 175, 178, 191, 228, 230
　love and, 140
　personal, 123
　relational, 123
　sanctifying, 114
　social, 124
　supernatural, 117
　theologies of, 3, 171–74, 175, 195, 196
　transactional understandings of, 88, 90, 95, 98, 102, 114
　universality of, 143–44
Graubner, Archbishop Jan, 48
Gregory XVI, Pope, 134
Grotius, Hugo, 124
Grulae (*Grupo de Libertação Alternativa Estudantil*), *viii–ix*

Index

Guardian, The, 63
Guardini, Romano, 163, 165
    On opposites (*Gegensatzlehre*), 163–64
Gutiérrez, Gustavo, 31, 148, 159
    on "non-persons," 69

Hapsburgs, 4, 34
Haddad, Fernando, 27
Hagin, Kenneth, 89–90, 103
Halík, Tomáš, 48, 149
Havel, Václav, 37–38, 39, 61, 130–31, 196, 208
hedonism, 95
Hegel, Georg Wilhelm Friedrich, Hegelian, 53, 93, 163
hegemonic discourse, 62–65, 125, 130, 157, 158, 177, 189, 191, 215, 225, 227, 228
    Christianity as a, 142, 225
    competing, 77, 197
    entitlement, 112, 114, 226
    faith as basis for, 80
    Pope Francis, 195
    populist, 116, 117, 121, 183, 216
    preaching as, 95
    prosperity theology as, 91, 92
    on society, 58
    and theology of grace, 175
    universalizing tendencies of, 67, 70
hegemony, hegemonic 41, 57, 59, 62–63, 67, 70–73, 79, 132, 157, 159, 209, 230
    identity. *See* Identity, hegemonic.
Hegemony and Socialist Strategy, 57–59, 74–75
Helsinki Accords, 38
heterogeneity, 69, 70, 71, 74
history, non-linear, 70–71
Hitler, Adolf, 36
Horsley, Richard, 120
Holy Spirit, 14, 165
    fruits of, 207
    gifts of, 220–27
    giver of life, 214–17
    unity and diversity, 218–19
Howard, SJ, Damian, 82, 83
human rights, 180–83
Hummes, Dom Claudio, 147–48

Hus, Jan, 33

identity, 29, 133, 154
    differential, 66
    hegemonic, 66
idolatry, 102, 218
ideology, 54–55, 189
    thin, 54, 64, 125
"idology," 12
Ignatius of Loyola, Saint, 7, 104, 178, 198, 221–22
Illich, Ivan, 203
individual, individuals, individualism, 124, 191, 197
injustice, 5, 9, 10, 31, 83, 112, 119, 127, 128, 141, 145, 208, 209, 215, 218, 222
Ivereigh, Austin, 146, 147, 172, 178

Jeremiah, 226–27
Jesus (Christ), 90, 104, 108–9, 138, 160, 202
    body of, 144, 149
    death on cross, 86
    faith in, 97, 145
    followers of, 223, 224
    headship of, 14
    law of, 141, 142
    life in, 8, 50, 117, 139, 142, 225
    praxis of, 141–42
    resurrection of, 84
    shalom, 209
    and unmasking of sin, 129
Jesuits. *See* Society of Jesus.
Jiří of Poděbrad, King, 34
John, Gospel of, 31, 129
John Paul II, Pope, 158, 181
justice, 8, 9, 10, 14, 55, 67, 75, 79, 96, 97, 119, 145, 156, 173, 179, 207, 209, 215, 219

Kingdom of God, 3, 10, 98, 100, 109, 141, 142, 171, 173, 189, 202, 215, 219, 222
Klaus, Václav, 39, 41, 179
Köstenberger, Andreas, 106, 107
knowledge as gift of Spirit, 225–26
Kubitschek, Juscelino, 49
Kuyper, Abraham, 113

Lacan, Jacques, 65
Laclau, Ernesto, 6, 55–56, 64, 65, 68, 69, 74, 91, 142, 153, 154, 155, 164, 191, 197
Latin America, 16–18
   thinking from, 18
Laudato Si', 175, 176, 191
Lava jato (Operation Car Wash), 24–26
left [wing], 31, 79
Levinas, Emmanuel, 82–83, 97, 192, 218
liberation theology, 3, 5, 50, 57, 64, 78, 80, 92, 103, 116, 117, 151, 155–56, 157, 168, 170, 225
   and politics, 119–21
liberty. *See* freedom.
Lifschitz, Joseph, 90, 91
locus theologicus, loci theologici, 155
loss, rhetoric of, 31
love, 4, 13, 97, 117, 123, 139–42, 158, 172, 176, 185, 186, 188, 189, 190, 205, 206, 207, 211, 216, 219, 228
   social, 14, 124, 145, 199–202
Luke, Gospel of, 97, 98, 103, 104, 106, 186, 190, 218
Lula (Luiz Inácio Lula da Silva), President, 19, 20, 24, 26, 29, 196, 225
Lumpenproletariat, 69
Luther, Martin, Lutheranism, 87–88, 133
Lyotard, Jean-François, 225

Macedo, Edir, 108
Malachi, 100
Mandela, Nelson, 196,
Marcel, Gabriel, 189
Marion, Jean-Luc, 83, 129
Mark, Gospel of, 6, 98, 100
Marx, Karl, 1, 70
   on religion, 1, 2
marxism, 153–54, 179
Masaryk, Tomáš Garrigue, President, 34–35
Master Signifier. *See* Empty Signifier.
Matthew, Gospel of, 6, 10, 98, 129, 144, 216
McClendon, James, 78
Mečiar, Vladimír, 39

Medellín (CELAM conference), 20, 152, 159
mensalão, 21, 24
Methodius. *See* Constantine (Cyril) and Methodius, Saints.
Metz, Johann Baptist, 2
migration, migrants, 44, 111, 133, 183, 185, 187, 193, 194
Miller, Daniel, 56
Million Moments Movement, 45, 62, 228
Miranda, Mario de França, 119, 126, 207
Mirari Vos. See Gregory XVI, Pope.
money, 99, 103
   love of, 98
morality, moral discourses, 30, 81
Moreira, Eduardo, 60
Morava, Greater, 33, 41
Mouffe, Chantal, 6, 55–56, 62, 71, 72, 74, 77, 91, 140, 142, 153, 164, 191, 197, 224
Mounier, Emmanuel, 75, 121, 122, 123
Movimento Sem Terra, 75
Mudde, Cas, 11, 54, 64
Munich Agreement, 36

NATO, 32
neo-pentecostalism, neo-pentecostal, 28
New Thought Movement, 89
Noble, Ivana, x, 13, 47, 61, 109, 112, 208, 220
Noble, Tim, 5, 13, 16, 22, 45, 58, 83, 102, 122, 129, 134, 153, 186, 194, 215
non-synthesizing dialectics, 13

Occupy, 76
Okamura, Tomio, 44, 185
Oliveira, Marcelo Rodrigues de, 96, 108–9
option for the poor, 8, 158
Orbán, Viktor, 44
Orthodoxy, 136–37
orthopraxis, 144, 170
Otto, Rudolf, 96
overdetermination, 58

Paul, Saint, 120, 130, 131, 137, 140–41, 218

Index

Pelagius, pelagianism, 138
pentecostalism. *See also* neo-pentecostalism. 92
people, the, 68, 153, 155–59, 161, 171, 177, 190, 196
   construction of, 64, 68–70, 74, 75, 162, 165, 197, 215
   in populism, 53, 64
   of God, 12, 156, 162
people, theology of the, 151–55, 177, 194, 202
perestroika, 38
Peronism, 153, 196
personalism, 75, 121–24
Petráček, Tomáš, 32, 33
Photios, Patriarch, 41
piety and fear of the Lord, 220–22
pink tide in Latin America, 16–17
Pius IX, Pope, 134–35
place and space, 165
plebs, 68, 70, 74
pleroma, 8, 165
Podemos, 72, 76
politics, 67, 80, 119, 133, 144, 201, 201, 219
political, the, 5, 156–57, 164, 178, 185, 224
polyhedron. *See under* Francis, Pope.
poor, the, 141–42, 155, 159–62, 215, 217
   as subjects, 160–61
   preferential love for, 148, 149
populism, populisms, 3, 11, 12, 31, 43, 53, 183, 196–97, 200
   common understandings of, 53, 63
   ideational approach to, 53, 54
   left, 52, 74–76, 77, 80
   Manichean form of, 53, 54, 81
Populus, 68, 69
positive confession, 84, 88, 89–90
post-Marxist, 64, 69, 154, 157
poverty, 22–23
proletariat, 68–69, 180
prosperity, theologies of, 84, 88–91, 103–4, 132
   exegetical approach, 90, 95, 96, 101–2
   problems of, 94–100
   strengths of, 91–94

PT (*Partido dos Trabalhadores*), 5, 17, 20–21, 222, 225
   election history, 17, 20–21
   Christian role in foundation of, 20
Puebla (CELAM conference), 20, 182
Pueblo, teología del. See people, theology of the.

Quimby, Phineas, 89
Qui Pluribus. See Pius IX, Pope.
Qur'an, 218, 219

Rahner, Karl, 113, 126, 138, 143, 198
Ratzinger, Joseph (Pope Benedict XVI), 124, 149–50, 158, 181
reality over idea, 162, 168–70, 176, 200
religion, religiosity, religious, 28–32
   popular, 78, 156
resilience, 227
responsibility, theologies of, 116
restitution, 110
right [wing], 31, 77
Roman Catholic Church, 46, 182, 188, 190
Roman Catholics, Brazilian, 30, 31
Roman Catholics, Czech, 46, 109–10
Rovira Kaltwasser, Cristóbal, 53, 54
Rules for Discernment. *See* Spiritual Exercises, The.

Sacks, Jonathan, 216, 218–19
sacrifice, 103–4, 114
salvation, 84, 95
Sattler, Michael. *See* Schleitheim Confession.
Scannone, Juan Carlos, 64, 152, 155, 161, 170
Schleitheim Confession, 133–34
Scott, Peter, 55
See—Judge—Act, 16, 177, 186
Segundo, Juan Luis, 54–55, 117, 118, 120, 122, 135–36, 138, 141, 143, 144
service, 13, 116
shalom, 2, 3, 10, 14, 113, 142, 166, 193–94, 196, 197, 206, 207–9, 211, 212, 215, 219, 226, 231
Silva, Fabricio Pereira da, 17

sin, social sin, 13, 124–27, 132, 145, 160, 178
　masking and unmasking, 13, 126, 127–31, 183
Singh, Devin, 85
slavery, 126–27, 188
Slavophiles, 41
Slovakia, Slovak, 31, 35, 36, 38, 39, 42, 44, 60, 61, 179
Sobrino, Jon, 141, 142, 148–49, 189
social democracy, 5
social media, 186, 198
social order, 58, 59
society, 57–58, 59, 125, 195
Society of Jesus, 50
solidarity, 140, 158, 167, 170, 192–93
Somos 70 por cento, 60
Soviet Union, 4
Spiritual Exercises, The, 178, 198, 201–2
　Rules for Discernment in, 7
Stalin, Joseph, 36, 74
StB (*Státní bezpečnost*), 42
subordination, 74
Superior Electoral Court, Brazil (TSE), 26
symbols, 102
synodality, 165

Teixeira, Faustino, 95
Tello, Rafael, 152, 156
telos, teloi, 94
Temer, Michel, President, 26
Thatcher, Margaret, 57
theological anthropology, 10
theosis, 8, 165, 225
Third, the. *See* Levinas, Emmanuel.
time superior to space, 3, 162, 164–66, 176, 180, 187, 207, 208, 212
tithing, tithes, 95, 105–9
　Scriptures on, 105–6
Tiso, Jozef, 36
totalitarian, 218
Tracy, David, 135
tremendum, 96
Trinity, 84, 142, 160, 165, 214, 215, 226
Trump, Donald, 185, 188
truth, 31, 62, 73, 92, 189, 203, 204, 206, 208, 222
　hierarchy of, 158
　living in, 38
　masking and unmasking of, 126, 130, 183
　people of, 228
　speaking in love, 4
　speaking of, 226–27
Tyrrell, George, 143, 144

Uber, 15
understanding as gift of Spirit, 223, 224
Ungrund, 137
United Kingdom, 3, 5, 6, 28, 47, 61, 70, 79, 127, 198–99
United States of America (USA), 15, 47, 61, 70, 71, 121, 127, 190
unity over conflict, 162, 166–68, 176, 183–84
Universal Church of the Kingdom of God (*Igreja Universal do Reino de Deus*—IURD), 29, 100, 108
USSR, Union of Soviet Socialist Republics. *See* Soviet Union.
utopia, utopias, utopianism, 31, 139, 177, 198

Venezuela, 16
Vigil, José María, 9
Villas Boas, Alex, 177
Vinicius de Moraes, 205–6

wealth, 43, 60, 84, 87, 88, 90, 91, 95–96, 98
Westernizers, 41
White Mountain, Battle of, 34
whole superior to part, 158, 162, 170–71, 191, 192, 195, 223
Wilberforce, William, 128
wisdom as gift of Spirit, 222–23, 224
Wogaman, Philip, 132
women's rights, 181–83, 193
Workers' Party. *See* PT, *Partido dos Trabalhadores*.
Wright, Christopher, 95–96

Zahradnik, Isidor, 34
Zeman, Miloš, 39, 196

www.ingramcontent.com/pod-product-compliance
Lightning Source LLC
Chambersburg PA
CBHW071934240426
43668CB00038B/1642